JÜRGEN KL LIVERPOOL ATTACKING TACTICS

Tactical Analysis and Sessions to Practice Klopp's 4-3-3

WRITTEN BY
MICHAIL TSOKAKTSIDIS

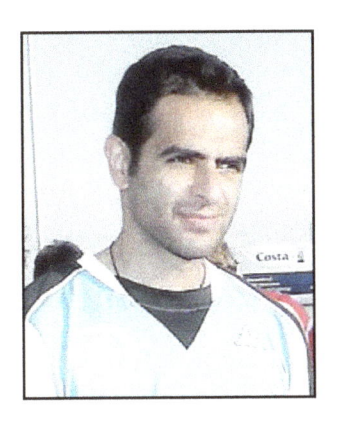

PUBLISHED BY
SoccerTutor.com

JÜRGEN KLOPP LIVERPOOL ATTACKING TACTICS

Tactical Analysis and Sessions to Practice Klopp's 4-3-3

First Published April 2021 by SoccerTutor.com
info@soccertutor.com | www.SoccerTutor.com

UK: 0208 1234 007 | **US:** (305) 767 4443 | **ROTW:** +44 208 1234 007

ISBN: 978-1-910491-48-5

Copyright: SoccerTutor.com Limited © 2021. All Rights Reserved.

All rights reserved. No part of this publication may be reproduced, stored in a retrieval system, or transmitted in any form or by any means, electronic, mechanical, photocopy, recording or otherwise, without prior written permission of the copyright owner. Nor can it be circulated in any form of binding or cover other than that in which it is published and without similar condition including this condition being imposed on a subsequent purchaser.

Author
Michail Tsokaktsidis © 2021

Editor
Alex Fitzgerald - SoccerTutor.com

Cover Design
Alex Macrides, Think Out Of The Box Ltd.
Email: design@thinkootb.com | Tel: +44 (0) 208 144 3550

Diagrams
Diagram designs by SoccerTutor.com. All the diagrams in this book have been created using SoccerTutor.com Tactics Manager Software available from www.SoccerTutor.com

Note: While every effort has been made to ensure the technical accuracy of the content of this book, neither the author nor publishers can accept any responsibility for any injury or loss sustained as a result of the use of this material.

CONTENTS

Meet The Author: Michail Tsokaktsidis 09
Jürgen Klopp's Achievements 10
Liverpool's Trophies and Records (2018-2020)..11
Liverpool's Match Statistics (2018-2019)...12
Liverpool's Match Statistics (2019-2020)...13
Introduction 14
Jürgen Klopp's 4-3-3 Formation and Liverpool Players' Attacking Roles........................15
Coaching Format 17
Key 17

THE ATTACKING PHASE 18

JÜRGEN KLOPP TACTICAL ANALYSIS - SOLUTION 1:
Build-up Against a High Press and Play Forward Quickly 19

Build-up Against a High Press and Play Forward Quickly 20
Target Areas (to Forward's Feet or in Behind) 20
Tactical Solution A: Build-up Against a High Press and Pass into Forward's Feet + Finish Attack Quickly 21
Tactical Solution B: Build-up Against a High Press and Direct Forward Pass in Behind the Defensive Line 22
Tactical Solution C: Playing Quickly in Behind the Defensive Line After a Throw-in (High Press)..................23
Statistical Analysis of Liverpool Building Up Play Against a High Press and Playing Forward Quickly 24
Analysis from Liverpool 3-1 Arsenal (Salah Goal 58') - 24th Aug 2019, Premier League 25
Analysis from Liverpool 2-1 Leicester City (Mané Goal 40') - 5th Oct 2019, Premier League 27
Analysis from Liverpool 3-0 Bournemouth (Salah Goal 48') - 9th Feb 2019, Premier League 28

SESSION 1A BASED ON THE TACTICS OF JÜRGEN KLOPP:
Build-up Against a High Press and Pass into Forward's Feet + Finish Attack Quickly 30

1. One-Touch Combination Play in a Continuous Short Passing Circuit (Support Angles) 31
2. Play Forward Quickly in a Dynamic Three Zone 6 v 6 (+4) Possession Game 33
3. Build-up Against a High Press and Pass to Forward + Finish Quickly in a Position Specific 2 Zone Game 34
4. Build-up Against a High Press and Pass to Forward + Finish Quickly in a Dynamic Zonal Game................35
5. Build-up Against a High Press and Pass to Forward + Finish Quickly in an 11v10 Tactical Game 36

SESSION 1B BASED ON THE TACTICS OF JÜRGEN KLOPP:
Build-up Against a High Press and Direct Forward Pass in Behind the Defensive Line 38

1. Build-up Through Press + Direct Forward Pass in Behind the Defensive Line in an 11v9 Dynamic Game.......39
2. Throw-in Under Press + Direct Forward Pass in Behind the Defensive Line in an 11v9 Dynamic Game........40
3. Build-up (or Throw-in) Through Press + Forward Pass in Behind the Defensive Line in 11v11 Tactical Game ...41

JÜRGEN KLOPP TACTICAL ANALYSIS - SOLUTION 2:
Break Through Pressing and Play in the Space Between the Lines 42

Break Through Pressing and Play in the Space Between the Lines 43
Target Areas (in Between the Lines)...43
Tactical Solution: Break Through Opponent's Pressing and Play Through the Midfield Line for a Fast Attack 44
Statistical Analysis of Liverpool Breaking Through Pressing and Playing in the Space Between the Lines.........45
Analysis from Liverpool 4-0 West Ham (Salah Goal 19') - 12th Aug 2018, Premier League......................46
Analysis from Liverpool 2-0 Watford (Salah Goal 90') - 14th Dec 2019, Premier League 48

SESSION 2 BASED ON THE TACTICS OF JÜRGEN KLOPP...50
1. Build-up Play Through the Lines in a Three Team Possession and Transition Game....................51
2. Break Through Pressing and Play in Between the Lines in a Position Specific Functional Game................53
3. Break Through Pressing and Play in Between the Lines in a 9v9 (+2) Dynamic Game 54
4. Break Through Pressing and Play in Between the Lines in a Tactical Zonal Game.........................55
5. Break Through Pressing and Play in Between the Lines in an 11v11 Tactical Game 56

JÜRGEN KLOPP TACTICAL ANALYSIS - SOLUTION 3:
Long Passes in Behind with All Opponents Behind the Ball 57

Long Passes in Behind with All Opponents Behind the Ball 58
Target Areas (Edge and Inside Box) 58
Tactical Solution: Long Aerial Forward Pass in Behind with All Opponents (5-4-1) Behind the Ball 59
Variation: Long Aerial Forward Pass in Behind when the Opposing Defensive Line (4-4-2) Pushes Up...........60
Statistical Analysis of Liverpool's Long Passes in Behind with All Opponents Behind the Ball 61
Analysis from Liverpool 5-2 Everton (Origi Goal 31') - 4th Dec 2019, Premier League..........................62
Analysis from Bournemouth 0-3 Liverpool (Chamberlain 35') - 7th Dec 2019, Premier League...................63
Analysis from Liverpool 1-0 Wolves (Mané Goal 42') - 29th Dec 2019, Premier League..........................64

SESSION 3 BASED ON THE TACTICS OF JÜRGEN KLOPP...65
1. Build-up Play from the Back + Long Pass in Behind in a Technical Passing Practice............................66
2. Build-up Play from the Back + Long Pass in Behind in a Functional Zonal Game 67
3. Build-up Play from the Back + Long Pass in Behind in a Conditioned 9v7 Zonal Game.....................68
4. Build-up Play from the Back + Long Pass in Behind in an 11v11 Tactical Zonal Game 69

JÜRGEN KLOPP TACTICAL ANALYSIS - SOLUTION 4:
Switch Point of Attack to Weak Side of Ball Oriented Opponents 70

Switch Point of Attack to Weak Side of Ball Oriented Opponents 71
Target Area (on Weak Side of Opponents)...71
Tactical Solution A: Switch Point of Attack to Weak Side of Ball Oriented Opponents (to Opposite Forward) 72
Tactical Solution B: Switch Point of Attack to Weak Side of Ball Oriented Opponents (to Opposite Full Back).....73
Statistical Analysis of Liverpool Switching Point of Attack to Weak Side of Ball Oriented Opponents.............74
Analysis from Liverpool 5-1 Arsenal (Mané 'Goal 32) - 29th Dec 2018, Premier League 75
Analysis from Liverpool 4-3 Crystal Palace (Salah Goal 75') - 19th Jan 2019, Premier League......................76
Analysis from Aston Villa 1-2 Liverpool (Robertson Goal 87') - 2nd Nov 2019, Premier League......................77

SESSION 4 BASED ON THE TACTICS OF JÜRGEN KLOPP...78
1. Combination Play on One Side + Switch to Weak Side, Low Cross and Finish in a Technical Practice 79
2. Combination Play on One Side + Switch to Weak Side in an Unopposed Pattern of Play Practice 82
3. Combination Play on One Side + Switch Point of Attack to Weak Side in a Dynamic Functional Game 85
4. Combination Play on One Side + Switch Point of Attack to Weak Side in a Dynamic Tactical Game 86
5. Combination Play on One Side + Switch Point of Attack to Weak Side in an 11 v 11 Tactical Game 87

JÜRGEN KLOPP TACTICAL ANALYSIS - SOLUTION 5:
Switch Play to the Full Back on the Weak Side for Early Cross..........................88

Switch Play to the Full Back on the Weak Side for Early Cross (Against Ball Oriented Opponents) 89
Target Areas (Receive Wide + Cross into Box)..89
Tactical Solution A: Switch Play to the Full Back on the Weak Side via Centre Back/s + Early Cross 90
Tactical Solution B: Switch Play to the Full Back on the Weak Side via Defensive Midfielder + Early Cross 91
Statistical Analysis of Liverpool Switching Play to the Full Back on the Weak Side for Early Cross.................92
Analysis from Liverpool 5-0 Huddersfield (Mané Goal 23') - 26th Apr 2019, Premier League 93
Analysis from Liverpool 5-3 Chelsea (Firmino Goal 54') - 22nd Jul 2020, Premier League 95
Analysis from Liverpool 2-1 Tottenham (Firmino Goal 16') - 31st Mar 2019, Premier League 96

SESSION 5 BASED ON THE TACTICS OF JÜRGEN KLOPP...98
1. Possession Play + Switch Play to Opposite Side in a 6 v 6 (+6) Dynamic 3 Zone Transition Game 99
2. Possession and Switch Play to Full Back on Weak Side for Early Cross in a Functional 8 v 8 (+2) Game........ 100
3. Possession and Switch Play to Full Back on Weak Side for Early Cross in a Functional 9 v 9 (+2) Game........ 101
4. Attack with Switch of Play to Full Back on Weak Side for Early Cross in a Tactical Zonal Game 102
5. Attack with Switch of Play to Full Back on Weak Side for Early Cross in an 11 v 11 Tactical Game 103

JÜRGEN KLOPP TACTICAL ANALYSIS - SOLUTION 6:
Technical Lofted Passes into the Box Against Deep Defences........................ 104

Technical Lofted Passes into the Box and in Behind the Opposition's Deep Defensive Line 105
Target Areas (in the Box) 105
Tactical Solution A: Technical Lofted Pass in Behind and into the Box from a Central Position 106
Tactical Solution B: Technical Lofted Pass in Behind and into the Box from a Wide Position.................... 106
Statistical Analysis of Liverpool's Technical Lofted Passes into the Box Against Deep Defences 107
Analysis from Liverpool 3-1 Man Utd (Mané Goal 24') - 16th Dec 2018, Premier League 108
Analysis from Liverpool 4-1 Norwich (Origi Goal 42') - 9th Aug 2019, Premier League......................... 110

SESSION 6 BASED ON THE TACTICS OF JÜRGEN KLOPP... 111
1. Combination Play with a Technical Lofted Pass into the Box + Finish in a Technical Practice 112
2. Maintain Possession and Switch Point of Attack with Lofted Pass into the Box in a Functional Rondo Game . 114
3. Maintain Possession and Switch Point of Attack with Lofted Pass into the Box in a Functional Game 115
4. Maintain Possession and Switch Point of Attack with a Lofted Pass into the Box in an 11 v 11 Tactical Game . 116

JÜRGEN KLOPP TACTICAL ANALYSIS - SOLUTION 7:
Combination Play with a Third Man Run Against Organised and Deep Defences ... 117

Combination Play with a Third Man Run Against Organised and Deep Defences ... 118
Target Areas ... 118
Tactical Solution A: Third Man Run to Receive in Behind the Defensive Line + Score (or Assist) ... 119
Tactical Solution B: Third Man Run to Receive in the Box in a 1v1 Situation, Beat the Opponent + Score ... 119
Tactical Solution C: Third Man Run to Receive in the Box + Pass Back for Oncoming Teammate to Shoot ... 120
Statistical Analysis of Liverpool's Combination Play with a Third Man Run Against Deep Defences ... 121
Analysis from Liverpool 4-0 Red Star Belgrade (Salah Goal 45') - 24th Oct 2018, Champions League ... 122
Analysis from Liverpool 4-3 Crystal Palace (Firmino 53') - 19th Jan 2019, Premier League ... 123
Analysis from Burnley 1-3 Liverpool (Milner Goal 62') - 5th Dec 2018, Premier League ... 125

SESSION 7A BASED ON THE TACTICS OF JÜRGEN KLOPP:
Third Man Run to Receive in Behind and Score Against Deep Defences ... 127

1. Combination Play with a Third Man Run in a Technical Passing Practice ... 128
2. Third Man Run to Receive in Behind and Score in a Technical Combination Play Practice ... 130
3. Combination Play with Third Man Run to Receive in Behind and Score in an 8 (+2) v 6 Tactical Game ... 131
4. Combination Play with Third Man Run to Receive in Behind and Score in a 10v8 Tactical Game ... 132
5. Combination Play with Third Man Run to Receive in Behind and Score in an 11v11 Tactical Game ... 133

SESSION 7B BASED ON THE TACTICS OF JÜRGEN KLOPP:
Three Player Combinations with a Third Man Run Against Deep Defences ... 134

1. Three Player Combinations in a Technical Practice with Finishing in a Large Goal ... 135
2. Three Player Combinations with a Third Man Run Against a Deep Defence in an 8 (+2) v 5 Zonal Game ... 138
3. Three Player Combinations with a Third Man Run Against a Deep Defence in a Dynamic Tactical Game ... 139

JÜRGEN KLOPP TACTICAL ANALYSIS - SOLUTION 8:
Attacking on the Flanks Against Deep and Compact Defences ... 140

Attacking on the Flanks Against Deep and Compact Defences ... 141
Target Areas (on the Flanks) ... 141
Tactical Solution A: Move the Ball Wide for the Full Back to Cross when Opponents are Deep Inside the Box ... 142
Tactical Solution B: Fast Combination Play for the Full Back to Receive in Behind when Opponents Defend Edge of Box ... 143
Tactical Solution C (1): Through Ball to Wide Forward in Behind when Opponents Defend with 2 Players Out Wide ... 144
Tactical Solution C (2): One-Two to Receive in Behind when Opponents Defend with 2 Players Out Wide ... 145
Tactical Solution C (3): Creating and Winning a 1v1 Duel when Opponents Defend with 2 Players Out Wide ... 146
Statistical Analysis of Liverpool Attacking on the Flanks Against Deep and Compact Defences ... 147
Analysis from Man Utd 1-1 Liverpool (Lallana Goal 85') - 20th Oct 2019, Premier League ... 149
Analysis from Liverpool 4-3 RB Salzburg (Robertson Goal 25') - 2nd Oct 2019, Champions League ... 150
Analysis from Watford 0-3 Liverpool (Salah Goal 67') - 24th Nov 2018, Premier League ... 151
Analysis from Liverpool 4-2 Burnley (Firmino Goal 19') - 10th Mar 2019, Premier League ... 152
Analysis from Liverpool 3-1 Man Utd (Shaqiri Goal 73') - 16th Dec 2018, Premier League ... 153

SESSION 8A BASED ON THE TACTICS OF JÜRGEN KLOPP:
Move the Ball Wide for the Full Back to Cross when Opponents are Deep Inside the Box 154
1. Move the Ball Wide for the Full Back to Cross in a Continuous High Intensity Game (+ Defend Mini Goals)... 155
2. Move the Ball Wide for the Full Back to Cross in a Continuous High Intensity Game (+ Defend Large Goals).. 156

SESSION 8B BASED ON THE TACTICS OF JÜRGEN KLOPP:
Fast Combination Play for the Advanced Full Back to Receive in Behind the Defensive Line ... 157
1. Combination Play for the Full Back to Receive in Behind Against a Compact Defence (Unopposed) 158
2. Combination Play for the Full Back to Receive in Behind Against a Compact Defence in a Time Limit Game . 161

SESSION 8C BASED ON THE TACTICS OF JÜRGEN KLOPP:
Attacking on the Flank when Opponents Defend with 2 Players Out Wide 162
1. Attacking on the Left Flank Against a Compact Defence in a Position Specific Conditioned Game........... 163
2. Attacking on the Right Flank Against a Compact Defence in a Position Specific Conditioned Game 164
3. Attacking on Both Flanks Against a Compact Defence in a Zonal 11 v 11 Tactical Game 165

TRANSITION FROM DEFENCE TO ATTACK 166

JÜRGEN KLOPP TACTICAL ANALYSIS - SOLUTION 9:
Exploit Free Spaces in the Opposition's Half During a Counter Attack from the Low Zone 167

Exploit Free Spaces in the Opposition's Half During a Counter Attack from the Low Zone 168
Target Areas (Wide Areas) 168
Target Area (Through the Centre).. 169
Tactical Solution A: Win the Ball, Pass Out Wide, Dribble the Ball Forward, and Cross into the Box 170
Tactical Solution B: Win the Ball, Pass Out Wide, Dribble the Ball Forward, One-Two to Get in Behind and Score 171
Tactical Solution C (1): Win the Ball, Pass into the Centre, Dribble the Ball Forward, and Pass in Behind for Supporting Runners 172
Tactical Solution C (2): Win the Ball and Pass in Behind to the Forward who Makes a Curved Run to Receive ... 173
Statistical Analysis of Liverpool Exploiting Free Spaces During Counter Attacks from the Low Zone 174
Analysis from Liverpool 5-3 Chelsea (Chamberlain Goal 84') - 22nd July 2020, Premier League 175
Analysis from Liverpool 2-0 Sheffield Utd (Mané Goal 64') - 2nd Jan 2020, Premier League.................... 177
Analysis from Liverpool 4-1 Cardiff (Mané Goal 87') - 27th Oct 2018, Premier League 178

SESSION 9 BASED ON THE TACTICS OF JÜRGEN KLOPP... 179
1. Fast Break Attack from a Wide Position in an Unopposed Finishing Practice 180
2. Fast Break Attack from a Wide Position in a High Intensity Functional Transition Game 182
3. Exploiting Free Space Out Wide During a Counter Attack from the Low Zone in an 11 v 11 Dynamic Game .. 183
4. Exploiting Free Space in Centre During a Counter Attack from the Low Zone in an 11 v 11 Two Zone Game.. 184

JÜRGEN KLOPP TACTICAL ANALYSIS - SOLUTION 10:
Exploit Unbalanced Opponents in the Transition to Attack from the Middle Zone 185

Exploit Unbalanced Opponents in the Transition to Attack from the Middle Zone 186
Target Areas (Between Full Back and Centre Back) 186
Target Areas (in Between the 2 Centre Backs) 187
Tactical Solution A: Win Ball in Middle Zone + Fast Break Attack to Exploit the Space in Between the Centre Back and Full Back 188
Tactical Solution B: Win Ball in Middle Zone + Direct Pass in Behind to Exploit Space Between the Centre Backs 189
Statistical Analysis of Liverpool Exploiting Unbalanced Opponents in Transition to Attack from Middle Zone .. 190
Analysis from Brighton 1-3 Liverpool (Henderson Goal 8') - 8th July 2020, Premier League 191
Analysis from Liverpool 3-0 Bournemouth (Wijnaldum Goal 34') - 9th Feb 2019, Premier League 192

SESSION 10 BASED ON THE TACTICS OF JÜRGEN KLOPP 193
1. One-Touch Combination Play in a Continuous Short Passing Circuit 194
2. One-Touch Combination Play in a Continuous Finishing Circuit 196
3. Continuous 3v2 Attacking Overloads in a Fast Break Attack Dual Game 197
4. Win the Ball in the Middle Zone and Fast Break Attack in a 3 Zone Dynamic Transition Game (10v9 +GK) ... 198
5. Win the Ball in the Middle Zone and Fast Break Attack in a 3 Zone Dynamic Transition Game (11v9 +GK) ... 199

JÜRGEN KLOPP TACTICAL ANALYSIS - SOLUTION 11:
Fast Break Attack After Winning the Ball in the High Zone 200

Fast Break Attack After Winning the Ball in the High Zone (Opponent with Unbalanced Defence) 201
Target Areas (Spaces to Exploit High Up the Pitch) 201
Tactical Solution: Fast Break Attack After Winning the Ball in the High Zone to Finish Quickly Before Opponents Reorganise 202
Statistical Analysis of Liverpool's Fast Break Attacks After Winning the Ball in the High Zone 203
Analysis from Liverpool 4-0 Red Star Belgrade (Mané Goal 80') - 24th Oct 2018, Champions League 204
Analysis from Liverpool 1-0 Brighton (Salah Goal 23') - 25th Aug 2018, Premier League 205

SESSION 11 BASED ON THE TACTICS OF JÜRGEN KLOPP 206
1. High Intensity Transition Play in a 3v3 (+3) Dynamic Possession Game 207
2. High Intensity 6v10 Dynamic Transition Game with Mini Goals 208
3. High Intensity Transition Play in a 9v10 Position Specific Conditioned Game 209

MEET THE AUTHOR: MICHAIL TSOKAKTSIDIS

MICHAIL TSOKAKTSIDIS

- UEFA 'A' Coaching Licence
- BSc Sports Science & Physical Education
- BSc Soccer Coaching & Performance Training
- **10 years as a professional player in Greece**
  (Doxa Dramas, Iltex Likoi (Wolves), Olympiakos Volou, Agrotikos Asteras, Ethnikos K. and Pandramaikos).
- **16 years as a Coach in** Youth, Amateur, and Semi-Pro Level in Greece
- A coach and man who passionately loves the game

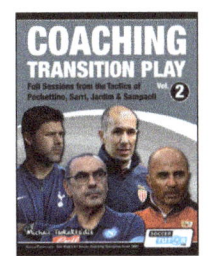

m.tsokaktsidis@gmail.com

- Author: **Coaching Transition Play Vol.2** (2018)
- Learn to "Coach Transition Play" with 83 Practices based on 22 Transition Game Situations from the Tactics of Mauricio Pochettino, Maurizio Sarri, Leonardo Jardim and Jorge Sampaoli

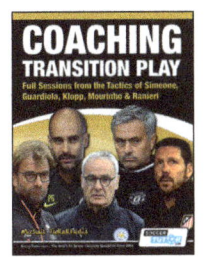

- Author: **Coaching Transition Play Vol.1** (2017)
- Learn to "Coach Transition Play" with 98 Practices based on 32 Transition Game Situations from the Tactics of Diego Simeone, Pep Guardiola, Jürgen Klopp, José Mourinho and Claudio Ranieri

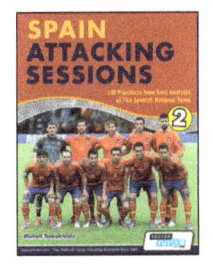

- Author: **Spain Attacking Sessions** (2014)
- 140 Practices from Goal Analysis of the Spanish National Team
- Learn how to coach your team to play like "one of the best national teams in history" with 31 ready-made sessions

- Author: **José Mourinho Attacking Sessions** (2013)
- 114 Practices from Goal Analysis of Real Madrid's 4-2-3-1
- Learn how to coach your team to play like "the best counter attacking team in the world" with 30 ready-made sessions

JÜRGEN KLOPP'S ACHIEVEMENTS

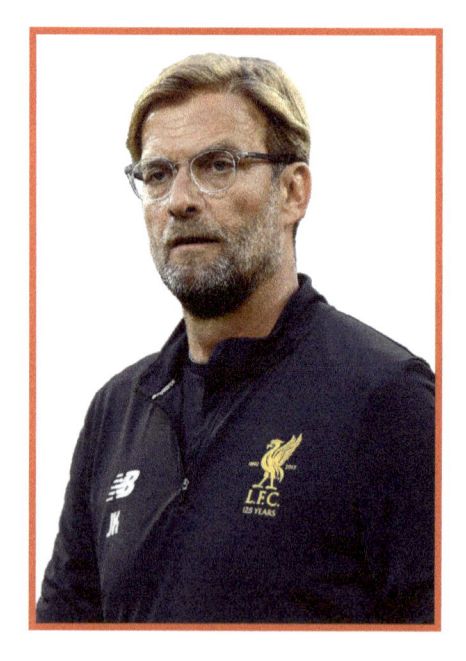

COACHING ROLES

- Liverpool F.C. (2015 - Present)
- Borussia Dortmund (2008 - 2015)
- Mainz 05 (2001 - 2008)

HONOURS (Europe/World)

- UEFA Champions League (2019)
- UEFA Champions League Runner-up x 2 (2013, 2018)
- UEFA Europa League Runner-up (2016)
- FIFA Club World Cup (2019)
- UEFA Super Cup (2019)

HONOURS (Domestic Leagues)

- English Premier League (2020)
- German Bundesliga x 2 (2011, 2012)
- Promotion to Bundesliga (2004)

HONOURS (Domestic Cups)

- German DFB-Pokal (2012)
- German DFL-Supercup x 2 (2013, 2014)

INDIVIDUAL AWARDS

- The Best FIFA Men's Coach x 2 (2019, 2020)
- Onze d'Or Coach of the Year (2019)
- IFFHS World's Best Club Coach (2019)
- World Soccer Awards World Manager of the Year (2019)
- Globe Soccer Awards Best Coach of the Year (2019)
- Premier League Manager of the Season (2020)
- LMA Manager of the Year (2020)
- BBC Sports Personality of the Year Coach Award (2019)
- German Football Manager of the Year (2011, 2012, 2019)

LIVERPOOL'S TROPHIES AND RECORDS

2018-2019
UEFA Champions League

2019-2020
Premier League  + **UEFA Super Cup** 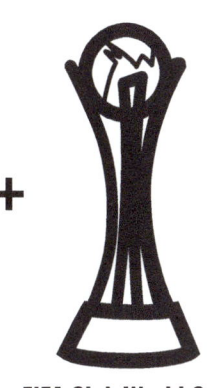 + **FIFA Club World Cup**

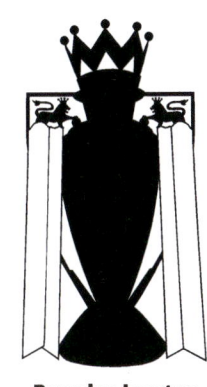

In the 2018-2019 season, Jürgen Klopp's Liverpool team won the **UEFA Champions League** and also came close to winning the Premier League, finishing with a record breaking runner-up total of 97 points (losing only 1 game), just 1 point short of champions Manchester City.

To win the UEFA Champions League, Liverpool beat **Bayern Munich**, **Porto**, **FC Barcelona**, and **Tottenham** with high intensity, attacking and exciting football.

In the 2019-2020 season, Jürgen Klopp's Liverpool team won the **UEFA Super Cup**, the **FIFA World Club Cup**, and the **Premier League** title with 7 games still to be played and another incredible great points total of 99.

Across these 2 Premier League seasons (2018/2019 & 2019/2020), Klopp's Liverpool had a record of 62 wins, 10 draws and only 4 losses (of which 2 losses were after they were already crowned Premier League Champions in 2020).

Jürgen Klopp's Liverpool have also achieved the following league records:

- Joint-record for **most Premier League wins in a season (32)** - 2019/2020.
- February 2019 to July 2020, Liverpool **won 24 consecutive Premier League home matches**.
- Joint-record for **most Premier League home wins in a season (18)** - 2019/2020.
- Joint-record for **fewest Premier League home defeats in a season (0)** - 2018/2019 and 2019/2020.
- October 2019 to February 2020, Liverpool **won 18 consecutive league matches**, a joint-record in English top-flight history.
- Liverpool remained **undefeated in 68 consecutive league games at home** (April 2017 - January 2021) - the third longest run in English top-flight history.

* Trophy images from PIXSECTOR.com

LIVERPOOL'S MATCH STATISTICS (2018-2019)

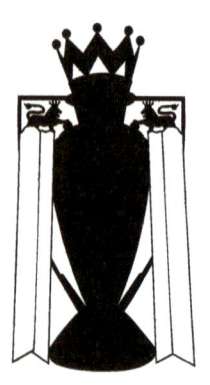

PREMIER LEAGUE

PLAYED	W	D	L	GF	GA	GD	PT
38	30	7	1	89	22	+67	97

AVERAGE GOALS PER GAME   2.34

UEFA CHAMPIONS LEAGUE

PLAYED	W	D	L	GF	GA	GD
13	8	2	3	24	12	+12

AVERAGE GOALS PER GAME   1.85

TOTAL (PREMIER LEAGUE + CHAMPIONS LEAGUE)

PLAYED	W	D	L	GF	GA	GD
51	38	9	4	113	34	+79

AVERAGE GOALS PER GAME   2.22

LIVERPOOL'S MATCH STATISTICS (2019-2020)

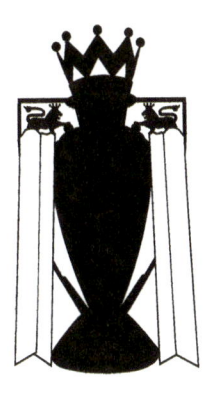

PREMIER LEAGUE

PLAYED	W	D	L	GF	GA	GD	PT
38	32	3	3	85	33	+52	99

AVERAGE GOALS PER GAME   2.24

UEFA CHAMPIONS LEAGUE

PLAYED	W	D	L	GF	GA	GD
8	4	1	3	15	12	+3

AVERAGE GOALS PER GAME   1.88

TOTAL (PREMIER LEAGUE + CHAMPIONS LEAGUE)

PLAYED	W	D	L	GF	GA	GD
46	36	4	6	100	45	+55

AVERAGE GOALS PER GAME   2.17

INTRODUCTION

Jürgen Klopp became known as a coach for the style of play he established at **Borussia Dortmund** which was characterised by **intensity**, **rhythm**, **energy**, and **speed**, with the main exponent of all of these features being used in the transition phases, both from attack to defence and defence to attack. The famous gegenpressing (counter pressing) was and still is a big weapon for Klopp. When his teams lose the ball, he wants to apply an immediate and synchronised high press to win the ball back as soon as possible. He then wants to exploit the unbalanced positioning of the opposition to finish the attack in seconds (with a few passes and a final action).

Jürgen Klopp arrived in Liverpool in October 2015 and implemented this style of play immediately, and he did it successfully. However, he realised that perhaps this way alone cannot lead him to his main goal for which he went to England for; to win the Premier League title. Therefore, Klopp developed his team's style of play so that it became more flexible and Liverpool found easier solutions to the regular problems they face from different types of opponents in the Premier League, where the previous more simplistic tactics may have been less successful.

This book focuses on the period of 2018-2020, in which Liverpool have further evolved their game and become a lethal and dominant force in England and Europe. In this period Jürgen Klopp's Liverpool team faced and found solutions against opponents that used many different tactics:

- Opponents who defend deep in the low zone with many players in front of the box
- Opponents with many players on the ball side of the pitch to create a strong defensive side
- Opponents who defend in the middle zone with all their players behind the ball
- Opponents that tried to apply high pressing
- + More...

In this book, we will try to present all of these situations and show the solutions Liverpool used to overcome these tactical problems to become the dominant team in Europe with all these achievements:

- **UEFA Champions League** winners (2019)
- **UEFA Champions League** runners-up (2018)
- **Premier League** winners (2019-2020)
- **Premier League** runners-up (2018-2019)
- **FIFA World Club Cup** winners (2019)
- **UEFA Super Cup** winners (2019)

During the last **two Premier League seasons combined (76 matches)**, Jürgen Klopp's Liverpool team have a record of **62 wins**, 10 draws, and only 4 losses, and have scored an incredible **174 goals**.

For this book, I have analysed how Liverpool score their goals and provided evidence and presented detailed examples. This analysis is then used to create full training sessions, so you the coach can implement Jürgen Klopp and Liverpool's tactics into your training sessions.

JÜRGEN KLOPP'S 4-3-3 FORMATION AND LIVERPOOL PLAYERS' ATTACKING ROLES

CENTRE BACKS

The 3 main centre backs are **van Dijk (4)**, **Gomez (12)**, and **Matip (32)**. **Lovren (6)** provided cover. The centre backs take part in building up play from the back when ball circulation is necessary to transfer the ball from one side of the pitch to the other. The aim is to pass the ball forward to a midfielder between the lines, or diagonally to an advanced full back out wide. They also play long passes (especially **van Dijk**) in behind the opposition's defensive line, into space for the front 3 to exploit. They have a special role for set-pieces and score many goals from them.

FULL BACKS

The full backs use the full width of the pitch and give the team rhythm and energy. With non-stop running up and down the pitch, both full backs provide clear support angles in 2/3 of the pitch, while bringing out the aggression and creativity of their game.

The full backs deliver a lot of crosses (early or delayed depending on the situation) and constantly make runs with and without the ball, combining with the midfielders and forwards to break through the opposition's defence. **Alexander-Arnold (66)** and **Robertson (26)** also take part in a lot of individual plays by attacking and winning 1v1 situations in wide positions.

Finally, they make a lot of diagonal runs in behind the defensive line to exploit the weak side of the opposition, to either pass the ball to an oncoming teammate (assist) or finish the attack themselves.

DEFENSIVE MIDFIELDER

The defensive midfielder is the "connecting player," directs the game, and is the most responsible player for setting the rhythm and the intensity for the team. In Klopp's Liverpool team, this is most often **Fabinho (3)**.

The defensive midfielder's decision making plays a decisive role in the team's game. He moves continuously with good body positioning, to provide the correct supporting angles to the back four and help in the first and second stages of building the attack.

This key role includes many different requirements depending on the situation; receiving many passes, helping to circulate and transfer the ball from one side of the pitch to the other (switch), passing the ball forward directly to a forward, carrying the ball forward into space (dribbling), making fast runs from deep, shooting from distance, and winning second balls in around the opponent's penalty box.

CENTRAL MIDFIELDERS

The 2 central midfielders are perhaps the most versatile and hard-working players on the pitch in Klopp's Liverpool team. They move and create the correct angles to receive passes from the centre backs in between the lines or to receive diagonal inside passes from the full backs. The players to play in these positions most frequently were **Henderson (14)**, **Keïta (8)**, **Wijnaldum (5)**, **Chamberlain (15)**, and **Milner (7)**.

The aim is to be aggressive, creative, to provide rhythm and energy, and to play forward as quickly as possible. They run and move in most areas of the pitch. They create numerical advantages at the sides when cooperating and combining with the full backs and wide forwards.

They move in vertical lines with and without the ball to combine with the forwards. They provide support in and around the box and create overloads in the final third (to score or assist).

FORWARDS

The 3 Liverpool forwards **Salah (11)**, **Mané (10)** and **Firmino (9)** create and score the majority of the goals. They all make fast runs in behind the defensive line to receive the ball, and they are all adept at dribbling at opponents. When they do this, they force a defender to close them down and move out of position - from there, they either play to a teammate in the space created or use combination play (e.g. one-two or third man runs) to exploit the space themselves.

The Liverpool forwards are also great in 1 v 1 situations in wide areas. They support the full backs and central midfielders on the flanks to help create a numerical superiority there. They create a lot of goals and score even more.

2018-2019 Statistics in All Competitions:

- **Salah** = 27 goals, 12 assists (52 games)
- **Mané** = 26 goals, 5 assists (50 games)
- **Firmino** = 16 goals, 8 assists (48 games)

2018-2019 Statistics in All Competitions:

- **Salah** = 23 goals, 13 assists (48 games)
- **Mané** = 22 goals, 12 assists (47 games)
- **Firmino** = 12 goals, 13 assists (52 games)

In the 2017/2018 Champions League campaign (which Liverpool won), all 3 forwards **Salah**, **Mané** and **Firmino** were joint-top scorers in the competition with 10 goals each.

In the 2018/2019 Premier League campaign, **Salah** and **Mané** were joint-top scorers (with Aubameyang) in the competition with 22 goals each.

In the 2019/2020 Premier League campaign (which Liverpool won), **Salah** scored 19 goals and **Mané** scored 18 goals.

Origi (27) was mostly used as a substitute.

COACHING FORMAT

1. TACTICAL SITUATION AND GOAL ANALYSIS

2. TRAINING SESSION BASED ON JÜRGEN KLOPP'S TACTICS

- Technical Practices and Functional Practices/Games
- Conditioned Games and Tactical Games
- Rules, Coaching Points, Variations, and Progressions (if applicable)

DIAGRAM KEY

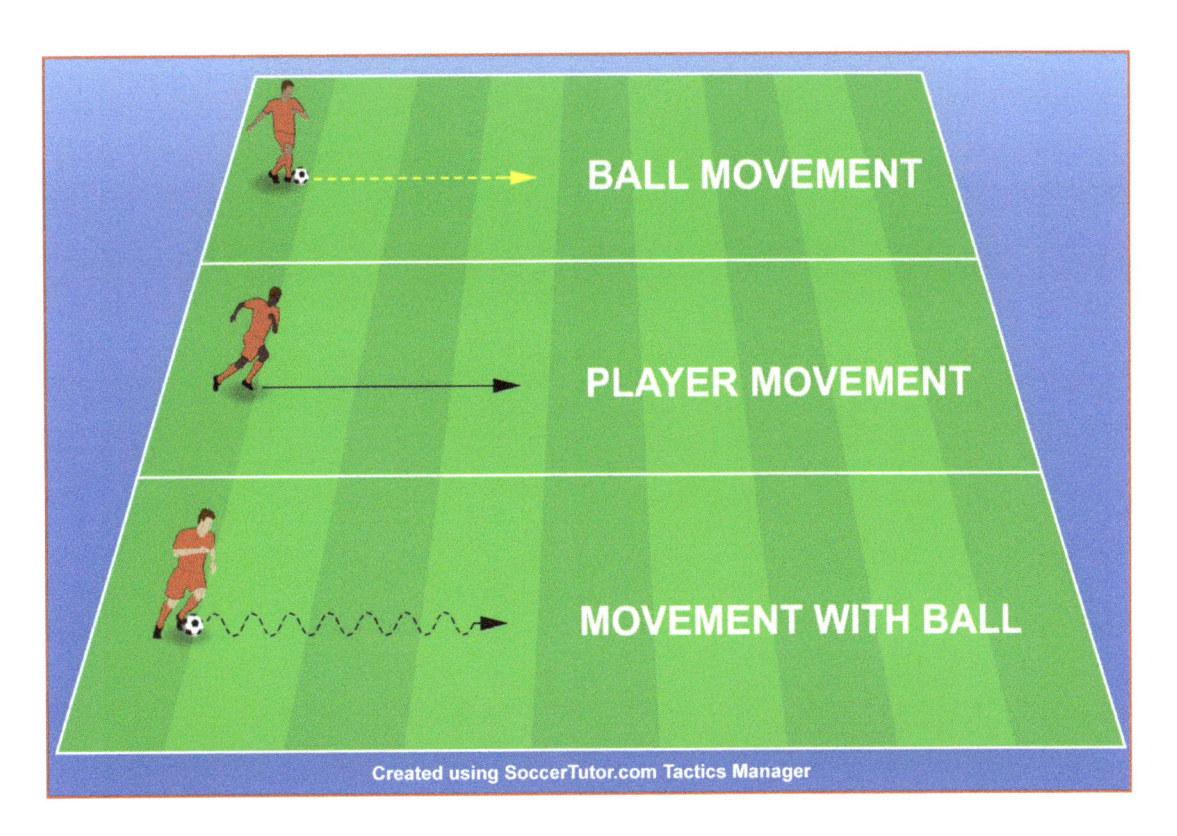

- BALL MOVEMENT
- PLAYER MOVEMENT
- MOVEMENT WITH BALL

THE ATTACKING PHASE

JÜRGEN KLOPP TACTICAL ANALYSIS

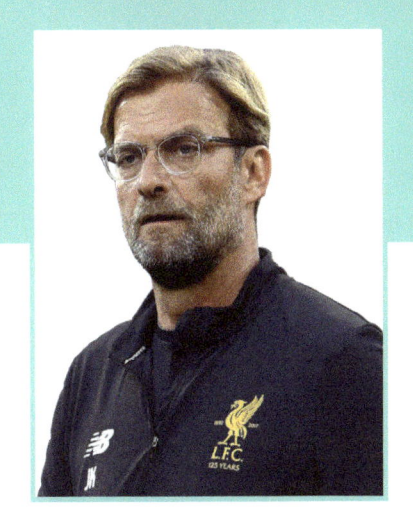

SOLUTION 1

Build-up Against a High Press and Play Forward Quickly

Content from analysis of Liverpool F.C. during the 2018-2019 Champions League winning season and the 2019-2020 Premier League winning season

- Analysis based on recurring patterns of play observed within the Liverpool team.
- Tactical solutions displayed as examples of the team's tactics being used effectively.
- Real match examples of Liverpool scoring a goal using this specific attacking tactical solution.
- Each action, pass, individual movement with or without the ball, and the positioning of each player on the pitch including their body shape, are presented.
- The analysis is then used to create a full progressive session to coach this tactical situation.

Tactical Solution 1 - Build-up Against a High Press and Play Forward Quickly

Build-up Against a High Press and Play Forward Quickly

What?

Liverpool look to play through the opposition's high press during build-up play in their own half, play a direct forward pass, and then attack their defence to score.

Why?

The opponents are positioned high up the pitch and there is a lot of space in their half to exploit if the ball can be moved forward quickly (neutralising their midfielders).

How?

Playing forward as fast as possible directly to the forwards feet or in behind the defensive line to exploit the forwards' speed and quality against the opposing defenders.

Target Areas (to Forward's Feet or in Behind)

Against high pressing teams, Liverpool play forward quickly (to forward's feet or in behind)

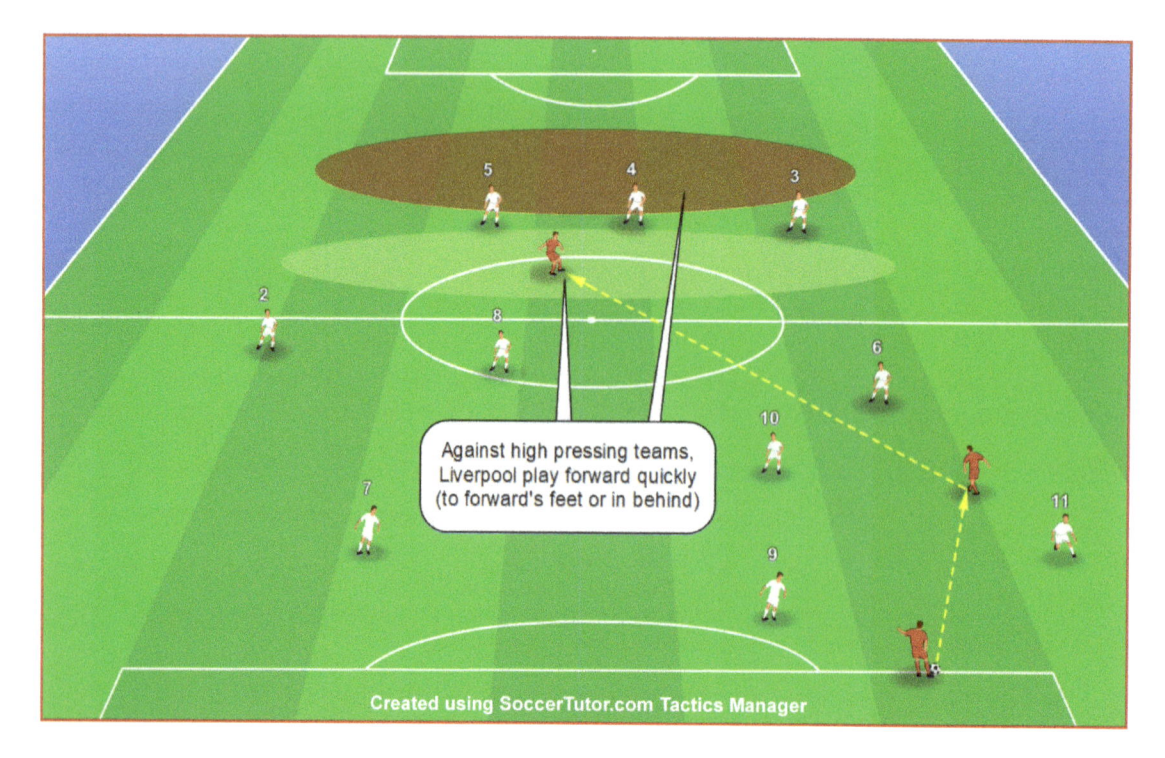

Tactical Solution 1 - Build-up Against a High Press and Play Forward Quickly

Tactical Solution A: Build-up Against a High Press and Pass into Forward's Feet + Finish Attack Quickly

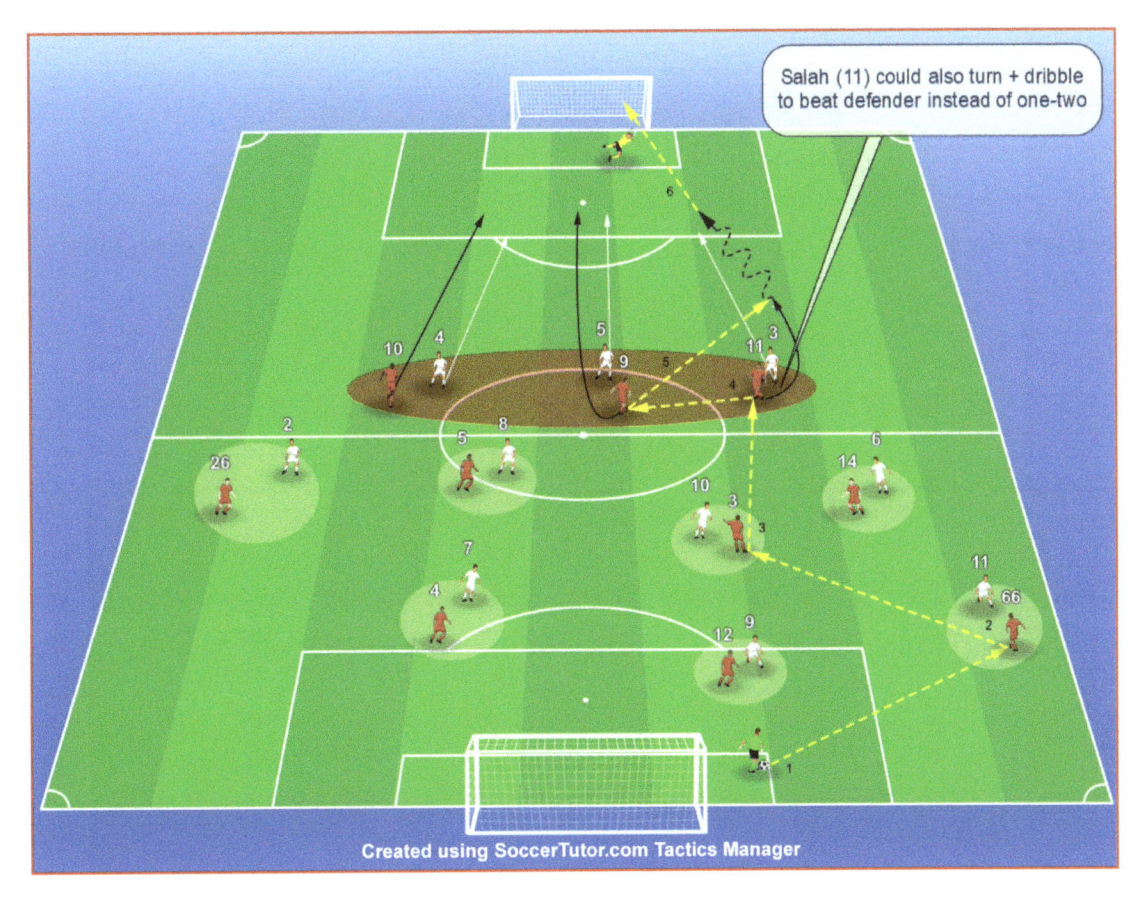

Salah (11) could also turn + dribble to beat defender instead of one-two

Liverpool are building up play from the GK and their opponents apply a high press. There are multiple 1 v 1 situations, as shown.

The Liverpool players are trying to pass the ball quickly from one player to another with good player positioning, making sure to protect the ball from their opponents with good body shape.

The aim is to pass to a forward in the attacking half as quickly as possible.

When one of the 3 forwards receives to feet, they all then look to exploit the space with the high quality and speed they have.

The Liverpool forwards **Salah (11)**, **Firmino (9)** and **Mané (10)** often choose to attack in 1 v 1 situations which they are very likely to win.

They also combine using one-two combinations or create 2 v 1 situations to neutralise their opponents and pass the ball in behind them to finish the attack.

In this example, the defensive midfielder **(3)** plays a forward pass to the feet of the right forward **(11)**, who plays a one-two combination with the centre forward **(9)** to receive in behind. From there, **No.11** dribbles into the box and scores past the GK. Alternatively, he could cut the ball back for one of his teammates.

Tactical Solution 1 - Build-up Against a High Press and Play Forward Quickly

Tactical Solution B: Build-up Against a High Press and Direct Forward Pass in Behind the Defensive Line

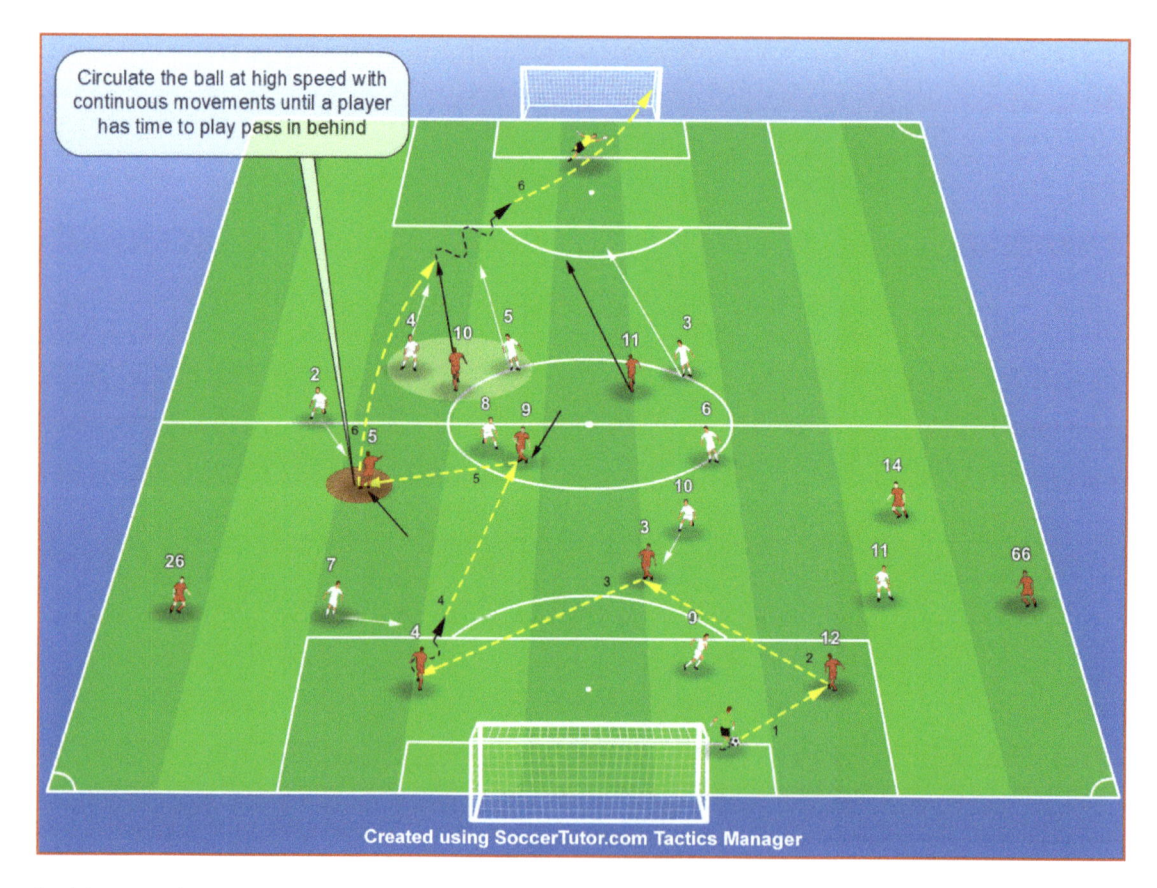

Circulate the ball at high speed with continuous movements until a player has time to play pass in behind

In this second situation, Liverpool are again building up from the back under a high press from their opponents.

They circulate the ball at a high speed and use continuous movements.

The key is to use the correct angles to provide support and good passing options for the ball carrier until one of them has the opportunity (time and space) to play a forward pass into the attacking half.

Liverpool look to play a direct forward pass in behind the defensive line instead of playing into a forward's feet like they do in Tactical Solution A.

By playing a pass in behind the defensive line, Liverpool can exploit the space in behind their opponent's high line. There is a lot of space in the opponent's half which the 3 Liverpool forwards can exploit with their high quality and superior speed that they have.

In this example, the centre forward (**9**) drops back to provide support and lays the ball off for the central midfielder (**5**) to play a pass in behind the defensive line. The left forward (**10**) times his run well and uses his speed to get to the ball ahead of the defenders, dribbles into the box and scores past the GK. Alternatively, he could cut the ball back for **No.11** to score.

Tactical Solution 1 - Build-up Against a High Press and Play Forward Quickly

Tactical Solution C: Playing Quickly in Behind the Defensive Line After a Throw-in (High Press)

In this third situation, Liverpool have a throw-in deep in their half. Their opponents have many players in and around this space and high up the pitch. They also have a very high defensive line, which is 8 yards short of the halfway line.

The aim for Liverpool is to move the ball to a player with free space and time. This can be directly from the throw-in or after a short combination between 2-3 players. From there, that player looks to pass in behind the defensive line to exploit the large amount of space available in the attacking half.

The 3 Liverpool forwards **Salah (11)**, **Firmino (9)** and **Mané (10)** are very good at exploiting the space in behind a high defensive line with their high quality and speed.

In this example, the right central midfielder **(14)** moves towards the side-line and drags his marker with him. This creates space for the left central midfielder **(5)** to move into and receive the throw-in from the right back **(66)**.

With time on the ball, the central midfielder **(5)** plays an aerial pass in behind the defensive line. The centre forward **(9)** times his run well and uses his speed to get to the ball ahead of the opponent, dribbles into the box and cuts the ball back for **No.10** to score.

Tactical Solution 1 - Build-up Against a High Press and Play Forward Quickly

Statistical Analysis of Liverpool Building Up Play Against a High Press and Playing Forward Quickly

Liverpool scored **11 goals** in this tactical situation
(Premier League and Champions League 2018-2019 and 2019-2020 seasons)

VS. OPPONENT'S HIGH PRESS
BUILD-UP THROUGH PRESSING AND PLAY FORWARD QUICKLY

DATE	HOME	AWAY	SCORE	GOAL (MIN)	SCORER	ASSIST
8th Dec 2018	Bournemouth	Liverpool	0-4	0-4 (77')	**Salah**	Lallana
19th Jan 2019	Liverpool	Crystal Palace	4-3	4-2 (90 +3')	**Mané**	Robertson
9th Feb 2019	Liverpool	Bournemouth	3-0	3-0 (48')	**Salah** *	Firmino
5th Apr 2019	Southampton	Liverpool	1-3	1-3 (86')	**Henderson**	Firmino
24th Aug 2019	Liverpool	Arsenal	3-1	3-0 (58')	**Salah** *	
5th Oct 2019	Liverpool	Leicester City	2-1	1-0 (40')	**Mané** *	Milner
10th Dec 2019	RB Salzburg	Liverpool	0-2	0-2 (58')	**Salah**	
26th Dec 2019	Leicester City	Liverpool	0-4	0-4 (78')	**A-Arnold**	Mané
1st Feb 2020	Liverpool	Southampton	4-0	3-0 (71')	**Salah**	Henderson
11th Mar 2020	Liverpool	Atlético Madrid	2-3	2-0 (90 +4')	**Firmino**	Wijnaldum
26th Jul 2020	Newcastle	Liverpool	1-3	1-3 (89')	**Mané**	

* The full analysis of these goals is shown on the following pages...

Tactical Solution 1 - Build-up Against a High Press and Play Forward Quickly

Analysis from Liverpool 3-1 Arsenal (Salah 58') - 24th Aug 2019, Premier League

Tactical Solution A: Build-up Against a High Press and Pass into Forward's Feet + Finish Attack Quickly

Arsenal press high and right back **A-Arnold (66)** receives near the side-line pressed by an Arsenal forward. **A-Arnold (66)** protects the ball and passes inside to defensive midfielder **Fabinho (3)**, who is also pressed.

Fabinho (3) recognises the situation and plays a clever first time pass to **Salah (11)**, which takes all but 3 Arsenal players out of the game. This is because they had many players pushed high up in Liverpool's half.

All 3 Liverpool forwards **Salah (11)**, **Firmino (9)** and **Mané (10)** have 1 v 1 situations against Arsenal's 2 centre backs and right back.

This creates a very dangerous 3 v 3 situation for them to finish the attack.

The Liverpool forwards are very fast and **Salah (11)** exploits his speed advantage against the Arsenal centre back. He beats him in the 1 v 1 situation with good skill and then looks to dribble quickly towards the goal.

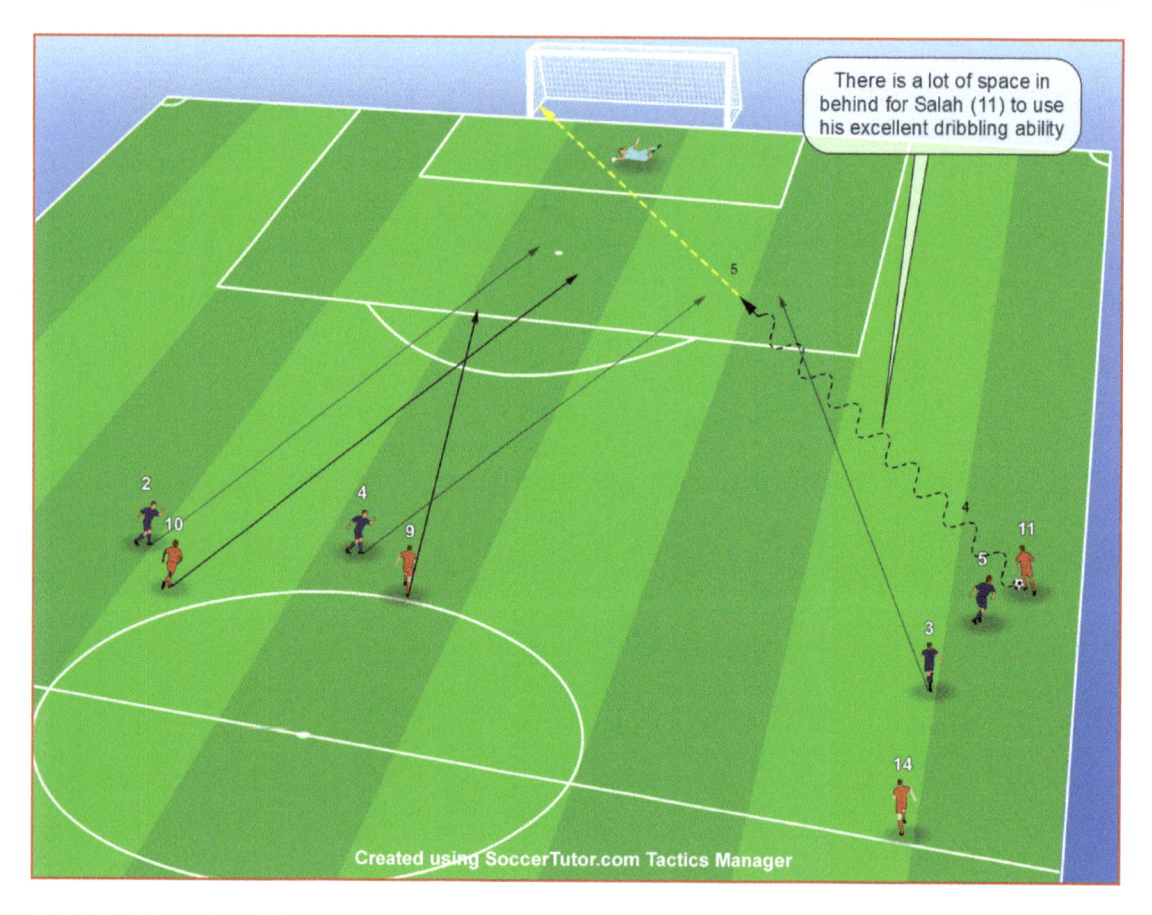

Tactical Solution 1 - Build-up Against a High Press and Play Forward Quickly

There is a lot of space in behind for Salah (11) to use his excellent dribbling ability

Salah (11) has a lot of free space to exploit in front of him, which is due to Arsenal's high defensive line. He dribbles very quickly towards the goal.

Salah (11) dribbles into the box by cutting across the recovering left back and then scores into the far corner with his left foot.

Tactical Solution 1 - Build-up Against a High Press and Play Forward Quickly

Analysis from Liverpool 2-1 Leicester City (Mané 40') - 5th Oct 2019, Premier League

Tactical Solution B: Build-up Against a High Press and Direct Forward Pass in Behind the Defensive Line

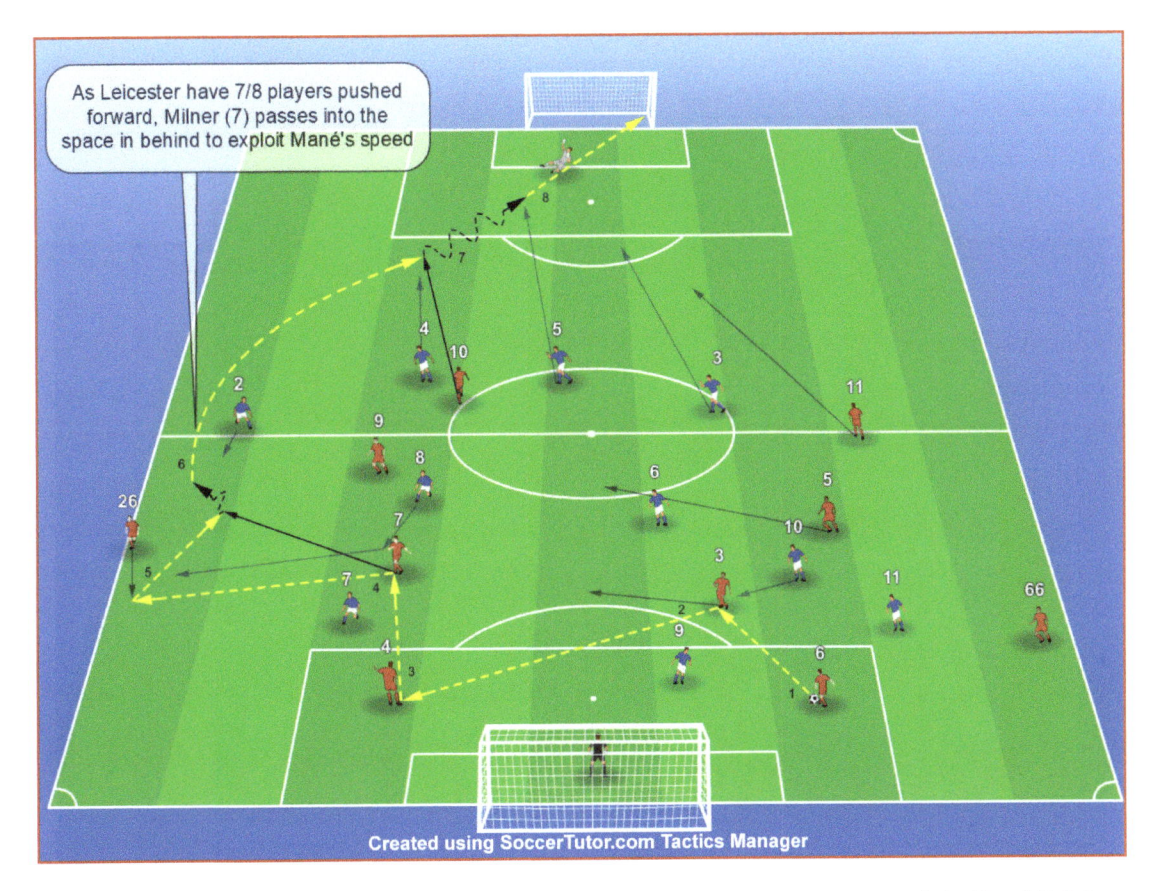

As Leicester have 7/8 players pushed forward, Milner (7) passes into the space in behind to exploit Mané's speed

Leicester press high up the pitch. The 2 centre backs **Lovren (6)** and **van Dijk (4)**, and the defensive midfielder **Fabinho (6)** create a triangle shape to move the ball easily to left centre back **van Dijk (4)** in space, who passes forward to left central midfielder **Milner (7)** in behind the front line of Leicester's press.

Milner (7) is pressed from behind and passes to the left back **Robertson (26)**, who drops back. **Milner (7)** immediately moves forward at a good angle to receive the return pass. **Robertson (26)** passes to **Milner (7)**, who now has more space and time.

With 7-8 Leicester in Liverpool's half and **Salah (11)** and **Mané (10)** in front of him, the central midfielder **Milner (7)** plays a pass into the space in behind Leicester's defensive line.

The aim is to exploit the left forward **Mané's (10)** speed and ability in 1 v 1 situations.

Mané (10) times his run well and beats his opponent to the ball showing great speed and receives just outside the box. He dribbles towards goal keeping the ball very close to his feet and slots the ball past the GK to score.

Tactical Solution 1 - Build-up Against a High Press and Play Forward Quickly

Analysis from Liverpool 3-0 Bournemouth (Salah 48') - 9th Feb 2019, Premier League

Tactical Solution C: Playing Quickly in Behind the Defensive Line After a Throw-in (High Press)

LB Milner (7) throws the ball to LF Mané (10), who is positioned between 2 opponents

Liverpool have a throw-in on the right side in their own half. The right back **Milner (7)** throws the ball to the left forward **Mané (10)** in between 2 opponents.

Mané (10) produces a nice turn and protects the ball while drawing 2 opponents towards him.

He then passes inside to the unmarked central midfielder **Keïta (8)**, who moves forward.

Keïta (8) takes a good first touch forward into the opposition's half and has 8 Bournemouth players within 15-20 yards of him.

The centre forward **Firmino (9)** and right forward **Salah (11)** provide an attacking solution to play quickly forward into the space in behind Bournemouth's defensive line.

Keïta (8) chooses the best solution and passes the ball in between 2 Bournemouth defenders, and into a channel for centre forward **Firmino (9)** to run into.

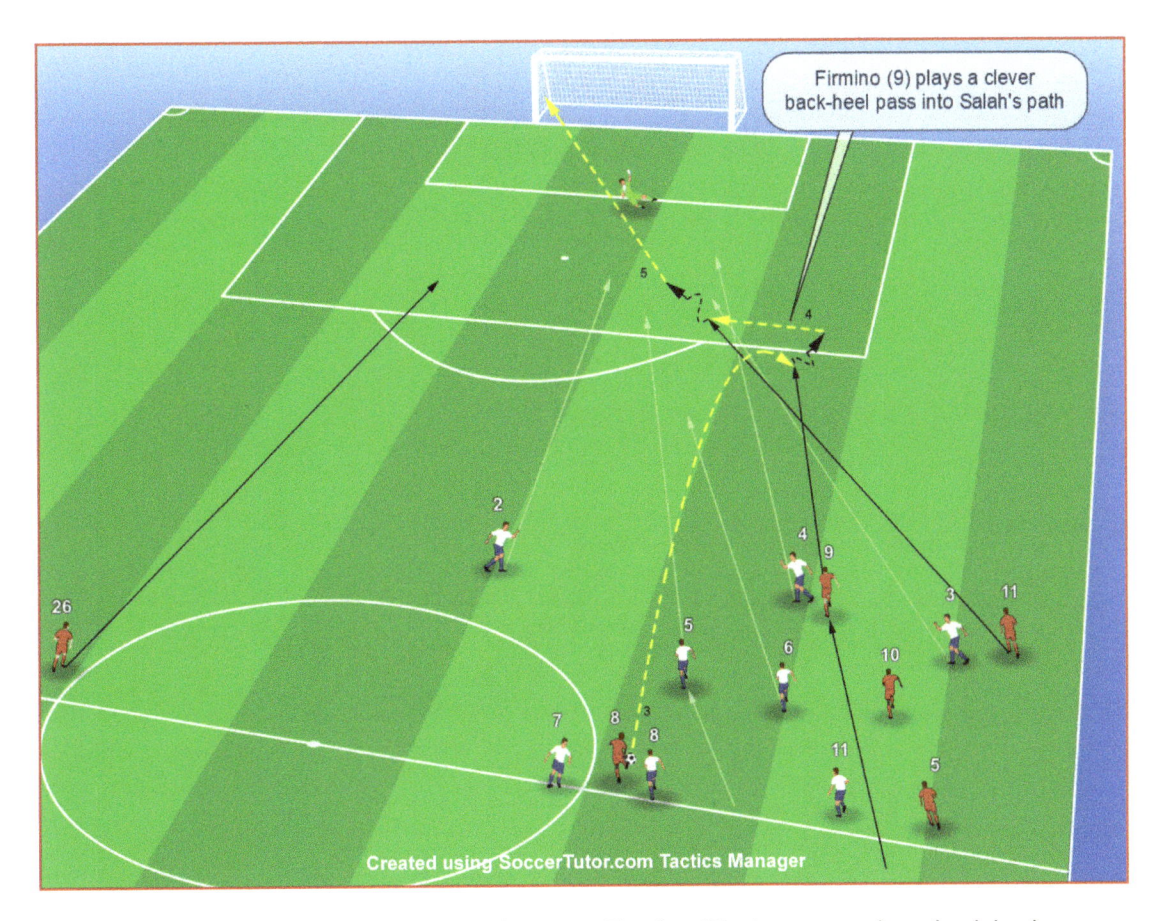

Tactical Solution 1 - Build-up Against a High Press and Play Forward Quickly

Firmino (9) plays a clever back-heel pass into Salah's path

Firmino (9) shows good speed and strength against his opponent in a 1v1 situation to gain control of the ball.

The right forward **Salah (11)** makes a well-timed movement and asks for the ball.

Firmino (9) plays a very clever back-heel pass into the path of **Salah (11)**, who takes it in his stride with a good first touch and finishes well into the far corner with his left foot.

SESSION 1A BASED ON THE TACTICS OF JÜRGEN KLOPP

Build-up Against a High Press and Pass into Forward's Feet + Finish Attack Quickly

Session for JÜRGEN KLOPP Tactics - Build-up Against a High Press and Play Forward Quickly

SESSION FOR THIS TACTICAL SITUATION (5 PRACTICES)

1. One-Touch Combination Play in a Continuous Short Passing Circuit (Support Angles)

1a: Finish with Dribble and Short Pass

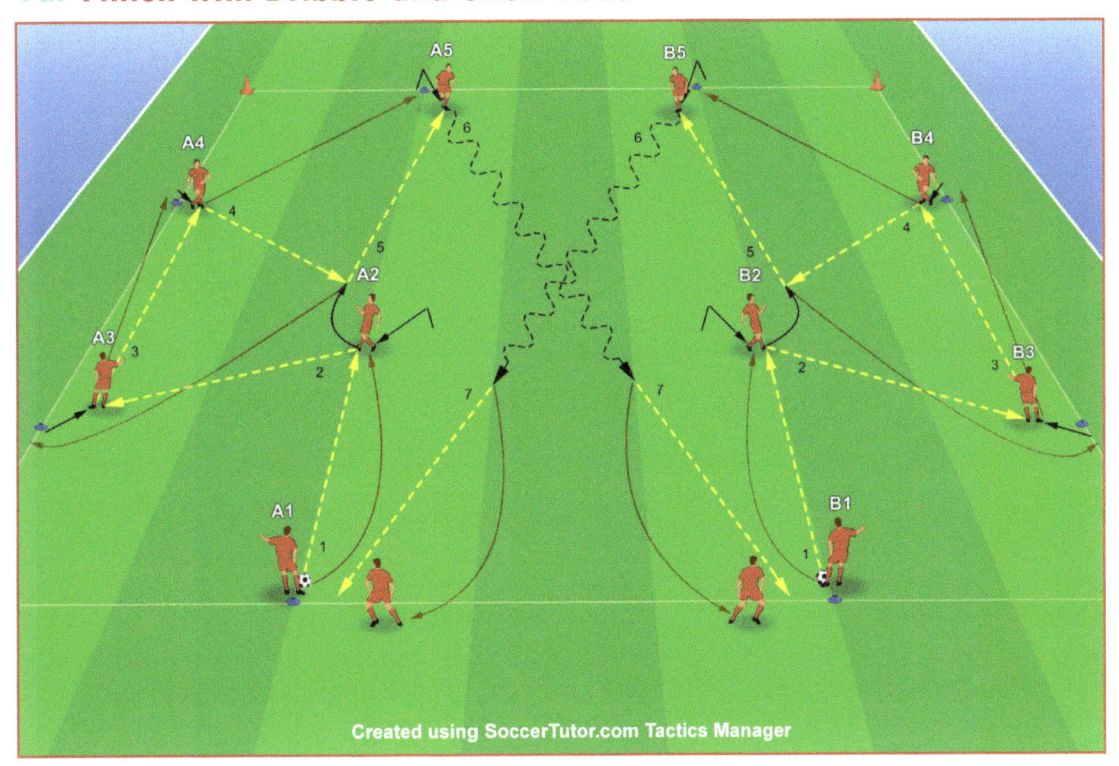

Description (1a)

In a 20 x 30 yard area, we work with 12 players split into 2 groups (A and B).

The sequence starts simultaneously with 2 balls from Player 1 in each group.

1. Player 1 passes forward to Player 2.
2. Player 2 plays back and across to Player 3.
3. Player 3 passes forward to Player 4.
4. Player 4 lays the ball back for Player 2, who turns to receive.
5. Player 2 passes forward to Player 5.
6. Player 5 takes a first touch out in front and dribbles forward quickly at an angle, as shown.
7. Player 5 passes to the next player waiting in the opposite group and the practice continues.

Rotation

All players move to the next position:
1 -> 2 -> 3 -> 4 -> 5 -> Opposite group

Session for **JÜRGEN KLOPP** Tactics - Build-up Against a High Press and Play Forward Quickly

1b: Finish with Movement to Receive and Long Pass (Progression)

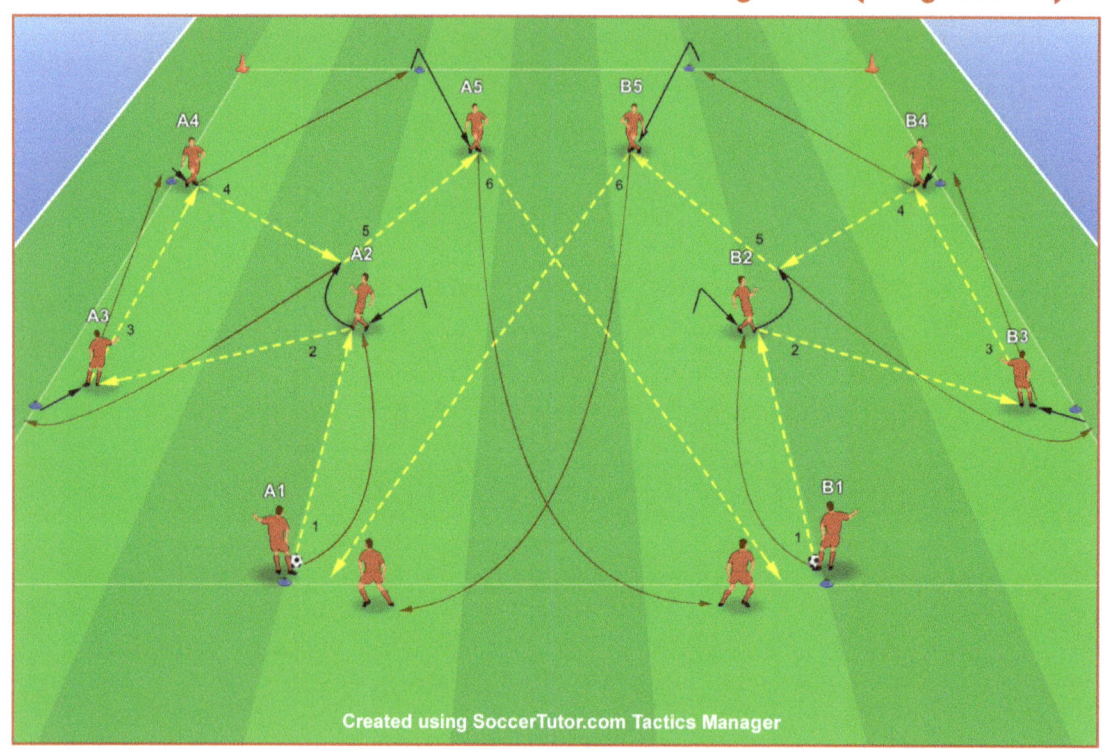

Description (1b)

- In the progression of the passing circuit on the previous page (1a), we now add more rhythm and speed to the passing combination.
- The sequence is the same except for the last 2 passes.
- Player 2 now plays his pass to Player 5 in front of him, so he can run forward onto it and **receive** (pass 5 in diagram).
- Also, there is no dribbling as part of the final action. Instead, Player 5 plays a longer pass to the start position of the opposite group to complete the sequence.

Rotation

All players move to the next position:
1 -> 2 -> 3 -> 4 -> 5 -> Opposite group

Coaching Points

1. Passes need to be well-weighted and aimed just in front of their teammates to step forward up to.
2. Make sure the players communicate with their teammates (visual and verbal) and heads are always up.
3. The practice should be done at a high tempo throughout.
4. The key is the rhythm and timing of the movement, together with the pass.
5. Synchronisation in the movements and actions of all players.

Session for JÜRGEN KLOPP Tactics - Build-up Against a High Press and Play Forward Quickly

PROGRESSION
2. Play Forward Quickly in a Dynamic Three Zone 6v6 (+4) Possession Game

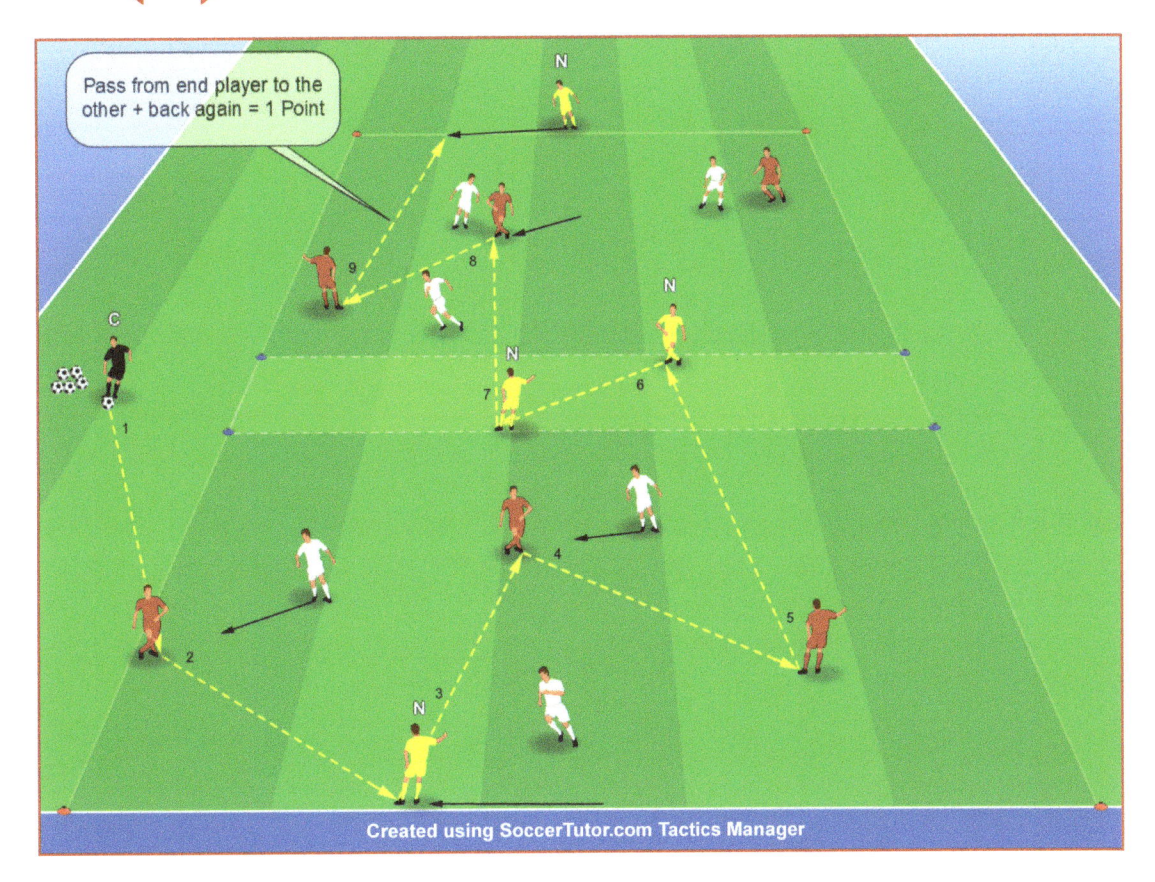

Pass from end player to the other + back again = 1 Point

Description

- In a total area of 15 x 35 yards, mark out 3 zones with a small middle zone.
- We play a 6v6 (+4) possession game across the 3 zones.
- There are 3 players from each team in each end zone. The 4 yellow neutral players all play along the zones' outer lines, as shown.
- The practice starts with the Coach's pass into an end zone and one team in possession.
- The aim is to exploit the numerical advantage with help from the neutral players to move the ball from the bottom neutral player to the top neutral player and back again (1 point).
- If they do this quickly (within 15 seconds), they score 2 points.
- If the defending team win the ball or the ball goes out of play, the teams switch roles.
- For each team, 3 players in one zone can be defenders and midfielders, and the 3 in the other zone can be midfielders and forwards.
- **RULES:** Red and white players are limited to 2 or 3 touches and the neutral players are limited to 1 or 2 touches.

Session for **JÜRGEN KLOPP** Tactics - Build-up Against a High Press and Play Forward Quickly

PROGRESSION

3. Build-up Against a High Press and Pass to Forward + Finish Quickly in a Position Specific 2 Zone Game

Forward decides whether to beat defender in 1v1 or combine with teammate

5 (+5) v 5

Description

- We split the marked out area into 2 halves and play an 8v8 (+5) game. The neutrals **(N)** play in the low zone with the team in possession (2 on each end line and 1 in the middle).

- The practice starts with the GK and the reds must build up play through a high press, and then pass to a forward in the other half where there is a 2v2 situation.

- The 2 forwards must find a solution to finish the attack quickly (individual or combine). In this example, they use a one-two combination to get in behind and score.

- If the attack finishes or the ball goes out of play, the teams switch roles, and we start from the white GK. The aims are exactly the same but going in the opposite direction with the whites attacking, and the reds defending.

- If the defending team wins possession at any time, they try to score on the counter attack within 8-10 seconds. The neutral players do not participate in this phase.

Rules

1. Players in the low zone limited to 2/3 touches.
2. Neutral players limited to 1 touch.
3. The forwards have unlimited touches.

©SOCCERTUTOR.COM

JÜRGEN KLOPP LIVERPOOL ATTACKING TACTICS

PROGRESSION
4. Build-up Against a High Press and Pass to Forward + Finish Quickly in a Dynamic Zonal Game

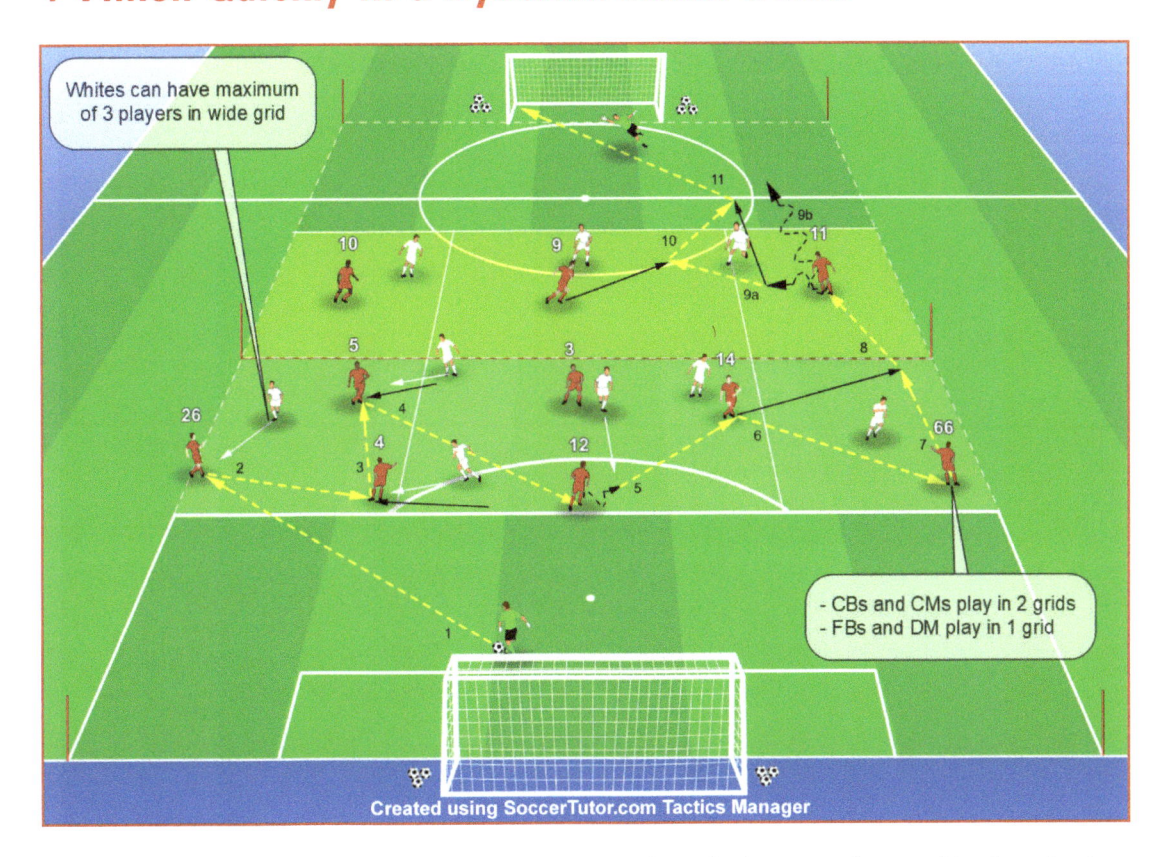

Whites can have maximum of 3 players in wide grid

- CBs and CMs play in 2 grids
- FBs and DM play in 1 grid

Description

- The 4 side grids are 12 x 12 yards, and the 2 central grids are 20 x 12 yards. The reds are in Liverpool's 4-3-3 formation and the whites have 10 players in a 3-2-3-1 (missing full back).
- The practice always starts from the red GK with a 7 v 6 situation across the first 3 grids.
- The red left centre back (**4**) and left central midfielder (**5**) can only move in the left and centre grids, and vice versa on the other side.
- The red full backs (**26 and 66**) and the defensive midfielder (**3**) can only move within their grids. The whites can defend with any 3 players in a side grid and 4 in the centre grid.
- The reds aim to use fast combination play to move the ball to one of their 3 forwards, who are all in 1 v 1 situations. The 3 red forwards must find a solution to play into the end zone and finish the attack. This can be done with individual play or by combining e.g. one-two in diagram.
- If the white team win the ball, they must try to score within 10 seconds (no zone restrictions).

Different Rules

1. The forwards move freely across all grids and the defenders stay within their grids.
2. The forwards and the defenders stay within their grids.

Session for **JÜRGEN KLOPP** Tactics - Build-up Against a High Press and Play Forward Quickly

PROGRESSION

5. Build-up Against a High Press and Pass to Forward + Finish Quickly in an 11v10 Tactical Game

5a: Versus 10 Players in 3-2-3-1 (Missing Full Back)

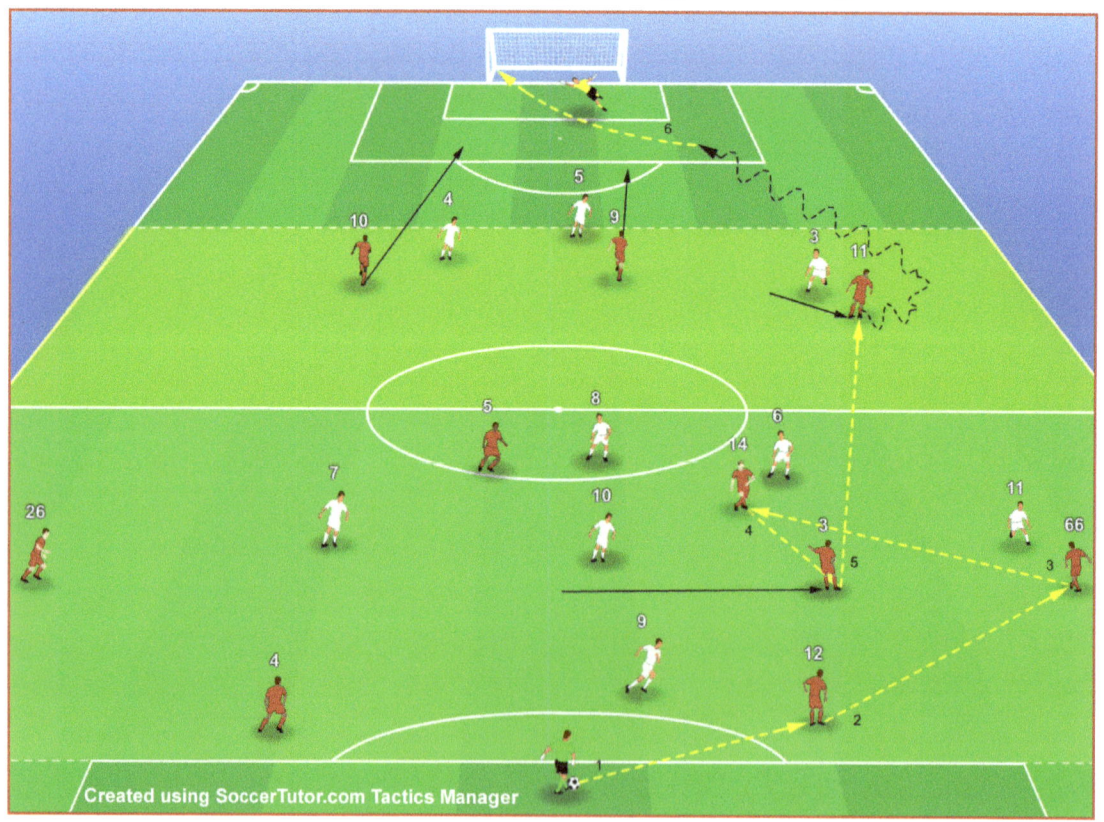

Description

- On a full pitch, mark out 2 large zones as shown in the diagram + 2 end zones. The reds have all 11 players from Liverpool's 4-3-3 formation and the whites have 10 players in a 3-2-3-1 formation (left back or right back missing from the 4-2-3-1).

- The game starts with the red GK's pass into Zone 1. The white defending team apply a high press in a 2-3-1 formation.

- The reds aim to build up play through the pressing and pass to a forward in Zone 2.

- The 3 red forwards must find a solution to play into the end zone and finish the attack. This can be done with individual play or by combining e.g. one-two.

- In this example, the right forward **(11)** beats his direct opponent in a 1v1 situation, dribbles into the box and scores.

- If the white team win the ball, they must try to score within 12 seconds (no zone restrictions).

- **RULES:** The 7 reds in Zone 1 are limited to 2/3 touches and the 3 forwards are unlimited.

Session for JÜRGEN KLOPP Tactics - Build-up Against a High Press and Play Forward Quickly

5b: Versus 11 Players in 4-2-3-1

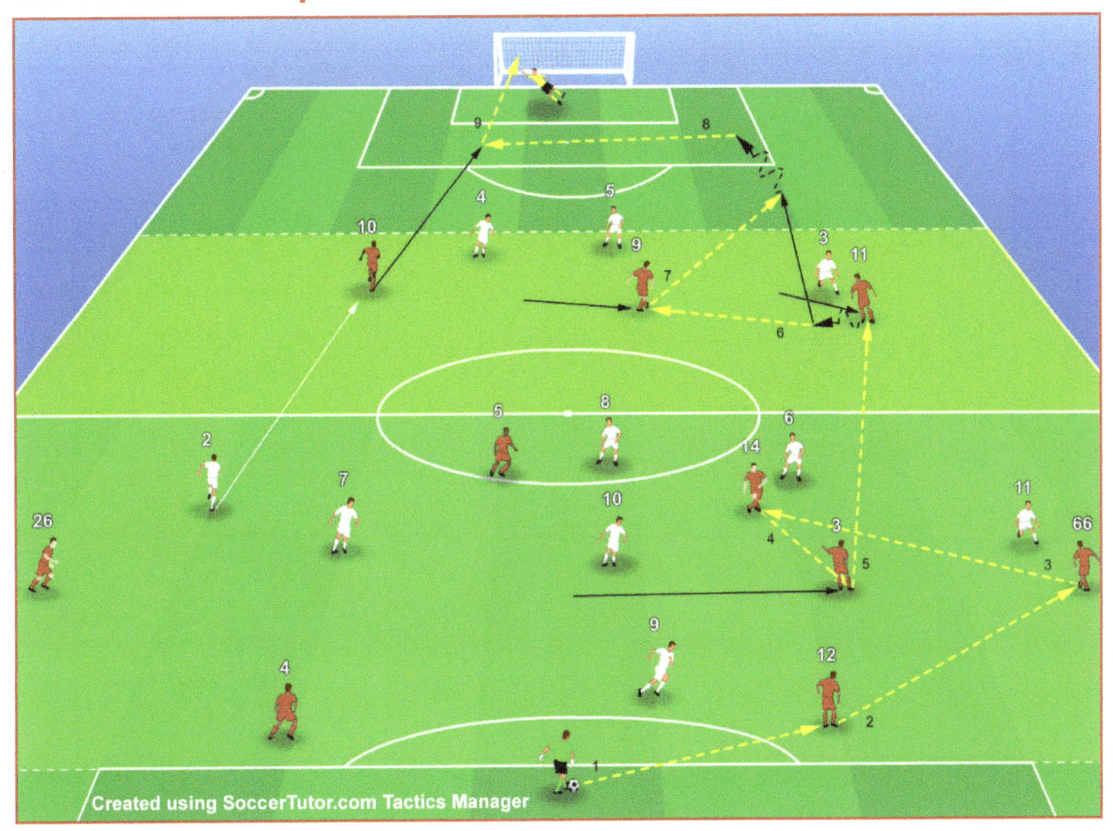

Description

- In this progression of Practice 5a on the previous page, we simply add the missing full back for the white team to complete their back 4.

- This full back is right back No.2 in the diagram example as the reds build up play on the other side. No.2 can move to support the white front 6 in Zone 1 by helping to apply a high press on the reds.

- If the reds successfully play forward into Zone 2, the white full back can run back to help the back 4 defend the attack.

- This creates a 3v4 situation for the reds instead of 3v3 and potentially makes it much more difficult to finish their attack quickly and score.

SESSION 1B BASED ON THE TACTICS OF JÜRGEN KLOPP

Build-up Against a High Press and Direct Forward Pass in Behind the Defensive Line

Session for **JÜRGEN KLOPP** Tactics - Build-up Against a High Press and Play Forward Quickly

SESSION FOR THIS TACTICAL SITUATION (3 PRACTICES)
1. Build-up Through Press + Direct Forward Pass in Behind the Defensive Line in an 11v9 Dynamic Game

As soon as an attack finishes, the Coach plays a new ball in

Description (1a)

- The low zone is 40 x 30 yards, the middle zone is 40 x 5 yards, and the high zone is 40 x 15 yards. The reds use Liverpool's 4-3-3 formation, and the whites have 9 players in a 3-2-3-1 formation (1 full back missing).

- The red GK starts, and the reds build up play through the white's high press (8v7 situation), as one of the red forwards (centre forward **No.9** in diagram) drops back to provide support.

- The aim is to play in behind the 2 white centre backs and into the high zone as quickly as possible for a red forward to run onto, receive, and score in any of the 3 mini goals (1 point).

- The practice works continuously. As soon as an attack is finished, the Coach passes a new ball into the red team. The 2 red forwards and the 2 white centre backs move back into the middle zone as quickly as possible to be ready.

- If the whites win the ball at any time, they try to score within 10 seconds (2 points).

Rules

1. Limit the time the reds have to play the ball into the high zone depending on the degree of difficulty you want to give to the practice.

2. Either all players are limited to 2 or 3 touches, or all players except the red forwards are limited to 2 to 3 touches.

Session for **JÜRGEN KLOPP** Tactics - Build-up Against a High Press and Play Forward Quickly

VARIATION
2. Throw-in Under Press + Direct Forward Pass in Behind the Defensive Line in an 11v9 Dynamic Game

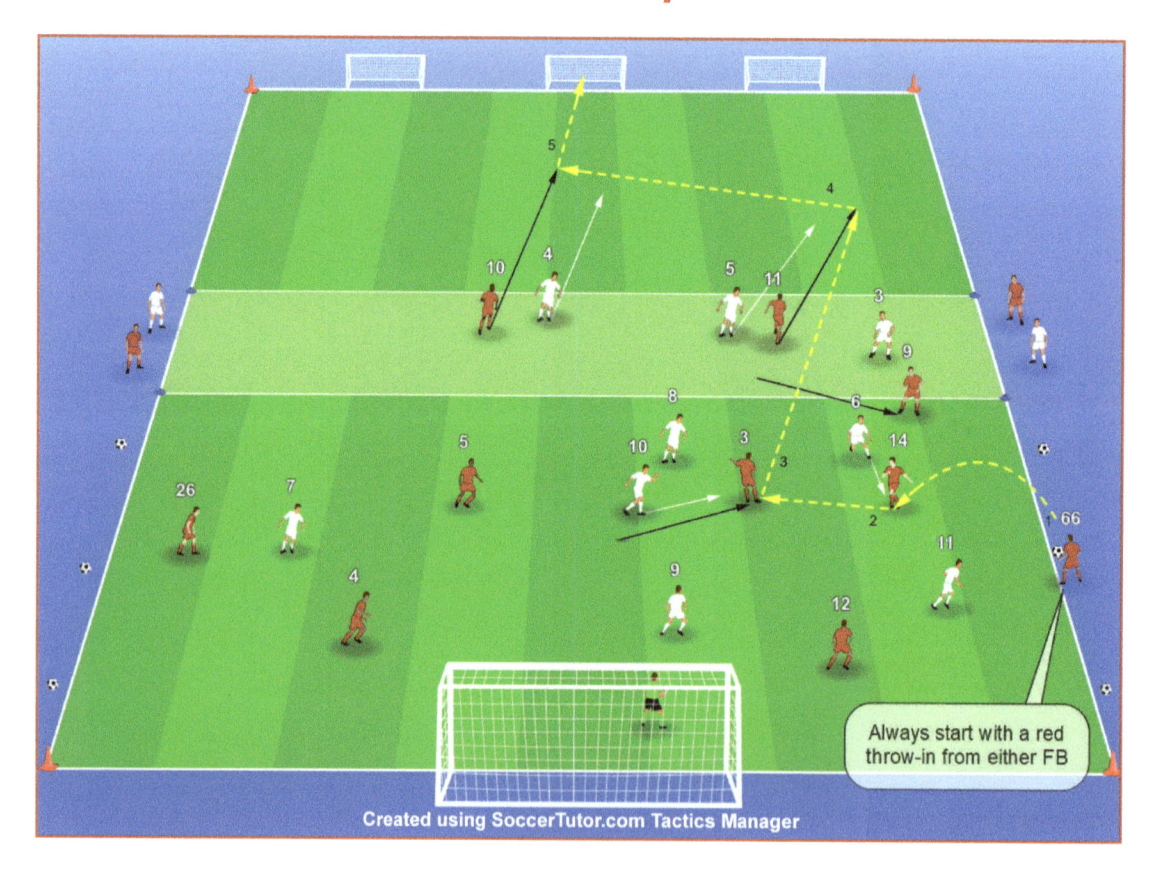

Always start with a red throw-in from either FB

Description

- In this variation of the previous practice, we move the white full back No.3 into the middle zone, as shown.

- The aims and rules for the practice are exactly the same, except now we start with a throw-in from within the low zone. The whites still implement a high press, but with one less player in the low zone.

- The reds must exploit their 8v6 numerical advantage to find a player in space who can pass in behind the 3 white defenders and into the high zone as quickly as possible.

- The aim is for a red forward to run onto the pass, receive, and then score in any of the 3 mini goals (1 point). He can score himself or combine with his teammate, as shown.

- If the whites win the ball at any time, they try to score on the counter attack within 10 seconds (2 points).

- In this variation, there are players waiting to move into the middle zone, so the practice continues without any stoppages (Coach plays new ball into reds in the low zone).

- Alternate starting with throw-ins from the full backs on both sides.

Session for **JÜRGEN KLOPP** Tactics - Build-up Against a High Press and Play Forward Quickly

PROGRESSION
3. Build-up (or Throw-in) Through Press + Forward Pass in Behind the Defensive Line in an 11v11 Tactical Game

Description
- Mark out 3 horizontal zones on a full pitch, as shown. The reds use Liverpool's 4-3-3 formation, and the whites use the 4-2-3-1.
- The practice starts with the red GK and the reds build up play through the white's high press in an 8v7 situation. One of the red forwards (**No.9** in diagram) drops back to provide support and one of the white full backs is pushed forward (left back No.3).
- The aim is to play in behind the 3 white defenders in the middle zone and into the high zone as quickly as possible for one of the 2 red forwards (**No.10** or **No.11**) to run onto.
- The forwards try to get to the ball ahead of the defenders and score either individually or by combining with their teammate.
- The practice works continuously but we **alternate between the GK starting and a full back starting with a throw-in**.
- As soon as the attack above is finished, a red full back will restart with a throw-in under a high press from the whites. The red forwards and white defenders move back into the middle zone as quickly as possible to be ready.
- If the whites win the ball at any time, they try to score on the counter attack.

JÜRGEN KLOPP TACTICAL ANALYSIS

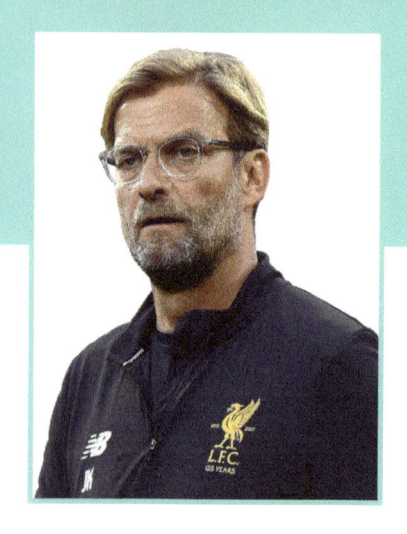

SOLUTION 2

Break Through Pressing and Play in the Space Between the Lines

Content from analysis of Liverpool F.C. during the 2018-2019 Champions League winning season and the 2019-2020 Premier League winning season

- Analysis based on recurring patterns of play observed within the Liverpool team.
- Tactical solutions displayed as examples of the team's tactics being used effectively.
- Real match examples of Liverpool scoring a goal using this specific attacking tactical solution.
- Each action, pass, individual movement with or without the ball, and the positioning of each player on the pitch including their body shape, are presented.
- The analysis is then used to create a full progressive session to coach this tactical situation.

Tactical Solution 2 - Break Through Pressing and Play in the Space Between the Lines

Break Through Pressing and Play in the Space Between the Lines

What?

Liverpool look to play through their opponent's pressing and into the space between their midfield and defensive lines.

Why?

When opponents press in the middle and high zones, but they have a large distance between their midfield and defensive lines (which can be exploited).

How?

Liverpool circulate the ball in their half with the aim to pass in behind the opponent's midfielders, which neutralises 6 players and leads to an attack against just the back 4.

Target Areas (in Between the Lines)

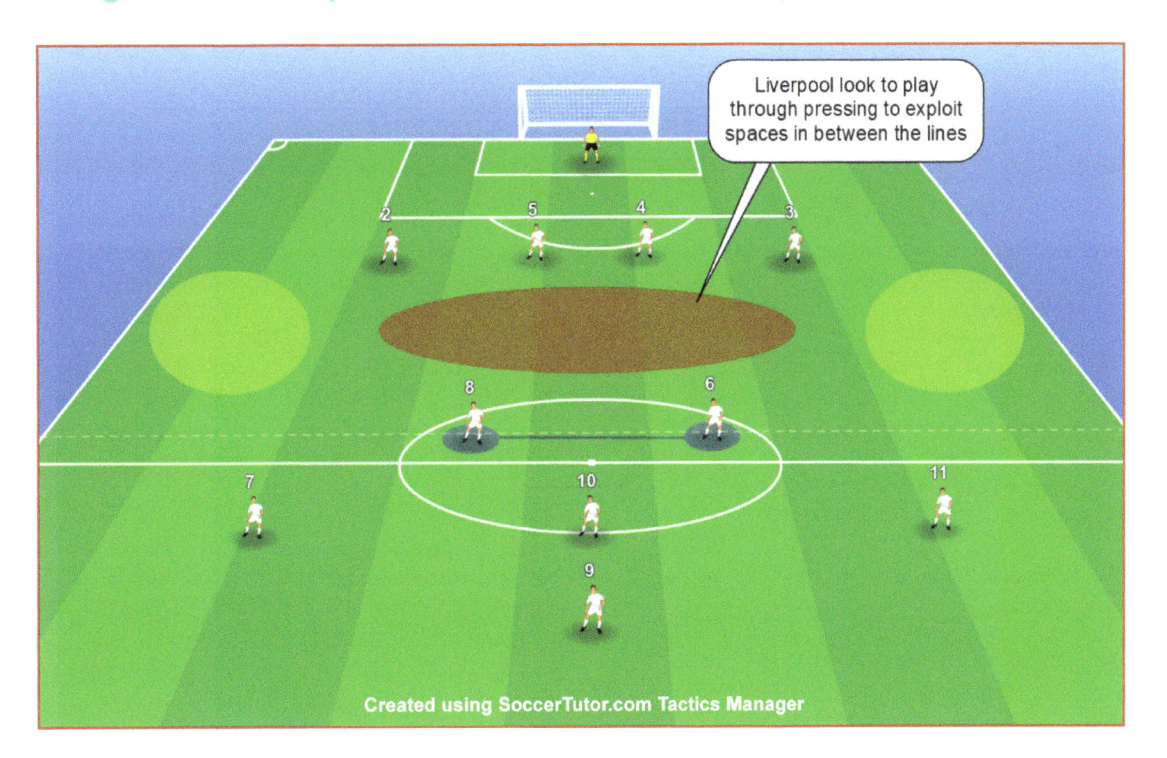

Liverpool look to play through pressing to exploit spaces in between the lines

Tactical Solution 2 - Break Through Pressing and Play in the Space Between the Lines

Tactical Solution: Break Through Opponent's Pressing and Play Through the Midfield Line for a Fast Attack

In this tactical situation, Liverpool (4-3-3) are building up play from the back and their opponents (4-2-3-1) apply pressing in the middle and high zone.

This pressing tactic leaves a large space for Liverpool to exploit in between the opposition's midfield and defensive lines.

The aim for Liverpool is to play an incisive forward pass to one of the central midfielders in behind the 2 opposing defensive midfielders, which takes 6 players out of the game and leaves a potential 4v4 attack, as shown.

This can also be a 3v4 (+1), 3v4 (+2), 4v4 (+1) or 4v4 (+2) attack depending on the situation and positioning of Liverpool's players.

Liverpool's right back **Alexander-Arnold** is very adept at playing these kinds of incisive passes, which are shown in the game analysis pages to follow.

In this example, the full back **(66)** plays inside to the central midfielder **(14)**, who then plays an incisive forward pass beyond the opposition's midfield line and into the large space between the lines.

The other central midfielder **(5)** receives on the half-turn and dribbles forward to try and finish a quick 4v4 attack with the front 3 against the opposition's back 4. As explained, this can be a 4v4 (+1) or 4v4 (+2) attack if the full backs sprint forward quickly to provide support.

Statistical Analysis of Liverpool Breaking Through Pressing and Playing in the Space Between the Lines

Liverpool scored **8 goals** in this tactical situation
(Premier League and Champions League 2018-2019 and 2019-2020 seasons)

VS. OPPONENTS PRESSING IN MIDDLE & HIGH ZONES
BREAK THROUGH PRESS AND PLAY IN SPACE BETWEEN THE LINES

DATE	HOME	AWAY	SCORE	GOAL (MIN)	SCORER	ASSIST
12th Aug 2018	Liverpool	West Ham	4-0	1-0 (19')	**Salah** *	Robertson
12th Aug 2018	Liverpool	West Ham	4-0	3-0 (53')	**Mané**	Firmino
20th Oct 2018	Huddersfield	Liverpool	0-1	0-1 (24')	**Salah**	Shaqiri
8th Dec 2018	Bournemouth	Liverpool	0-4	0-1 (25')	**Salah**	
29th Dec 2018	Liverpool	Arsenal	5-1	1-1 (13')	**Firmino**	
10th Mar 2019	Liverpool	Burnley	4-2	4-2 (90 +3')	**Mané**	Sturridge
26th Apr 2019	Liverpool	Huddersfield	5-0	5-0 (83')	**Salah**	Robertson
14th Dec 2019	Liverpool	Watford	2-0	2-0 (90')	**Salah** *	Origi

* The full analysis of these goals is shown on the following pages...

Tactical Solution 2 - Break Through Pressing and Play in the Space Between the Lines

Analysis from Liverpool 4-0 West Ham (Salah 19') - 12th Aug 2018, Premier League

Tactical Solution (1): Incisive Pass Through the Opponent's Midfield Line for a Fast Attack (Cross from Left)

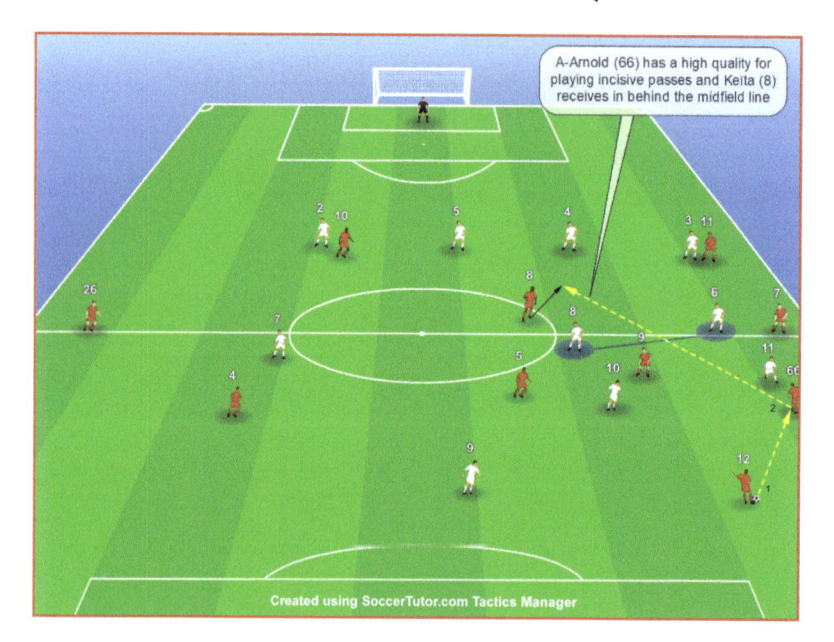

Liverpool are building up play and the centre back **Gomez (12)** passes to right back **A-Arnold (66)** near to the side-line.

As **A-Arnold (66)** has a high quality for playing incisive passes, central midfielder **Keïta (8)** moves in behind to receive.

A-Arnold's (66) pass neutralises 6 opponents, as they are all now behind the ball.

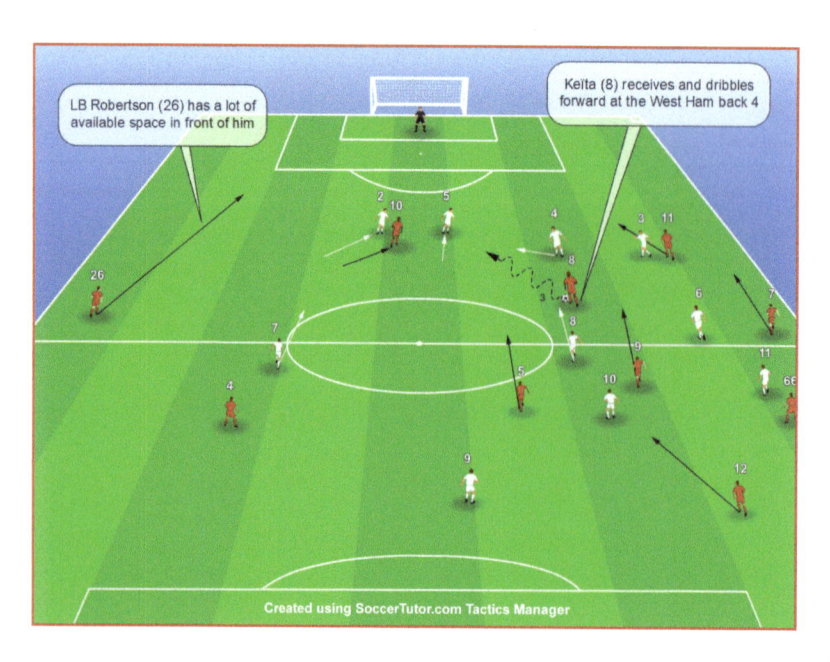

Left central midfielder **Keïta (8)** receives and dribbles forward at the opposition's back 4 with the following support:

- 2 forwards **Mané (10)** and **Salah (11)** in front of him.
- Right central midfielder **Milner (7)** to the right.
- Left back **Robertson (26)** to the left.

This creates a 3v4 (+2) situation for Liverpool to finish the attack. Centre forward **Firmino (9)** is in a deep position in this particular example.

Tactical Solution 2 - Break Through Pressing and Play in the Space Between the Lines

Robertson (26) has the momentum and advantage against opponents

Keïta (8) dribbles at West Ham's back line who move backwards towards the edge of their box.

At the correct time, he passes into the wide channel for the advanced run of the left back **Robertson (26)**, who receives in the box and in behind the defensive line.

Robertson (26) has the advantage and momentum against the opponents who are simply reacting to the situation (delay).

With his first touch, **Robertson (26)** passes the ball across the 6-yard box to the right forward **Salah (11)**, who scores with an easy finish.

Tactical Solution 2 - Break Through Pressing and Play in the Space Between the Lines

Analysis from Liverpool 2-0 Watford (Salah 90') - 14th Dec 2019, Premier League

Tactical Solution (2): Incisive Pass Through the Opponent's Midfield Line for a Fast Attack (Cut Back from Right)

Liverpool's GK **Alisson** throws the ball out to the right back **A-Arnold (66)**.

A-Arnold (66) is pressed by a Watford player and quickly plays an incisive pass in behind the midfield line.

Liverpool's central midfielder **Chamberlain (15)** has moved into the area between the midfield and defensive lines to receive the pass.

Chamberlain (15) receives and only has 4 Watford players (back 4) ahead of him.

Salah (11) and **Mané (10)** are positioned well between the defenders to provide support and attacking options.

Chamberlain (15) decides to pass immediately into the channel between the left back and centre back, which **Mané (10)** moves into and asks for the ball with a good side-on body position.

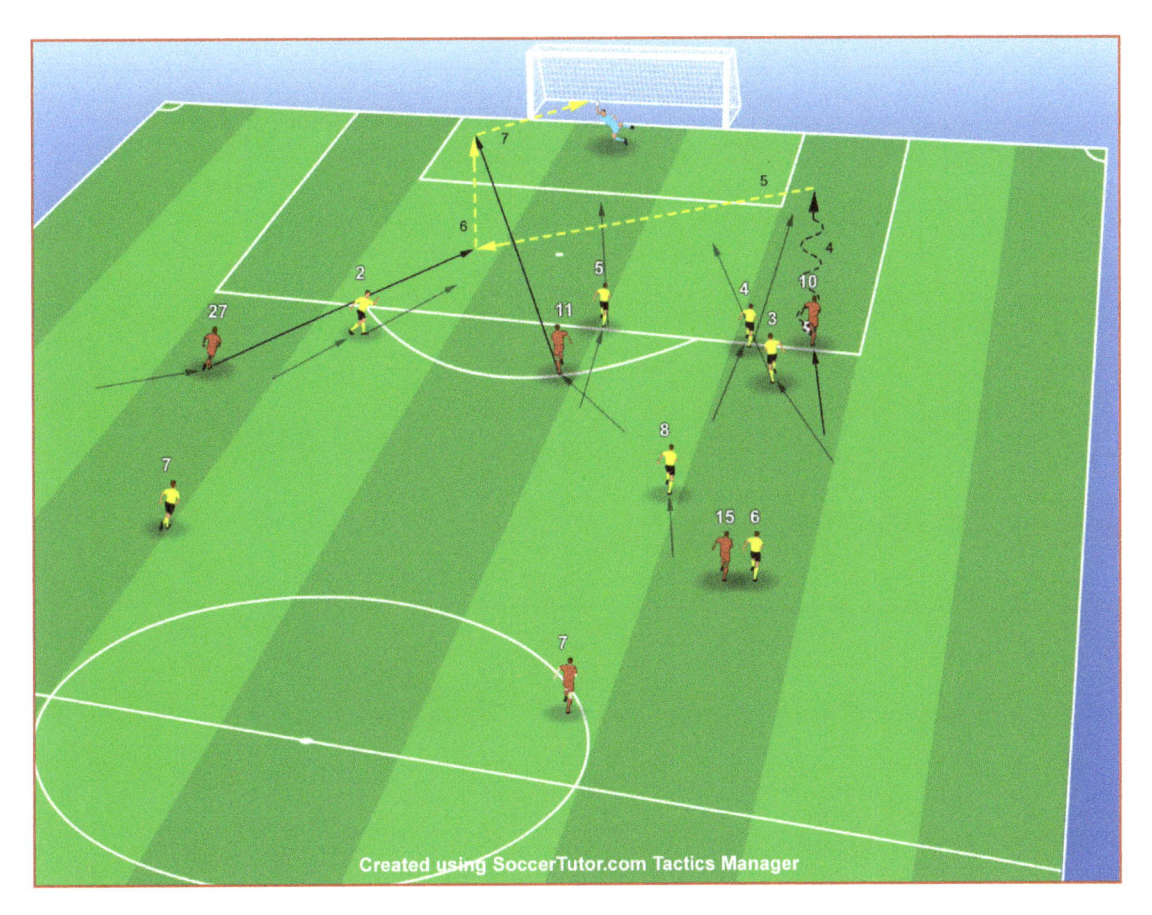

Tactical Solution 2 - Break Through Pressing and Play in the Space Between the Lines

Mané (10) exploits his speed advantage to beat the Watford centre back to the ball and receives inside the box. He then dribbles the ball forward before cutting the ball back for the oncoming run of the other forward **Origi (27)** approaching from the left side.

Origi (27) tries to shoot at goal but instead drags his shot to the left towards **Salah (11)** near the by-line, who reacts quickly and scores from a tight angle with a clever back heel.

SESSION 2 BASED ON THE TACTICS OF JÜRGEN KLOPP

Break Through Pressing and Play in the Space Between the Lines

Session for JÜRGEN KLOPP Tactics - Break Through Pressing and Play in Between the Lines

SESSION FOR THIS TACTICAL SITUATION (5 PRACTICES)
1. Build-up Play Through the Lines in a Three Team Possession and Transition Game

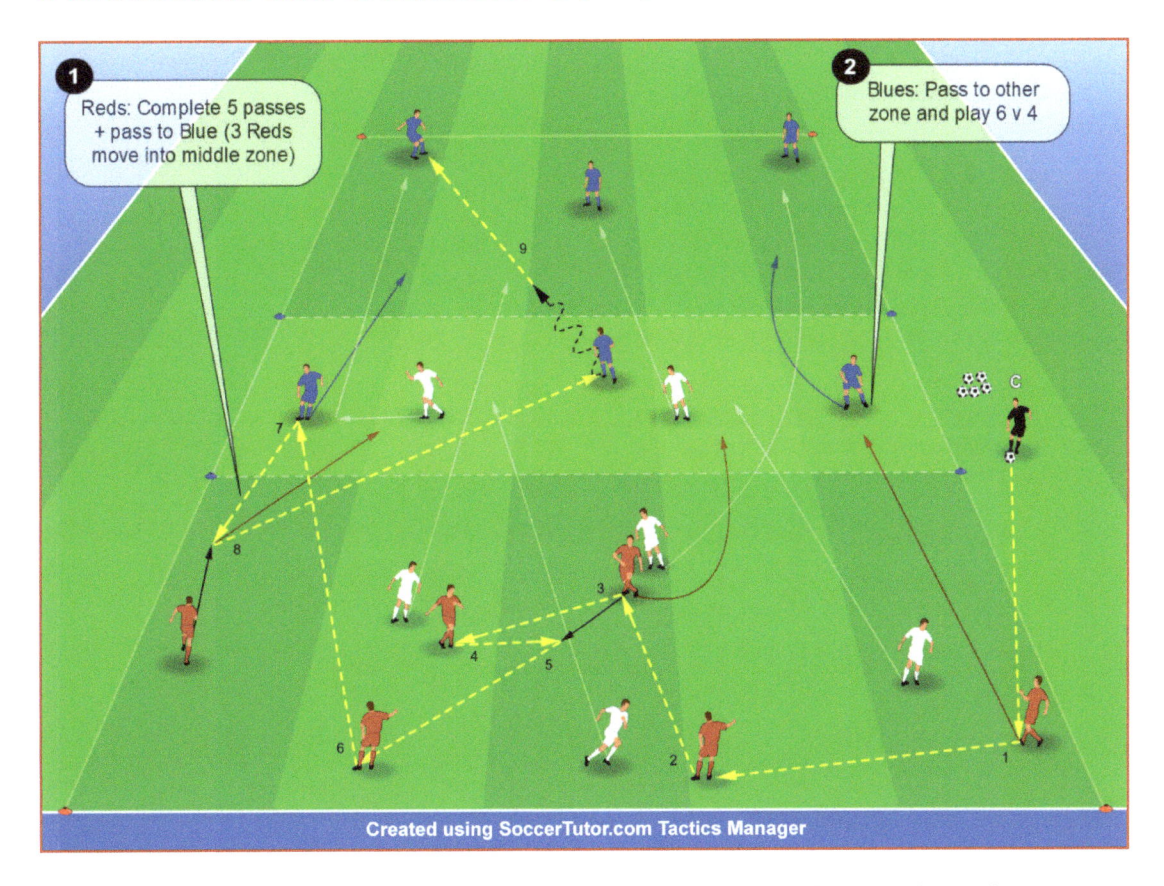

1. Reds: Complete 5 passes + pass to Blue (3 Reds move into middle zone)

2. Blues: Pass to other zone and play 6 v 4

Description

- The two end zones are 20 x 15 yards, and the middle zone is 20 x 5 yards. We have 3 teams of 6 players (red, white, and blue).

- The practice starts with the Coach's pass to the reds, who have a 6v4 situation within the end zone vs. 4 white players.

- The other 2 white players and 3 blue players are in the middle zone. The remaining 3 blue players are in the opposite end zone.

- The reds aim to complete 5 passes and then pass to a blue player in behind the 2 white middle players. The blue player who receives in behind dribbles into the opposite end zone and passes to one of his 3 teammates.

- **NOTE**: The 3 blue players can pass back to a red player if they are marked or pressed. In this example, a blue player passes back when pressed, and this then creates space for the blue player in the middle to receive in behind from the next pass.

- The 2 white players in the middle mark the 3 blue players and try to intercept any passes.

- Practice description continues on next page...

JÜRGEN KLOPP LIVERPOOL ATTACKING TACTICS

Session for JÜRGEN KLOPP Tactics - Break Through Pressing and Play in Between the Lines

Description (Continued...)

- All the blue players from the middle zone move into the end zone.
- The 2 white middle zone players also move into the end zone + 2 more white players from the opposite zone.
- The other 2 white players move into the middle zone, as shown.
- The blue team now play 6v4 in the opposite end zone with the same aim to complete 5 passes before moving the ball to a red player in the middle zone (in behind 2 white middle players), and then moving the ball to the opposite end zone for a new 6v4 for the reds.
- If the whites win the ball at any point, they switch roles with the team that lost the ball, and the practice continues with the same aims, but the roles reversed.

Coaching Points

1. Correct body shape (open up and half turn) and positioning is important to view the options for where the next pass is going.
2. The correct angles, distances and movement are required to provide good support.
3. Players should check away from their marker before moving to receive (create space).
4. Encourage quick one touch combination play.
5. The players must communicate (visually and verbally) with their heads up.
6. The practice must be executed with high rhythm and synchronisation of all movements.

Session for JÜRGEN KLOPP Tactics - Break Through Pressing and Play in Between the Lines

PROGRESSION
2. Break Through Pressing and Play in Between the Lines in a Position Specific Functional Game

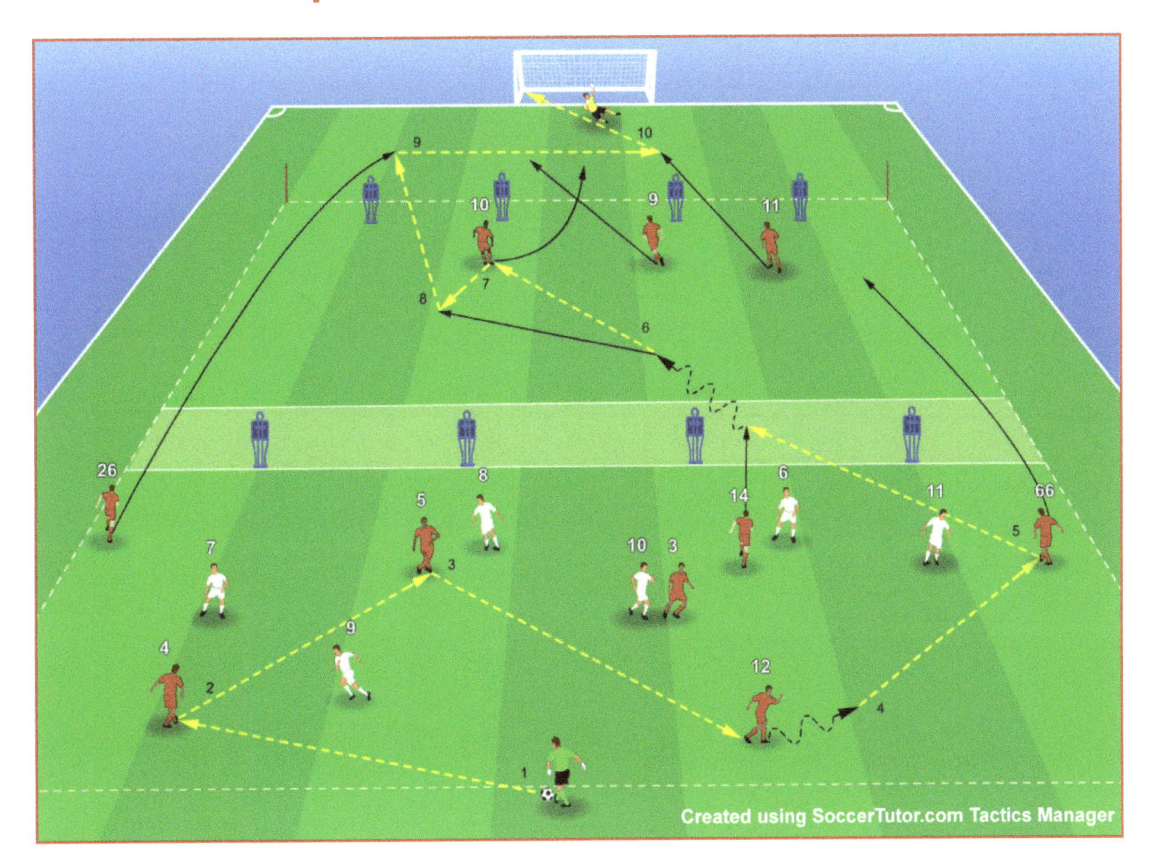

Description

- The low zone is 40 x 15 yards, the middle zone is 40 x 5 yards, and the high zone is 40 x 15 yards. The two end zones are 40 x 10 yards.
- There are 2 goals with GKs, 4 mannequins in the middle zone (midfield line) and 4 mannequins in the high zone (defensive line).
- The red attacking team use Liverpool's 4-4-3 formation and the white defending team have the front 7 players in a 2-3-1 formation.
- The practice always starts from the red team's GK and the reds aim to build-up play through the low zone against the white's pressing.
- The reds then aim to pass into the middle zone, where one of the central midfielders moves in behind the midfield line (mannequins) to receive.
- The player that receives (**No.14** in diagram) dribbles into the high zone. The 2 full backs make advanced runs into the high zone.
- The reds use predetermined patterns of play **(see analysis pages in this section for examples)** to get in behind the defensive line and score past the GK in the end zone.

Progression: Remove the predetermined patterns and play freely to finish the attacks.

JÜRGEN KLOPP LIVERPOOL ATTACKING TACTICS

Session for **JÜRGEN KLOPP** Tactics - Break Through Pressing and Play in Between the Lines

PROGRESSION

3. Break Through Pressing and Play in Between the Lines in a 9v9 (+2) Dynamic Game

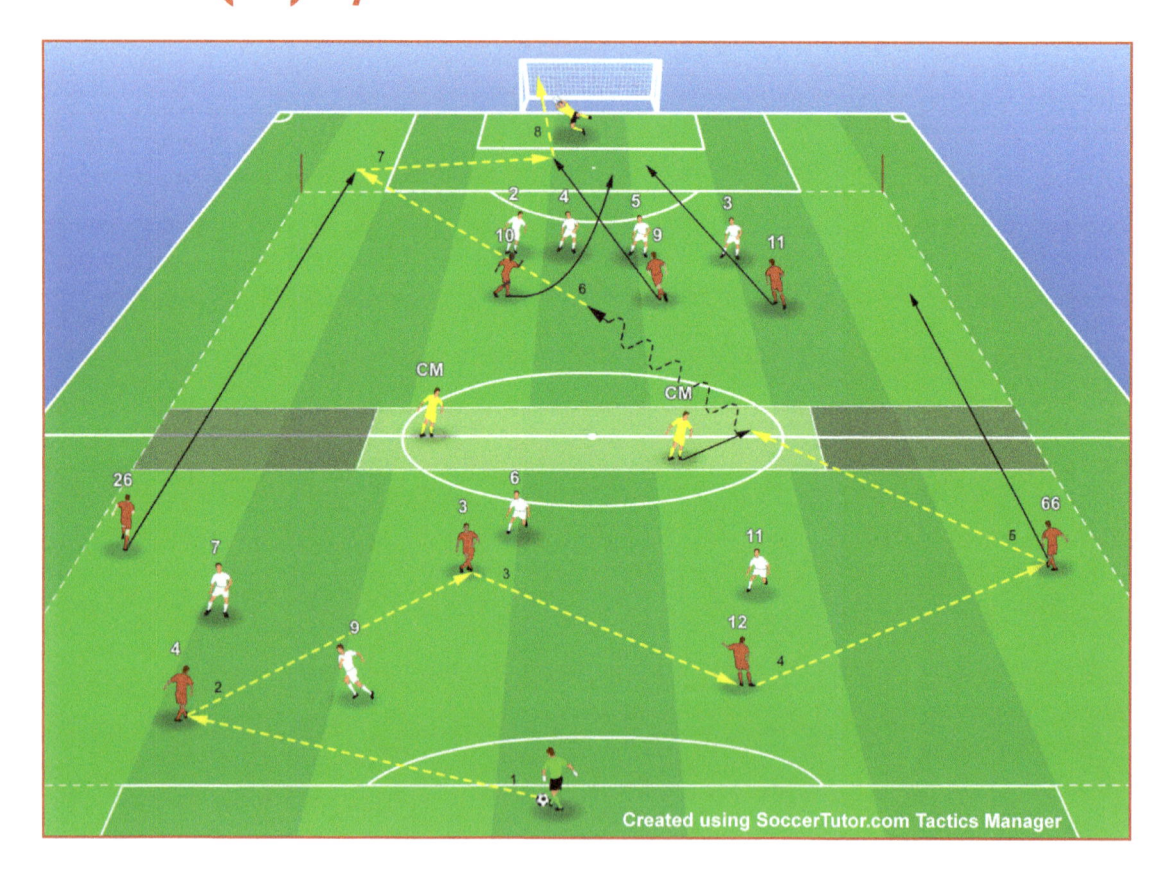

Description

- In this progression of the previous practice, we play in a larger area and add a back 4 for the white team. Both teams use the 4-3-3 formation, with the neutral players taking the role of 2 central midfielders for either team when they are in possession.

- Either GK starts (red in example) by passing into the low zone. The red back 4 and the defensive midfielder (3) build up play against 3 white forwards and 1 defensive midfielder.

- The aim is to pass to either CM in the middle zone (in behind the opposition's midfield line) and then finish the attack in the other half.

- It becomes a 4 (+2) v 4 situation with the 2 red full backs making advanced runs to provide support.

- When the attack finishes or the ball goes out of play, the game starts again from the white GK and the 2 teams switch roles.

- If the white front 4 win the ball, they try to score within 10 seconds.

- If a white defender wins the ball, they pass back to their GK and the 2 teams switch roles.

Progression: The white front 4 are able to run back and help their back 4 defend as soon as the ball is played into their half.

Session for **JÜRGEN KLOPP** Tactics - Break Through Pressing and Play in Between the Lines

PROGRESSION
4. Break Through Pressing and Play in Between the Lines in a Tactical Zonal Game

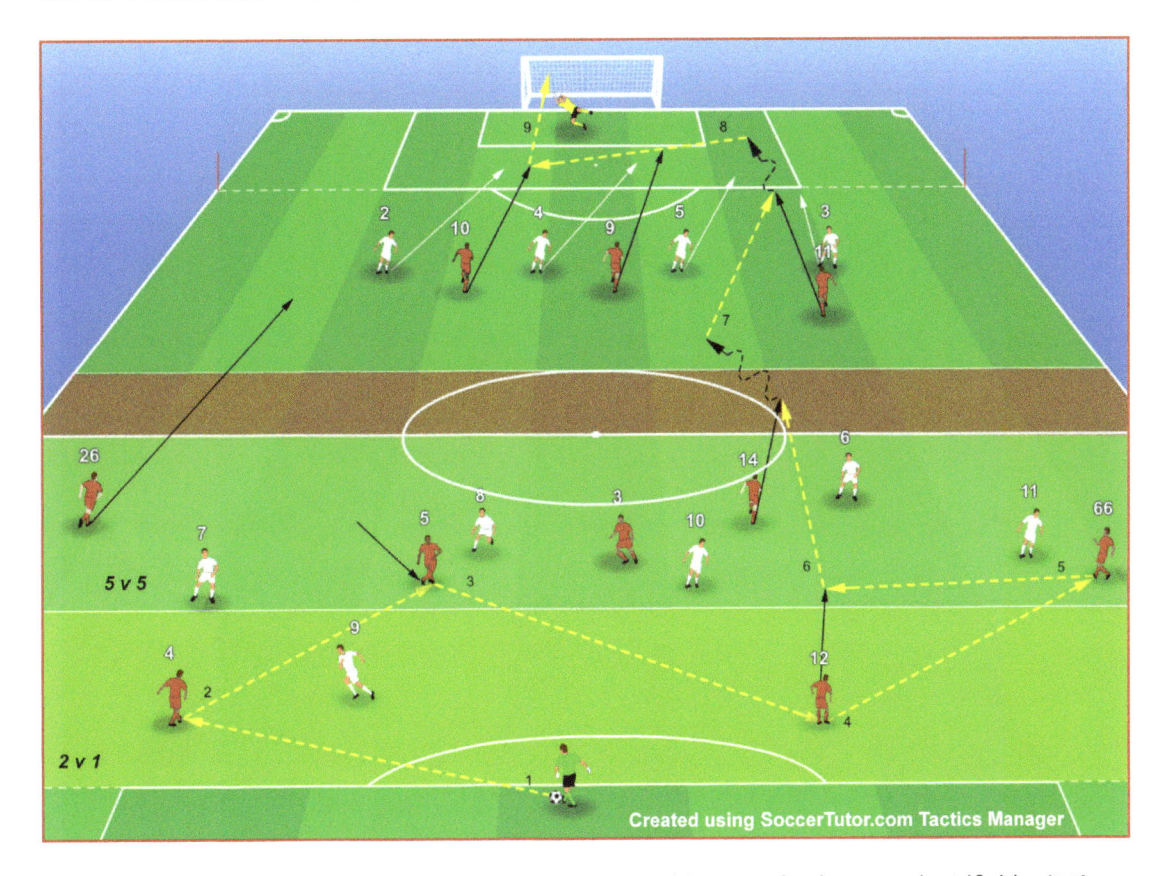

Description
- On a full pitch, mark out 4 horizontal zones + 2 end zones. Play a normal 11 v 11 game with the reds in a 4-3-3 and the whites in a 4-2-3-1.
- The game starts from the red GK's pass into the first zone (2 v 1) and the red centre backs play into the second zone (5 v 5). The aim is to play through the white team's high press and one of the central midfielders (**No.14** in diagram) moves into the third zone to receive in behind the midfield line.
- The reds launch a fast attack with at least 5 players (including a full back) to quickly get in behind the defensive line and score.

- In this example, the central midfielder (**14**) receives and passes in the channel between the white left back and centre back for the run of the red right forward (**11**).
- The right forward (**11**) receives, dribbles forward and cuts the ball back for the left forward (**10**) to score at the back post.
- The white front 6 can run back to defend as soon as the ball is played into their half. All of the red players can also move freely to attack.
- When the attack finishes or the ball goes out of play, all players return to their starting positions within their zones, and we start again from the red GK.

JÜRGEN KLOPP LIVERPOOL ATTACKING TACTICS

Session for **JÜRGEN KLOPP** Tactics - Break Through Pressing and Play in Between the Lines

PROGRESSION
5. Break Through Pressing and Play in Between the Lines in an 11v11 Tactical Game

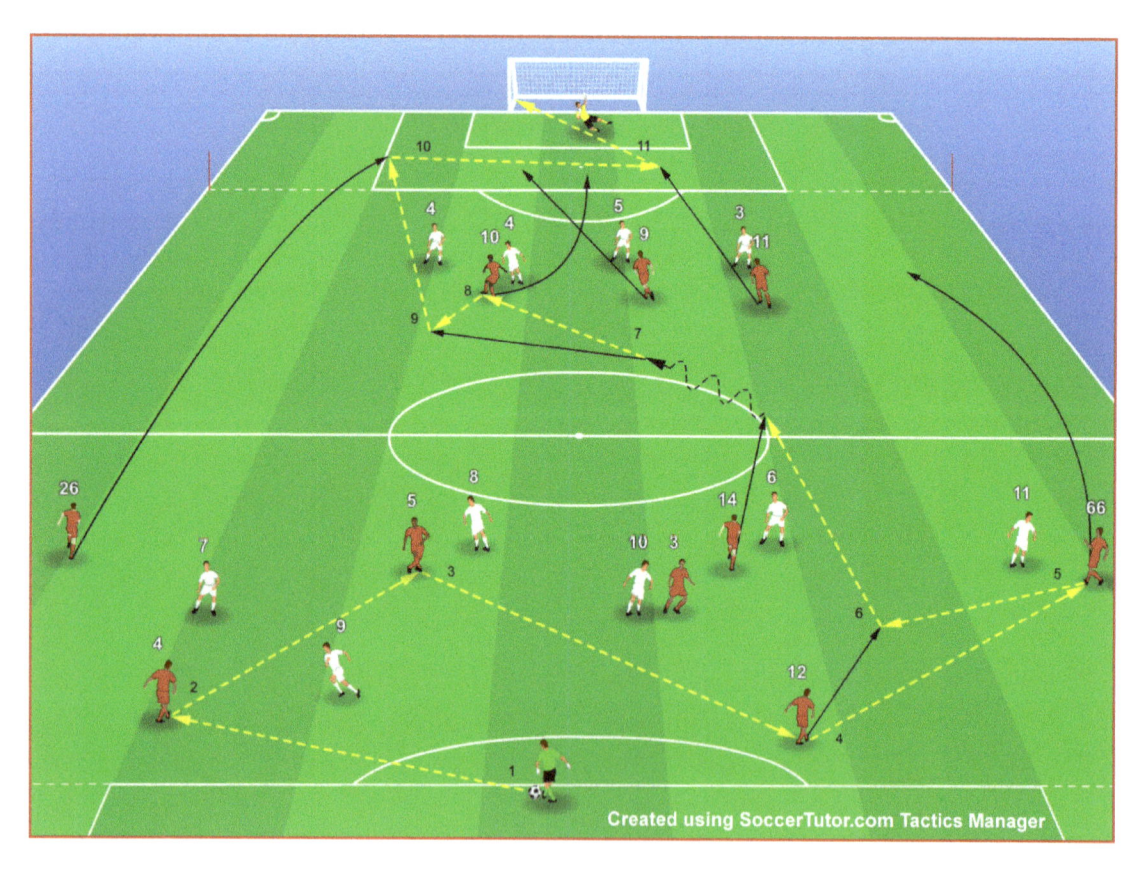

Description

- In this final practice and progression of the previous game, we only keep the 2 end zones and play a normal 11v11 game. Both teams use the 4-3-3 formation.

- Instruct the defending team's front 6 to press high up the pitch and the back 4 to be deep, so that there is a big gap between the midfield and defensive lines.

- The game starts with either GK (red in diagram) passing to a defender. The reds must play through the white team's high press and pass to a central midfielder (**No.14** in diagram), who moves to receive in behind the midfield line. From there, they try to finish the attack quickly.

- The reds must try to find the best solution to play in behind the defensive line e.g. If the white back 4 are compact, the reds can utilise their full backs who make advanced runs. This forces the whites to defend realistically.

- If the reds score directly from this type of attack, they get 2 points. If the whites win the ball, they try to score within 14 seconds (counter attack) - the reds must make a fast transition from attack to defence.

JÜRGEN KLOPP TACTICAL ANALYSIS

SOLUTION 3

Long Passes in Behind with All Opponents Behind the Ball

Content from analysis of Liverpool F.C. during the 2018-2019 Champions League winning season and the 2019-2020 Premier League winning season

- Analysis based on recurring patterns of play observed within the Liverpool team.
- Tactical solutions displayed as examples of the team's tactics being used effectively.
- Real match examples of Liverpool scoring a goal using this specific attacking tactical solution.
- Each action, pass, individual movement with or without the ball, and the positioning of each player on the pitch including their body shape, are presented.
- The analysis is then used to create a full progressive session to coach this tactical situation.

Tactical Solution 3 - Long Passes in Behind with All Opponents Behind the Ball

Long Passes in Behind with All Opponents Behind the Ball

What?

Liverpool play through the opposition's defence by playing a direct long aerial forward pass in behind the defensive line and into the target area shown in the diagram below.

Why?

The opposing defensive line need to be at least 10-15 yards in front of the box so there is space to exploit in behind, but their attacking players are not advanced enough to press the Liverpool centre backs and prevent them from playing long passes.

How?

Liverpool use a direct game with a long aerial forward pass from their centre backs (or defensive midfielder) to their forwards into the highlighted target area.

Target Areas (Edge and Inside Box)

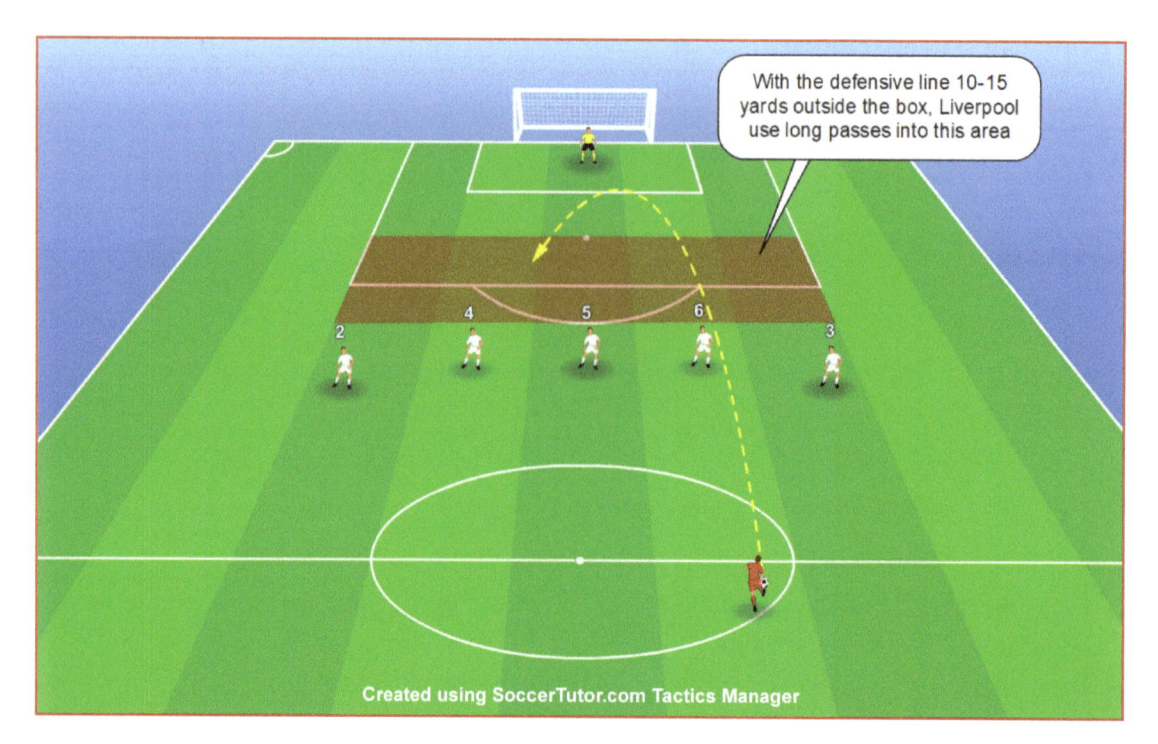

With the defensive line 10-15 yards outside the box, Liverpool use long passes into this area

Tactical Solution 3 - Long Passes in Behind with All Opponents Behind the Ball

Tactical Solution: Long Aerial Forward Pass in Behind with All Opponents (5-4-1) Behind the Ball

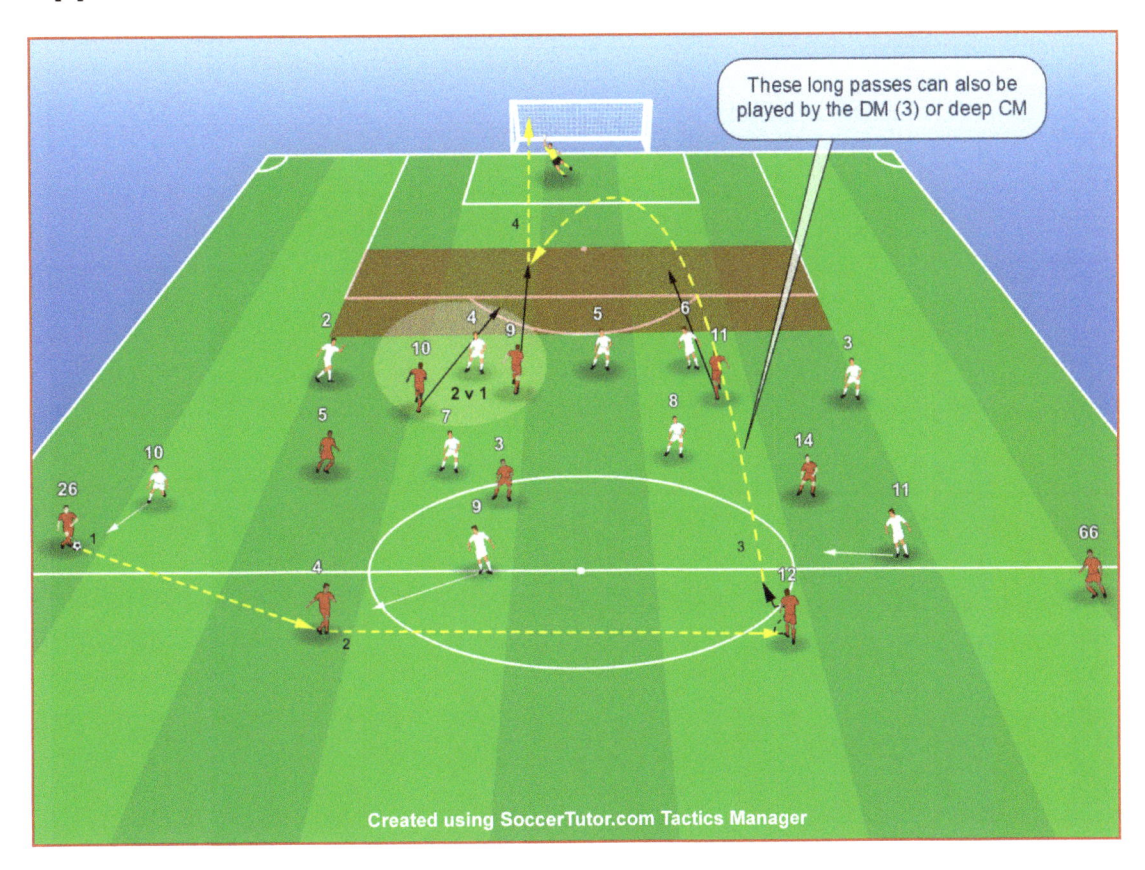

The opposition are defending with all of their players behind the ball in a 5-4-1 defensive formation, and they wait to apply collective pressing until the ball is played into their half.

Liverpool's back 4 circulate the ball and the 3 forwards take up positions in between the defenders.

In some cases, Liverpool would position 2 forwards up against 1 defender to create a 2 v 1 situation when the ball is played in behind.

At the right time, a Liverpool player (who has time and space on the ball and sees a forward who is ready to move) plays a long aerial forward pass into the space in behind the defensive line.

This is normally a centre back, as shown with **No.12's** pass towards the centre forward **No.9**. However, these passes can also be played by the defensive midfielder **(3)** or a deep positioned central midfielder **(5 or 14)**.

The forward (**No.9** in diagram example) times his run well, receives the pass in the box and scores past the GK. This is unless the forward sees a teammate in a better position and passes to them for a tap-in.

Tactical Solution 3 - Long Passes in Behind with All Opponents Behind the Ball

Variation: Long Aerial Forward Pass in Behind when the Opposing Defensive Line (4-4-2) Pushes Up

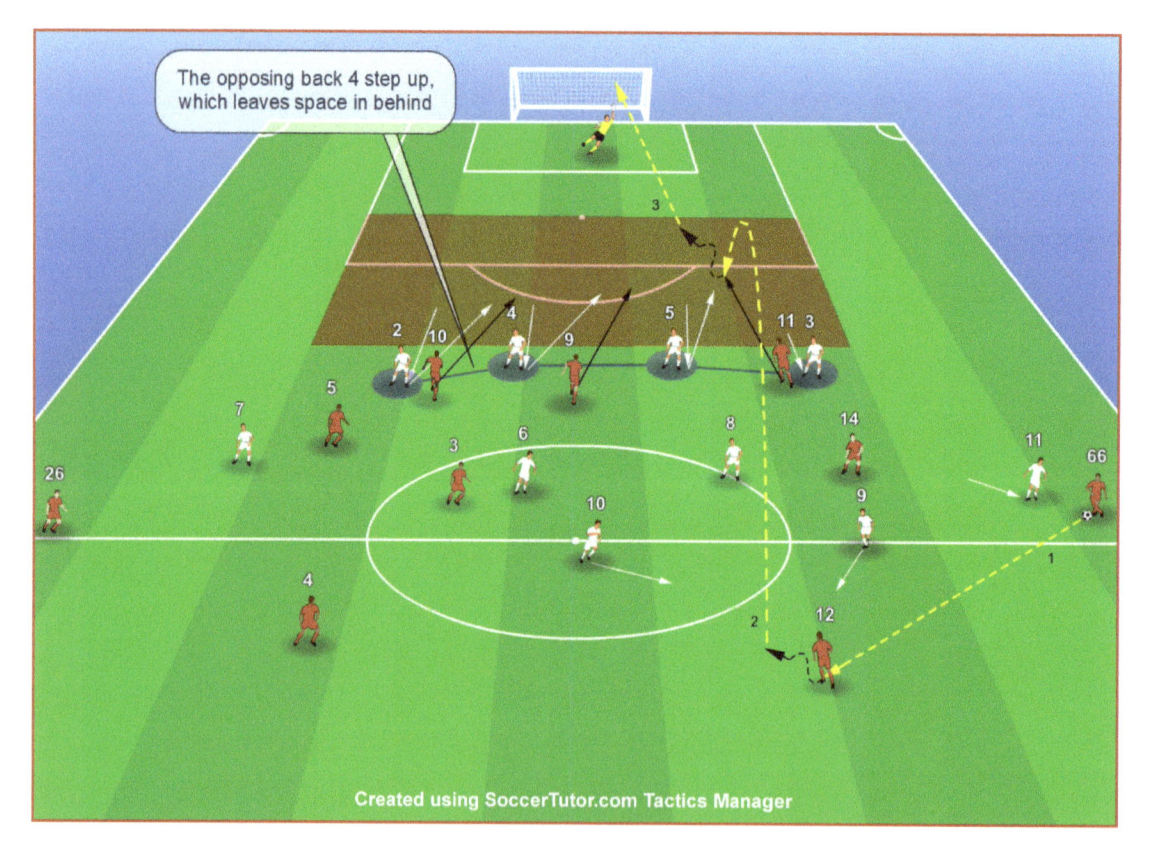

In this variation of the previous example, Liverpool's opponents are in a 4-4-2 formation and push forward to close the space and press the ball, which forces the play backwards.

As the opposing defensive line steps forward together, more space is created to exploit in behind.

When the opponents move forward while the ball was travelling from one player to another, Liverpool would use a long aerial forward pass to quickly exploit their temporary weakness.

In this example, the right back (66) is forced to play backwards and the opposing defensive line all push forward.

To exploit this situation, the Liverpool centre back **(12)** acts quickly to play a long aerial forward pass into the space created in behind (red highlighted area in diagram).

Liverpool also used this tactical solution when their opponent's press the ball and force Klopp's players to play backwards to control the game.

This space was often exploited by the speed and abilities of Liverpool's front 3 **Salah (11)**, **Mané (10)**, and **Firmino (9)**.

In this example, the right forward **Salah (11)** times his run well, receives the pass, moves into the box and scores.

Tactical Solution 3 - Long Passes in Behind with All Opponents Behind the Ball

Statistical Analysis of Liverpool's Long Passes in Behind with All Opponents Behind the Ball

Liverpool scored **8 goals** in this tactical situation
(Premier League and Champions League 2018-2019 and 2019-2020 seasons)

ALL OPPONENTS BEHIND THE BALL
TACTICAL SOLUTION = LONG PASSES IN BEHIND DEFENSIVE LINE

DATE	HOME	AWAY	SCORE	GOAL (MIN)	SCORER	ASSIST
13th Mar 2019	Bayern Munich	Liverpool	1-3	0-1 (26')	**Mané**	van Dijk
5th Apr 2019	Southampton	Liverpool	1-3	1-3 (86')	**Henderson**	Firmino
26th Apr 2019	Liverpool	Huddersfield	5-0	3-0 (45+1')	**Salah**	A-Arnold
4th Dec 2019	Liverpool	Everton	5-2	3-1 (31')	**Origi** *	Lovren
7th Dec 2019	Bournemouth	Liverpool	0-3	0-1 (35')	**Chamberlain** *	Henderson
29th Dec 2019	Liverpool	Wolves	1-0	1-0 (42')	**Mané** *	Lallana
2nd Jan 2020	Liverpool	Sheffield Utd	2-0	1-0 (4')	**Salah**	Robertson
15th Feb 2020	Norwich	Liverpool	0-1	0-1 (78')	**Mané**	Henderson

* The full analysis of these goals is shown on the following pages...

Tactical Solution 3 - Long Passes in Behind with All Opponents Behind the Ball

Analysis from Liverpool 5-2 Everton (Origi 31') - 4th Dec 2019, Premier League

Tactical Solution (1): Long Forward Pass in Behind with All Opponents Behind the Ball in a 5-4-1 Formation

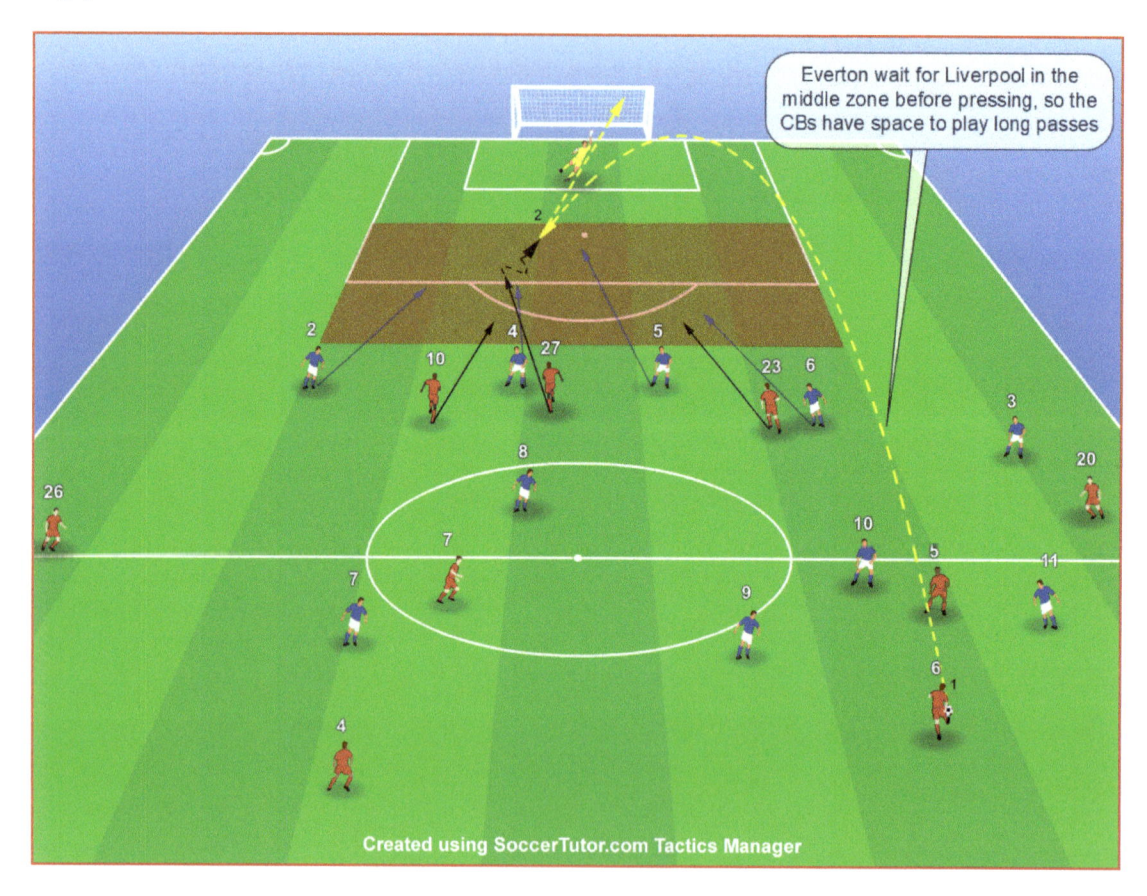

Everton wait for Liverpool in the middle zone before pressing, so the CBs have space to play long passes

Everton are organised in a 5-4-1 defensive shape with all players behind the ball and are waiting until Liverpool enter the middle zone before applying pressing. This means that Liverpool's centre backs **Lovren (6)** and **van Dijk (4)** have space to play without any pressure.

Lovren (6) has the ball unmarked and looks up to play a long pass in behind the defensive line.

The 3 forwards **Mané (10)**, **Origi (27)**, and **Shaqiri (23)** have taken up positions in the same line against Everton's back 4.

Centre back **Lovren (6)** plays a long aerial pass in behind the defensive line to neutralise all of Everton's players and exploit the speed of Liverpool's 3 forwards.

Centre forward **Origi (27)** makes a well-timed run at a great speed, takes an excellent first touch inside the box and scores with his second touch.

©SOCCERTUTOR.COM

JÜRGEN KLOPP LIVERPOOL ATTACKING TACTICS

Tactical Solution 3 - Long Passes in Behind with All Opponents Behind the Ball

Analysis from Bournemouth 0-3 Liverpool (Chamberlain 35') - 7th Dec 2019, Premier League

Tactical Solution (2): Long Forward Pass in Behind with All Opponents Behind the Ball in a 4-4-2 Formation

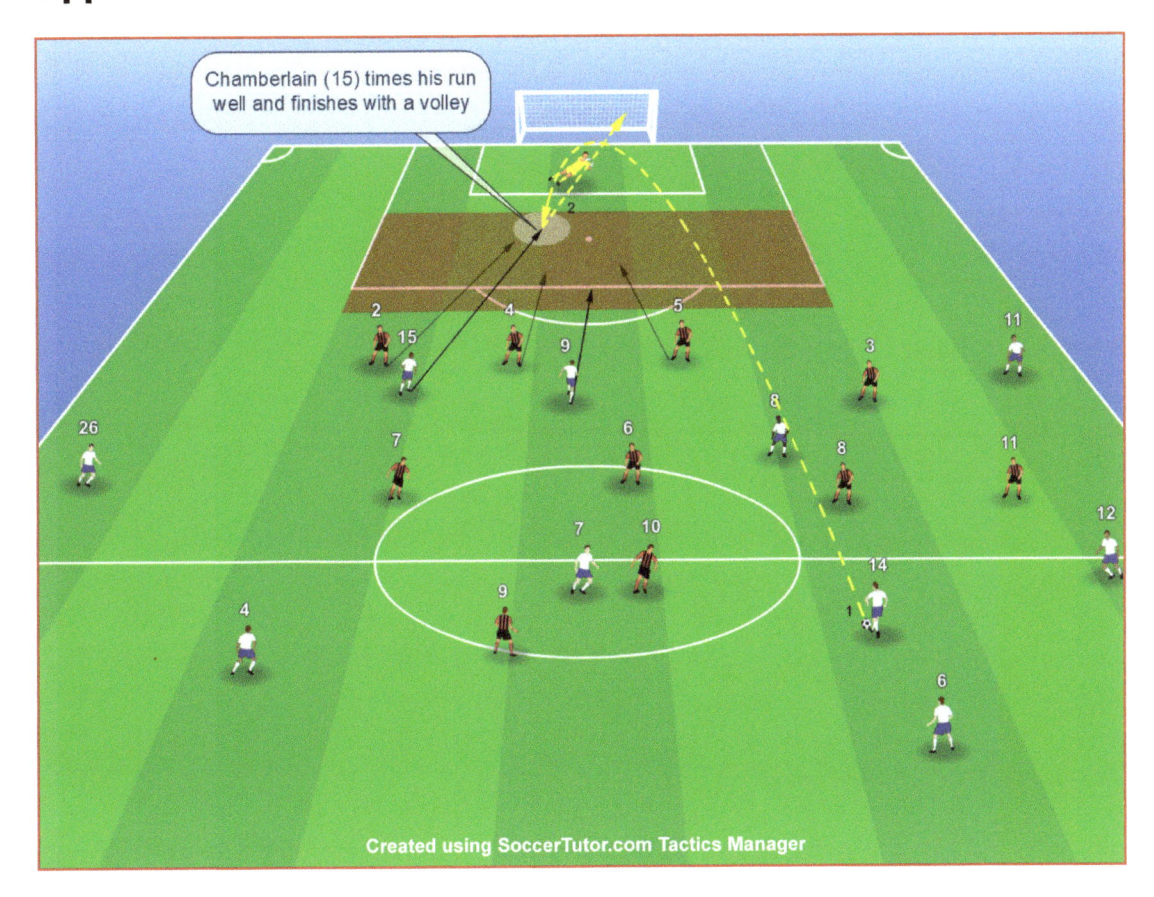

This is a similar situation to the previous example, with Bournemouth waiting to press if the ball enters their half of the pitch. However, they are in a 4-4-2 formation. The Liverpool players in the defensive half can play without pressure.

Defensive midfielder **Henderson (14)** has no opponent near him, so has all the time and space needed to hit a long pass in behind Bournemouth's defensive line.

The long aerial pass by **Henderson (14)** is played into the box precisely for the well-timed run of the left forward **Chamberlain (15)**, who sprints very quickly to get ahead of the defenders.

Chamberlain (15) displays excellent coordination and balance to score directly from the long pass with a volley on the run, with the GK coming out to close the angle.

Tactical Solution 3 - Long Passes in Behind with All Opponents Behind the Ball

Analysis from Liverpool 1-0 Wolves (Mané 42') - 29th Dec 2019, Premier League

Tactical Solution (3): Long Forward Pass in Behind with All Opponents Behind the Ball in a 3-5-2 Formation

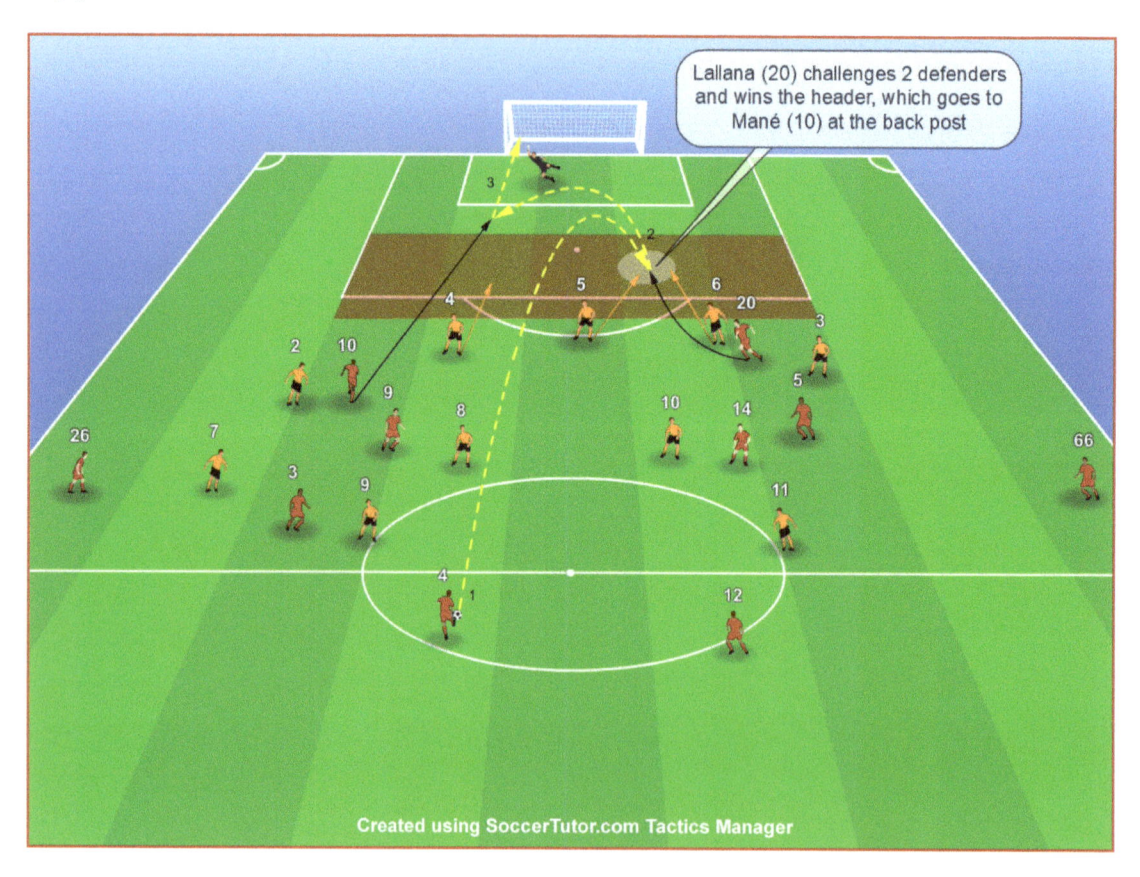

In this example, all of the Wolves players are defending in a 3-5-2 shape within their own half.

Liverpool's centre backs **van Dijk (4)** and **Gomez (12)** are allowed to have the ball without any pressure from their opponents, who are a good distance away from them. In this example, it is **van Dijk (4)** who plays the long forward pass into the space in behind Wolves' 3 centre backs.

Two of Liverpool's players **Lallana (20)** and **Mané (10)** are in advanced positions, ready to make runs in behind. In this example, van Dijk's (4) pass is aimed towards **Lallana (20)**, who makes a run in between 2 Wolves centre backs.

At the same time, the left forward **Mané (10)** moves to support **Lallana (20)**, who manages to get to the ball first and chest it into the path of **Mané (10)** on the left side of the box.

Mané (10) manages to finish first time (on the bounce) into the bottom left corner of the goal.

SESSION 3 BASED ON THE TACTICS OF JÜRGEN KLOPP

Long Passes in Behind with All Opponents Behind the Ball

Session for **JÜRGEN KLOPP** Tactics - Long Passes in Behind with All Opponents Behind the Ball

SESSION FOR THIS TACTICAL SITUATION (4 PRACTICES)
1. Build-up Play from the Back + Long Pass in Behind in a Technical Passing Practice

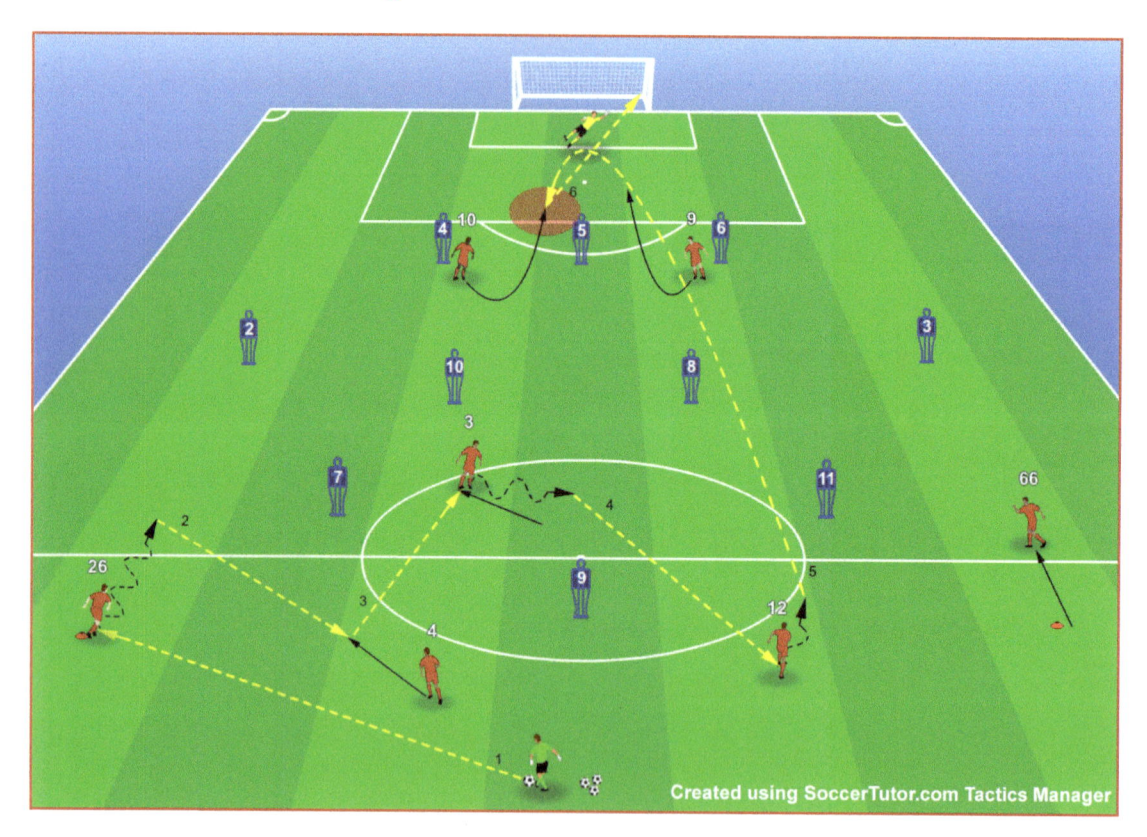

Description

- The 10 mannequins are in a 5-4-1 formation. With the wide midfielders (mannequins 7 and 11) tucked inside and the opponents meant to be pressing the red players, it takes more of a **3-4-2-1 defensive shape**. You can change to any formation you want to work against.

- The reds have a GK, the back 4, a defensive midfielder **(3)** and 2 forwards **(10 & 9)** from Liverpool's 4-3-3 formation.

- The practice starts with the GK's pass to a defender. The back 4 and defensive midfielder **(3)** circulate the ball. At the right moment, one of the centre backs (or defensive midfielder) plays a long pass in behind the defensive line and into an area for the 2 forwards to run into. They receive inside the box and try to score.

Coaching Points

1. The long passes in behind the defensive line need to have the correct accuracy and weight.
2. The runs in behind the defensive line need to be sharp (explosive), be made at the correct time to be onside and meet the pass.
3. The forwards need a quality first touch to control the ball in the box.
4. Quick, accurate and quality finishing with pressure if the GK closes them down.

Session for **JÜRGEN KLOPP** Tactics - Long Passes in Behind with All Opponents Behind the Ball

PROGRESSION
2. Build-up Play from the Back + Long Pass in Behind in a Functional Zonal Game

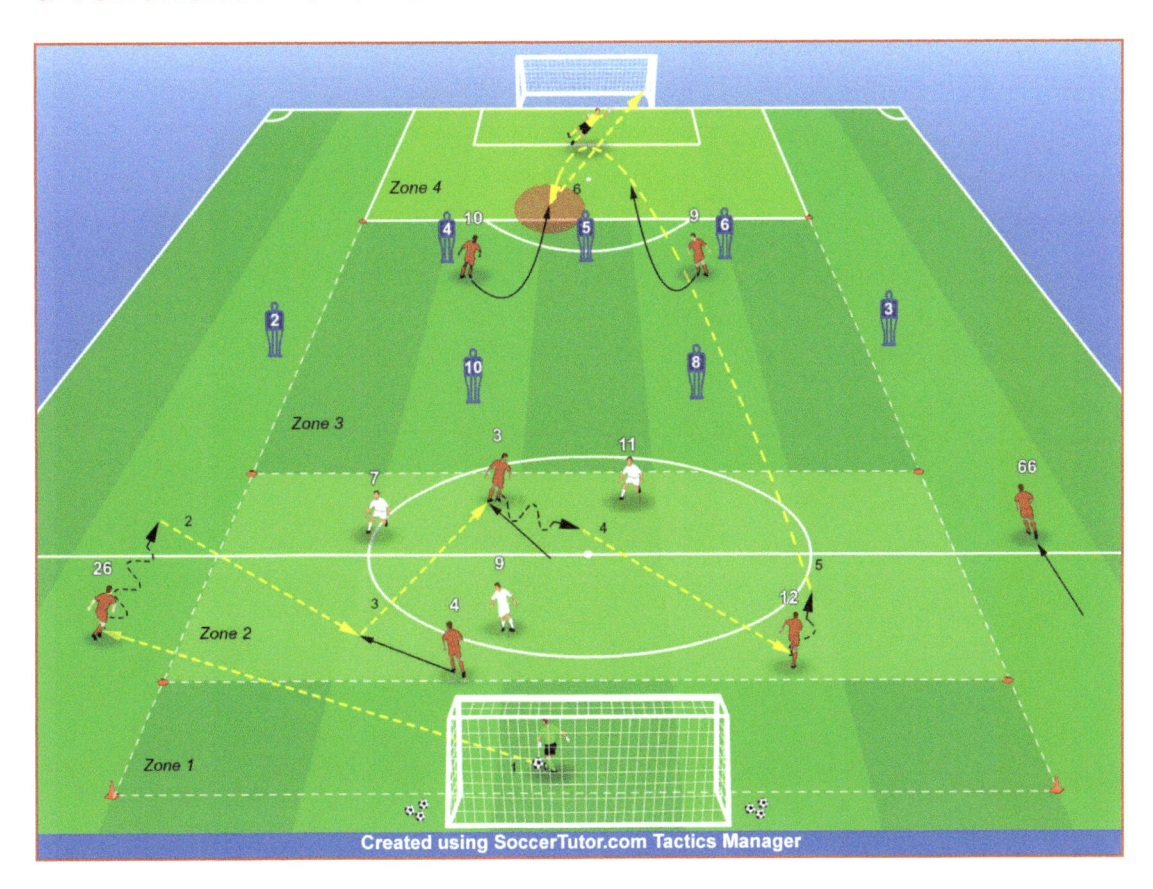

Description

- **Zone 1** = Red GK's zone.
- **Zone 2** = Red centre backs and defensive midfielder vs. 3 white players (3v3).
- **Zone 3** = 2 red forwards and 5 mannequins.
- **Zone 4** = Penalty box.
- There are also red full backs (**2** and **3**), who operate on the sides and provide support.
- The practice starts with the GK's pass to a defender. The red back 4 and defensive midfielder (**3**) circulate the ball under pressure from the 3 white players.

- The aim is to find space to play a long pass in behind the defensive line and into the box for the 2 forwards to run into, receive and score.
- In this example, centre back (**12**) receives in space and plays a long pass towards **No.10**.
- If the 3 white players win the ball, they try to score as quickly as possible.
- The game always restarts from the red's GK.

Progression

Add a white centre back in place of the No.5 mannequin to defend the long pass, making it more difficult for the forwards to score.

Session for **JÜRGEN KLOPP** Tactics - Long Passes in Behind with All Opponents Behind the Ball

PROGRESSION
3. Build-up Play from the Back + Long Pass in Behind in a Conditioned 9v7 Zonal Game

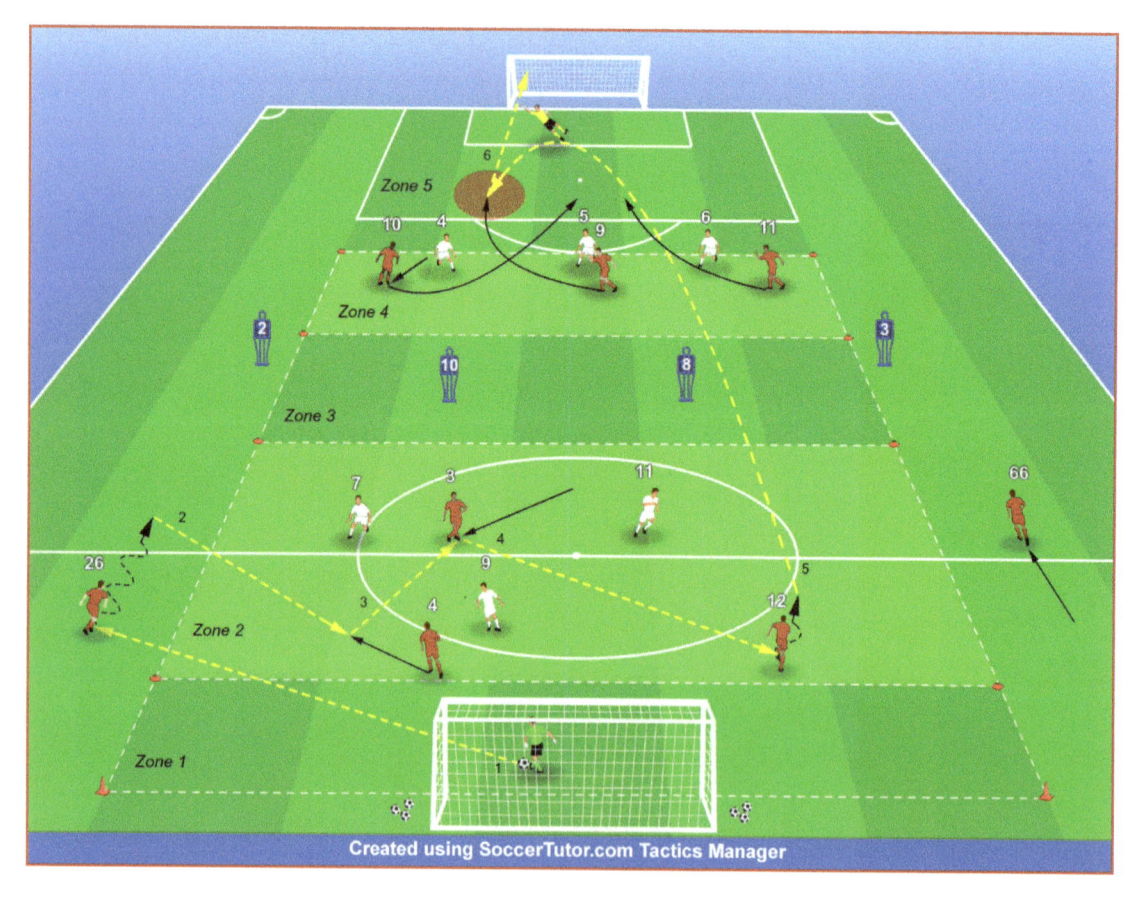

Description

- In this progression of the previous practice, we replace 3 of the mannequins with 3 active white defenders. There are also 3 red forwards instead of 2 (**No.11** has been added).

- There is 1 extra zone marked out, so we now have 5 zones in total.

- The practice works in the exact same way, but now there are 3 white centre backs defending the long passes and the runs in behind to try and prevent any goals from being scored.

- This makes it much more difficult for the reds, as they must really focus to play the correct passes at the right time, and the forwards must time their runs to perfection and finish quickly.

Session for **JÜRGEN KLOPP** Tactics - Long Passes in Behind with All Opponents Behind the Ball

PROGRESSION
4. Build-up Play from the Back + Long Pass in Behind in an 11v11 Tactical Zonal Game

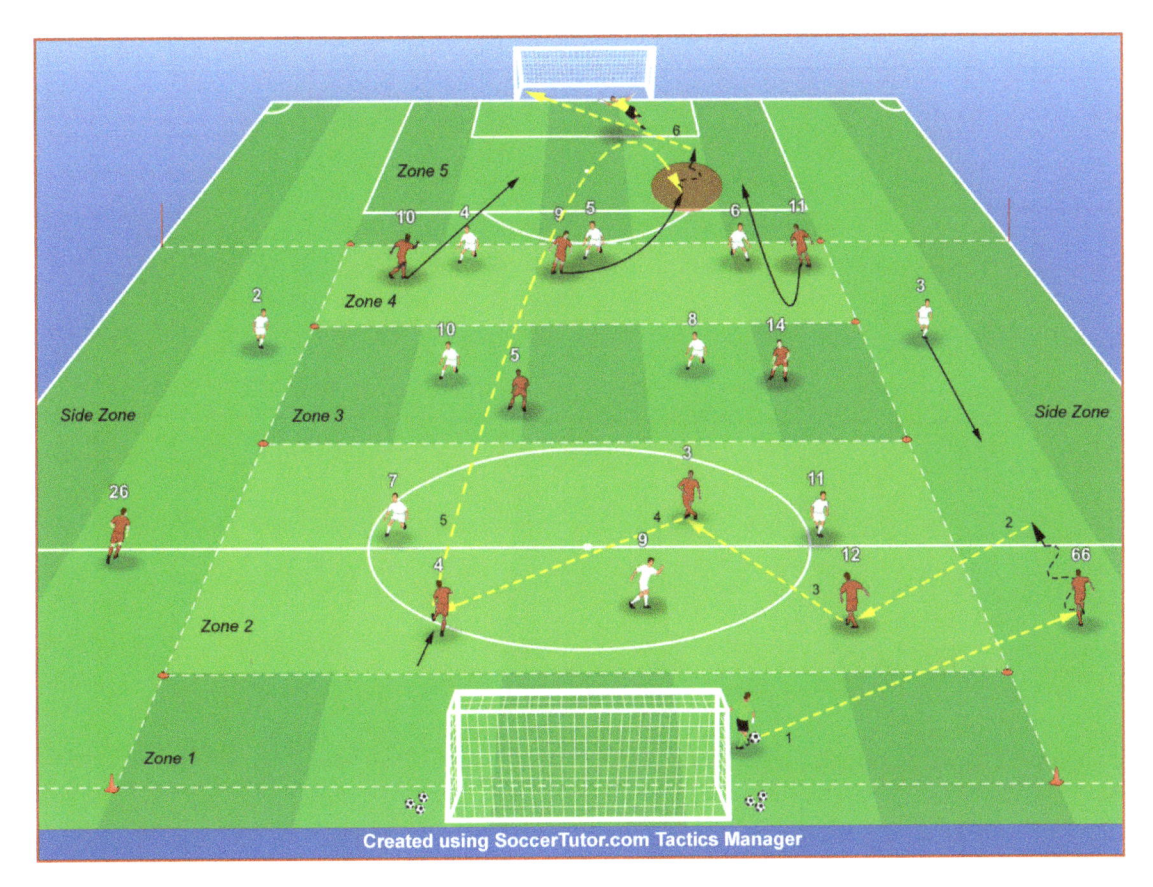

Description

- **Zone 1** = Red GK's zone.
- **Zone 2** = 2 red centre backs and defensive midfielder vs. 3 white players (3v3).
- **Zone 3** = 2 red central midfielders vs. 2 white central midfielders (2v2).
- **Zone 4** = 3 red forwards vs. 3 white centre backs (3v3).
- **Zone 5** = Final zone (penalty box).
- **Side Zones** = Red full back **(26/66)** vs. white full back (2/3).

- In this final practice, we play an 11v11 game. The red team are in a 4-3-3 formation and the whites are in a 5-4-1 (3-4-2-1 defensive shape).
- The practice always starts from the red GK and the reds circulate the ball. All players must stay within their zones during this phase.
- The reds wait for the right opportunity to play a long pass for one of the 3 forwards to run into Zone 5 (box) and score. The 3 white centre backs cannot move into Zone 5 until a long pass has been played by a red player.
- If the whites win the ball, they try to score with a counter attack (no zone restrictions).

JÜRGEN KLOPP TACTICAL ANALYSIS

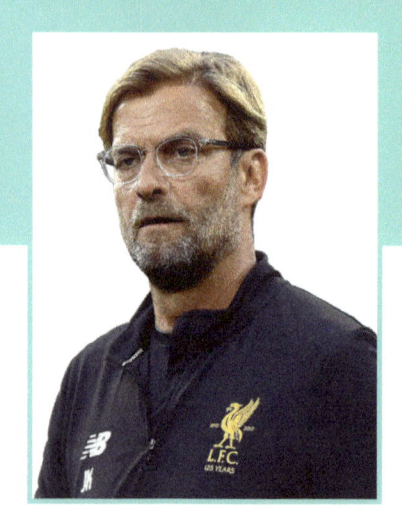

SOLUTION 4

Switch Point of Attack to Weak Side of Ball Oriented Opponents

Content from analysis of Liverpool F.C. during the 2018-2019 Champions League winning season and the 2019-2020 Premier League winning season

- Analysis based on recurring patterns of play observed within the Liverpool team.
- Tactical solutions displayed as examples of the team's tactics being used effectively.
- Real match examples of Liverpool scoring a goal using this specific attacking tactical solution.
- Each action, pass, individual movement with or without the ball, and the positioning of each player on the pitch including their body shape, are presented.
- The analysis is then used to create a full progressive session to coach this tactical situation.

©SOCCERTUTOR.COM

JÜRGEN KLOPP LIVERPOOL ATTACKING TACTICS

Tactical Solution 4 - Switch Point of Attack to Weak Side of Ball Oriented Opponents

Switch Point of Attack to Weak Side of Ball Oriented Opponents

What?

Liverpool switch play from a congested area to their opponent's weak side and into the target area shown - they then try to score quickly with a low cross and finish.

Why?

As the opposing players all move towards the ball together and create a strong side (ball oriented defence), there is available space to exploit on their weak side.

How?

Play a diagonal pass to the weak side for the opposite side forward or advanced full back (into highlighted area), who pass the ball across for a teammate or score themselves.

Target Area (on Weak Side of Opponents)

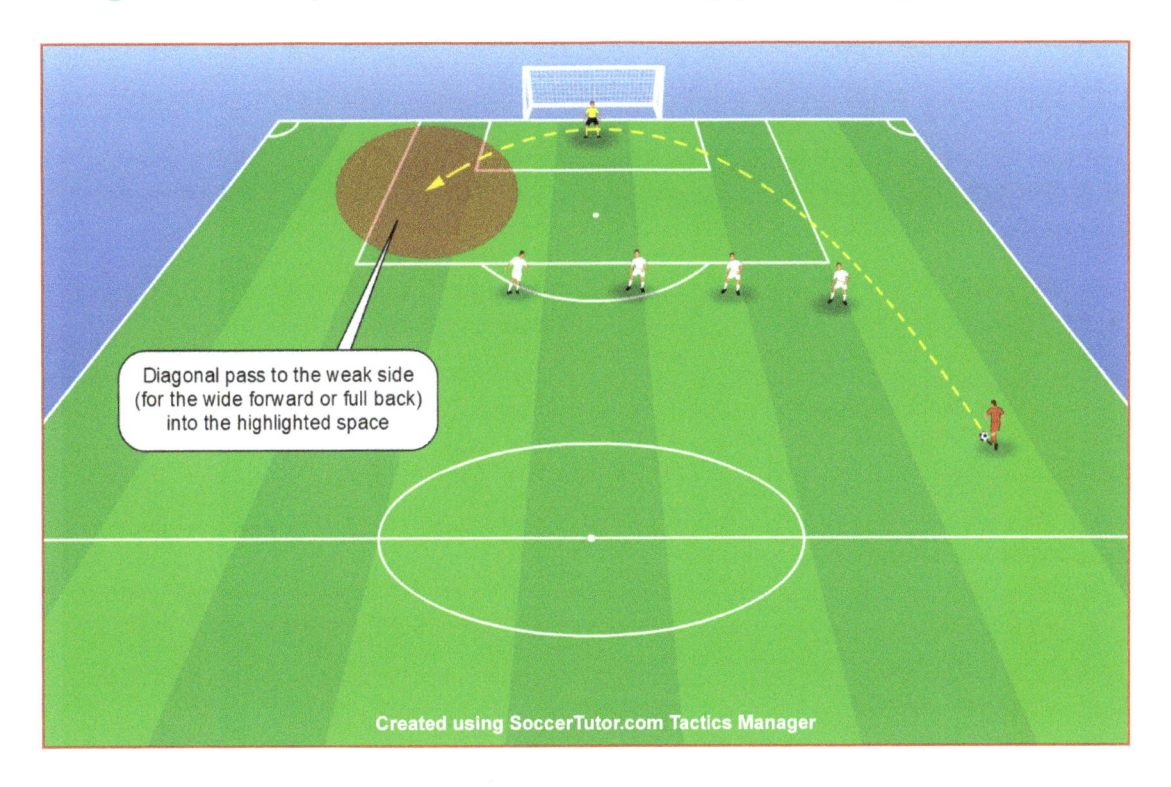

Diagonal pass to the weak side (for the wide forward or full back) into the highlighted space

Created using SoccerTutor.com Tactics Manager

JÜRGEN KLOPP LIVERPOOL ATTACKING TACTICS

Tactical Solution 4 - Switch Point of Attack to Weak Side of Ball Oriented Opponents

Tactical Solution A: Switch Point of Attack to Weak Side of Ball Oriented Opponents (to the Opposite Wide Forward)

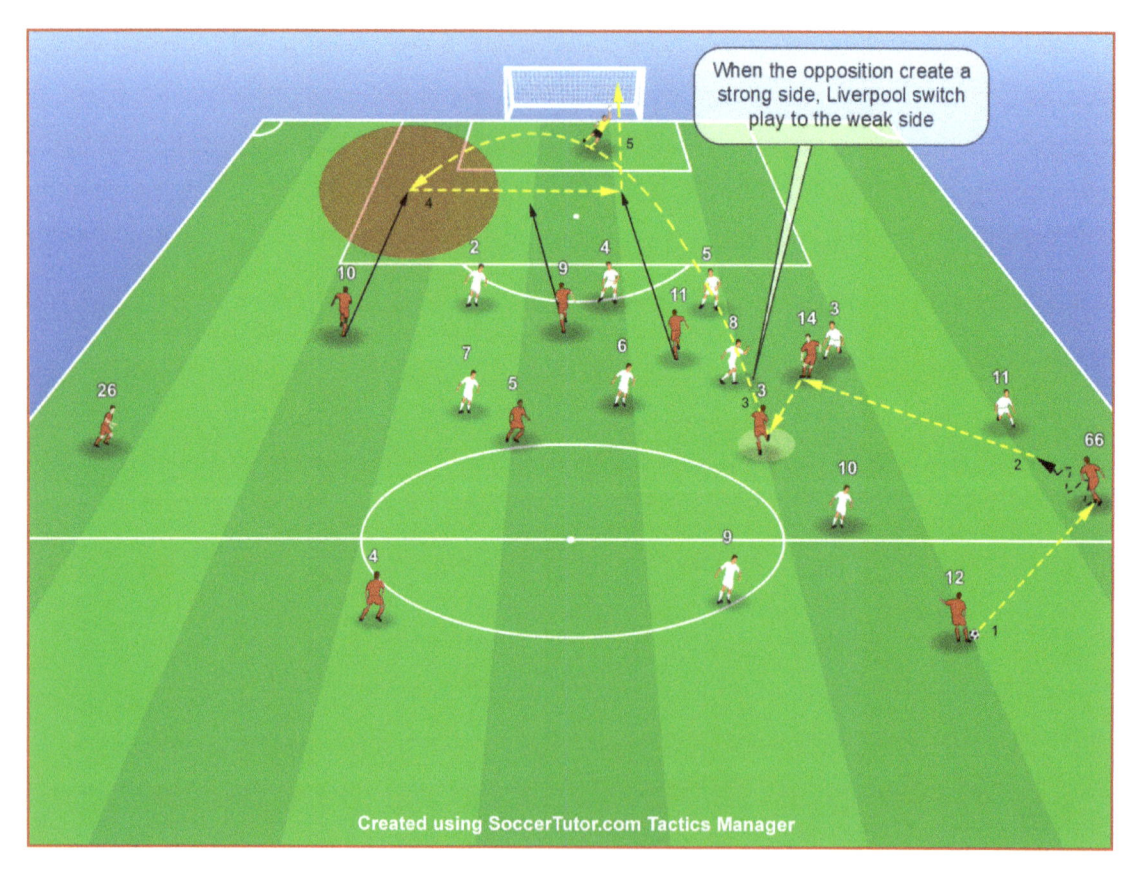

When the opposition create a strong side, Liverpool switch play to the weak side

The opposition are playing with a ball oriented defence (pressing collectively depending on where the ball is).

In this example, the opponents are trying to create a numerical advantage and a strong defensive side on their left side of the pitch (Liverpool's right).

When this happens, Jürgen Klopp's Liverpool team aim to transfer the ball to the weak side with a diagonal aerial pass in behind the defensive line.

Usually, this happens with a pass to the opposite forward (**No.10** in diagram).

The Liverpool players combine with the ball on the right side until the defensive midfielder (**3**) receives unmarked.

The defensive midfielder (**3**) looks up and plays an aerial diagonal pass for the run of the left forward (**10**) to receive in behind the defensive line and inside the box.

No.10 makes a fast run to meet the pass but is in a wide position. Therefore, he passes the ball across for one of the other 2 forwards (who also make fast runs into box for support) to score.

In this example, the right forward **No.11** times his run well and scores.

JÜRGEN KLOPP LIVERPOOL ATTACKING TACTICS

Tactical Solution 4 - Switch Point of Attack to Weak Side of Ball Oriented Opponents

Tactical Solution B: Switch Point of Attack to Weak Side of Ball Oriented Opponents (to the Opposite Full Back)

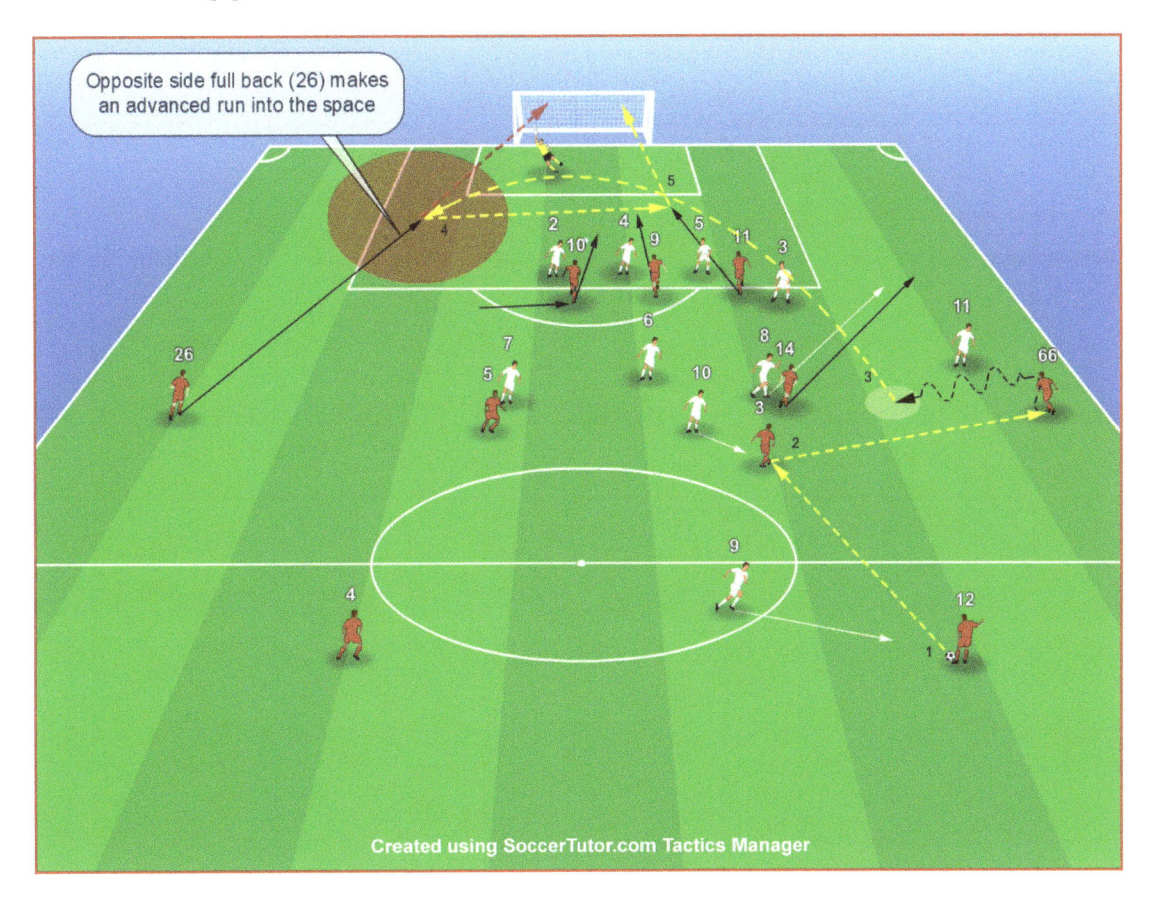

Opposite side full back (26) makes an advanced run into the space

For the second tactical solution of this game situation, the defending team are positioned deeper.

In this example, the right back **(66)** receives out wide and the central midfielder **(14)** makes a diagonal run into an advanced position on the right flank.

This movement creates space for the right back **(66)** to dribble inside and then play a diagonal aerial pass to the weak side of the opponents.

The right back's **(66)** pass is accurately played into the box for the very well-timed advanced run of the left back **(26)** on the weak side.

The left back **(26)** has **2 Options**:

1. Receive and deliver a low cross (or first time cross) across the box for an oncoming teammate to score easily.

2. Try to finish first time if the angle allows (see red arrow in diagram).

Tactical Solution 4 - Switch Point of Attack to Weak Side of Ball Oriented Opponents

Statistical Analysis of Liverpool Switching Point of Attack to Weak Side of Ball Oriented Opponents

Liverpool scored **11 goals** in this tactical situation
(Premier League and Champions League 2018-2019 and 2019-2020 seasons)

VS. BALL ORIENTED OPPONENTS CREATING STRONG SIDE
SWITCH POINT OF ATTACK TO WEAK SIDE (LOW CROSS OR DIRECT FINISH)

DATE	HOME	AWAY	SCORE	GOAL (MIN)	SCORER	ASSIST
12th Aug 2018	Liverpool	West Ham	4-0	2-0 (45'+2)	**Mané**	Milner
11th Nov 2018	Liverpool	Fulham	2-0	2-0 (53')	**Shaqiri**	Robertson
5th Dec 2018	Burnley	Liverpool	1-3	1-2 (69')	**Firmino**	van Dijk
29th Dec 2018	Liverpool	Arsenal	5-1	3-1 (32')	**Mané** *	Salah
3rd Jan 2019	Man City	Liverpool	2-1	1-1 (64')	**Firmino**	Robertson
19th Jan 2019	Liverpool	Crystal Palace	4-3	3-2 (75')	**Salah** *	Milner
31st Mar 2019	Liverpool	Tottenham	2-1	2-1 (90')	**Own Goal**	Salah
27th Oct 2019	Liverpool	Tottenham	2-1	1-1 (52')	**Henderson**	Fabinho
2nd Nov 2019	Aston Vila	Liverpool	1-2	1-1 (87')	**Robertson** *	Mané
26th Dec 2019	Leicester City	Liverpool	0-4	0-1 (31')	**Firmino**	A-Arnold
11th Jul 2020	Liverpool	Burnley	1-1	1-1 (34')	**Robertson**	Fabinho

* The full analysis of these goals is shown on the following pages...

Tactical Solution 4 - Switch Point of Attack to Weak Side of Ball Oriented Opponents

Analysis from Liverpool 5-1 Arsenal (Mané '32) - 29th Dec 2018, Premier League

Tactical Solution A: Switch Point of Attack to Weak Side of Ball Oriented Opponents (to the Opposite Wide Forward)

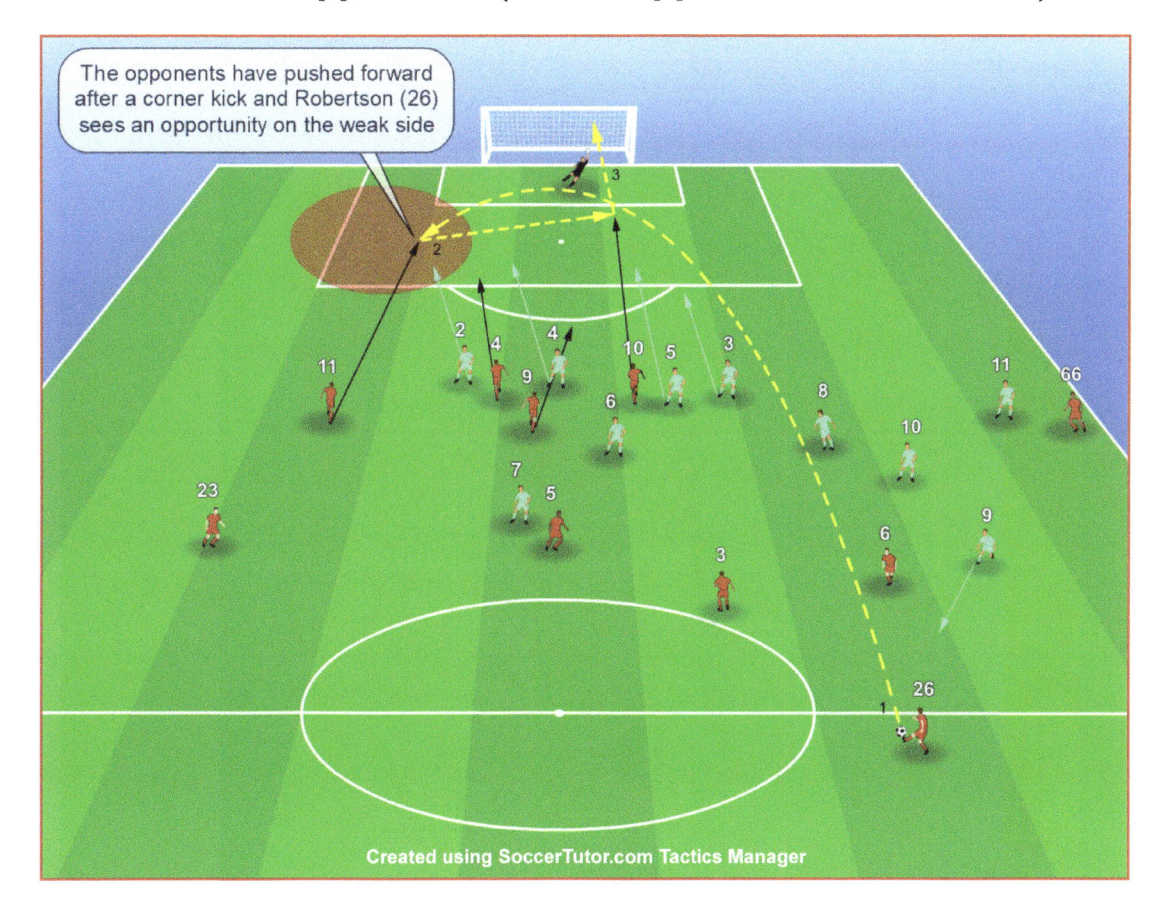

The Arsenal players have pushed forward after clearing the ball away from a corner and have most of their players on one side of the pitch. Liverpool's left back **Robertson (26)** has the ball just inside his own half.

Robertson (26) sees that the weak side of the opponent offers an attacking opportunity, so he plays a long high ball into the target area for the right forward **Salah (11)** to run onto. **Firmino (9)**, **van Dijk (4)**, and **Mané (10)** also run forward to provide support and give **Salah (11)** more options.

Salah (11) understands the situation and makes a good decision to pass with his first touch across the box for the oncoming **Mané (10)**, who is in a better position to finish.

Mané (10) scores past the GK with a one touch finish.

JÜRGEN KLOPP LIVERPOOL ATTACKING TACTICS

Tactical Solution 4 - Switch Point of Attack to Weak Side of Ball Oriented Opponents

Analysis from Liverpool 4-3 Crystal Palace (Salah 75') - **19th Jan 2019, Premier League**

Tactical Solution B (1): Switch Point of Attack to Weak Side of Ball Oriented Opponents (to the Opposite Full Back)

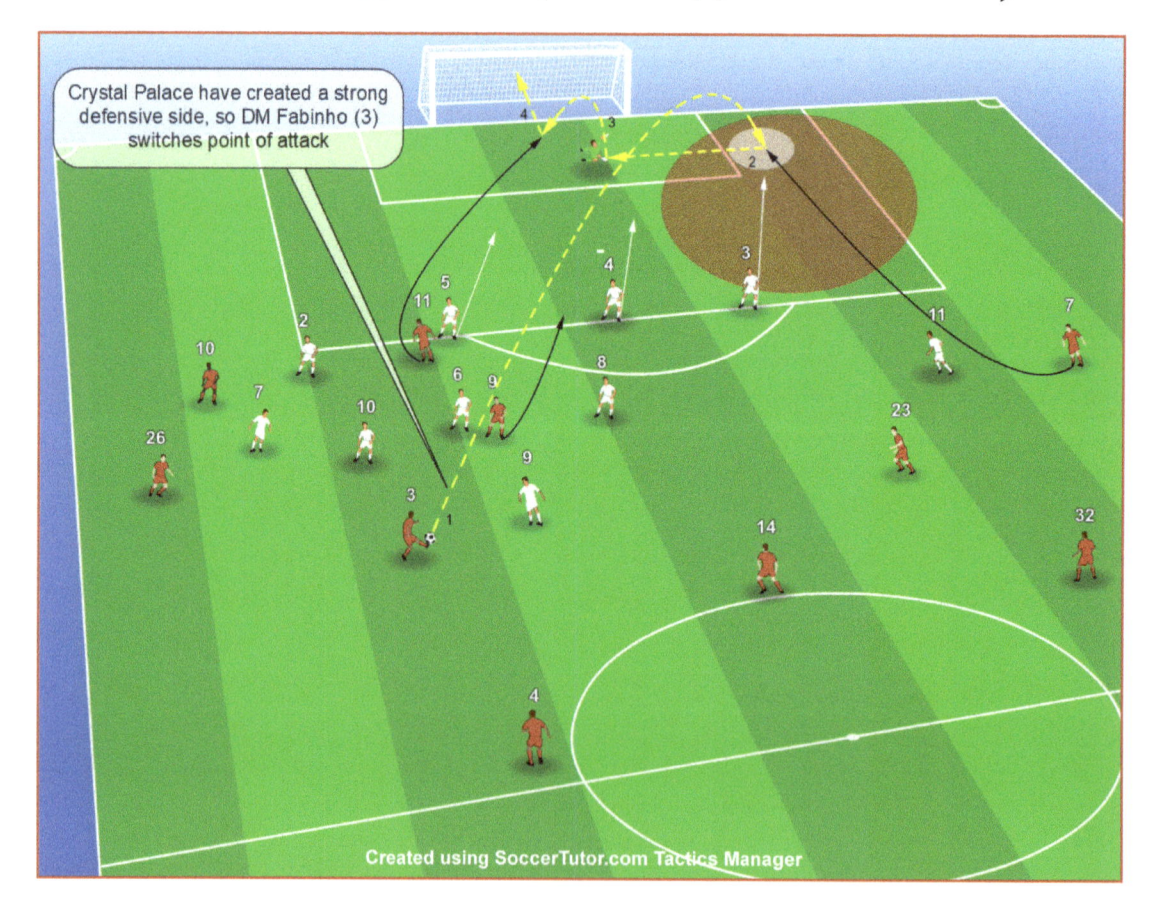

All of the Crystal Palace players (4-5-1 formation) are defending in the low zone and they have created a strong side on Liverpool's left. Liverpool have been keeping possession and the defensive midfielder **Fabinho (3)** ends up with the ball in space.

While Liverpool were successfully maintaining possession, the right back **Milner (7)** moved onto the weak side of his direct opponent.

Fabinho (3) plays a high diagonal pass towards **Milner (7)** into the box and in behind Crystal Palace's defensive line.

This means that all of the Palace players will be taken out of the game.

Milner (7) reads the flight of the ball and plays it across the box first time on the volley.

The GK tries to stop the ball but fumbles it and the ball bounces up towards the goal.

The forward **Salah (11)** is there to score an easy goal into an empty net.

Tactical Solution 4 - Switch Point of Attack to Weak Side of Ball Oriented Opponents

Analysis from Aston Villa 1-2 Liverpool (Robertson 87') - 2nd Nov 2019, Premier League

Tactical Solution B (2): Switch Point of Attack to Weak Side of Ball Oriented Opponents (Cross for Direct Finish)

Liverpool have many players on the right side and use a combination of short passes to try and find solutions to attack.

The defensive midfielder **Henderson (14)** passes to right back **A-Arnold (66)**, who moves the ball to forward **Mané (10)** on the side-line. Left back **Robertson (26)** is maximising the width on the weak side.

Mané (10) moves into a 1v1 and dribbles the ball inside onto his left foot.

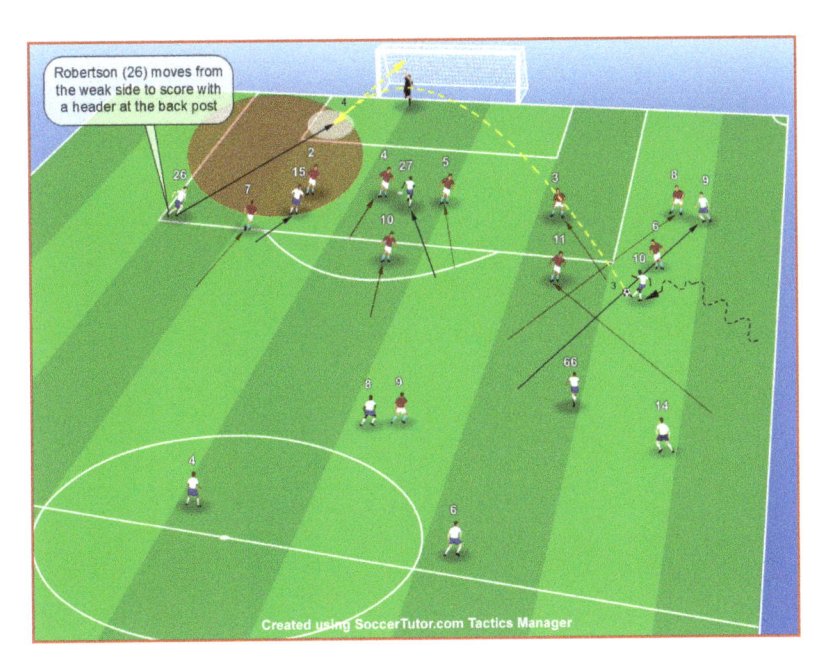

Mané (10) delivers a cross with his left foot into the 6-yard box and in behind Aston Villa's defensive line for the fast run of the opposite full back **Robertson (26)**, who has sprinted from the weak side.

Robertson (26) scores with a header in the 87th minute, and then **Mané (10)** scores a few minutes later to seal a 2-1 win.

This was one of the best Liverpool turnarounds on their way to the title.

JÜRGEN KLOPP LIVERPOOL ATTACKING TACTICS

SESSION 4 BASED ON THE TACTICS OF JÜRGEN KLOPP

Switch Point of Attack to Weak Side of Ball Oriented Opponents

Session for **JÜRGEN KLOPP** Tactics - Switch Attack to Weak Side of Ball Oriented Opponents

SESSION FOR THIS TACTICAL SITUATION (5 PRACTICES)
1. Combination Play on One Side + Switch to Weak Side, Low Cross and Finish in a Technical Practice

1a: Wide Forward's Lay-off for Full Back to Switch Point of Attack

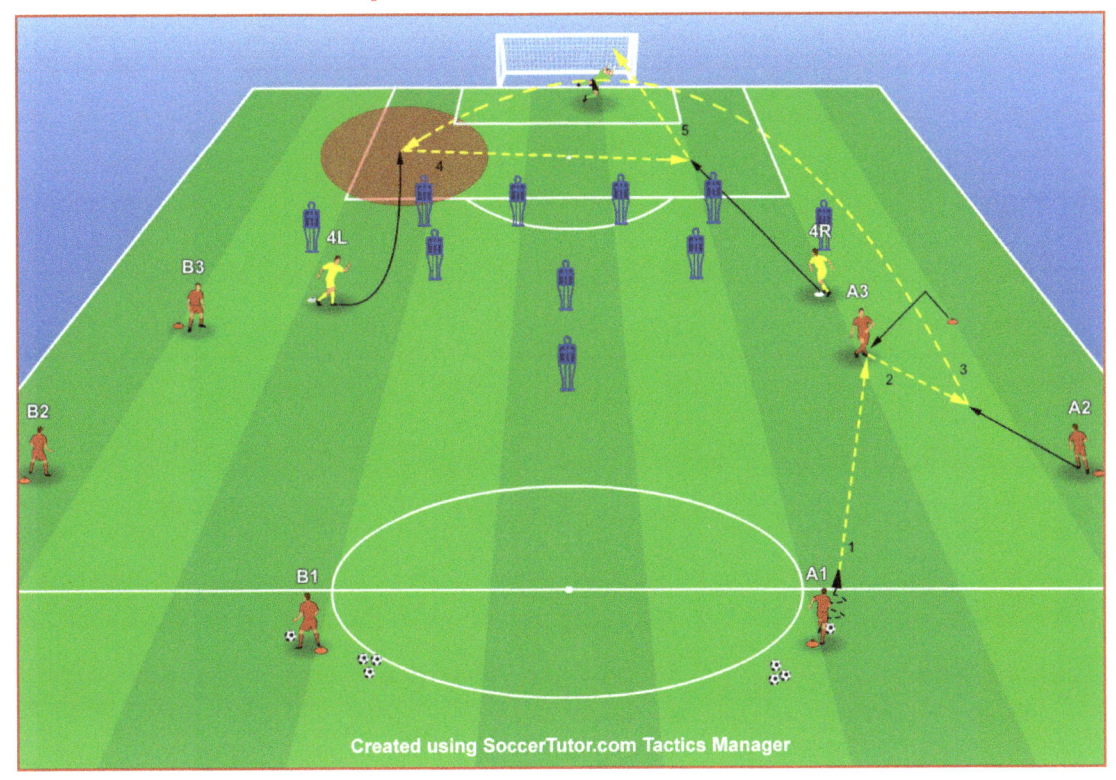

Objective: Combination play and switching point of attack to weak side of the opponent.

Description (1a)

- In half a pitch, we position 10 mannequins around the box as shown.
- We work with 8 players (3 red and 1 yellow on each side of the pitch).
- The practice starts on the right side with **Player 1 (central midfielder)** dribbling forward and passing to **Player 3 (right forward)**, who checks away before moving to receive and lay the ball back.
- **Player 2 (right back)** moves forward and inside to receive the lay-off and plays a first time long diagonal pass into the box on the opposite side.
- This diagonal pass is weighted correctly for the well-timed forward run of **Player 4L (left forward)** in this example.
- **Player 4L** receives or passes with one touch across the box for **Player 4R (centre forward)** to run onto and score.
- The same sequence repeats immediately from the left side of the pitch.

JÜRGEN KLOPP LIVERPOOL ATTACKING TACTICS

Session for **JÜRGEN KLOPP** Tactics - Switch Attack to Weak Side of Ball Oriented Opponents

1b: Wide Forward's Lay-off for Central Midfielder to Switch Attack

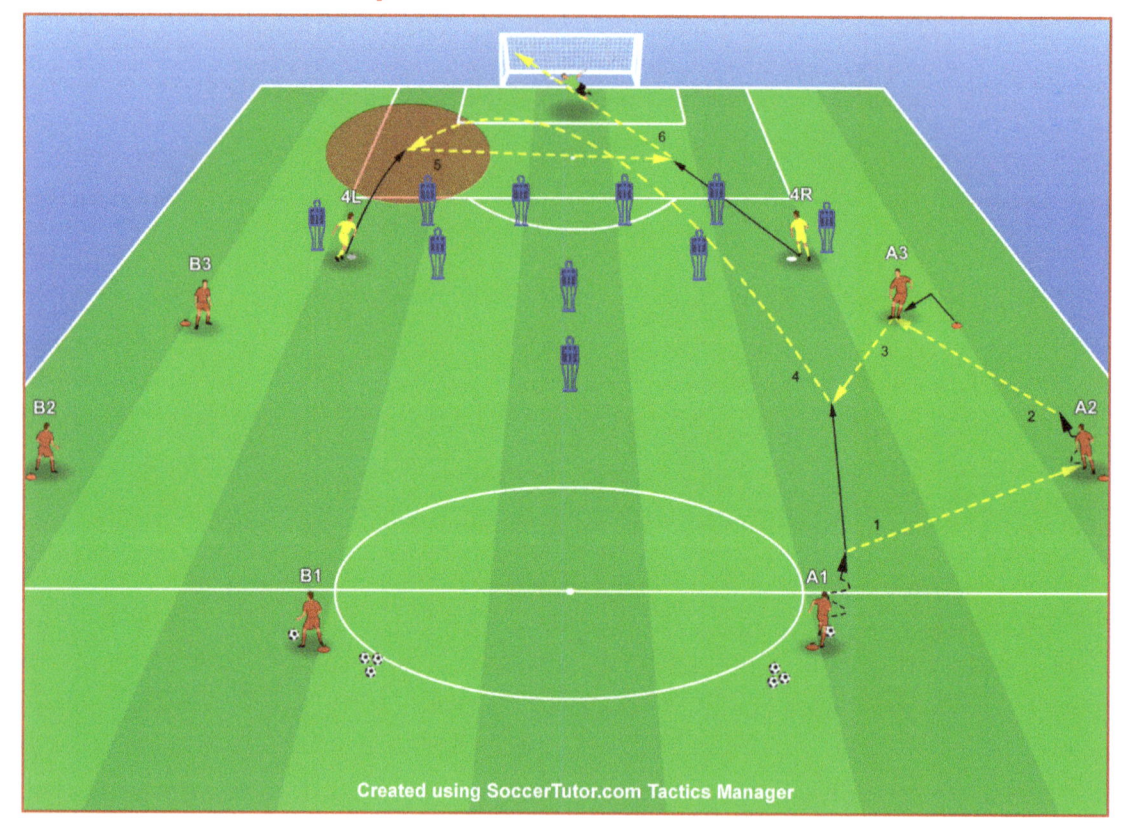

Description (1b)

- In this variation of the previous practice (1a), the combination and sequence changes.

- The practice starts on the right side with **Player 1 (central midfielder)** dribbling forward and passing to **Player 2 (right back)**, who takes a touch forward and passes to **Player 3 (right forward)**.

- **Player 1** moves forward to receive the lay-off from **Player 3** and then plays a first time aerial diagonal pass into the box on the opposite side.

- This diagonal pass is weighted correctly for the well-timed forward run of **Player 4L (left forward)** in this example.

- **Player 4L** receives or passes with one touch across the box for **Player 4R (centre forward)** to run onto and score.

- The same sequence repeats immediately from the left side of the pitch.

Session for **JÜRGEN KLOPP** Tactics - Switch Attack to Weak Side of Ball Oriented Opponents

1c: Wide Forward Dribbles Inside and Switches Point of Attack

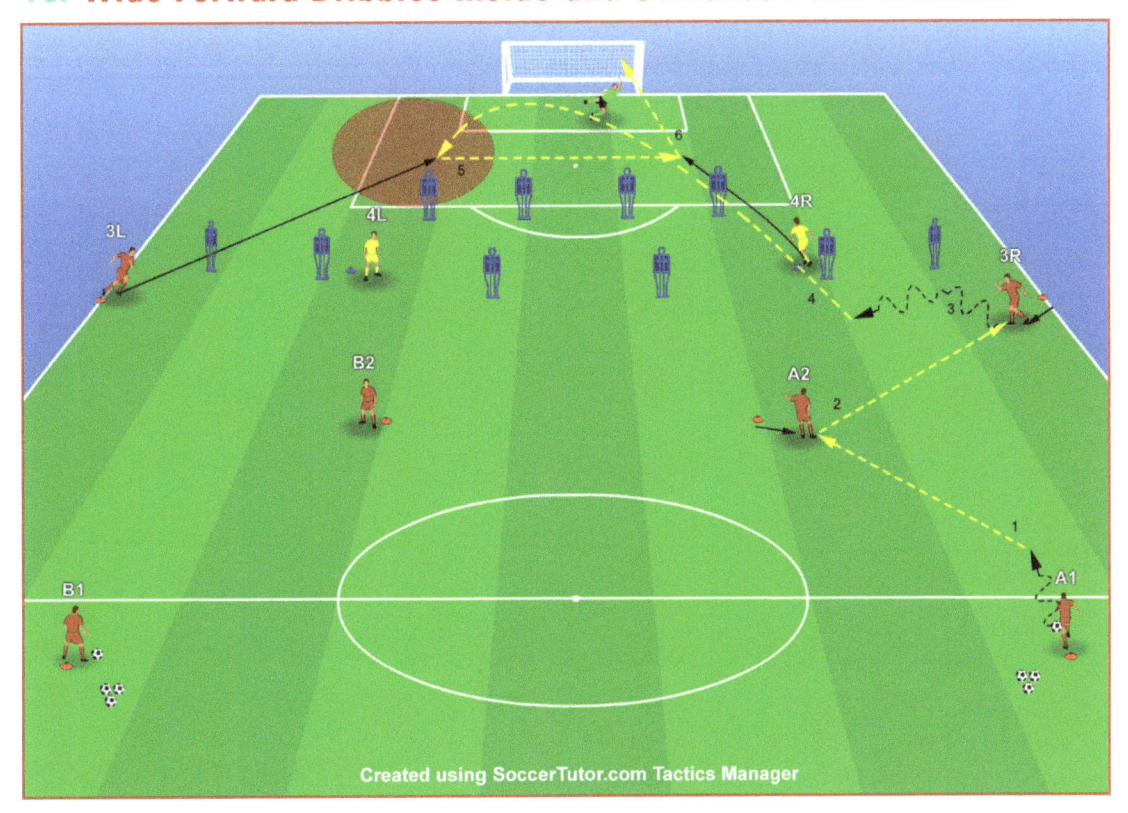

Description (1c)

- In the last variation, we work with the wide players on dribbling inside and crossing with the outside of the opposite foot.

- The practice starts on the right side with **Player 1 (full back)** dribbling forward and passing to **Player 2 (central midfielder)**, who passes first time out wide to **Player 3R (right forward)**.

- **Player 3R** uses a feint, dribbles inside, and then bends a cross towards the back post (near to the 6-yard box) with the outside of his right foot.

- **Player 3L (left forward)** times his run well to meet the cross and has **2 Options**:
  1. First time finish (shot or header).
  2. Pass the ball across for **Player 4R** to score.

Coaching Points

1. The accuracy and weight of the passes and crosses must be correct, played at the right moment and into the space required.

2. The timing of the movement from **3L** moving to meet the ball (as soon as **3R** moves inside) is very important as to whether the attack will be successful.

3. The runs in behind the defensive line need to be sharp and timed correctly to be onside and meet the pass.

4. The synchronisation, the rhythm and timing of the movement together with the pass is key to success in this practice.

5. Make sure the players communicate with their teammates and their heads are up (to maximise their game awareness).

Session for **JÜRGEN KLOPP** Tactics - Switch Attack to Weak Side of Ball Oriented Opponents

PROGRESSION
2. Combination Play on One Side + Switch to Weak Side in an Unopposed Pattern of Play Practice

Ball 1/3: Wide Forward's Lay-off for Central Midfielder to Switch

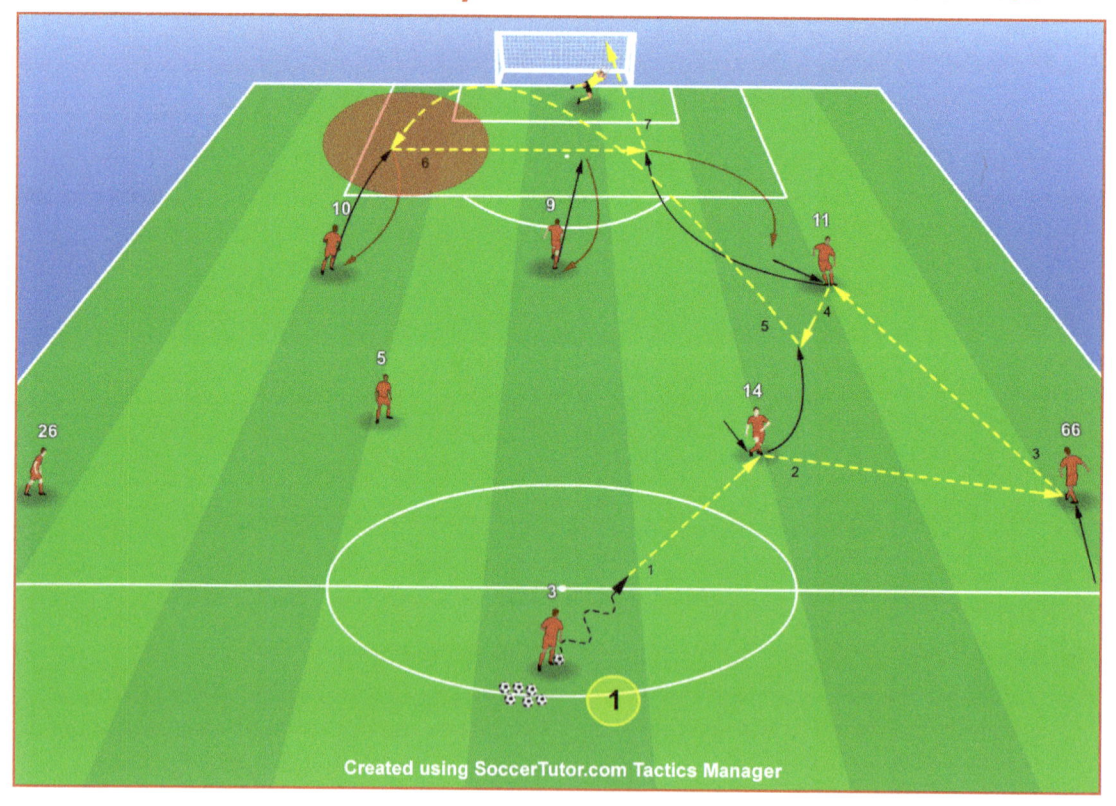

Objective: Continuous attacking combinations to switch point of attack (parts 1-3).

Description (Ball 1)

- In half a pitch, we have 2 red full backs, 1 defensive midfielder, 2 central midfielders and 3 forwards from Liverpool's 4-3-3 formation.
- The practice is continuous from one ball to the next without any stopping.
- The practice starts with the defensive midfielder (3) dribbling forward and passing to the right central midfielder (14), who passes out wide to the right back (66).
- The right back (66) passes forward to the right forward (11), who lays the ball back for the central midfielder (14) to run onto.
- The central midfielder (14) then plays a first time aerial diagonal pass into the box on the opposite side to switch the point of attack.
- This diagonal pass is weighted correctly for the well-timed forward run of the left forward (10) in this example.
- The left forward (10) passes across the box for either of the other 2 forwards (9 or 11), who make forward runs to help finish the attack.

Session for **JÜRGEN KLOPP** Tactics - Switch Attack to Weak Side of Ball Oriented Opponents

Ball 2/3: Wide Forward's Lay-off for Full Back to Switch

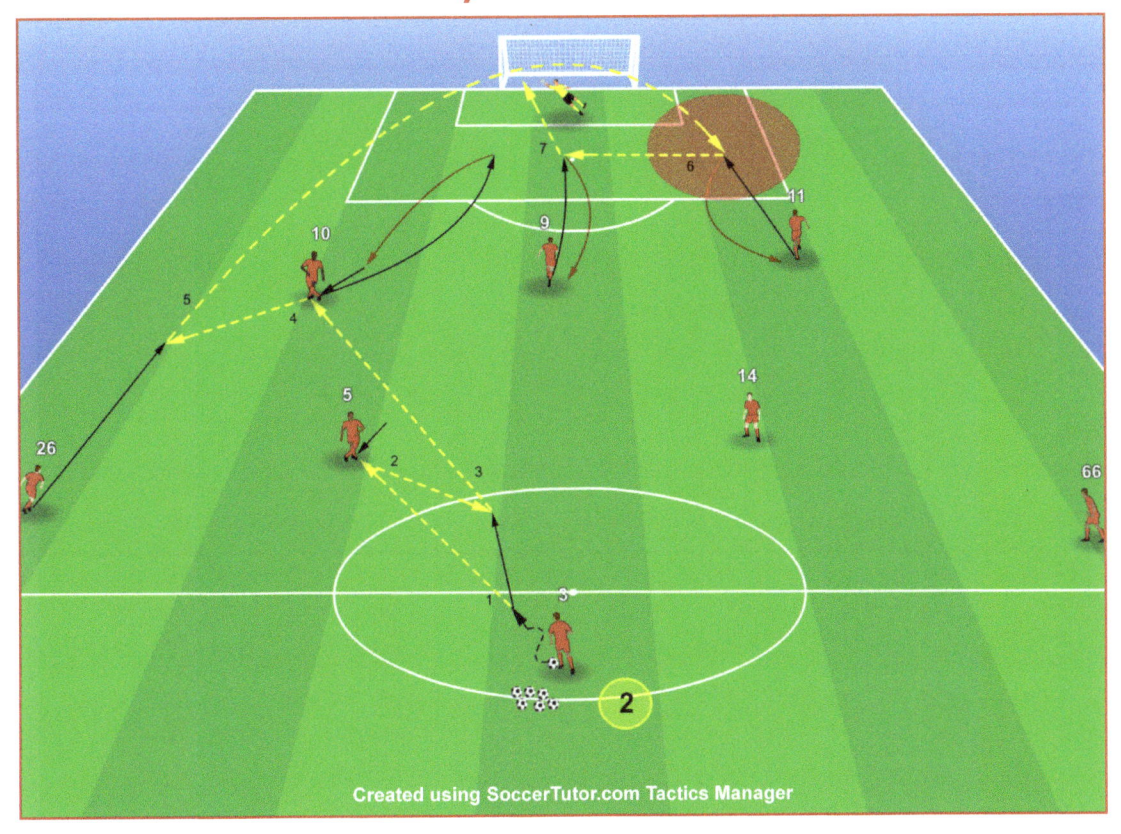

Description (Ball 2)

- Immediately following part 1, the defensive midfielder **(3)** dribbles a new ball forward and plays a one-two combination with the left central midfielder **(5)**.

- After receiving the return pass, the defensive midfielder **(3)** plays a diagonal forward pass to the left forward **(10)**.

- The left forward **(10)** passes back for the forward run of the left back **(26)**.

- The left back **(26)** then plays a first time long diagonal pass into the box on the opposite side to switch the point of attack.

- This diagonal pass is weighted correctly for the well-timed forward run of the right forward **(11)**.

- The right forward **(11)** passes across the box for either of the other 2 forwards **(9 or 10)**, who make forward runs to help finish the attack.

JÜRGEN KLOPP LIVERPOOL ATTACKING TACTICS

Session for **JÜRGEN KLOPP** Tactics - Switch Attack to Weak Side of Ball Oriented Opponents

Ball 3/3: Wide Forward Dribbles Inside + Switch to Weak Side

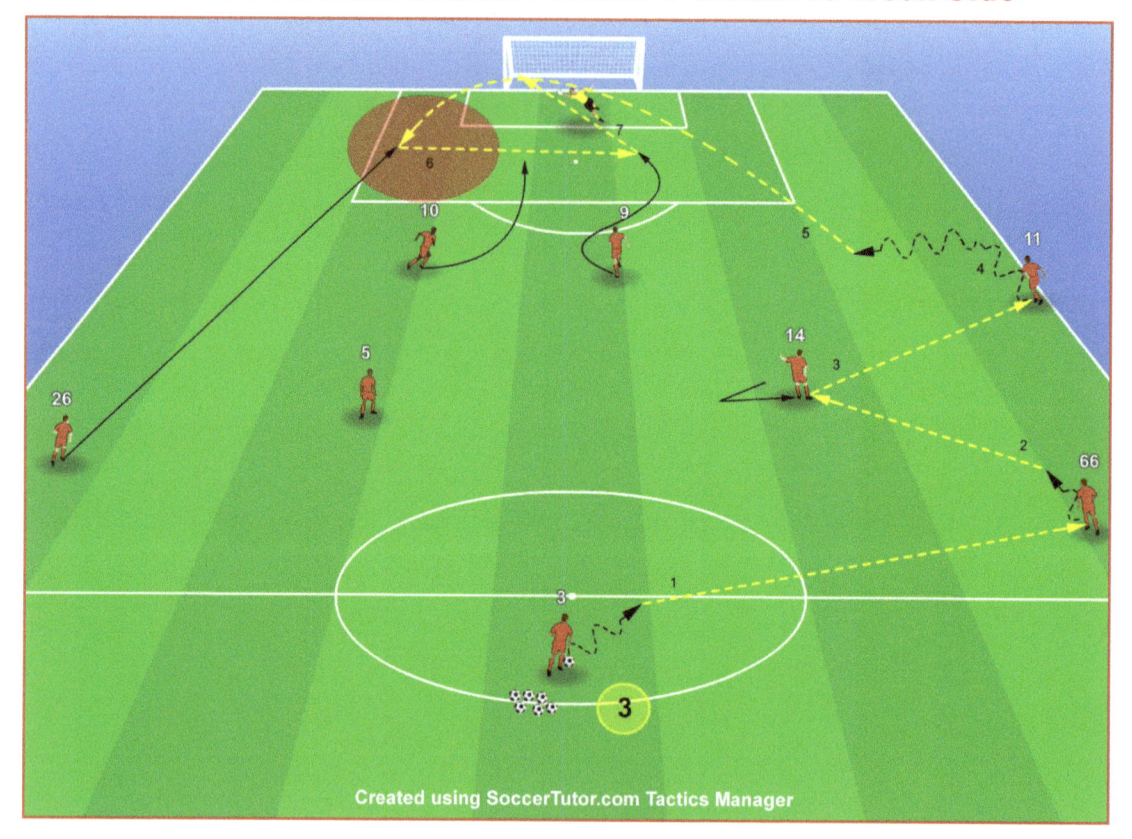

Description (Ball 3)

- Immediately following part 2, the defensive midfielder **(3)** dribbles a new ball forward and passes out wide to the right back **(66)**.

- The right back **(66)** takes a forward touch and passes to the right central midfielder **(14)**, who passes first time out wide to the right forward **(11)** on the side-line.

- The right forward **(11)** uses a feint, dribbles inside, and then bends a cross towards the back post.

- The left back **(26)** on the opposite side makes a long deep run and times it well to meet the cross. He has **2 Options**:

  a. First time finish (shot or header).

  b. Pass across for one of the 2 forwards.

Coaching Points

1. The final pass should be across the box parallel with the 6-yard box.

2. The forwards should make opposite runs with one moving into the centre or near post to finish, and the other moving towards the back post area.

Session for **JÜRGEN KLOPP** Tactics - Switch Attack to Weak Side of Ball Oriented Opponents

PROGRESSION
3. Combination Play on One Side + Switch Point of Attack to Weak Side in a Dynamic Functional Game

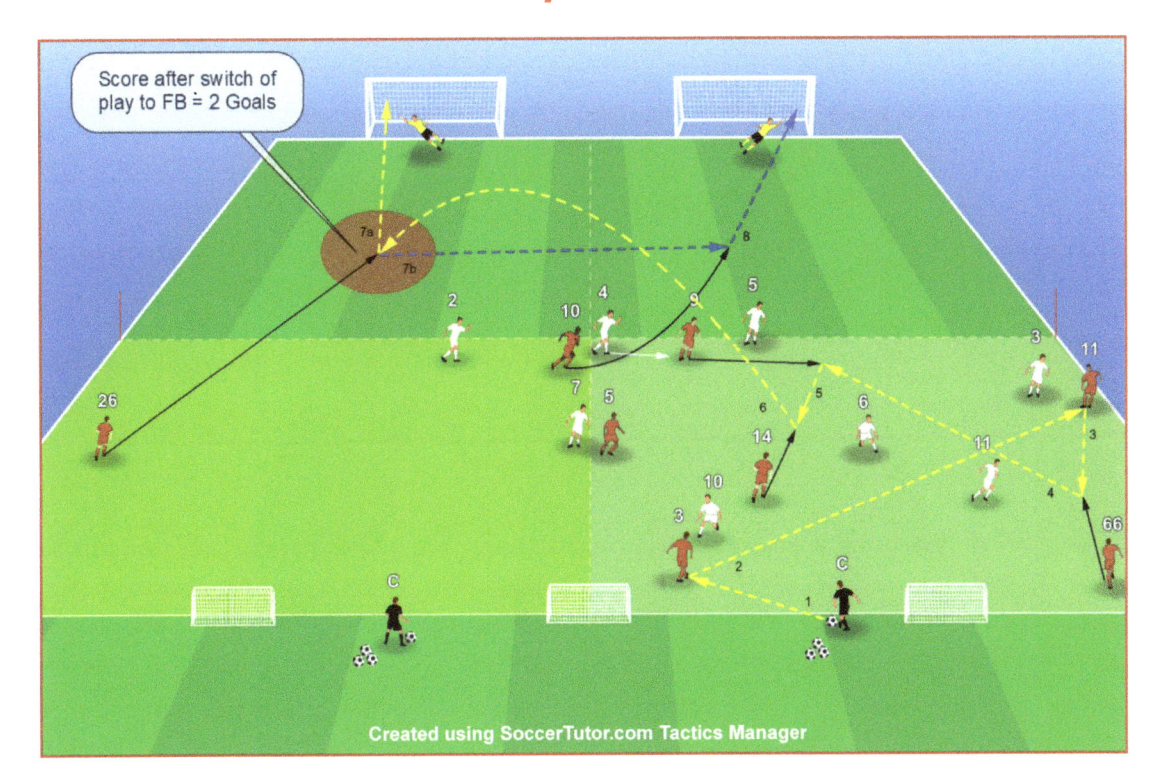

Description

- The 2 larger zones are 25 yard squares, and the 2 end zones are 25 x 15 yards.
- The red attacking team have 8 players in a 2-3-3 formation (from 4-3-3) with 2 full backs, 1 defensive midfielder, 2 central midfielders, and 3 forwards.
- The white defending team are in a 4-3-1 formation and have 2 GKs defending 2 goals.
- The practice starts with the reds in possession on one side (right in diagram example). If they find space, they attack the goal on the right side and try to score (1 point). However, if the whites defend well in this zone, the aim for the reds becomes to exploit the weak side.
- When a player finds space (right back **No.66** in diagram), he plays an aerial diagonal pass into the end zone for the forward run of the full back on the opposite side (left back **No.26**).
- The full back has **2 Options**:
    a. Try to score himself.
    b. Pass the ball across for a forward to score in the end zone on the opposite side.
- All players can move freely into the end finishing zones after the ball is played in there. If the attacking team score a goal after a diagonal pass to the opposite end zone, they get 2 points.
- If the whites win the ball at any point, they try to score in any of the 3 mini goals (2 points).

Session for JÜRGEN KLOPP Tactics - Switch Attack to Weak Side of Ball Oriented Opponents

PROGRESSION
4. Combination Play on One Side + Switch Point of Attack to Weak Side in a Dynamic Tactical Game

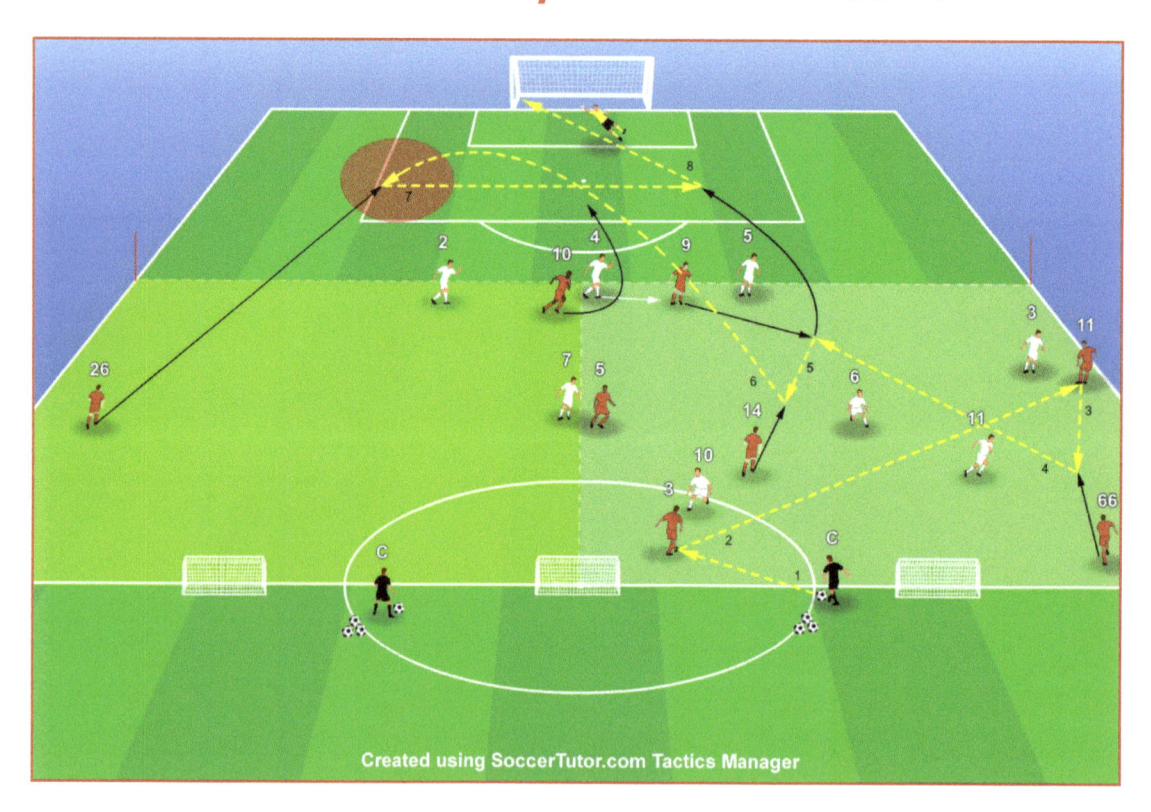

Description
- In this progression of the previous practice, we now use half a pitch with just 1 goal + GK.
- There is only 1 end zone instead of 2. Otherwise, it works in exactly the same way.
- The diagonal pass (switching to weak side) should be played into the box as shown.
- All players can move freely into the box after the ball is played in there.
- In this example, the diagonal pass is played to the full back (**26**), but it can also be played to the wide forward (**10**).

Rules
- Give the red players unlimited touches in the large zones or limit them to 2-3 touches.
- Limit the red players to 1 or 2 touches in the end zone (box).

Session for **JÜRGEN KLOPP** Tactics - Switch Attack to Weak Side of Ball Oriented Opponents

PROGRESSION
5. Combination Play on One Side + Switch Point of Attack to Weak Side in an 11 v 11 Tactical Game

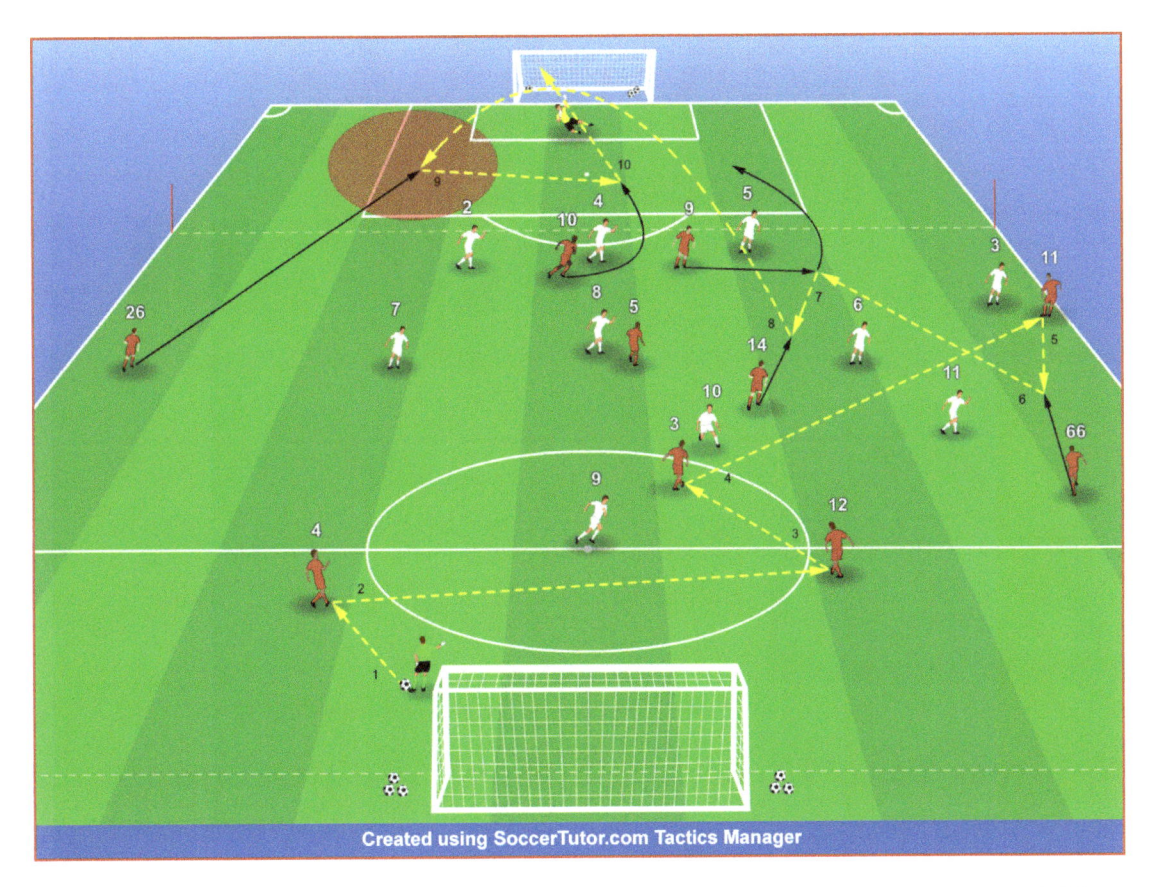

Description

- In this final practice of the session, we play an 11 v 11 game in 2/3 of a pitch. There is still an end zone (from just outside the box).
- The reds are in Liverpool's 4-3-3 formation and the whites are in a 4-2-3-1.
- We always start with the red team's GK and the reds build up play trying to score (1 point).
- As in the previous practices in this session, if the red attacking team score a goal after a diagonal pass to the weak side and in behind, they get 2 points.
- In this diagram example, a central midfielder **(14)** switches the point of the attack for the forward run of the left back **(26)**.
- The left back **(26)** has **2 Options**:
  1. Try to score himself.
  2. Pass the ball across for one of the forwards to score **(9 or 10)**.
- All players can move freely into the end finishing zone after the ball is played in there.
- If the whites win the ball at any point, they try to score with a counter attack (2 points).

JÜRGEN KLOPP LIVERPOOL ATTACKING TACTICS

JÜRGEN KLOPP TACTICAL ANALYSIS

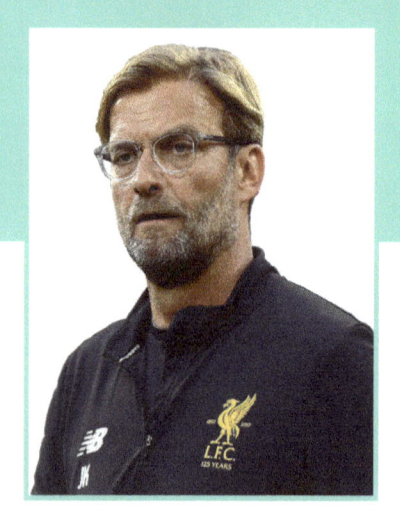

SOLUTION 5

Switch Play to the Full Back on the Weak Side for Early Cross

Content from analysis of Liverpool F.C. during the 2018-2019 Champions League winning season and the 2019-2020 Premier League winning season

- Analysis based on recurring patterns of play observed within the Liverpool team.
- Tactical solutions displayed as examples of the team's tactics being used effectively.
- Real match examples of Liverpool scoring a goal using this specific attacking tactical solution.
- Each action, pass, individual movement with or without the ball, and the positioning of each player on the pitch including their body shape, are presented.
- The analysis is then used to create a full progressive session to coach this tactical situation.

Tactical Solution 5 - Switch Play to the Full Back on the Weak Side for Early Cross

Switch Play to the Full Back on the Weak Side for Early Cross (Against Ball Oriented Opponents)

What?

Liverpool switch play to the opponent's weak side and then deliver an early cross to attack the space in the box and try to score.

Why?

As the opposing players all move towards the ball together and create a strong side (ball oriented defence), there is available space to exploit on the weak side. However, unlike the previous Tactical Solution 4, the run in behind is covered by an opposing player, which means the switch is played in front of the defensive line.

How?

Liverpool switch play to the full back on the weak side, who delivers an early cross into the box and in behind the defensive line for the forwards while the opposition are temporarily out of position.

Target Areas (Receive Wide + Cross into Box)

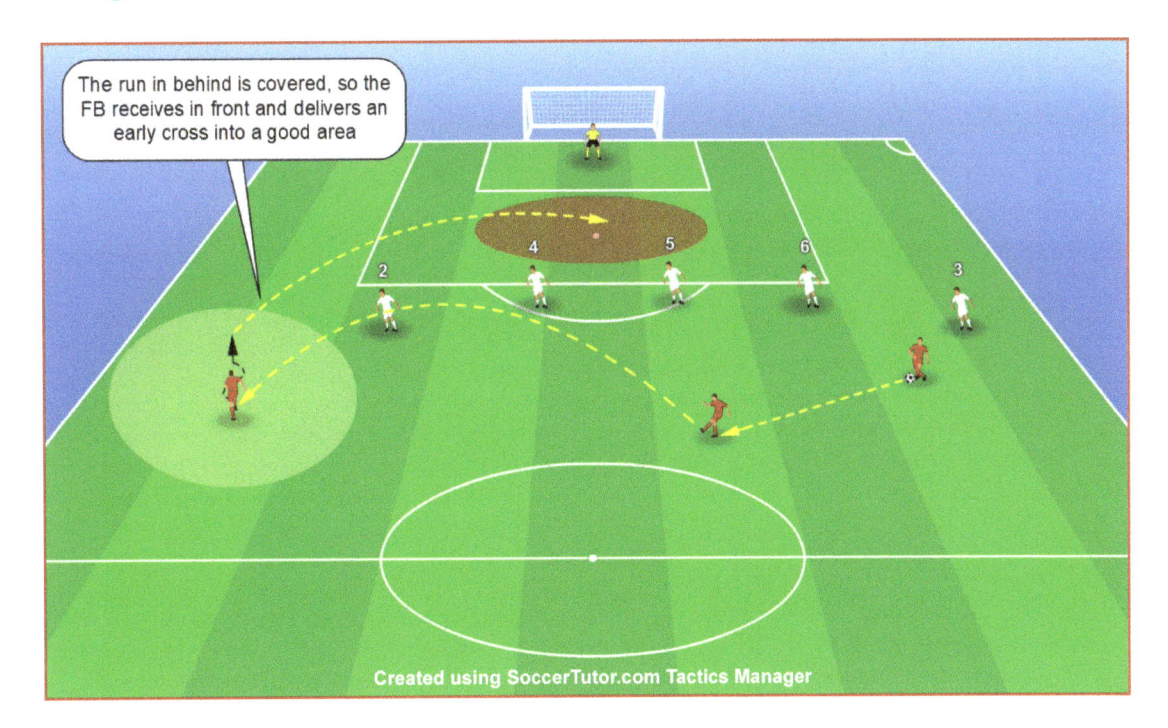

The run in behind is covered, so the FB receives in front and delivers an early cross into a good area

JÜRGEN KLOPP LIVERPOOL ATTACKING TACTICS

Tactical Solution 5 - Switch Play to the Full Back on the Weak Side for Early Cross

Tactical Solution A: Switch Play to the Full Back on the Weak Side via Centre Back/s + Early Cross

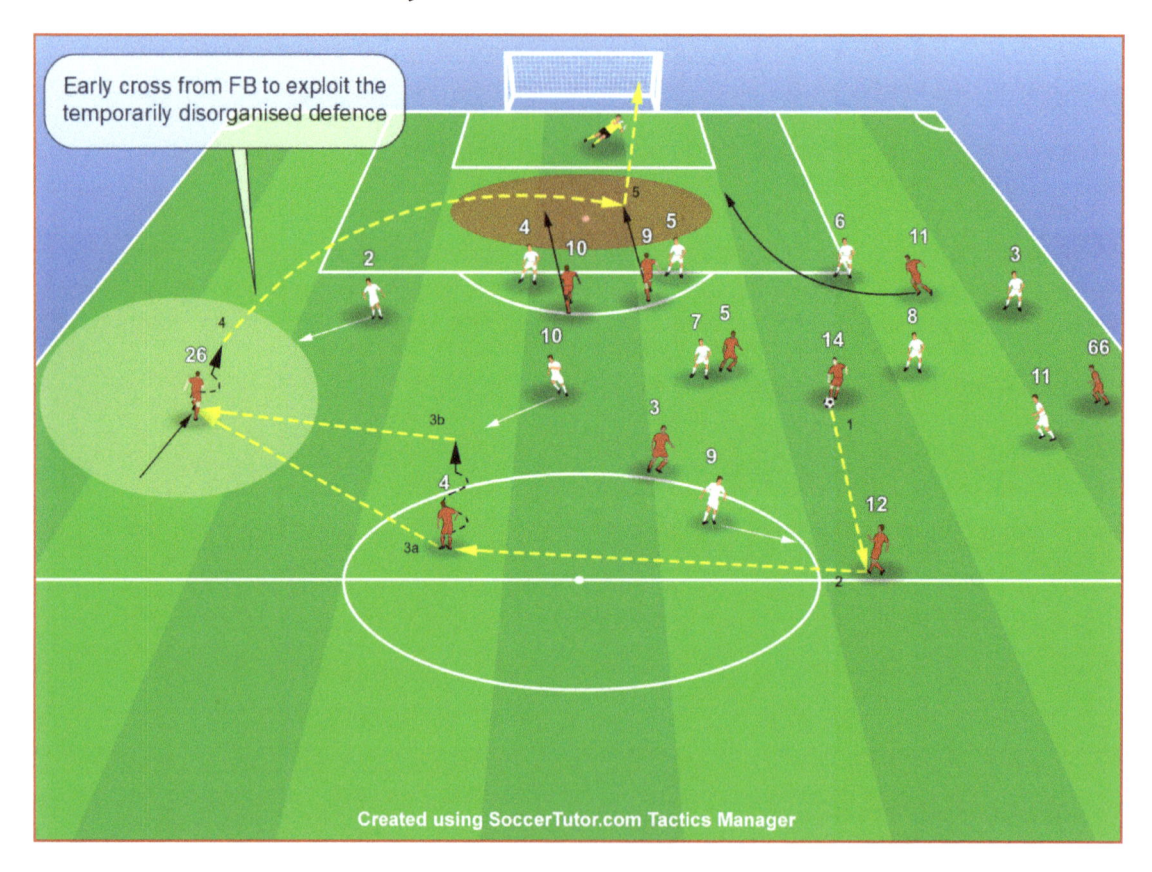

Liverpool are attacking on one side of the pitch (right in diagram example) with many players positioned there trying to create a numerical superiority.

If the opposition adapt to this situation and also have many players defending on this side of the pitch, then Liverpool's objective is to quickly change the point of attack and switch the play to the full back on the opposite side (from right to left or vice versa).

In this tactical example, we show how Liverpool move the ball to the full back on the weak side via the centre back/s. The central midfielder (**14**) passes back to the right centre back (**12**), who passes across to the other centre back (**4**).

The centre back (**4**) has **2 Options**:

A. Pass directly to the left back (**26**).

B. Dribble forward to attract the opponent in front (No.10) and then pass to the left back (**26**) before reaching him. This takes white No.10 out of the game.

The full back (**No.26** in diagram example) usually moves forward and delivers an early cross into the centre of the box and in behind the defensive line to exploit the temporarily disorganised defence.

At least 2 of the forwards (all 3 in diagram) make runs into the space to attack the cross and score. Here, the centre forward (**9**) scores.

Tactical Solution 5 - Switch Play to the Full Back on the Weak Side for Early Cross

Tactical Solution B: Switch Play to the Full Back on the Weak Side via Defensive Midfielder + Early Cross

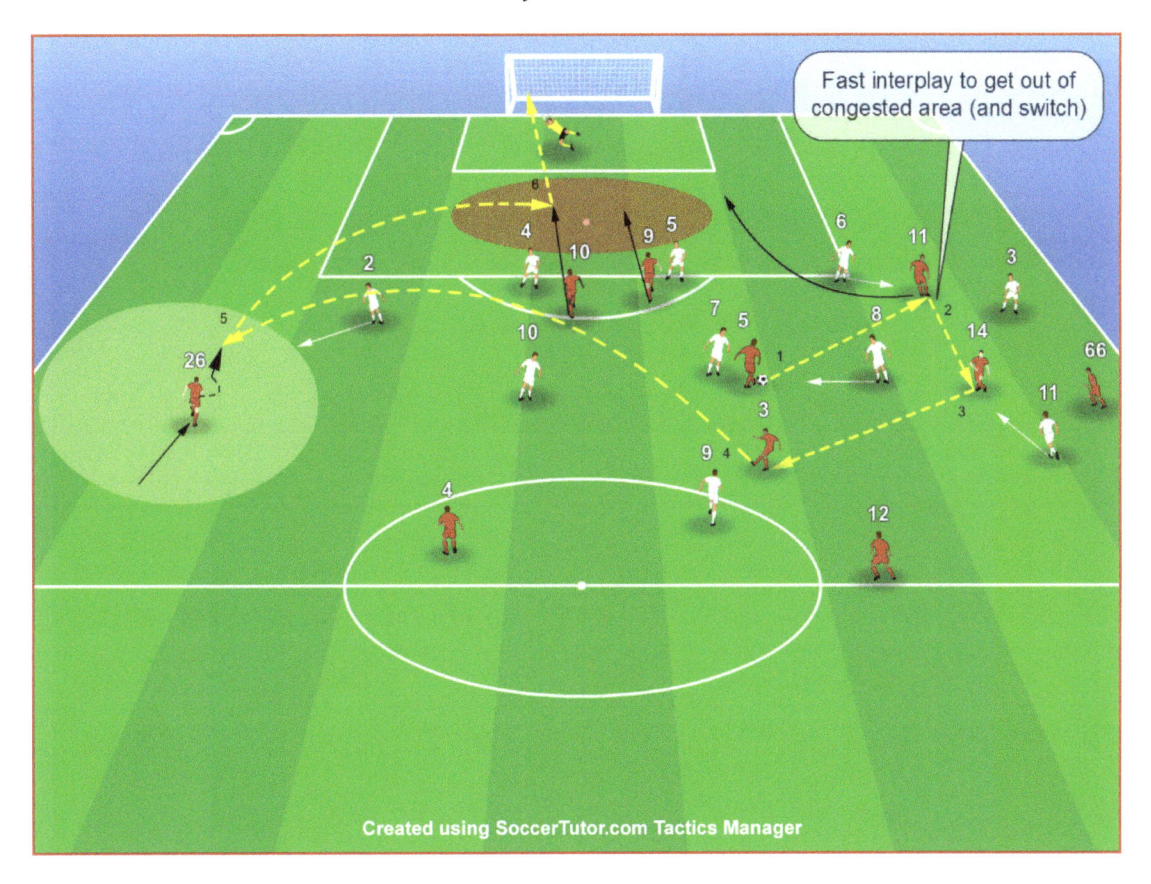

Tactical Solution B shows a variation of Tactical Solution A. In this tactical solution, we show how Liverpool move the ball to the full back on the weak side via the defensive midfielder **(3)**.

The central midfielder **(5)** passes to the right forward **(11)**, and without better options he passes back to the other central midfielder **(14)**.

When the central midfielder **(14)** receives, he sees the opportunity to switch the play to the opponent's weak side. He passes inside to the defensive midfielder **(3)**, who is unmarked and plays an aerial pass to switch the play to the full back **(26)** in space.

The left back **(26)** receives, moves forward, and delivers an early cross into the centre of the box and in behind the defensive line.

At least 2 of the forwards (all 3 in diagram) make runs into the space to attack the cross and score. Here, the left forward **(10)** scores.

Tactical Solution 5 - Switch Play to the Full Back on the Weak Side for Early Cross

Statistical Analysis of Liverpool Switching Play to the Full Back on the Weak Side for Early Cross

Liverpool scored **7 goals** in this tactical situation
(Premier League and Champions League 2018-2019 and 2019-2020 seasons)

VS. BALL ORIENTED OPPONENTS CREATING STRONG SIDE
SWITCH PLAY TO THE FULL BACK ON THE WEAK SIDE + EARLY CROSS

DATE	HOME	AWAY	SCORE	GOAL (MIN)	SCORER	ASSIST
27th Feb 2019	Liverpool	Watford	5-0	2-0 (20')	**Mané**	A-Arnold
27th Feb 2019	Liverpool	Watford	5-0	5-0 (82')	**van Dijk**	Robertson
31st Mar 2019	Liverpool	Tottenham	2-1	1-0 (16')	**Firmino** *	Robertson
17th Apr 2019	Porto	Liverpool	1-4	1-3 (77')	**Firmino**	Henderson
26th Apr 2019	Liverpool	Huddersfield	5-0	2-0 (23')	**Mané** *	Robertson
10th Nov 2019	Liverpool	Man City	3-1	2-0 (13')	**Salah**	Robertson
22nd Jul 2020	Liverpool	Chelsea	5-3	4-1 (54')	**Firmino** *	A-Arnold

* The full analysis of these goals is shown on the following pages...

Tactical Solution 5 - Switch Play to the Full Back on the Weak Side for Early Cross

Analysis from Liverpool 5-0 Huddersfield (Mané 23') - 26th Apr 2019, Premier League

Tactical Solution A (1): Switch Play to the Full Back on the Weak Side via Centre Back (Right to Left) + Early Cross

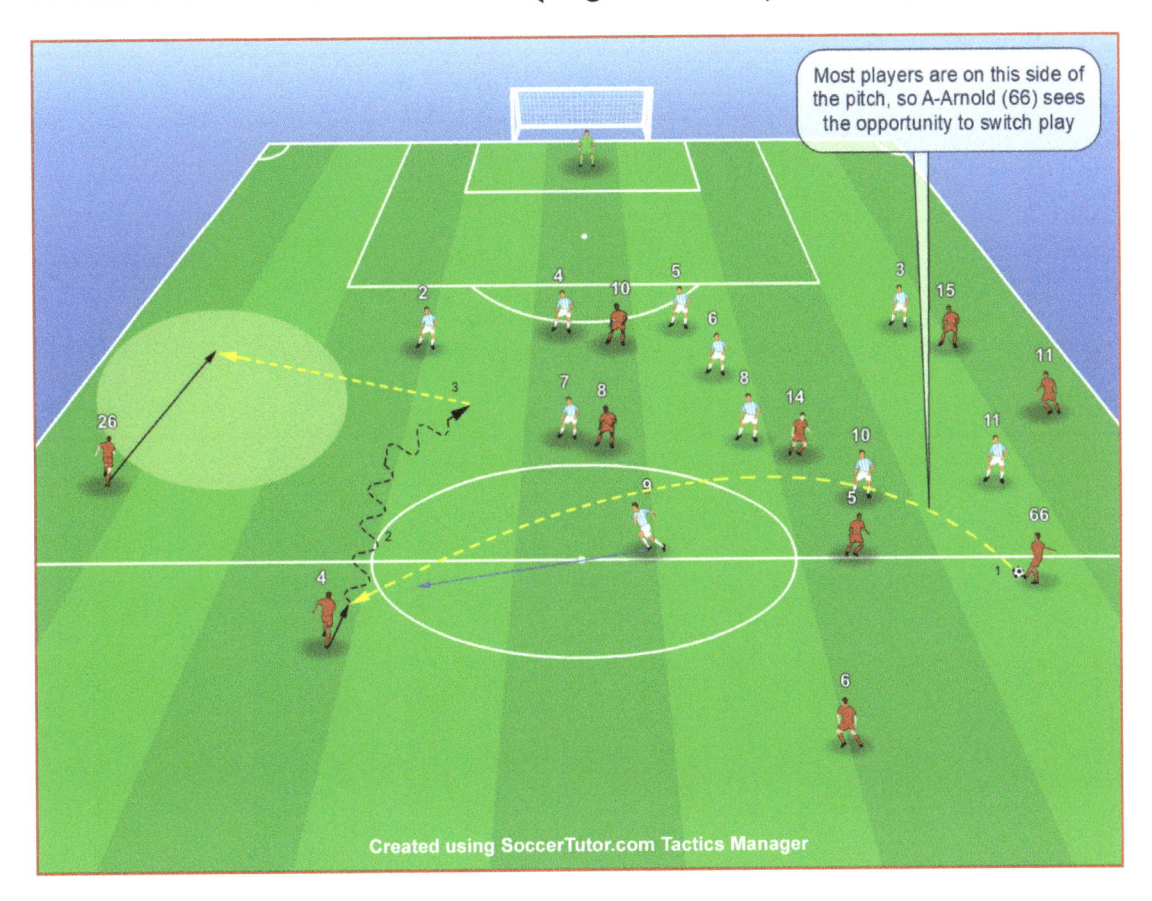

Most players are on this side of the pitch, so A-Arnold (66) sees the opportunity to switch play

Liverpool have the ball on the right side of the pitch. Most of the Liverpool players and most of their opponents are all on that side. The right back in possession **A-Arnold (66)** looks up and sees the opportunity to switch play to the opponent's weak side.

He plays an aerial pass to the left centre back **van Dijk (4)**, who has a lot of free space in front of him. When he receives, he dribbles forward to exploit the space. He dribbles up to the opponent in front of him, and then passes out wide to the left back **Robertson (26)** to complete the switch of play.

The aim now is to deliver an early cross into the centre of the box and in behind the defensive line to exploit the temporarily disorganised Huddersfield defence.

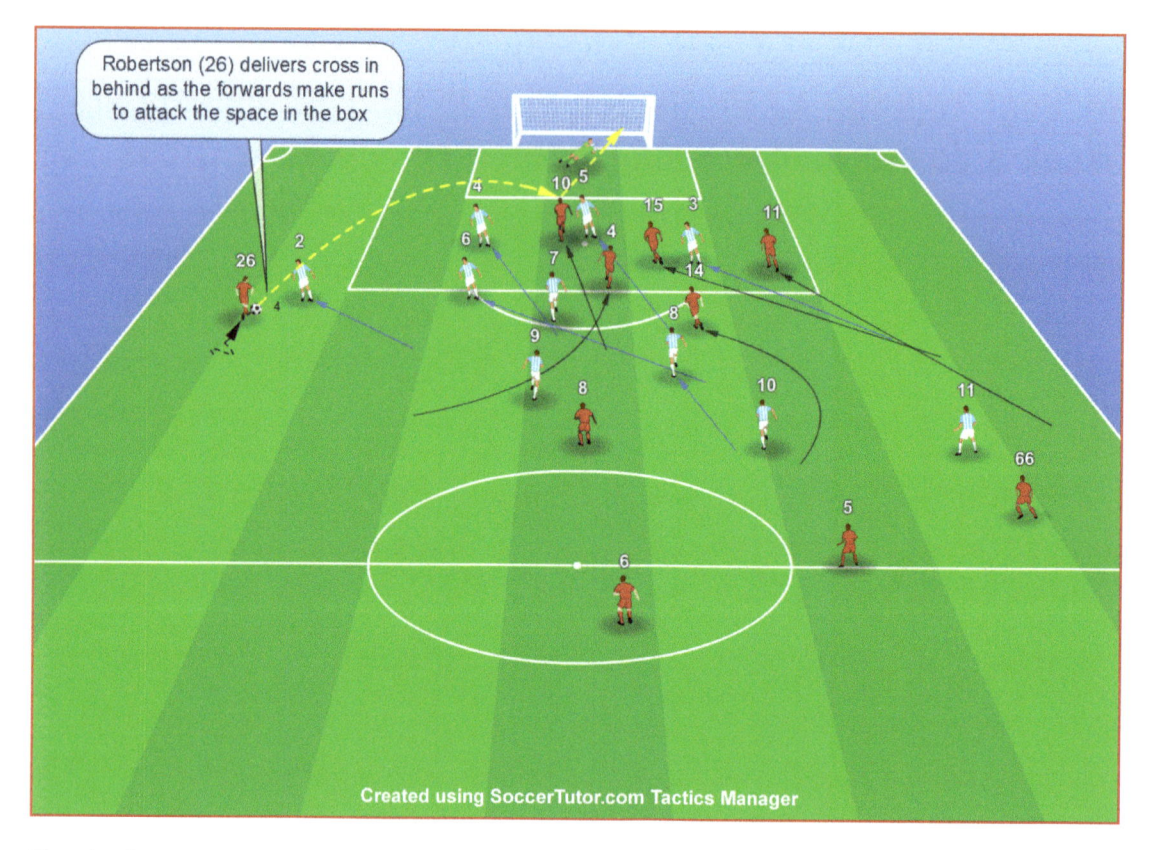

Tactical Solution 5 - Switch Play to the Full Back on the Weak Side for Early Cross

Robertson (26) delivers cross in behind as the forwards make runs to attack the space in the box

Shortly after receiving the ball, the left back **Robertson (26)** delivers an early cross in behind Huddersfield's defensive line as the forwards make runs into the box to attack the space and try to score.

The cross is aimed in behind the defensive line and into the space between the edge of the penalty area and the 6-yard box.

Mané (10) shows good timing and good coordination to get to the ball, jump up and head the ball past the Huddersfield GK to score.

Tactical Solution 5 - Switch Play to the Full Back on the Weak Side for Early Cross

Analysis from Liverpool 5-3 Chelsea (Firmino 54') - 22nd Jul 2020, Premier League

Tactical Solution A (2): Switch Play to the Full Back on the Weak Side via Centre Back (Left to Right) + Early Cross

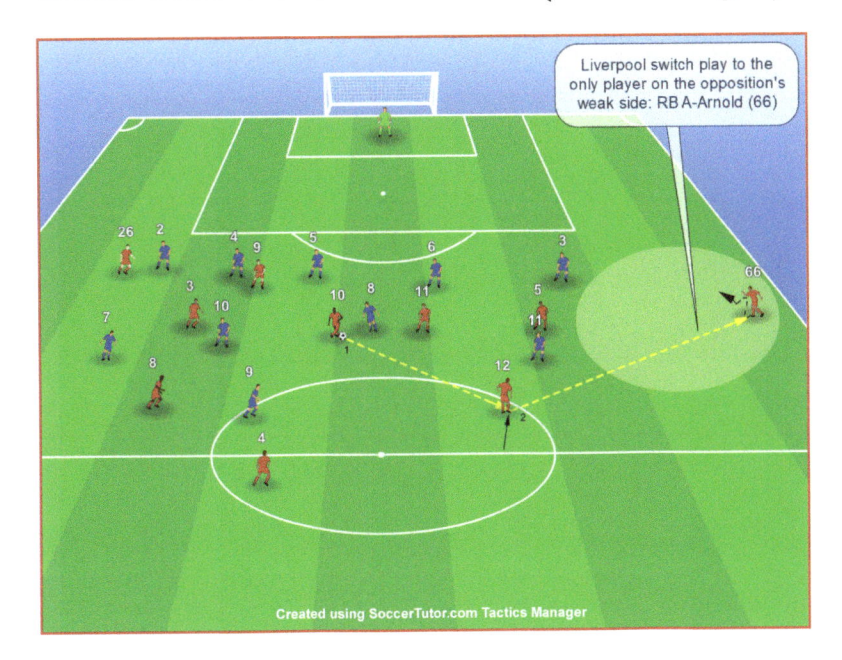

Liverpool had the ball on the left side of the pitch. Most of the Liverpool players and most of their opponents are all on that side. The ball is moved to centre back **Gomez (12)**.

All the players (except the Liverpool right back) are in the centre or left side of the pitch. **Gomez (12)** plays a quick pass to **A-Arnold (66)** and changes the direction/point of attack to the right side (weak side of the opponent).

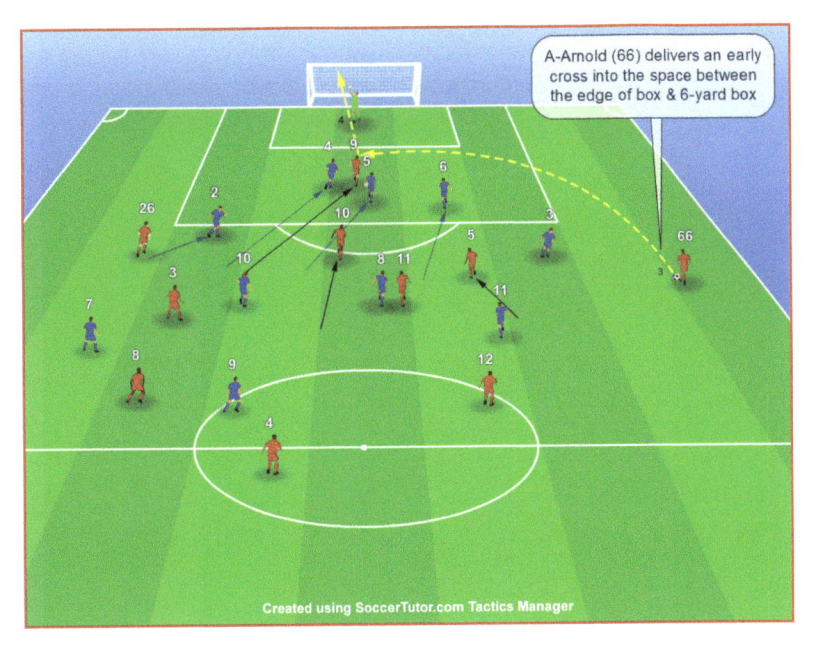

A-Arnold (66) receives on the right, takes a touch, and delivers an early technical cross in behind Chelsea's defensive line. The target area is the space between the edge of the penalty area and the 6-yard box.

Centre forward **Firmino (9)** sprints into the box. He shows very good timing and an excellent jump to beat the 2 Chelsea defenders in a 1v2 situation, and score with a header past the GK.

JÜRGEN KLOPP LIVERPOOL ATTACKING TACTICS

Tactical Solution 5 - Switch Play to the Full Back on the Weak Side for Early Cross

Analysis from Liverpool 2-1 Tottenham (Firmino 16') - 31st Mar 2019, Premier League

Tactical Solution B: Switch Play to the Full Back on the Weak Side via Defensive Midfielder + Early Cross

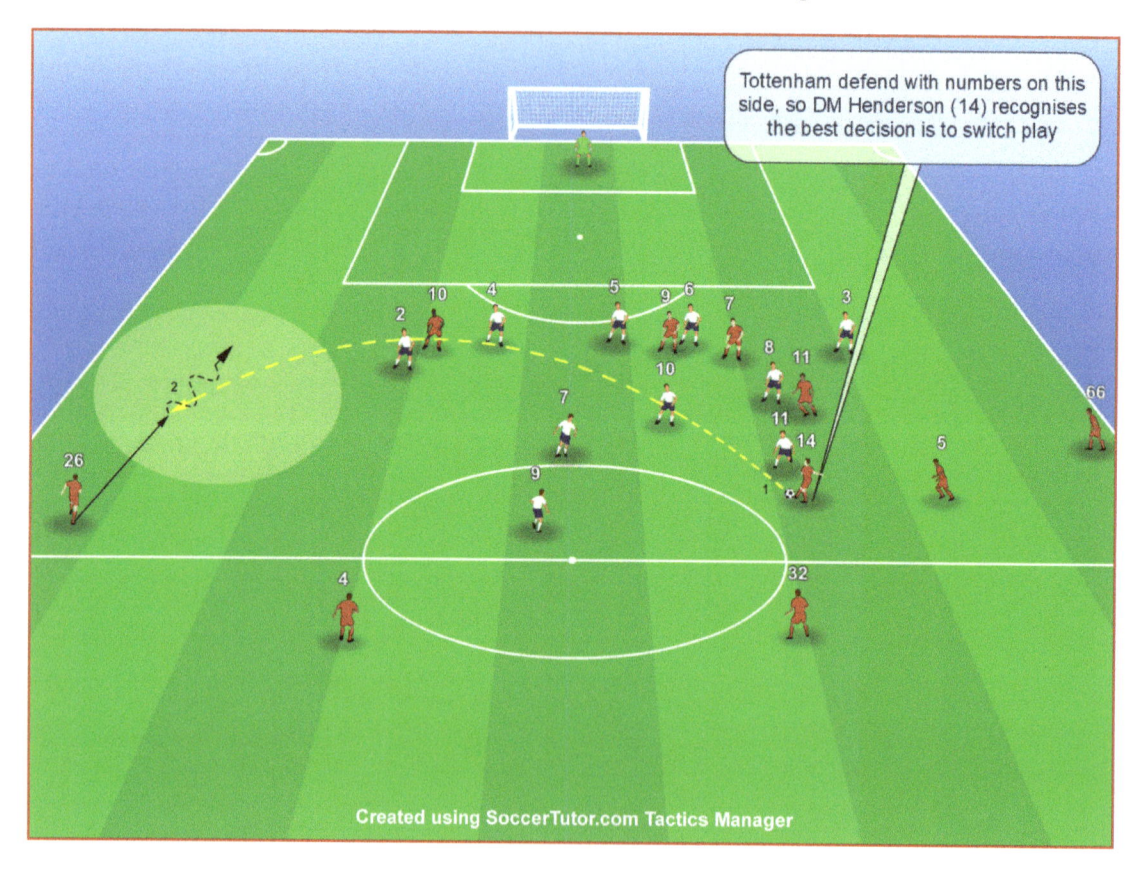

Tottenham defend with numbers on this side, so DM Henderson (14) recognises the best decision is to switch play

Liverpool are attacking on the right trying to create a numerical advantage there. Tottenham react to this and adapt to defend that side. Therefore, there are many players from both teams in this area of the pitch.

Defensive midfielder **Henderson (14)** recognises the situation and changes the direction of the attack to the left by playing a long aerial pass to left back **Robertson (26)**, who has a lot of free time and space to attack.

Robertson (26) receives and dribbles forward into the free space in front of him.

Tactical Solution 5 - Switch Play to the Full Back on the Weak Side for Early Cross

The left forward **Mané (10)** supports **Robertson (26)** by making a diagonal run in between the Tottenham centre back and right back, and into a wide position.

He asks for the ball but more importantly occupies the attention of the 2 Tottenham defenders who must cover **Mané's (10)** movement and mark him.

The left back **Robertson (26)** delivers an early cross in behind Tottenham's defensive line as the other 2 forwards **Firmino (9)** and **Salah (11)** make runs into the box to attack the space and try to score.

The cross is aimed in behind the defensive line and into the space between the edge of the penalty area and the 6-yard box.

Central midfielder **Milner (7)** moves to the edge of the box to collect any second balls.

Firmino (9) times his run perfectly for the cross and heads the ball down to score.

SESSION 5 BASED ON THE TACTICS OF JÜRGEN KLOPP

Switch Play to the Full Back on the Weak Side for Early Cross

Session for **JÜRGEN KLOPP** Tactics - Switch Play to Full Back on Weak Side for Early Cross

SESSION FOR THIS TACTICAL SITUATION (5 PRACTICES)
1. Possession Play + Switch Play to Opposite Side in a 6 v 6 (+6) Dynamic 3 Zone Transition Game

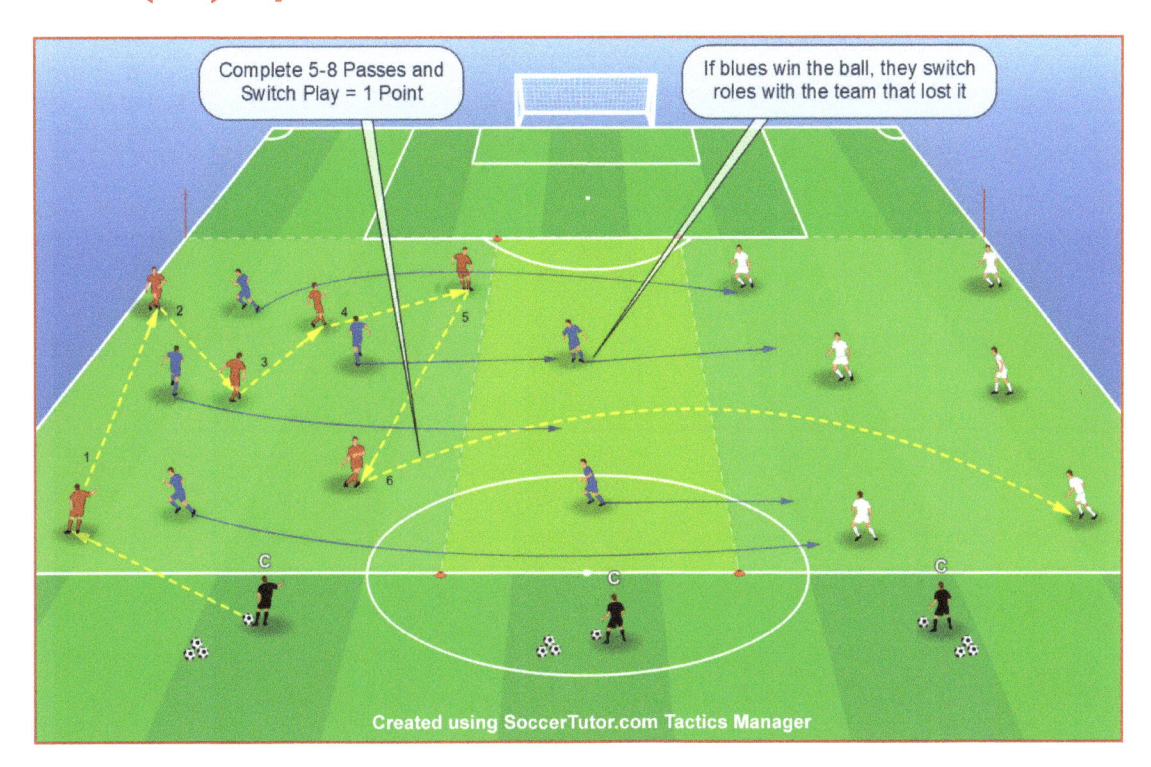

Complete 5-8 Passes and Switch Play = 1 Point

If blues win the ball, they switch roles with the team that lost it

Description

- Mark out 3 zones as shown. We work with 3 teams of 6 players. The practice starts with the Coach's pass to the red team and a 6 v 4 situation in one of the wide zones (left vs. blues in diagram example). The other 2 blue players are in the central zone and the white team are in the opposite wide zone.

- The aim is to exploit the numerical advantage to complete 5-8 passes, and then switch the play to the opposite wide zone. The 2 blue players in the central zone try to block/intercept the switch pass.

- If the blues win the ball either within the wide zone or intercept in the central zone, the red and blue teams immediately switch roles.

- If the switch to the white team is successful, the 2 central zone blue players + 2 more blue players move across to press the white team very quickly. The other 2 blue players move to the central zone.

- We have the same 6 v 4 situation, with the whites trying to complete 5-8 passes and switch back to the reds.

Coaching Points

1. Focus on accuracy and weight of passes under pressure, always provide support angles for ball carrier, and communicate with heads up.
2. Take first touches in the correct direction.
3. Good rhythm and synchronised movements.
4. Accurate aerial passing for switch of play.

Session for **JÜRGEN KLOPP** Tactics - Switch Play to Full Back on Weak Side for Early Cross

PROGRESSION
2. Possession and Switch Play to Full Back on Weak Side for Early Cross in a Functional 8 v 8 (+2) Game

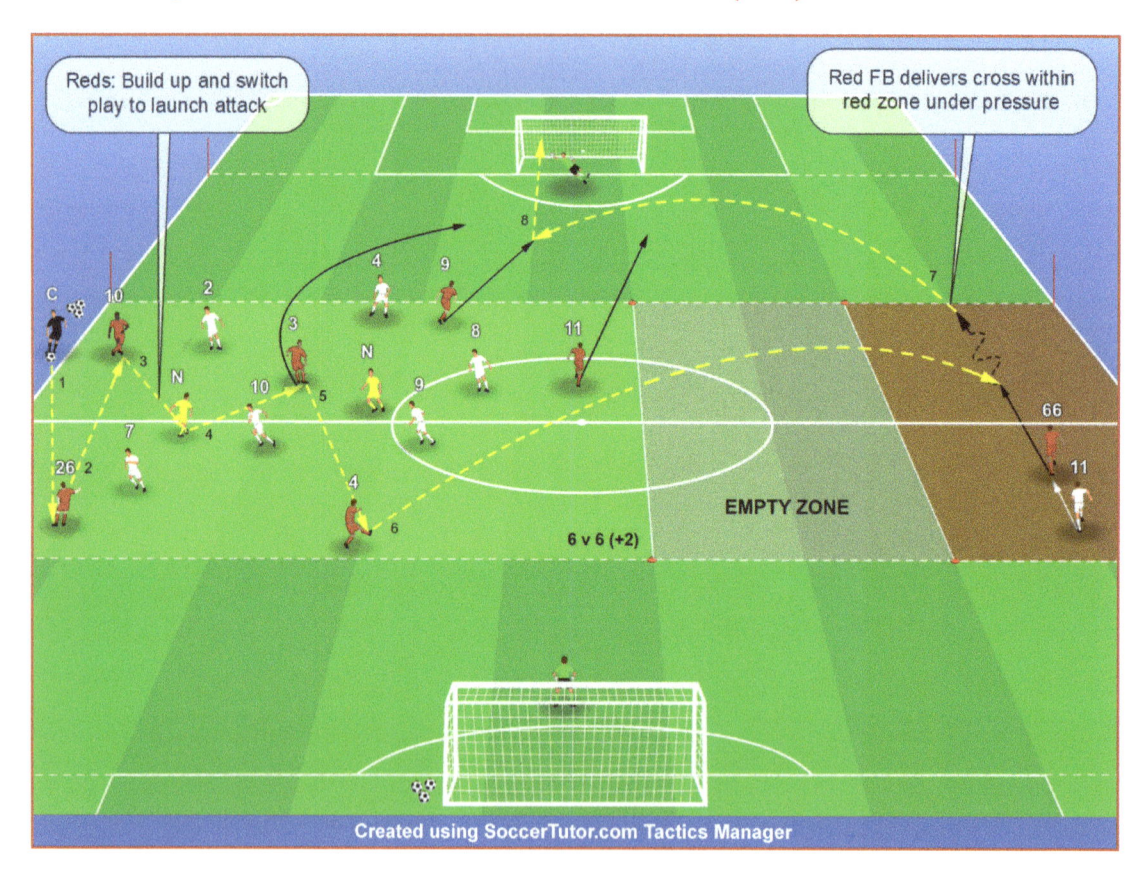

Reds: Build up and switch play to launch attack

Red FB delivers cross within red zone under pressure

EMPTY ZONE

6 v 6 (+2)

Description
- The total area is box to box, with 3 zones marked out as shown (40 yard depth).
- The practice starts with the Coach's pass to the reds into the large left zone where we have a 6 v 6 (+2) situation.
- The aim is to exploit the numerical advantage to complete 5-8 passes, and then switch the play to the opposite side zone (to **No.66**).
- The right back **(66)** receives, dribbles forward, and delivers an early cross from within his zone. At least 3 teammates make runs into the end zone to try and score from the cross.
- If the whites win the ball, the teams switch roles immediately with the same aims. After a set amount of time, move the large zone to the right so you work on both sides of pitch.

Coaching Points
1. All the coaching points from the previous practice also apply for this practice.
2. The accuracy and weight of the cross needs to be correct + aimed in the centre of the end zone and not too close to the GK.
3. Monitor the quality of the finishing, especially when trying to score with headers.

Session for **JÜRGEN KLOPP** Tactics - Switch Play to Full Back on Weak Side for Early Cross

PROGRESSION

3. Possession and Switch Play to Full Back on Weak Side for Early Cross in a Functional 9 v 9 (+2) Game

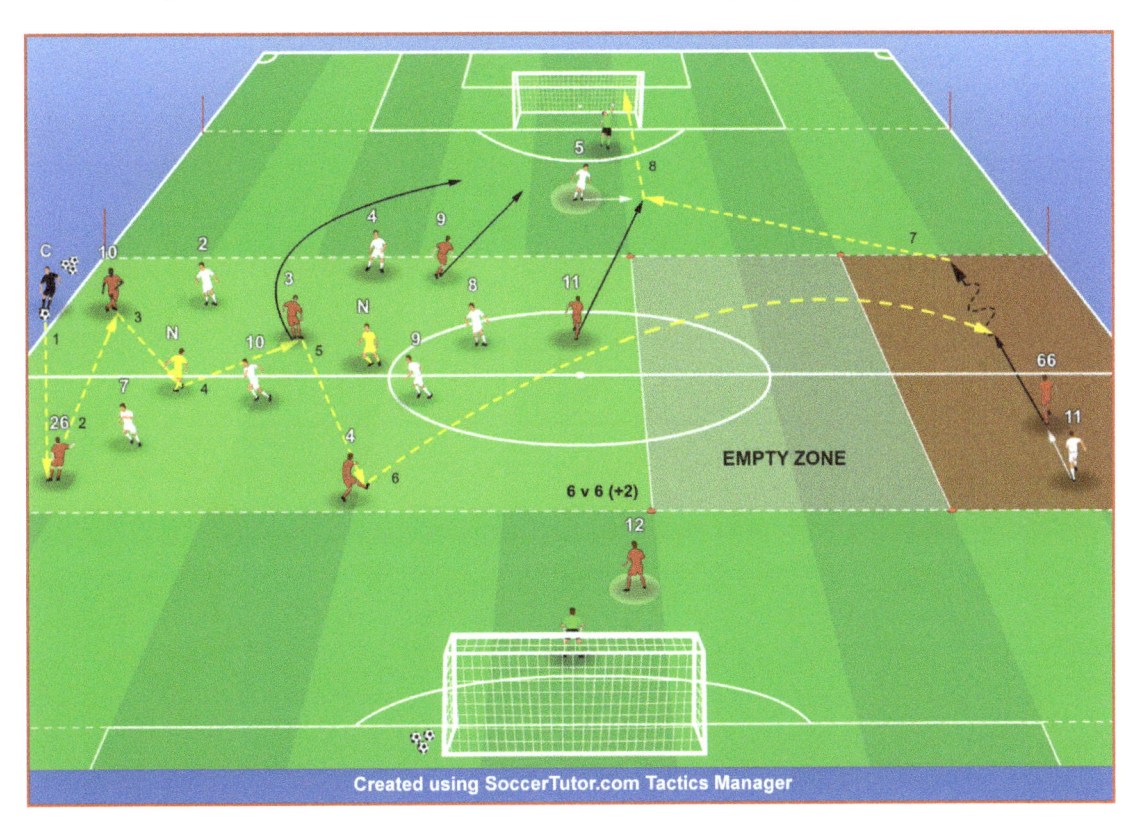

Description

- In the progression, we simply add a centre back for each team in the end zones, who are fully active to defend the crosses.

- This makes it more realistic, as the attackers have to time their runs better to avoid the defender and possibly compete with him in the air.

- In this example, the right back **(66)** delivers a low cross for the right forward **(11)** to score at the near post.

Session for **JÜRGEN KLOPP** Tactics - Switch Play to Full Back on Weak Side for Early Cross

PROGRESSION
4. Attack with Switch of Play to Full Back on Weak Side for Early Cross in a Tactical Zonal Game

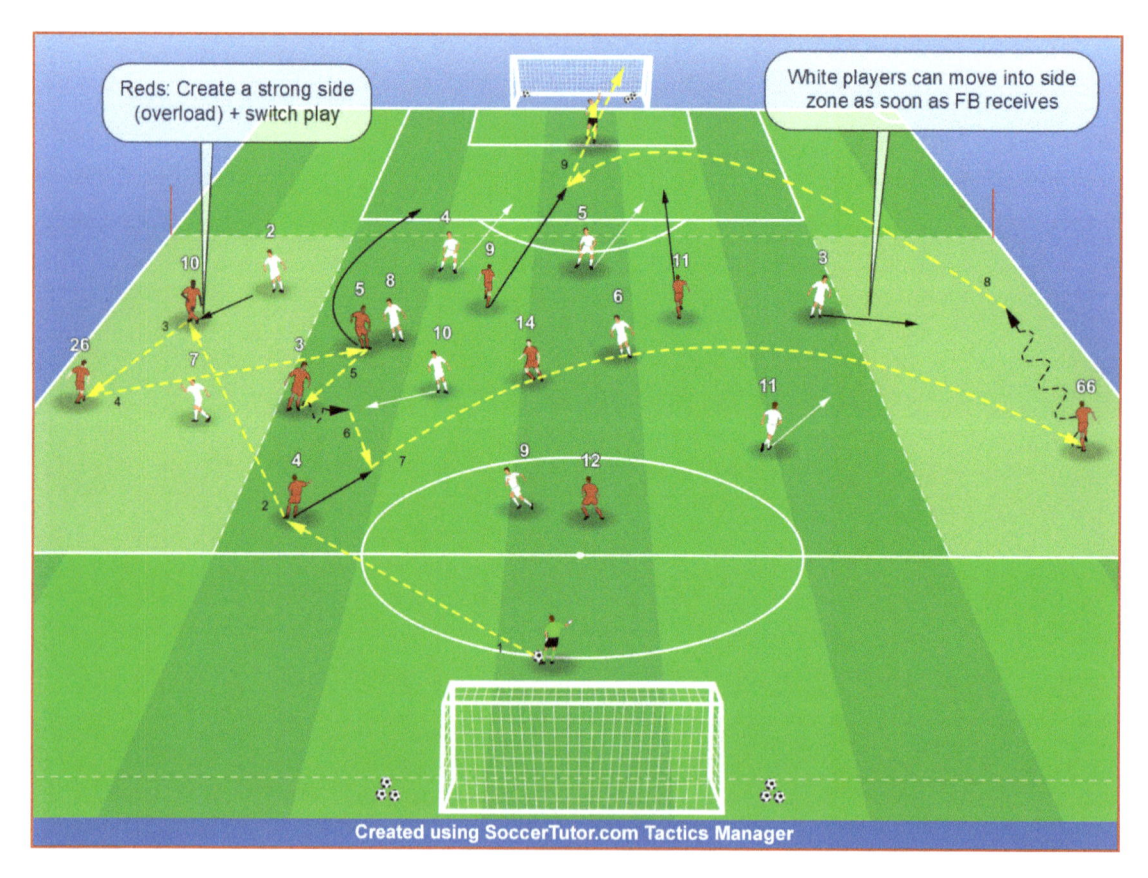

Reds: Create a strong side (overload) + switch play

White players can move into side zone as soon as FB receives

Description

- Mark out 3 vertical zones as shown + 2 end zones. The reds are in Liverpool's 4-3-3 formation and the whites are in a 4-2-3-1.
- The red GK starts by passing into the central zone and the reds aim to play in behind the defensive line (into the end zone) and score.
- The reds create a strong side on one side of the pitch (left), with only the opposite full back **(66)** in the opposite side zone (right).
- If the reds can play through the white team's pressing, they can attack on the left side normally and try to score (1 point).
- If the whites adapt to the situation and defend with many players on that side, the second aim is to switch the play to the weak side full back **(66)**, who dribbles forward and delivers an early cross from behind the end zone line.
- At least 3 teammates make runs into the end zone to try and score (2 points) from the cross into the space between the edge of the penalty area and the 6-yard box. As soon as red **No.66** receives, the white players can move to defend in the end zone.
- If the white team win the ball, they try to score with a counter attack (2 points).

Session for **JÜRGEN KLOPP** Tactics - Switch Play to Full Back on Weak Side for Early Cross

PROGRESSION
5. Attack with Switch of Play to Full Back on Weak Side for Early Cross in an 11 v 11 Tactical Game

Reds: Create a strong side (overload) + switch play

Description

- In the final practice of this session and progression of the previous practice, we remove the vertical zones in the middle and just have one large central zone, as shown.
- Everything else about the practice is the same.
- The red GK starts, and the reds try to create a strong side and score (1 point).
- If the whites adapt well and defend with numbers on that side, the reds switch play to the full back (**66**) on the weak side.
- The full back (**66**) receives and delivers an early cross for his teammates to score in the end zone (2 points).
- As soon as red **No.66** receives, the white players can move to defend in the end zone. Alternatively, the Coach can decide when/if the white players can defend in the end zone.
- If the white team win the ball, they try to score with a counter attack (2 points).

JÜRGEN KLOPP LIVERPOOL ATTACKING TACTICS

JÜRGEN KLOPP TACTICAL ANALYSIS

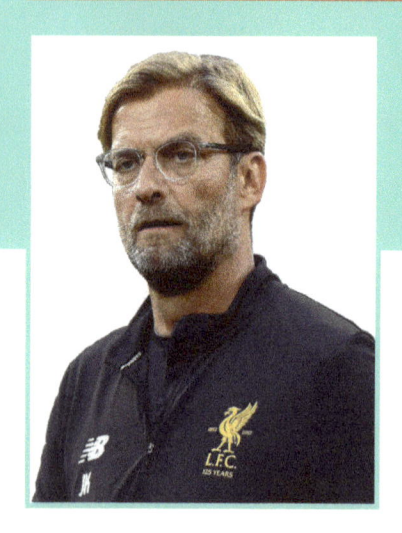

SOLUTION 6

Technical Lofted Passes into the Box Against Deep Defences

Content from analysis of Liverpool F.C. during the 2018-2019 Champions League winning season and the 2019-2020 Premier League winning season

- Analysis based on recurring patterns of play observed within the Liverpool team.
- Tactical solutions displayed as examples of the team's tactics being used effectively.
- Real match examples of Liverpool scoring a goal using this specific attacking tactical solution.
- Each action, pass, individual movement with or without the ball, and the positioning of each player on the pitch including their body shape, are presented.
- The analysis is then used to create a full progressive session to coach this tactical situation.

Tactical Solution 6 - Technical Lofted Passes into the Box Against Deep Defences

Technical Lofted Passes into the Box and in Behind the Opposition's Deep Defensive Line

What?
Liverpool want to get in behind their deep opponents and specifically get the ball to their attacking players in the box (highlighted area shown in diagram).

Why?
When the opposition have a compact defence and don't use collective team pressing around the ball area (waiting defence), it makes it difficult to play forward passes, penetrating passes, or to utilise individual attacking without losing the ball.

How?
Liverpool used technical lofted passes over the top to their attackers in behind their opponent's defensive line.

Target Area (in the Box)

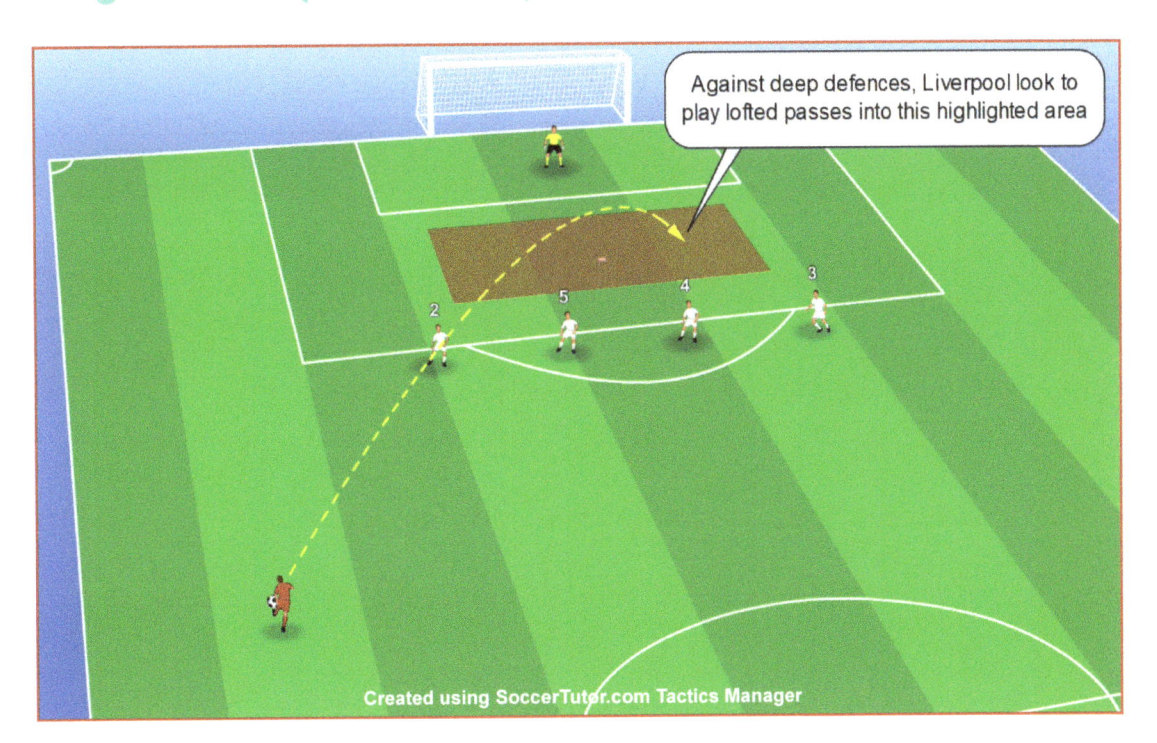

Against deep defences, Liverpool look to play lofted passes into this highlighted area

Tactical Solution 6 - Technical Lofted Passes into the Box Against Deep Defences

Tactical Solution A: Technical Lofted Pass in Behind and into the Box from a Central Position

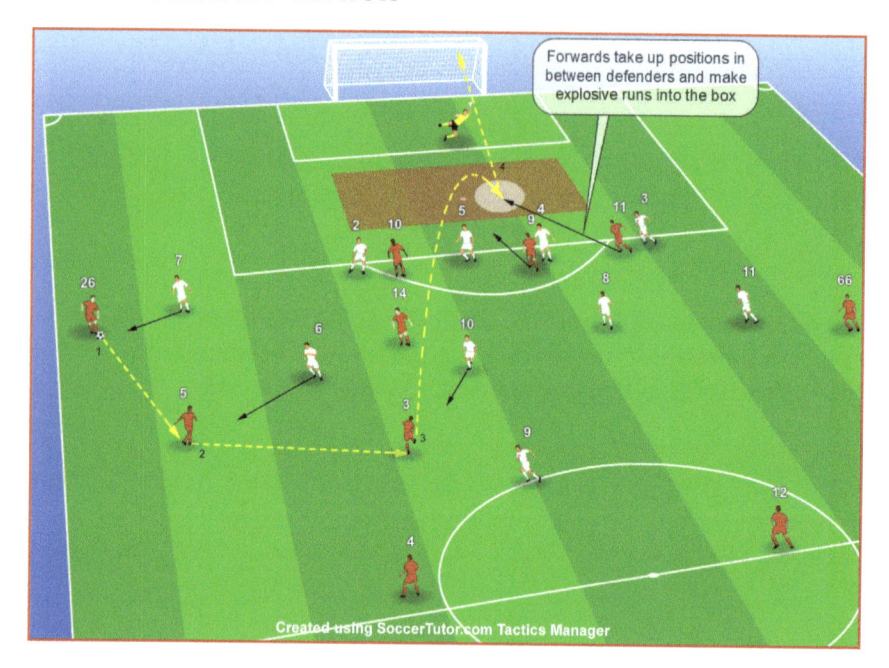

Forwards take up positions in between defenders and make explosive runs into the box

With the opponents deep and positioned around the box, Liverpool circulate the ball from the flank to the centre. When this happens, the attackers take up positions between the defenders and are ready to make explosive runs into the box and in behind. The defensive midfielder (**3**) plays a technical lofted pass for the right forward (**11**) to score.

Tactical Solution B: Technical Lofted Pass in Behind and into the Box from a Wide Position

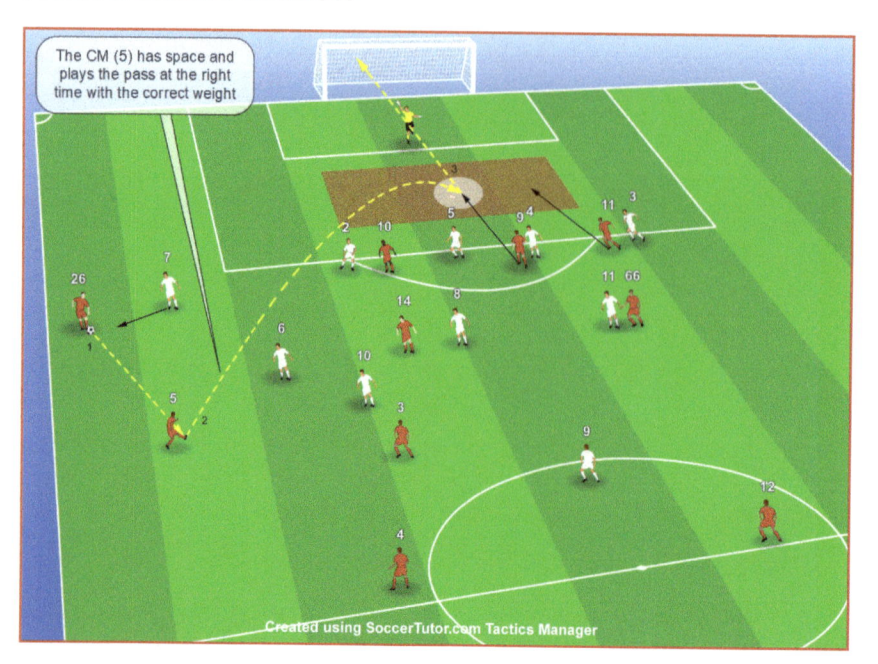

The CM (5) has space and plays the pass at the right time with the correct weight

When the ball goes back or inside, the players recognise the situation and play the pass at the right time with the correct weight and loft. There is also good communication and synchronisation of the actions and movements. In this second example, central midfielder **No.5** plays a technical lofted pass from a wide position for **No.9** to score.

Statistical Analysis of Liverpool's Technical Lofted Passes into the Box Against Deep Defences

Liverpool scored **7 goals** in this tactical situation
(Premier League and Champions League 2018-2019 and 2019-2020 seasons)

VS. ORGANISED AND DEEP DEFENCES

TACTICAL SOLUTION = TECHNICAL LOFTED PASSES INTO THE BOX

DATE	HOME	AWAY	SCORE	GOAL (MIN)	SCORER	ASSIST
16th Dec 2018	Liverpool	Man Utd	3-1	1-0 (24')	**Mané** *	Fabinho
21st Dec 2018	Wolves	Liverpool	0-2	0-2 (68')	**van Dijk**	Salah
31st Mar 2019	Bayern Munich	Liverpool	1-3	1-3 (84')	**Mané**	Salah
26th Apr 2019	Liverpool	Huddersfield	5-0	4-0 (66')	**Mané**	Henderson
12th May 2019	Liverpool	Wolves	2-0	2-0 (81')	**Mané**	A-Arnold
9th Aug 2019	Liverpool	Norwich	4-1	4-0 (42')	**Origi** *	A-Arnold
24th Jun 2020	Liverpool	Crystal Palace	4-0	2-0 (44')	**Salah**	Fabinho

* The full analysis of these goals is shown on the following pages...

Tactical Solution 6 - Technical Lofted Passes into the Box Against Deep Defences

Analysis from Liverpool 3-1 Man Utd (Mané 24') - 16th Dec 2018, Premier League

Tactical Solution A: Technical Lofted Pass in Behind and into the Box from a Central Position

The left back **Robertson (26)** throws the ball to the centre forward **Firmino (9)**, who plays it back to **Robertson (26)**.

Firmino (9) then moves back into a supporting position to provide a new angle to the right of **Robertson (26)**. He is also now facing the opposition's goal.

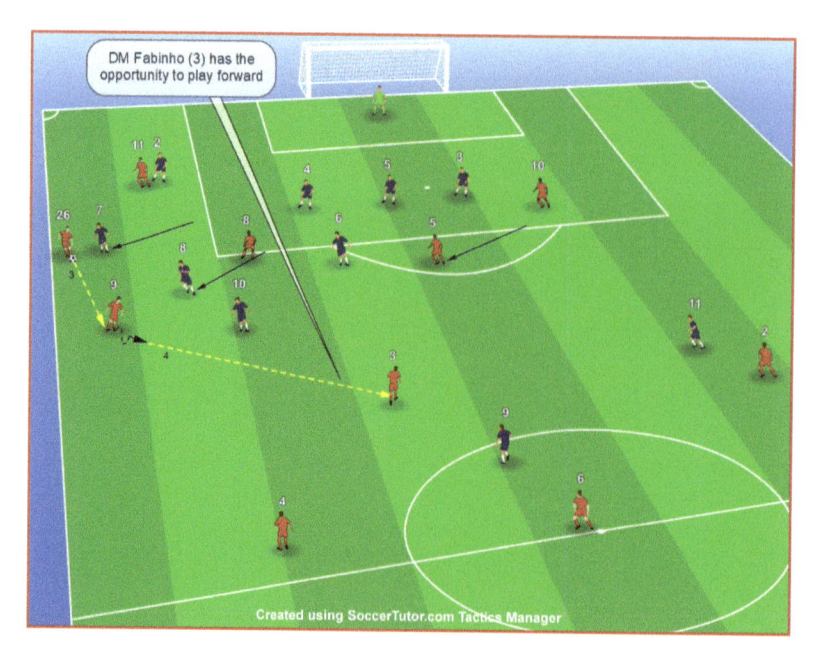

Robertson (26) is closed down and passes back to **Firmino (9)**, who's in a better position with more passing options.

Firmino (9) takes his first touch to the right and decides to pass the ball into the centre of the pitch to defensive midfielder **Fabinho (3)**, who has the opportunity to play forward or switch play to the weak side of the opposition's defence.

©SOCCERTUTOR.COM

JÜRGEN KLOPP LIVERPOOL ATTACKING TACTICS

Tactical Solution 6 - Technical Lofted Passes into the Box Against Deep Defences

Mané (10) chests the ball and scores with a left foot volley

Fabinho (3) has 4 teammates in front of him around the edge of the box: **Salah (11)**, **Keïta (8)**, **Wijnaldum (5)**, and **Mané (10)**. Right back **Clyne (2)** is another potential option on the right side of the pitch.

All of the 4 players around the edge of the box and especially the 2 to the right (**Wijnaldum** and **Mané**) have a side-on body position so they are ready to run in behind the defensive line and receive the ball inside the box.

Mané (10) has the better position and angle to make an effective diagonal run. **Fabinho (3)** delivers a technical lofted pass into the highlighted space at the correct time with perfect synchronisation for the run of **Mané (10)**.

Mané (10) sprints ahead of his direct opponent, receives the ball with his chest to bring the ball down in front of him and finishes into the bottom corner with his second touch.

Tactical Solution 6 - Technical Lofted Passes into the Box Against Deep Defences

Analysis from Liverpool 4-1 Norwich (Origi 42') - 9th Aug 2019, Premier League

Tactical Solution B: Technical Lofted Pass in Behind and into the Box from a Wide Position

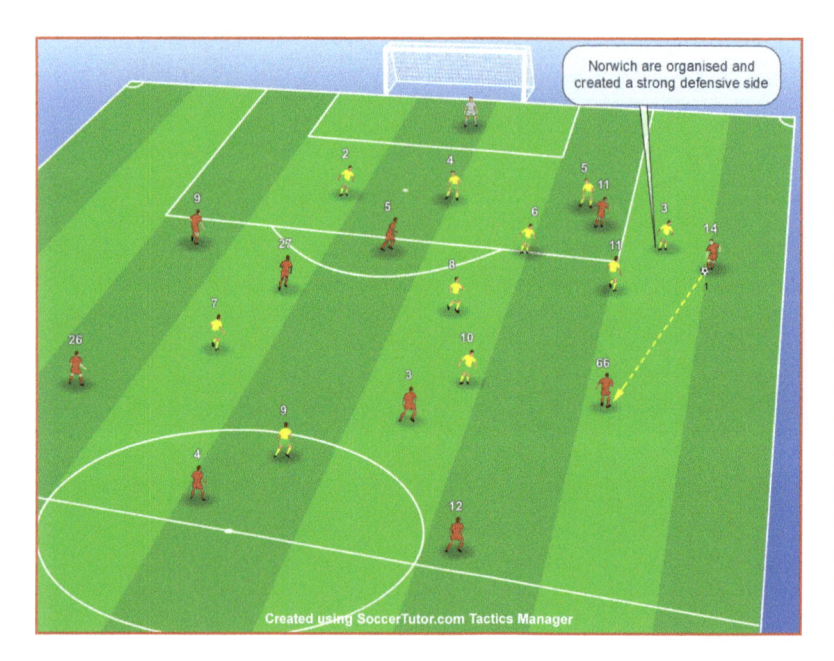

Norwich are organised, have many players in the low zone, and have created a strong defensive side on their left side of the pitch.

Liverpool's central midfielder **Henderson (14)** has the ball on the right flank. He recognises the tactical situation and that he has 2 Norwich players close to him, so passes back to the right back **A-Arnold (66)**, who provides supports from behind.

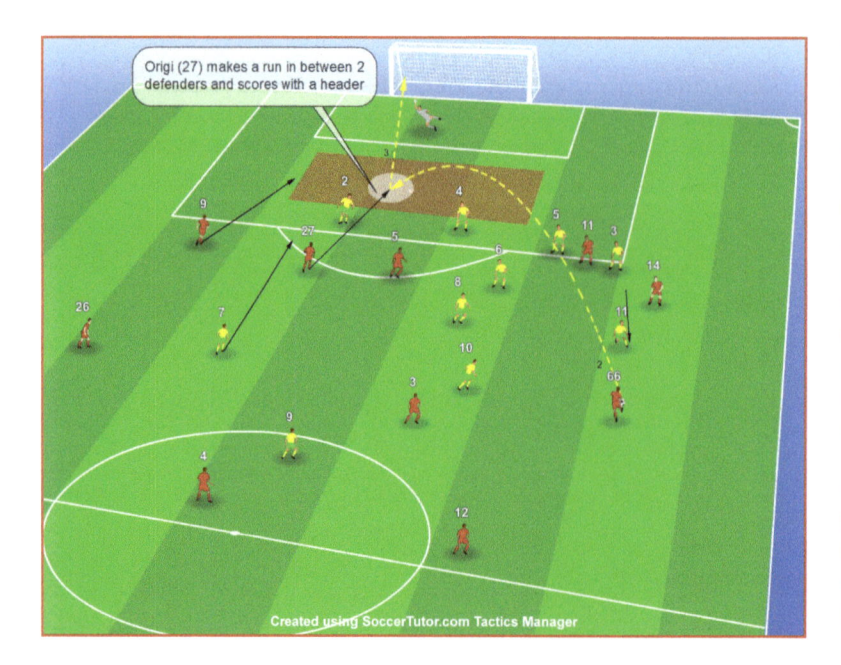

Norwich are using ball oriented defence on this side of the pitch, so there is space to exploit in the centre of their defensive line and on their weak side. **A-Arnold (66)** understands the situation, takes a first touch out in front and then uses his second touch to deliver a technical lofted pass into the centre of the box.

Centre forward **Origi (27)** makes a good run in between 2 defenders and scores with an excellent header.

SESSION 6 BASED ON THE TACTICS OF JÜRGEN KLOPP

Technical Lofted Passes into the Box Against Deep Defences

Session for JÜRGEN KLOPP Tactics - Technical Lofted Passes into the Box Against Deep Defences

SESSION FOR THIS TACTICAL SITUATION (4 PRACTICES)

1. Combination Play with a Technical Lofted Pass into the Box + Finish in a Technical Practice

1a: Technical Lofted Pass into the Box from a Central Position

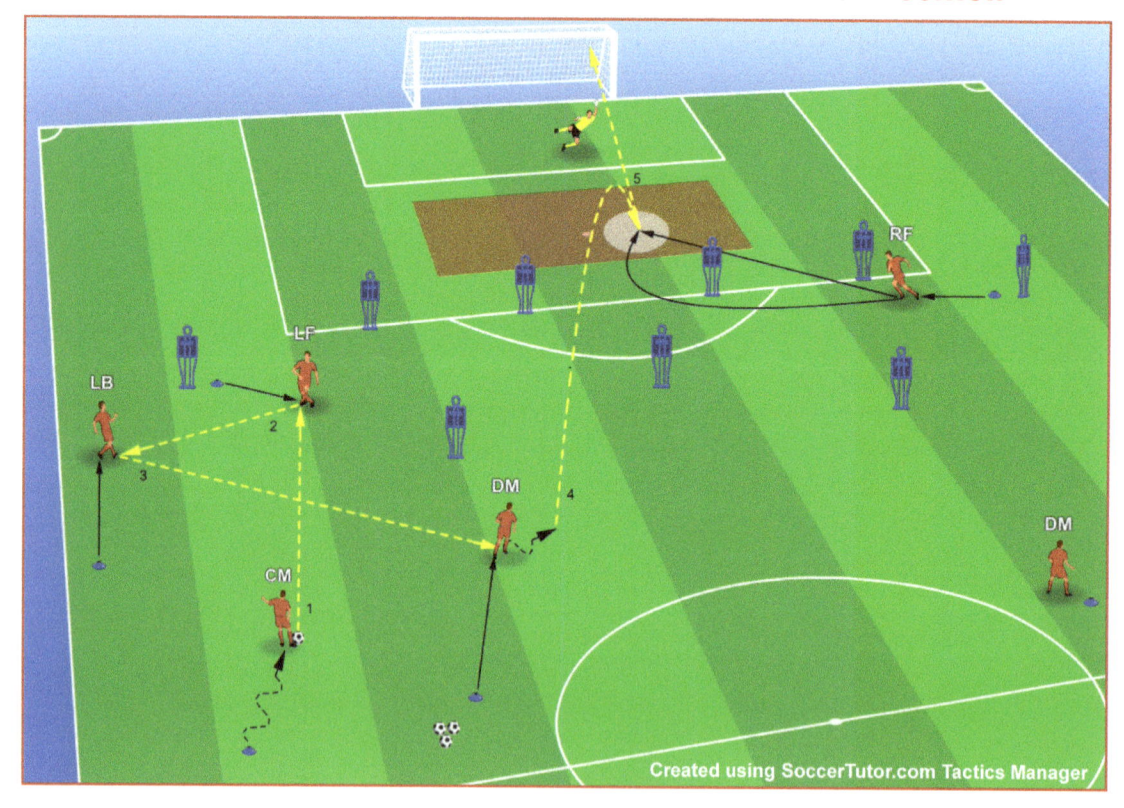

Objective: One-touch passing combinations + switching point of attack in behind.

Description (1a)

- Using half a pitch, we have 8 players across both sides starting from the cones. You can have 10 players so there is 1 spare player on each side.

- The practice starts with **the central midfielder (CM)** dribbling the ball forward and passing the ball to the **left forward (LF)**, who checks away to the outside and then moves inside to receive the pass.

- LF passes to the **left back (LB)**, who makes a forward run to provide support. **LB** changes the point of attack by passing back and inside to the **defensive midfielder (DM)**.

- **DM** receives, takes a touch to the right and plays a technical lofted pass to switch the point of attack in behind the defensive line.

- The **right forward (RF)** on the other side moves inside and in behind to receive the pass in the box and try to score past the GK.

- Restart with the **central midfielder (CM)** from the right side.

JÜRGEN KLOPP LIVERPOOL ATTACKING TACTICS

Session for **JÜRGEN KLOPP** Tactics - Technical Lofted Passes into the Box Against Deep Defences

1b: Technical Lofted Pass into the Box from a Wide Position

Description (1b)

- In this variation, the play starts from a more central position with the **defensive midfielder (DM)**. He dribbles forward and passes the ball to the **left forward (LF)**, who checks away to the outside and then moves inside to receive the pass.

- **LF** passes to the **left back (LB)**, who makes a forward run up the line, and then checks back to provide support. **LB** passes back to the central midfielder **(CM)**, who moves forward.

- **CM** receives and plays a technical lofted pass to switch the point of attack in behind the defensive line.

- The **right forward (RF)** on the other side moves inside and in behind to receive the lofted pass in the box and try to score past the GK.

- Restart with the **defensive midfielder (DM)** from the right side.

Coaching Points

1. The accuracy and weight of all the passes needs to be correct and closely monitored, as well as the rhythm and timing of the movement together with the passes.

2. The timing of the movement of the player on the opposite side (RF in diagram) to meet the final ball is very important, so that the attack can be successful.

3. The runs in behind the defensive line need to be sharp and timed correctly to be onside and meet the lofted pass.

4. Make sure the players communicate with their teammates and their heads are up (to maximise their game awareness).

Session for JÜRGEN KLOPP Tactics - Technical Lofted Passes into the Box Against Deep Defences

PROGRESSION
2. Maintain Possession and Switch Point of Attack with a Lofted Pass into the Box in a Functional Rondo Game

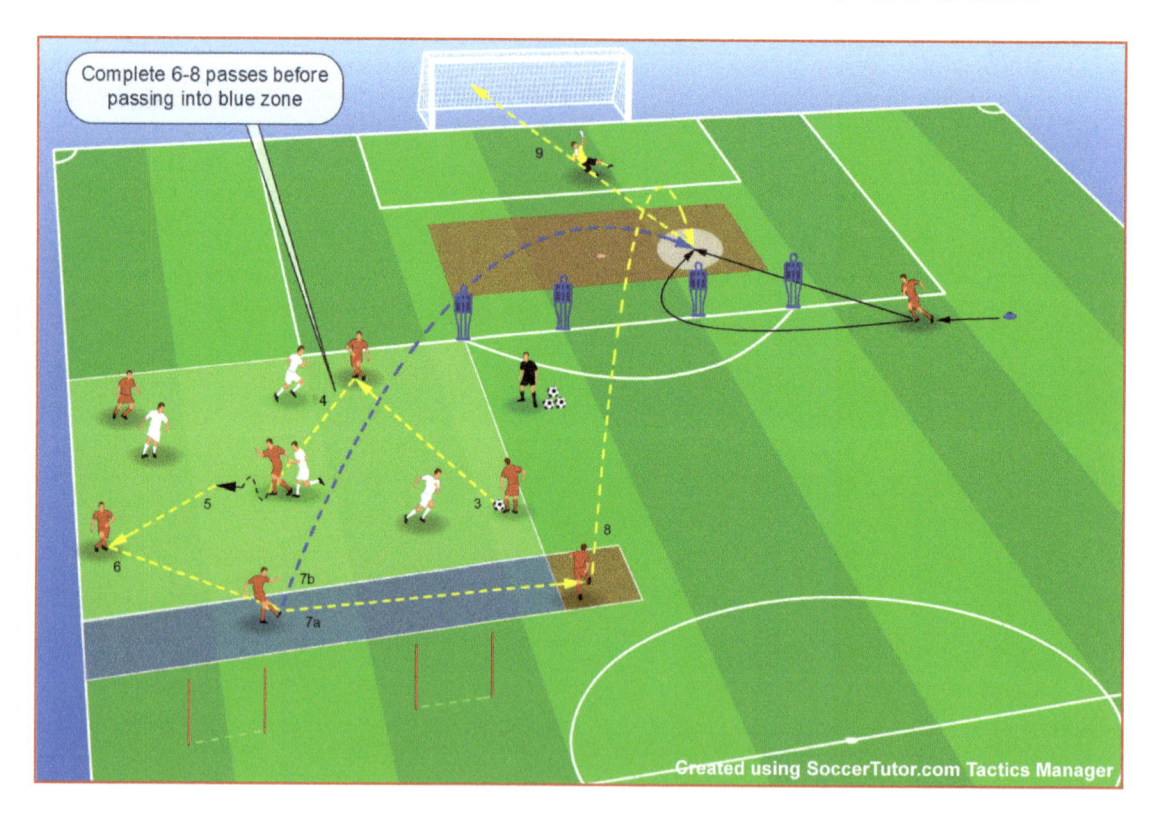

Complete 6-8 passes before passing into blue zone

Description

- We create an area on the left side of the pitch as shown. The small red extra zone on the side is a 2 x 2 yard square. The reds have 5 players in the large zone, 1 player in each of the smaller zones, and 1 player on the opposite side. The whites have 4 players in the large zone.

- The practice starts with the reds in possession (5v4) trying to complete 6-8 passes. They can then pass to the support player in the blue zone. He can play a technical lofted pass into the box. If a white player presses him, he passes to his teammate in the small red zone.

- That player can then play a technical lofted pass into the box and in behind for the run of the player on the opposite side of the pitch, who tries to score.

- If the 4 white players win the ball, they try to score through either pole gate.

- Practice on both sides of the pitch.

- **RULE**: Coach can decide whether the 2 red outside players take part in possession phase.

Coaching Points

1. See coaching points from previous practice.
2. Correct angles and distances to support the player in possession is very important.
3. Quality and accurate technical lofted pass in behind the defensive line.

Session for **JÜRGEN KLOPP** Tactics - Technical Lofted Passes into the Box Against Deep Defences

PROGRESSION
3. Maintain Possession and Switch Point of Attack with a Lofted Pass into the Box in a Functional Game

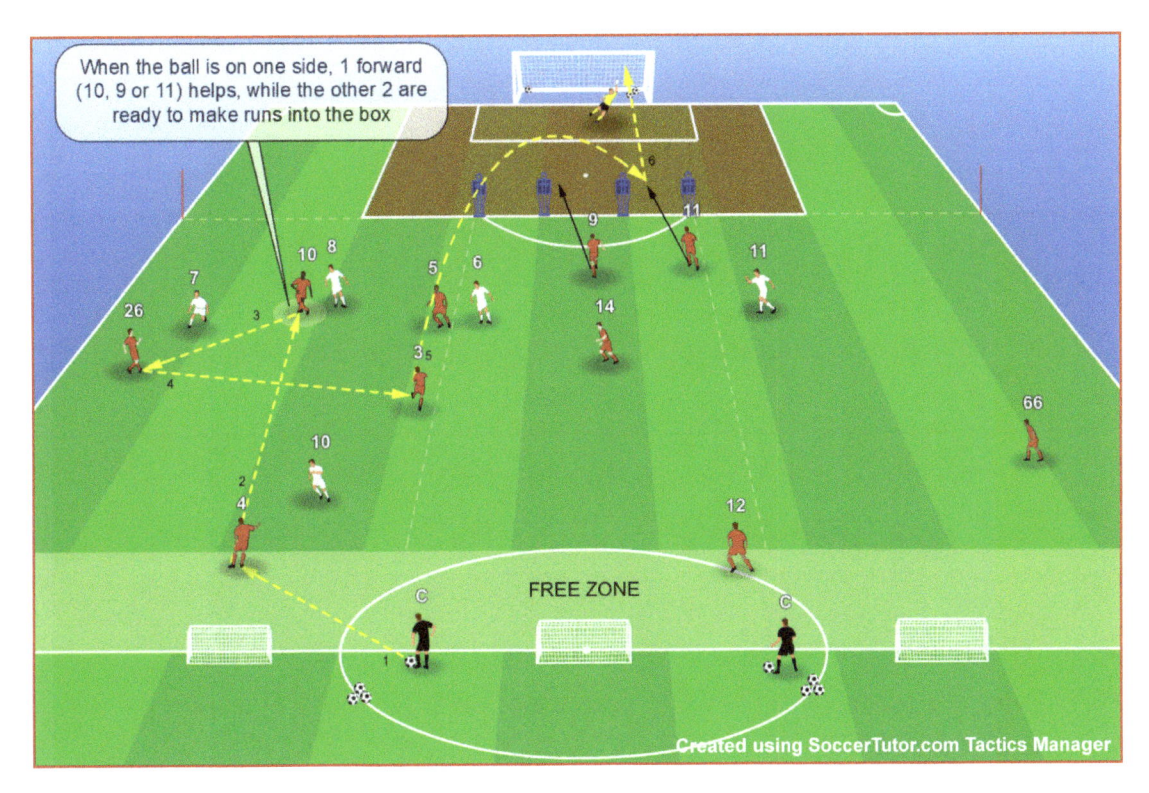

When the ball is on one side, 1 forward (10, 9 or 11) helps, while the other 2 are ready to make runs into the box

FREE ZONE

Description
- Divide the main zone into 3 vertical zones and position 3 mini goals on the halfway line.
- The reds have 10 players (4-3-3) against 5 active white players, 4 mannequins (narrow back 4) + a GK forming a 4-4-1.
- The practice starts with the Coach's pass to the reds who keep possession in a wide zone, trying to find a free player to play a technical lofted pass in behind for the run of the forwards into the box, who try to score.
- When the ball is on one side of the pitch, one of the forwards (11, 9 or 10) helps in the possession phase (**No.10** in diagram), and the other 2 are ready to make runs in behind.
- The whites aim to win the ball and score in any of the 3 mini goals within 10-15 seconds. This forces the reds to make a very quick transition from attack to defence (high press).

Rules
1. White players cannot defend in the "Free Zone." This zone is only for the red centre backs No.4 and No.5.
2. The reds are limited to 2 or 3 touches, and the whites have unlimited touches. Alternatively, all players can have unlimited touches.
3. You can restrict the red players to only being allowed to play the final pass from the wide zone or central zone (depending on what you are practicing).

Session for JÜRGEN KLOPP Tactics - Technical Lofted Passes into the Box Against Deep Defences

PROGRESSION

4. Maintain Possession and Switch Point of Attack with a Lofted Pass into the Box in an 11v11 Tactical Game

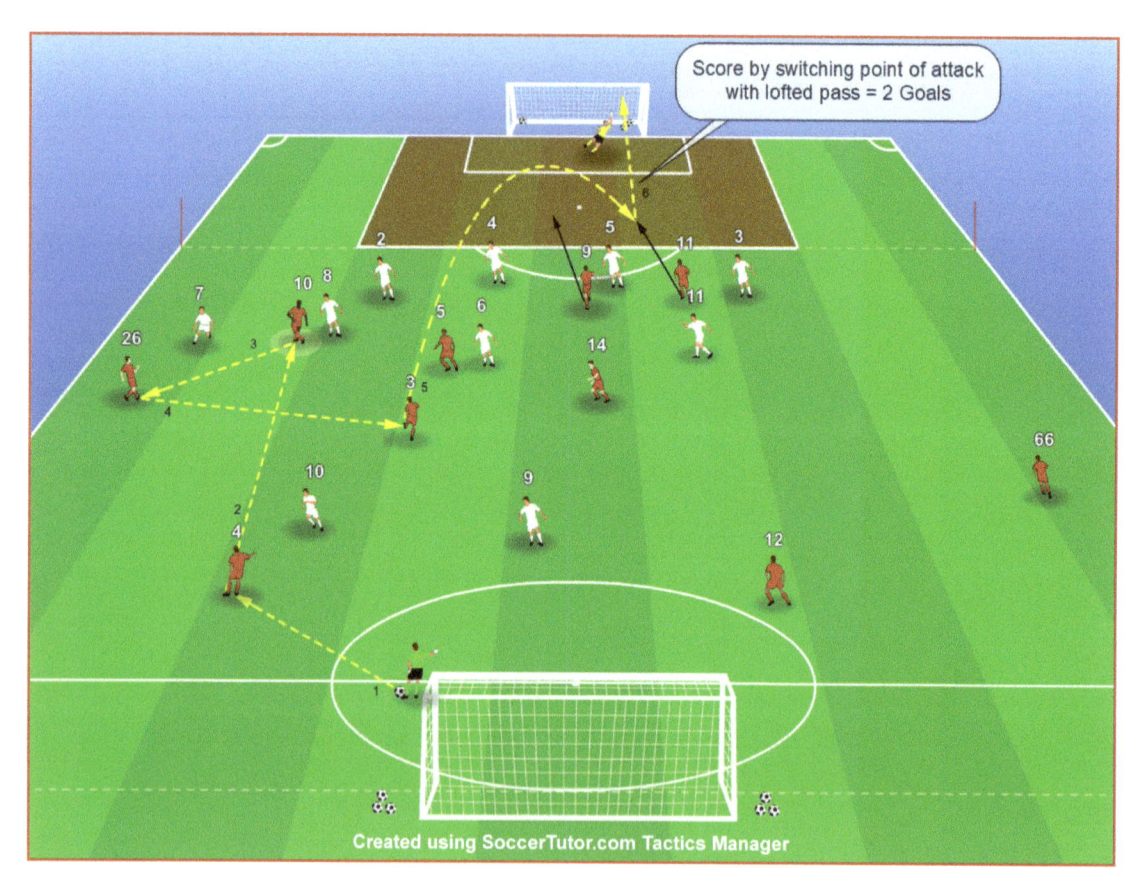

Score by switching point of attack with lofted pass = 2 Goals

Description

- In the final practice of this session, we play an 11v11 game in the area shown.

- The practice starts from the red team's GK, and the attacking team build up play and can score in any way (1 point).

- If the reds score after switching the point of attack and delivering a technical lofted pass into the box and in behind (from out wide or central position), they get 2 points.

- The whites aim to win the ball and score within 12 seconds (2 points).

- This forces the reds to make a very quick transition from attack to defence (high press) to stop the counter attack and try to win the ball back as quickly as possible.

- If a goal is scored or the ball goes out of play, restart the game from the red team's GK.

JÜRGEN KLOPP LIVERPOOL ATTACKING TACTICS

JÜRGEN KLOPP TACTICAL ANALYSIS

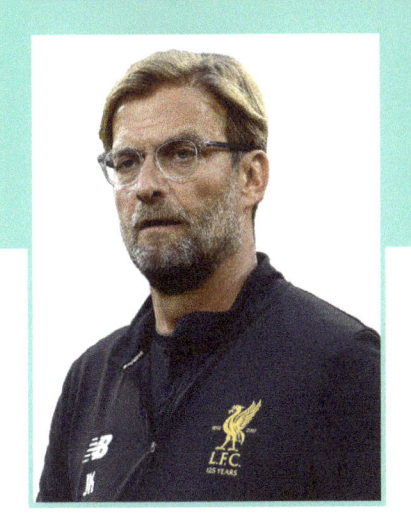

SOLUTION 7

Combination Play with a Third Man Run Against Organised and Deep Defences

Content from analysis of Liverpool F.C. during the 2018-2019 Champions League winning season and the 2019-2020 Premier League winning season

- Analysis based on recurring patterns of play observed within the Liverpool team.
- Tactical solutions displayed as examples of the team's tactics being used effectively.
- Real match examples of Liverpool scoring a goal using this specific attacking tactical solution.
- Each action, pass, individual movement with or without the ball, and the positioning of each player on the pitch including their body shape, are presented.
- The analysis is then used to create a full progressive session to coach this tactical situation.

Tactical Solution 7 - Combination Play with a Third Man Run Against Deep Defences

Combination Play with a Third Man Run Against Organised and Deep Defences

What?

Liverpool play through their opposition's defence by passing the ball (hopefully in behind the defensive line) into the two red target areas shown in the diagram below.

Why?

When opponents have a weakness in the centre of their defence (width of box), especially when 2-3 defenders try to cooperate with defensive actions such as "press and cover."

How?

Liverpool use quick combination play with a third man run into the highlighted areas.

Target Areas

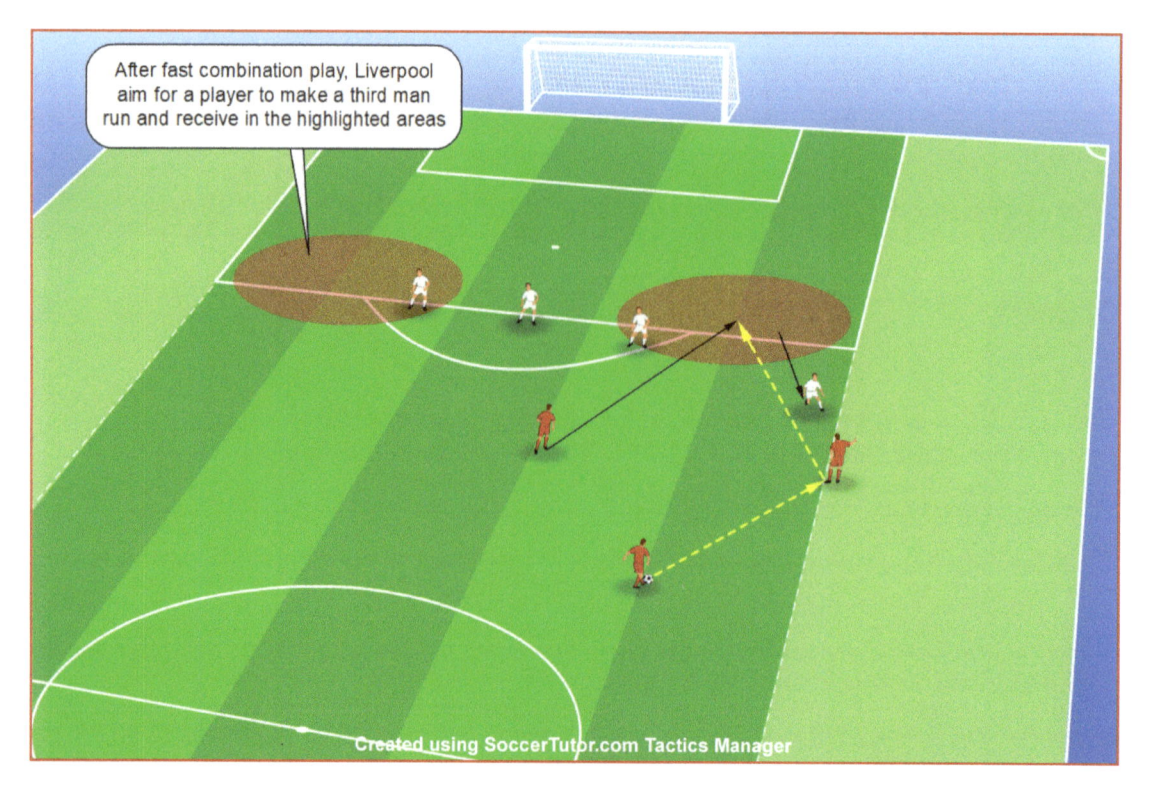

After fast combination play, Liverpool aim for a player to make a third man run and receive in the highlighted areas

Tactical Solution 7 - Combination Play with a Third Man Run Against Deep Defences

Tactical Solution A: Third Man Run to Receive in Behind the Defensive Line + Score (or Assist)

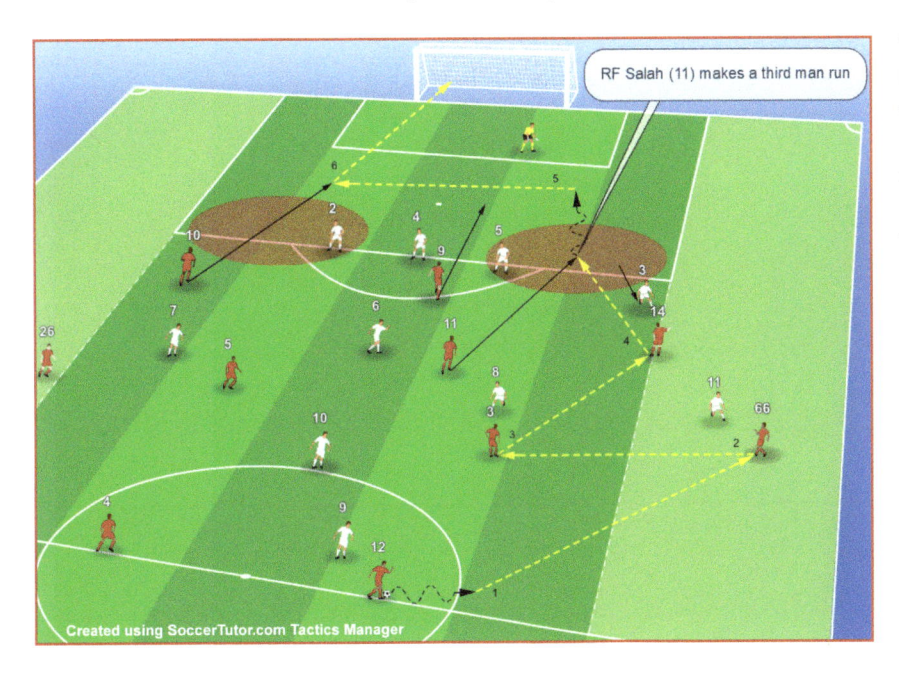

RF Salah (11) makes a third man run

The Liverpool full backs provide the width, and the other players work in the centre of the pitch (width of box). In this first tactical solution, the players use short passes and apply quick combination play ending with a third man run from a wide forward or central midfielder to receive in behind the defensive line (and into highlighted areas).

Tactical Solution B: Third Man Run to Receive in the Box in a 1v1 Situation, Beat the Opponent + Score

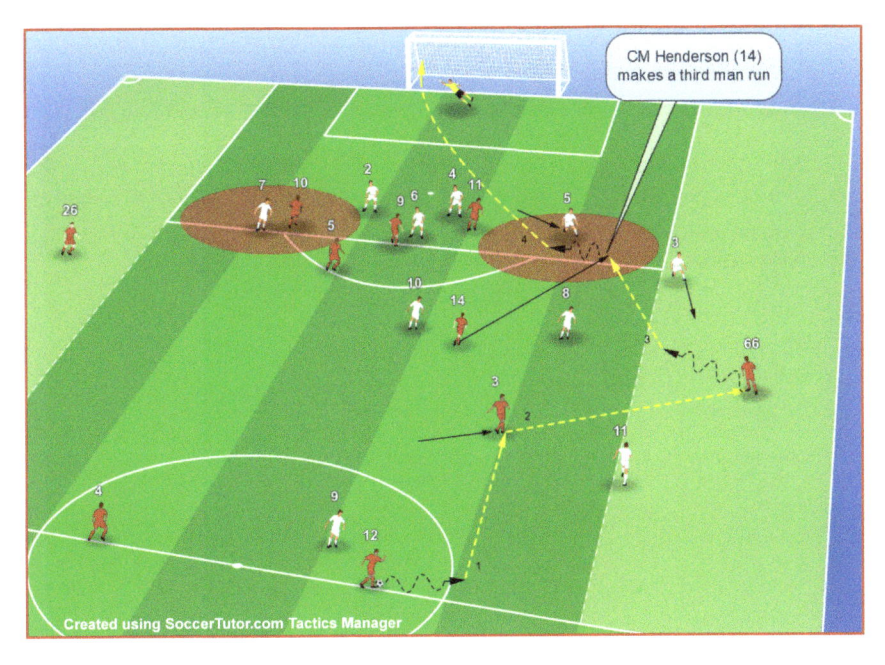

CM Henderson (14) makes a third man run

In this second tactical solution, we have the same starting point, but the aim is not to play in behind the defensive line. However, a Liverpool player does make a third man run to receive in the same target area again, but now uses his technical and tactical ability (speed of action) to beat an opponent in restricted space and score.

Tactical Solution 7 - Combination Play with a Third Man Run Against Deep Defences

Tactical Solution C: Third Man Run to Receive in the Box + Pass Back for Oncoming Teammate to Shoot

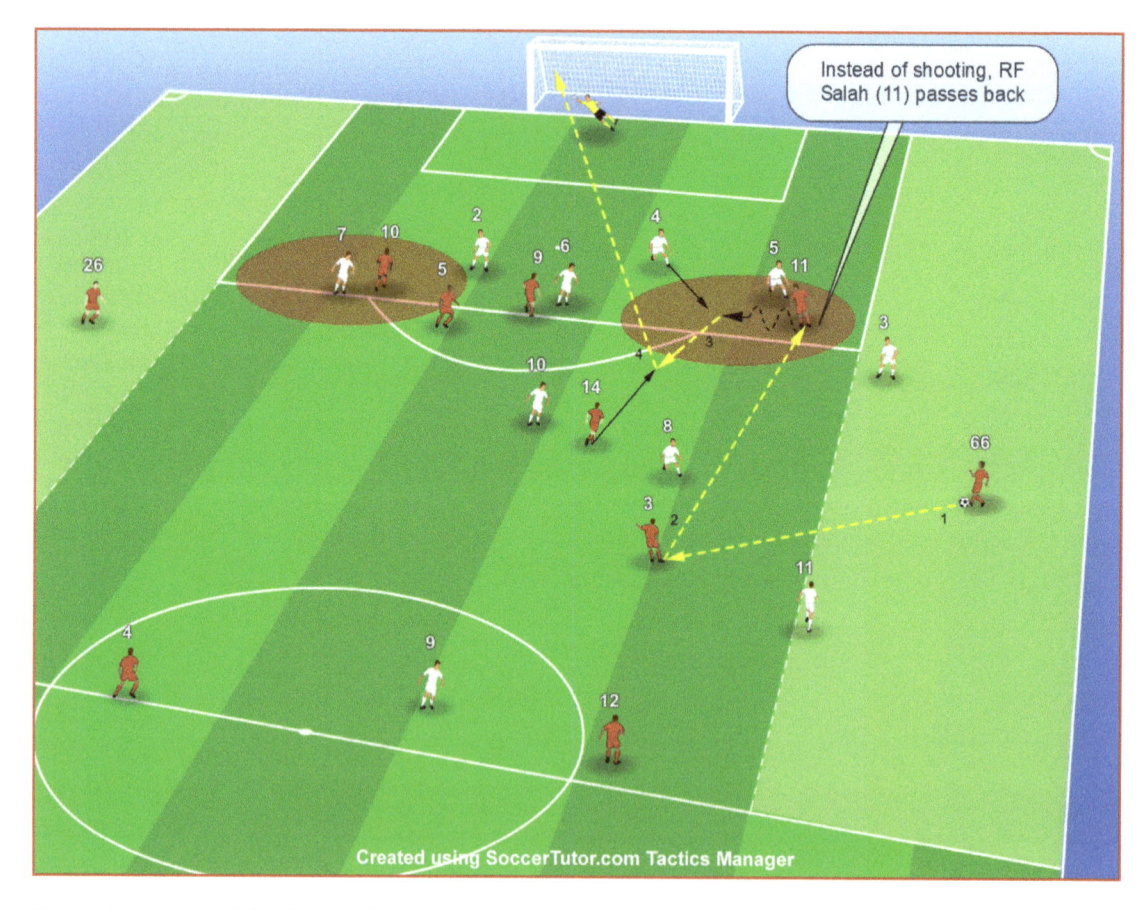

This is the third and final tactical solution for using combination play with a third man run against deep defences, and it's a variation of Tactical Solution B on the previous page.

This time, the player that receives in the box (**No.11** in diagram) tries to attack in a 1 v 1 situation but has less space and is closed down/blocked off successfully by an opponent.

No.11 plays the ball back to an unmarked teammate (**central midfielder - No.14**), who is moving forward to receive and shoot at goal (from 18-25 yards).

Tactical Solution 7 - Combination Play with a Third Man Run Against Deep Defences

Statistical Analysis of Liverpool's Combination Play with a Third Man Run Against Deep Defences

Liverpool scored **15 goals** in this tactical situation
(Premier League and Champions League 2018-2019 and 2019-2020 seasons)

VS. ORGANISED AND DEEP DEFENCES
TACTICAL SOLUTION = COMBINATION PLAY WITH THIRD MAN RUN

DATE	HOME	AWAY	SCORE	GOAL (MIN)	SCORER	ASSIST
24th Oct 2018	Liverpool	Red Star Belgrade	4-0	2-0 (45')	**Salah** *	Shaqiri
27th Oct 2018	Liverpool	Cardiff	4-1	2-0 (66')	**Mané**	
27th Oct 2018	Liverpool	Cardiff	4-1	3-1 (84')	**Shaqiri**	Salah
5th Dec 2018	Burnley	Liverpool	1-3	1-1 (62')	**Milner** *	Origi
11th Dec 2018	Liverpool	Napoli	1-0	1-0 (34')	**Salah**	Milner
16th Dec 2018	Liverpool	Man Utd	3-1	3-1 (80')	**Shaqiri**	Firmino
19th Jan 2019	Liverpool	Crystal Palace	4-3	2-1 (53')	**Firmino** *	Keïta
30th Jan 2019	Liverpool	Leicester City	1-1	1-0 (03')	**Mané**	Robertson
9th Apr 2019	Liverpool	Porto	2-0	1-0 (05')	**Keïta**	Firmino
14th Sep 2019	Liverpool	Newcastle	3-1	3-1 (72')	**Salah**	Firmino
23rd Oct 2019	Genk	Liverpool	1-4	0-2 (57')	**Chamberlain**	Firmino
23rd Oct 2019	Genk	Liverpool	1-4	0-4 (87')	**Salah**	
5th Nov 2019	Liverpool	Genk	2-1	2-1 (53')	**Chamberlain**	Salah
7th Dec 2019	Bournemouth	Liverpool	0-3	0-2 (44')	**Keïta**	Salah
5th Jul 2020	Liverpool	Aston Villa	2-0	1-0 (71')	**Mané**	Keïta

* The full analysis of these goals is shown on the following pages...

Tactical Solution 7 - Combination Play with a Third Man Run Against Deep Defences

Analysis from Liverpool 4-0 Red Star Belgrade (Salah 45') - 24th Oct 2018, Champions League

Tactical Solution A: Third Man Run to Receive in Behind the Defensive Line + Score (or Assist)

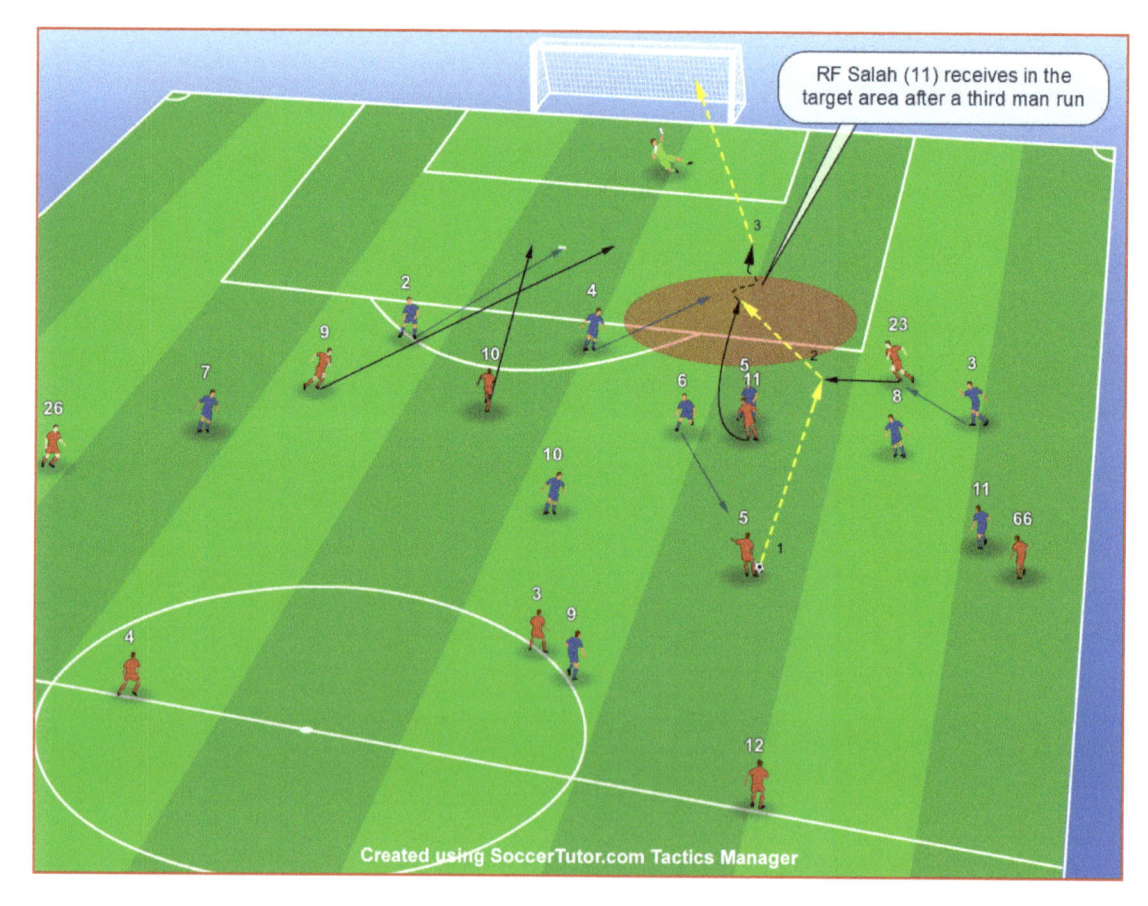

RF Salah (11) receives in the target area after a third man run

In this situation, the opponents Red Star Belgrade (Crvena Zvezda) defend in numbers just in front of the box, shifting collectively to the position of the ball.

Firstly, **Salah (11)** drops off and is followed by the centre back. This creates space in behind.

Central midfielder **Wijnaldum (5)** has the ball and **Salah (11)** then makes a run into the space into the box and in behind his direct opponent.

This run opens the opportunity for **Wijnaldum (5)** to play a forward pass to **Shaqiri (23)**.

As **Shaqiri (23)** is about to receive the pass, **Salah (11)** is left unmarked inside the box.

Shaqiri (23) recognises that his teammate is in a better position after his third man run, and therefore passes to him with his first touch.

Salah (11) takes a good first touch to receive the pass and scores with his second touch.

Tactical Solution 7 - Combination Play with a Third Man Run Against Deep Defences

Analysis from Liverpool 4-3 Crystal Palace (Firmino 53') - 19th Jan 2019, Premier League

Tactical Solution B: Third Man Run to Receive in the Box in a 1v1 Situation, Beat the Opponent + Score

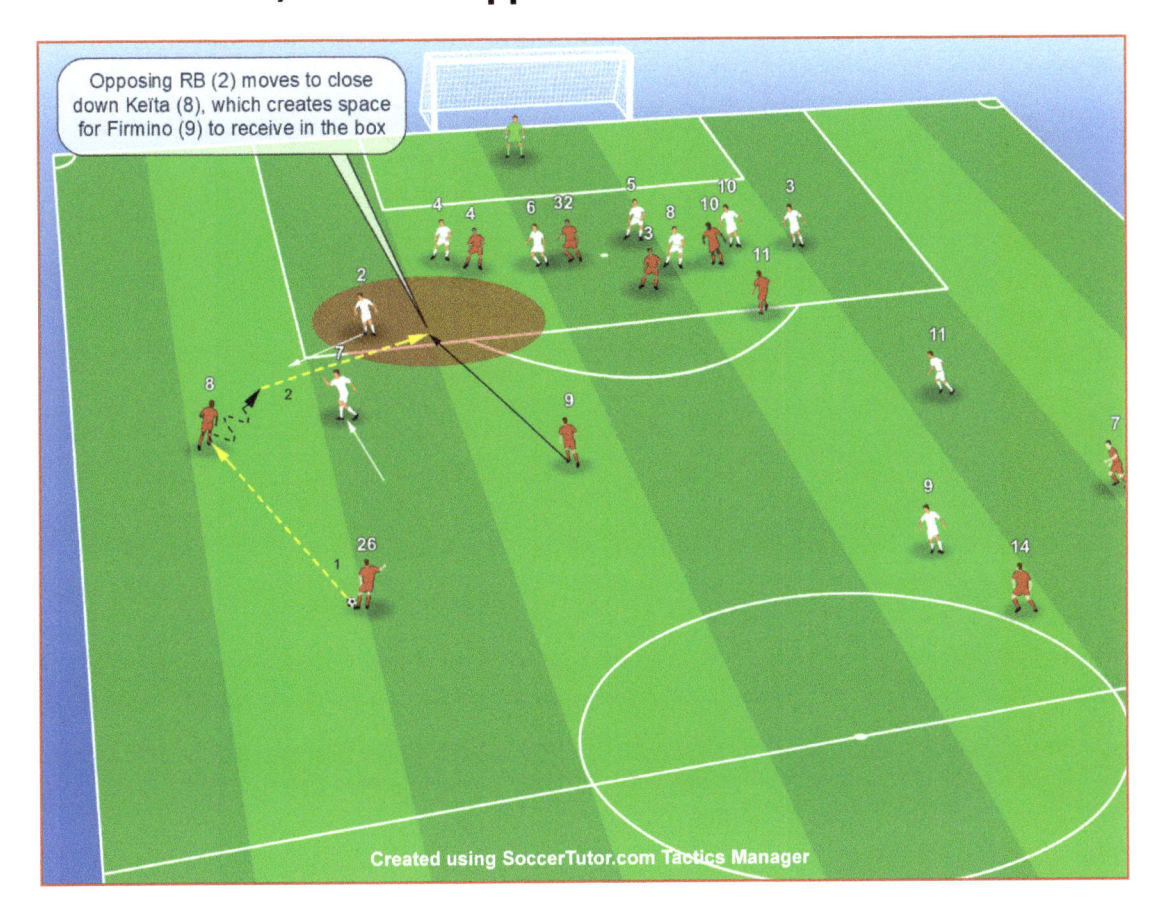

Opposing RB (2) moves to close down Keïta (8), which creates space for Firmino (9) to receive in the box

Left back **Robertson (26)** has possession with 9 Crystal Palace players behind the ball.

Robertson (26) passes to **Keïta (8)** on the left, who moves inside with the ball.

As **Keïta (8)** moves forward, the opposing right back (2) moves across to close him down, which creates space in behind him (highlighted area inside the box).

Firmino (9) makes a third man run to receive the next pass from **Keïta (8)** in the available space created by the Palace defender's movement.

Keïta (8) passes in between the 2 Crystal Palace players No.2 and No.7, and in behind them for the third man run of **Firmino (9)** into the box.

JÜRGEN KLOPP LIVERPOOL ATTACKING TACTICS

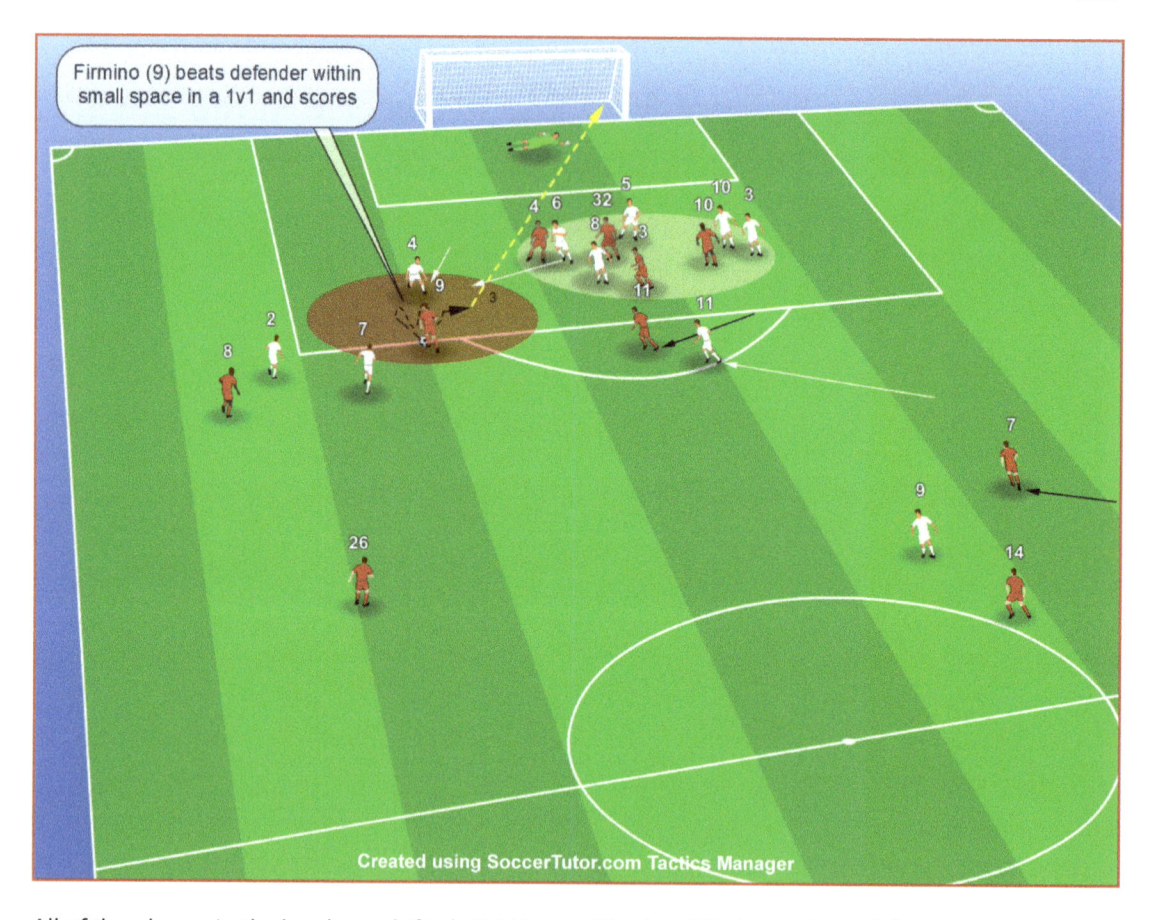

Tactical Solution 7 - Combination Play with a Third Man Run Against Deep Defences

Firmino (9) beats defender within small space in a 1v1 and scores

All of the players in the box have shifted slightly and are in a small space altogether (white highlighted area). This creates more space for **Firmino (9)** to exploit.

Firmino (9) receives and is closed down by the Crystal Palace centre back (4).

He turns slightly to his left, before then quickly changing direction to the right and away from the defender to win the 1v1.

Firmino (9) shoots through bodies as No.6 closes him down and scores past the GK.

Tactical Solution 7 - Combination Play with a Third Man Run Against Deep Defences

Analysis from Burnley 1-3 Liverpool (Milner 62') - 5th Dec 2018, Premier League

Tactical Solution C: Third Man Run to Receive in the Box + Pass Back for Oncoming Teammate to Shoot

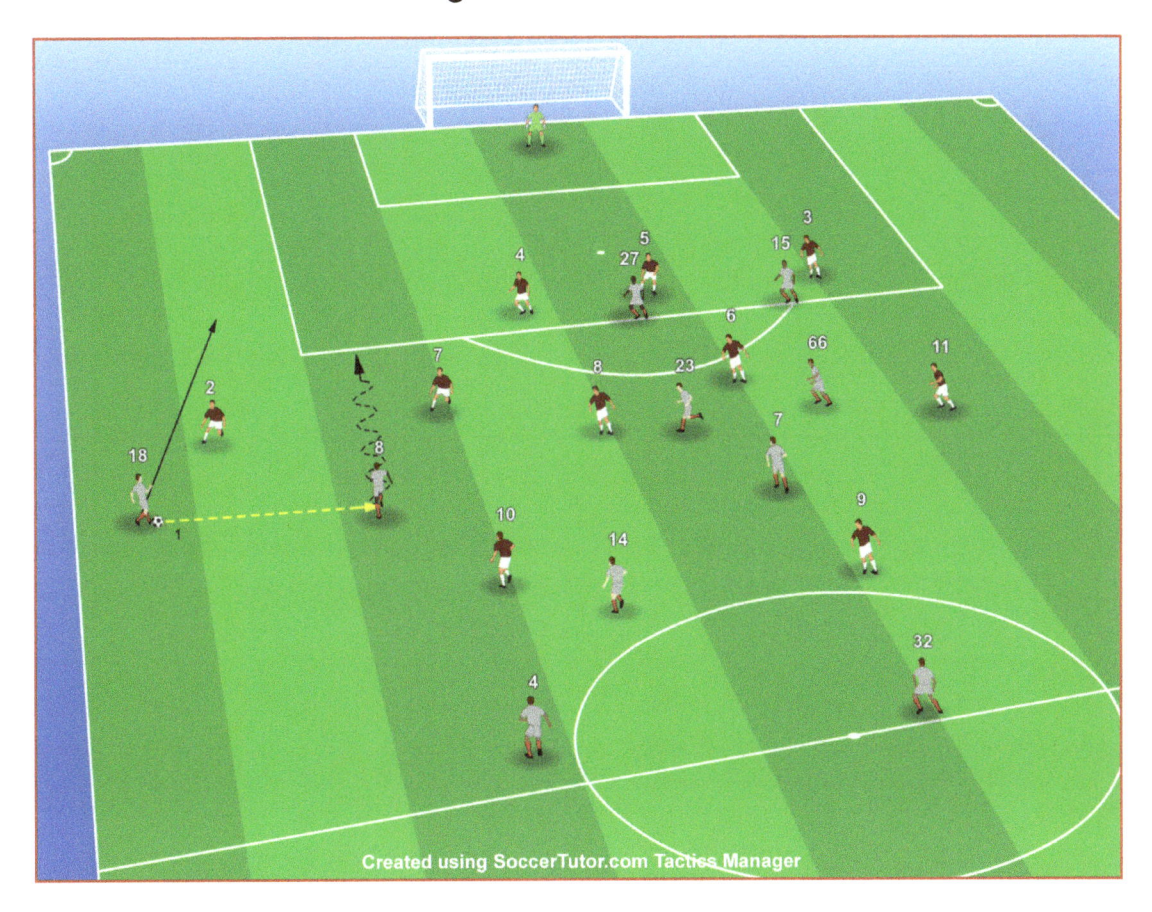

The left back **Moreno (18)** has the ball high up on the left flank and passes inside to central midfielder **Keïta (8)**.

As soon as he plays the pass, **Moreno (18)** makes a run to receive a return pass in the space behind the Burnley right back (2).

Keïta (8) is closed down and decides to dribble forward at the opponent.

He reaches the edge of the box with the ball still in his possession.

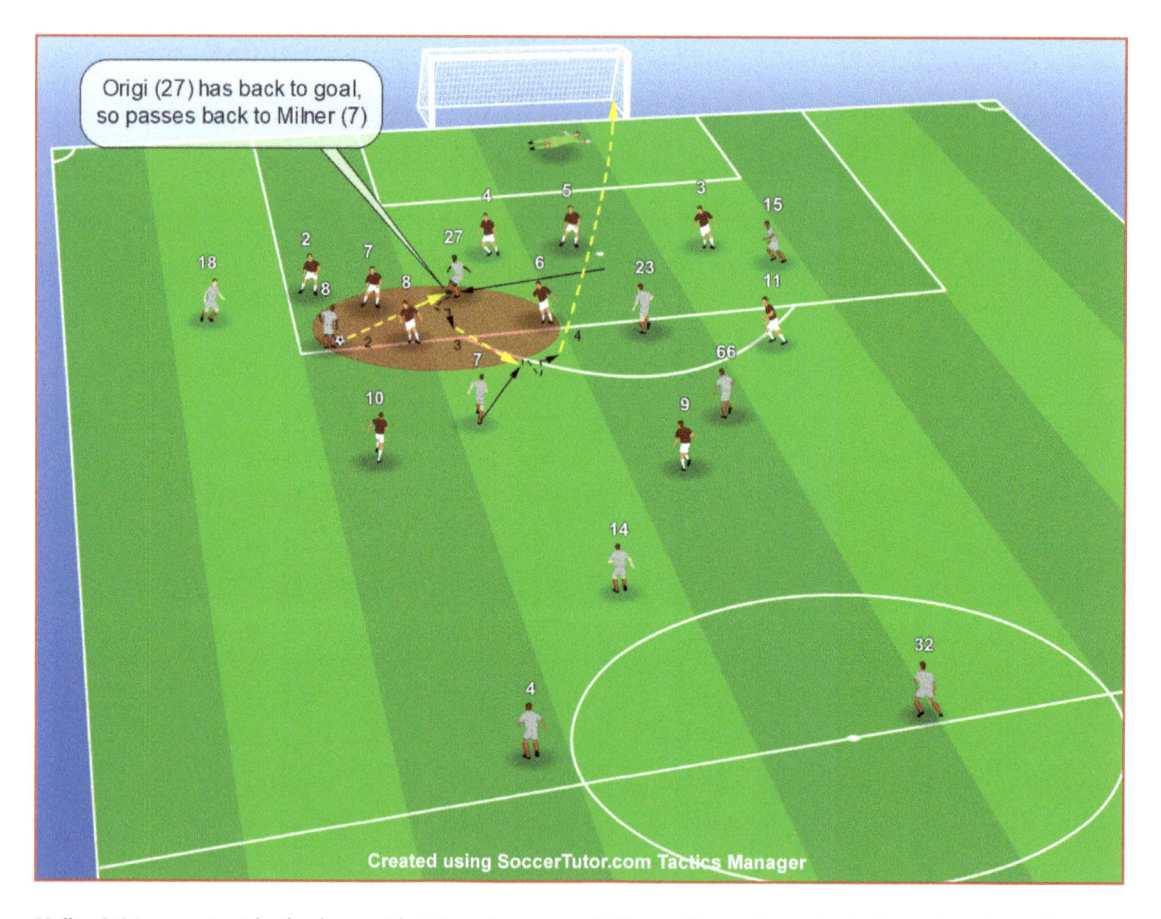

Tactical Solution 7 - Combination Play with a Third Man Run Against Deep Defences

Origi (27) has back to goal, so passes back to Milner (7)

Keïta (8) is now inside the box with 3 Burnley players around him, 2 of which have moved to close him down.

This means that there is space left behind the Burnley players to exploit.

The centre forward **Origi (27)** moves across to provide support and receive from **Keïta's (8)** pass.

Origi (27) has his back to goal and many opposing players around him. He therefore cannot turn towards goal without being dispossessed.

He looks up and sees central midfielder **Milner (7)** moving forward to support him and passes back to him.

Milner (7) receives the ball on the edge of the box (opens up) and shoots into the far corner, scoring an excellent goal.

SESSION 7A BASED ON THE TACTICS OF JÜRGEN KLOPP

Third Man Run to Receive in Behind and Score Against Deep Defences

Session for JÜRGEN KLOPP Tactics - Third Man Run to Receive in Behind & Score Against Deep Defences

SESSION FOR THIS TACTICAL SITUATION (5 PRACTICES)
1. Combination Play with a Third Man Run in a Technical Passing Practice

1a: Rotating Circuit

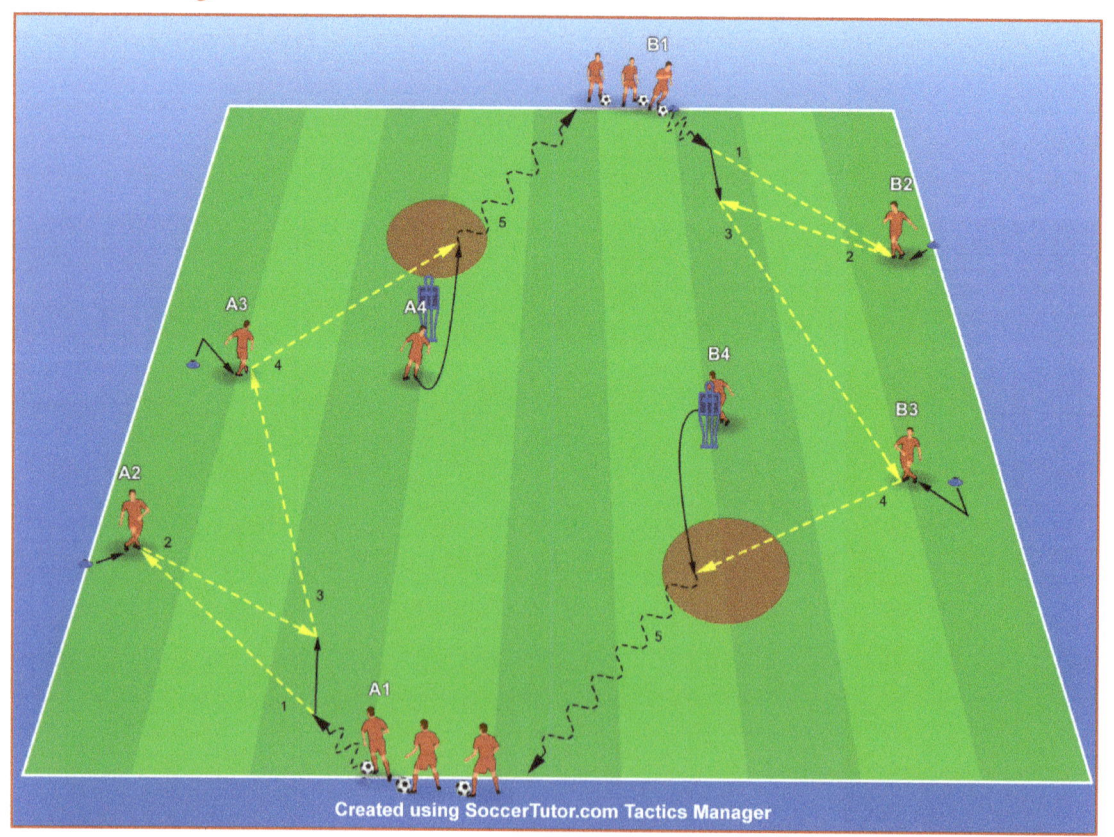

Description (1a)

- In a 20 x 30 yard area, we work with 12 players split into two equal groups. There are 3 cones and 1 mannequin marked out on each side, as shown in the diagram.

- We work with 2 balls simultaneously from A1 and B1 and the practice starts with Player 1's pass to Player 2.

- Player 1 plays a one-two with Player 2 and then passes to Player 3.

- Player 3 passes into the highlighted area (behind the mannequin) for the third man run of Player 4, who checks away from the mannequin (unmarking movement) first as the ball travels from Player 1 to Player 3.

- Player 4 receives the ball in the highlighted area and dribbles to the starting point of the other group. The players all rotate to the next position (1 -> 2 -> 3 -> 4 -> Other group).

- After a set amount of time, reverse the direction of the practice to anti-clockwise.

JÜRGEN KLOPP LIVERPOOL ATTACKING TACTICS

Session for **JÜRGEN KLOPP** Tactics - Third Man Run to Receive in Behind & Score Against Deep Defences

1b: Receive Final Pass and Score in Mini Goal

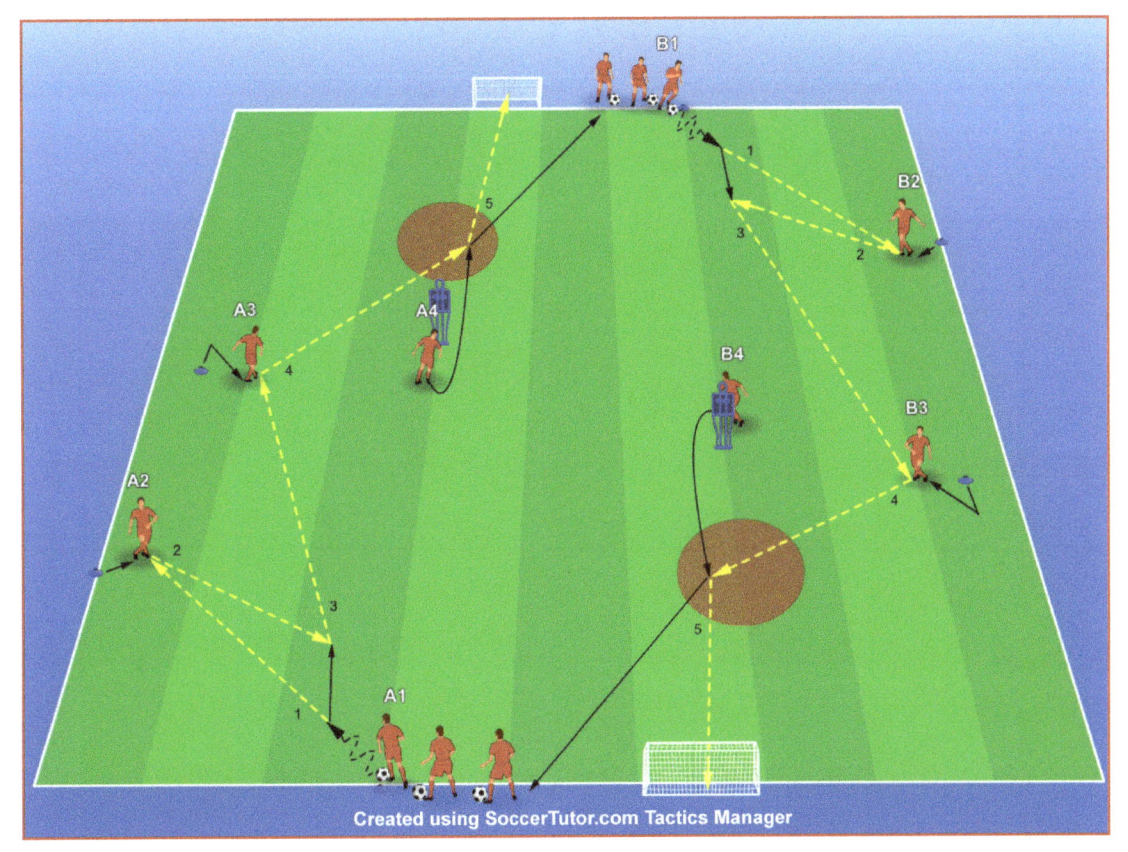

Description (1b)

In this variation of practice 1a, we now position two mini goals at the end of each group, as shown. The practice works in the same way except for one change.

When Player 4 receives the ball behind the mannequin, he tries to score in the mini goal with one touch (instead of dribbling) and then runs to the other group's starting position.

Coaching Points

1. The correct accuracy and weight of the final pass is the main focus for this practice.
2. Passes need to be well-weighted and aimed just in front of their teammates to step forward onto.
3. Make sure the players communicate with their teammates and their heads are up (to maximise their game awareness).
4. The practice should be done at a high tempo throughout.
5. The key is the rhythm and timing of the movement, together with the pass, and the synchronisation in the movements and actions of all the players.

Session for **JÜRGEN KLOPP** Tactics - Third Man Run to Receive in Behind & Score Against Deep Defences

PROGRESSION

2. Third Man Run to Receive in Behind and Score in a Technical Combination Play Practice

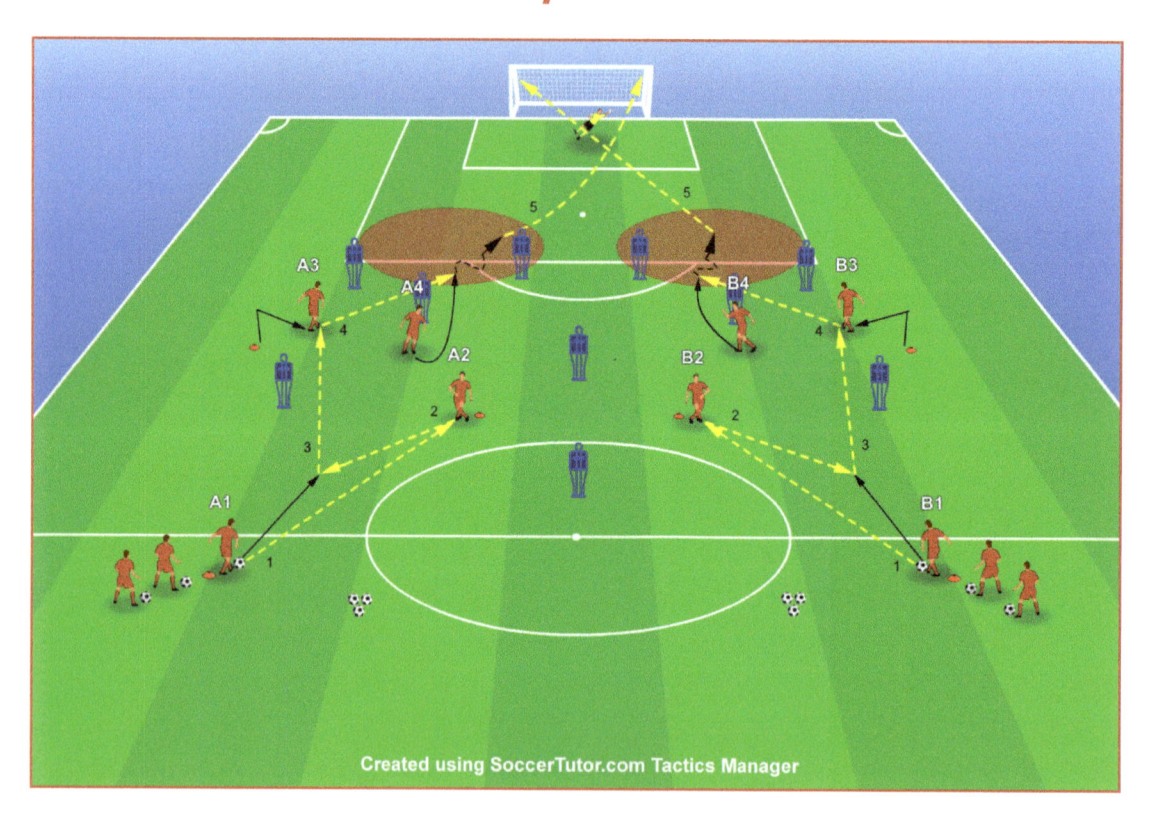

Description

- In the progression, we work in half a full pitch and practice combinations in the actual areas we want to play in competitive matches.

- We have a large goal with a goalkeeper, and 10 mannequins to represent opponents in a 4-2-3-1 formation (compact in width of box).

- We work with 12 outfield players split into two equal groups. There are 3 cones marked out on each side, as shown in the diagram.

- The sequence is exactly the same as the previous practice (see previous page), but now Player 4 takes a touch into the box and tries to score past the GK.

Coaching Points

1. All 5 coaching points from the previous practice apply for this practice too.

2. Player 4 needs a fast and quality directional first touch, and an accurate finish to score.

Session for JÜRGEN KLOPP Tactics - Third Man Run to Receive in Behind & Score Against Deep Defences

PROGRESSION
3. Combination Play with Third Man Run to Receive in Behind and Score in an 8 (+2) v 6 Tactical Game

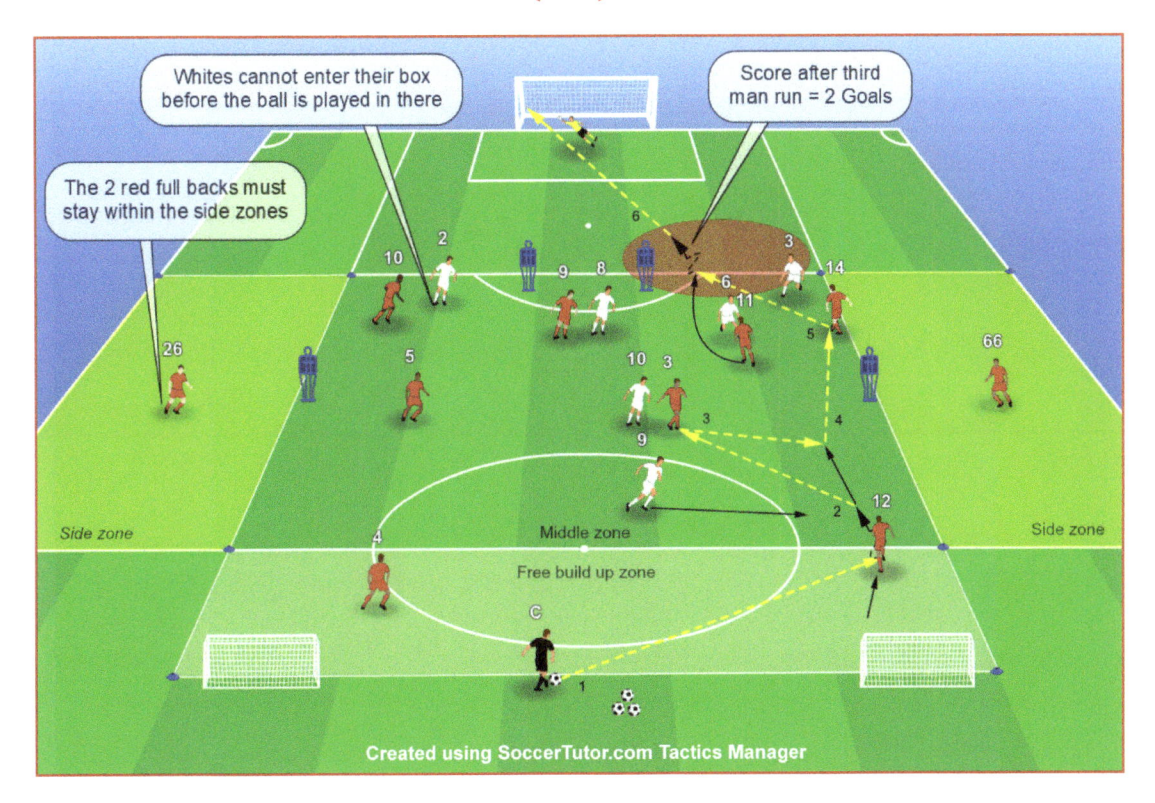

Description

- The large middle zone is split into 3 zones with 2 side zones, as shown. There is also a free build up zone + end zone (penalty box).

- The red team are in a 4-3-3 formation including 2 full backs, who must stay within their side zones. The white team are in a 4-2-3-1 formation with 6 active players and 4 mannequins representing the centre backs and the wingers.

- The practice starts with the Coach's pass to a centre back (No.12 in diagram) and the reds build up play. The aim for the reds is to play the ball in behind the defensive line within the width of the box and score a goal.

- If the reds manage to score a goal using a third man run (as shown in diagram example), the goal counts double.

- The aim for the white defending team is to win the ball and then try to score in either of the 2 mini goals within 12-15 seconds (no zone restrictions apply).

- When the reds lose the ball, they are forced to make a very quick transition to defence and should apply a high press to win the ball back as soon as possible. The 2 red full backs are not allowed to take part in this phase.

- **RULE**: White players cannot enter their box before the ball is played in there.

Session for JÜRGEN KLOPP Tactics - Third Man Run to Receive in Behind & Score Against Deep Defences

PROGRESSION
4. Combination Play with Third Man Run to Receive in Behind and Score in a 10 v 8 Tactical Game

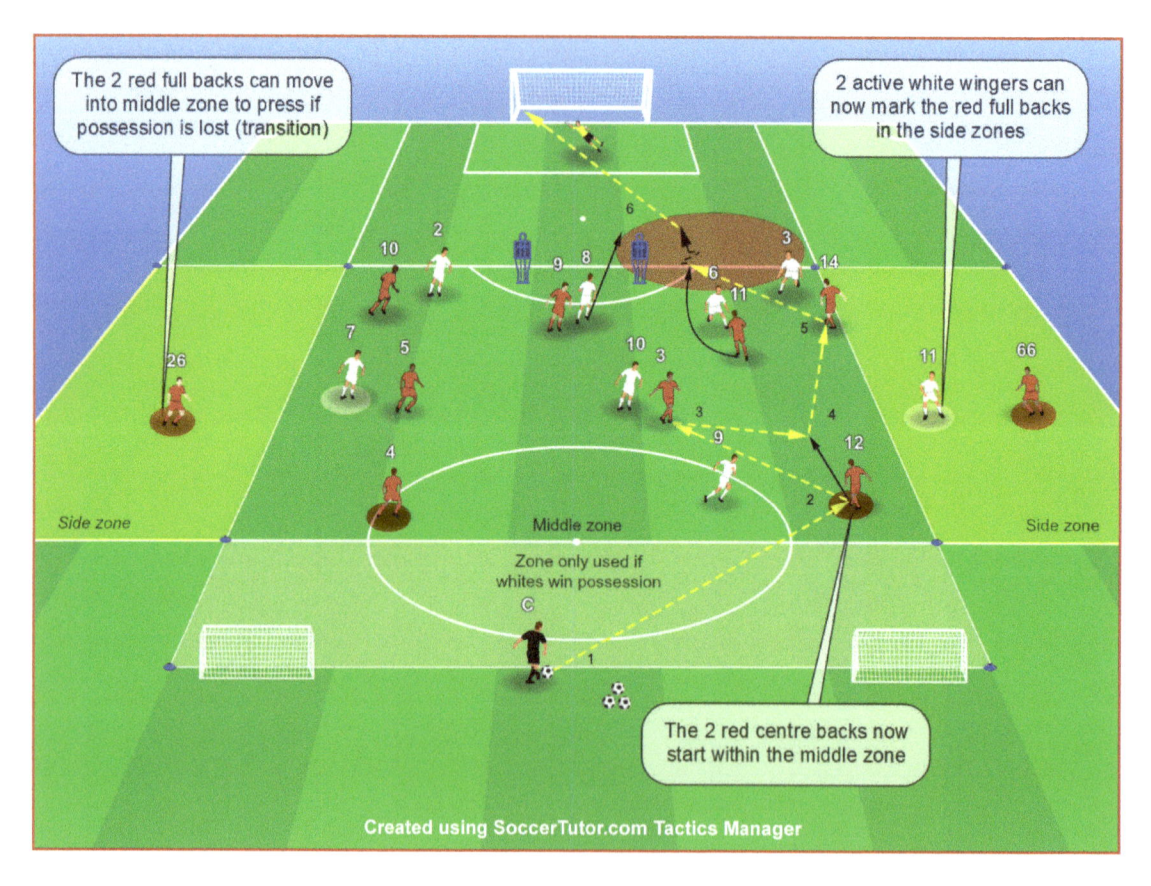

Annotations on diagram:
- The 2 red full backs can move into middle zone to press if possession is lost (transition)
- 2 active white wingers can now mark the red full backs in the side zones
- Side zone
- Middle zone
- Zone only used if whites win possession
- Side zone
- The 2 red centre backs now start within the middle zone

Created using SoccerTutor.com Tactics Manager

Description

- In the progression, we add 2 active wingers for the white defending team who replace the mannequins from the previous practice. They can now mark the red full backs in the side zones if necessary.

- The 2 red centre backs start within the middle zone now.

- **RULE CHANGE**: The 2 red full backs are allowed to participate in the transition from attack to defence, moving freely across all zones when possession is lost.

- Apart from this, the practice remains the same as described on the previous page.

- The white players still cannot enter their box before the ball is played in there.

Session for **JÜRGEN KLOPP** Tactics - Third Man Run to Receive in Behind & Score Against Deep Defences

PROGRESSION
5. Combination Play with Third Man Run to Receive in Behind and Score in an 11 v 11 Tactical Game

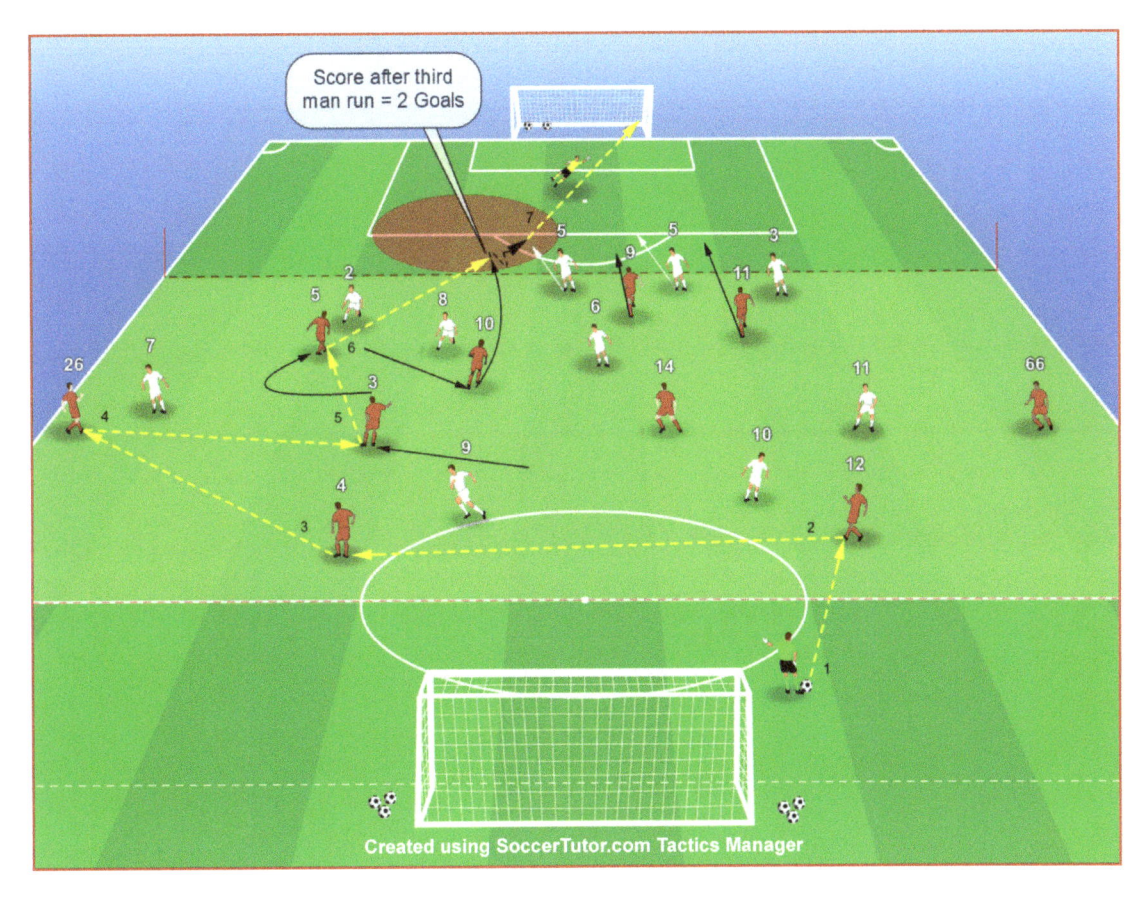

Score after third man run = 2 Goals

Description

- In the final practice of the session, we remove the side zones and just have 3 horizontal zones as shown.
- We also replace the 2 mini goals with a large goal + GK and add 2 active centre backs for the white defending team, who replace the mannequins from the previous practice.
- We play a normal 11 v 11 game. The practice starts with the red GK's pass into the middle zone and the reds build up play.

- The aim for the reds is to play the ball in behind the defensive line within the width of the box and score a goal.
- If the reds manage to score a goal using a third man run (as shown in diagram example), the goal counts double.
- The aim for the white defending team is to win the ball and then try to score a goal within 12-15 seconds (no zone restrictions).
- **RULE**: White players cannot enter their box before the ball is played in there.

SESSION 7B BASED ON THE TACTICS OF JÜRGEN KLOPP

Three Player Combinations with a Third Man Run Against Deep Defences

Session for JÜRGEN KLOPP Tactics - 3 Player Combinations with a Third Man Run Against Deep Defences

SESSION FOR THIS TACTICAL SITUATION (3 PRACTICES)

1. Three Player Combinations in a Technical Practice with Finishing in a Large Goal

Part 1/3: Turn and Shoot

Objective: Receiving and finishing in an around the box after a third man run.

Description (Part 1/3)

- We work in half a full pitch with a large goal and GK. The mannequins represent the compact and deep opponents within the width of the box.
- There are 2 groups of 3 players and the practice runs on both sides simultaneously.
- The practice starts from Player 1 who plays a forward pass to Player 2.
- Player 2 has his back to goal and the mannequin (defender) just inside the box.
- Player 2 receives, moves inside with the ball and past the mannequin (1 v 1 vs. defender), and then tries to score past the GK with a good shot at goal.
- This practice continues on the next page...

JÜRGEN KLOPP LIVERPOOL ATTACKING TACTICS

Session for JÜRGEN KLOPP Tactics - 3 Player Combinations with a Third Man Run Against Deep Defences

Part 2/3: Third Man Run, Dribble and Shoot

Description (Part 2/3)

- Immediately after shooting, Player 2 runs to the blue cone to receive a new ball from Player 1.

- While the ball is travelling from Player 1 to Player 2, Player 3 makes a cutting run through the mannequins to receive the next pass.

- Player 2 passes for the third man run of Player 3 into the highlighted space in the box.

- Player 3 receives, moves inside with the ball and past the mannequin (1 v 1 vs. defender), and then tries to score past the GK with a good shot at goal.

- This practice continues on the next page with the final part (3/3)...

Session for **JÜRGEN KLOPP** Tactics - 3 Player Combinations with a Third Man Run Against Deep Defences

Part 3/3: Pass Back for Oncoming Teammate to Shoot

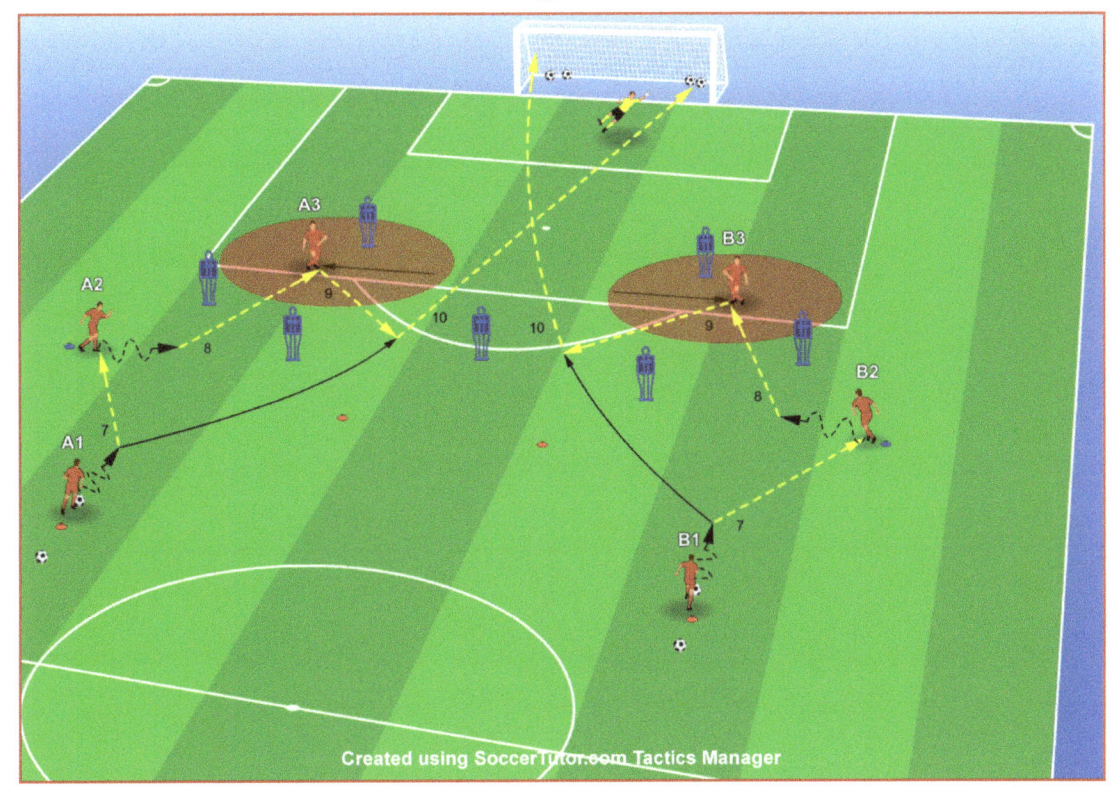

Description (Part 3/3)

- Immediately after shooting, Player 3 runs back and takes up a position in front of the mannequin with his back to goal.
- Player 1 dribbles a new ball forward, passes to Player 2, and then makes a forward run towards the box.
- Player 2 passes to Player 3, who receives with his back to the mannequin (defender) and the goal.
- Player 1 is still running forward and now moves to provide support for Player 3.
- We are practicing for a situation where Player 3 is unable to turn and shoot himself, so he passes back to Player 1 outside the box.
- Player 1 receives and shoots from outside the box, trying to score past the GK.

Coaching Points

1. Passes need to be well-weighted and aimed just in front of their teammates to step forward onto.
2. Make sure the players communicate with their teammates and their heads are up (to maximise their game awareness).
3. The practice should be done at a high tempo throughout.
4. The key is the rhythm and timing of the movement, together with the pass, and the synchronisation in the movements and actions of all the players.
5. There needs to be a quality directional first touch (if the player takes one) and accurate shooting to score a goal.

Session for **JÜRGEN KLOPP** Tactics - 3 Player Combinations with a Third Man Run Against Deep Defences

PROGRESSION

2. Three Player Combinations with a Third Man Run Against a Deep Defence in an 8(+2) v 5 Zonal Game

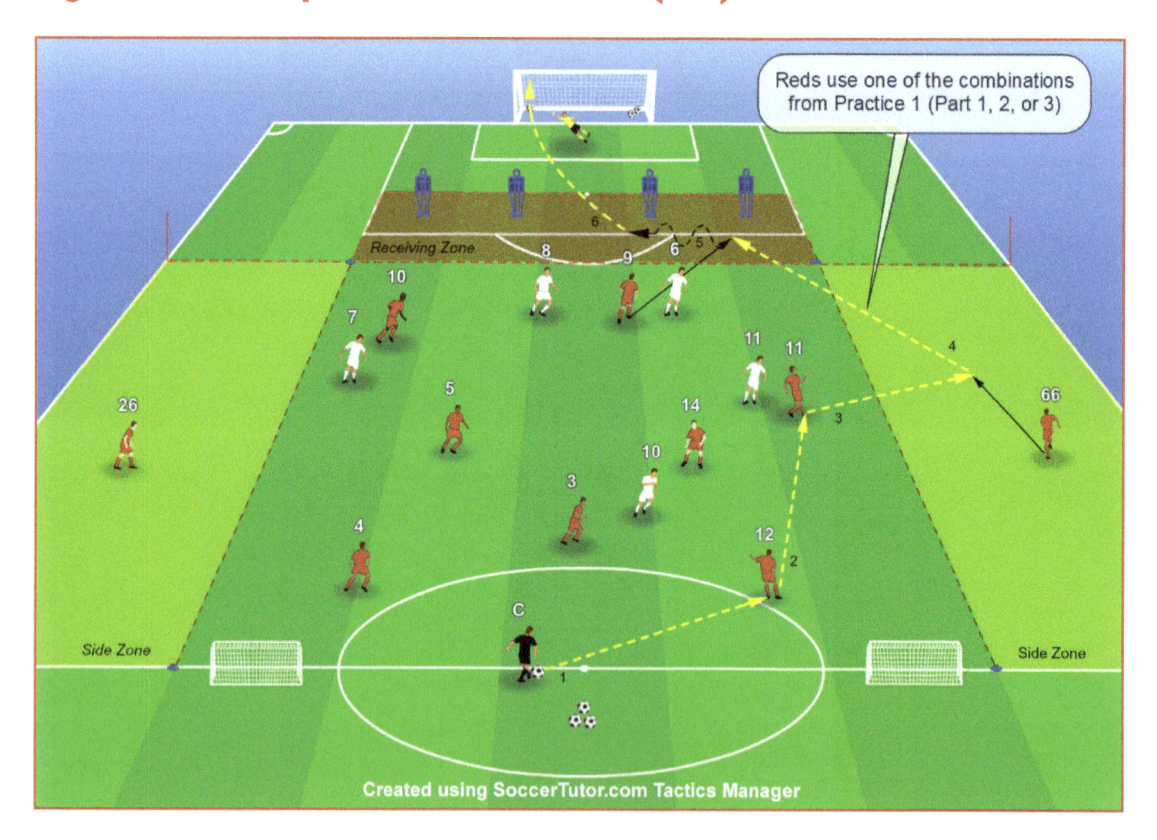

Reds use one of the combinations from Practice 1 (Part 1, 2, or 3)

Description

- Mark out a large zone from the halfway line to the edge of the box (width of box). Also mark out 2 side zones either side of this zone where the full backs **(26 & 66)** operate.

- In addition to this, there is a horizontal "Receiving Zone" from the "D" to the penalty spot, as shown.

- The red attacking team are in Liverpool's 4-3-3 formation.

- The white team have 5 players (4 midfielders and 1 forward) + 4 mannequins that represent their back 4.

- In the large central zone, we have an 8v5 situation. In the side zones, we have the full backs who are only active in the attacking phase and must stay within their zones.

- The practice starts with the Coach and the red attacking team build up play.

- The reds try to score using any of the 3 combinations fully described in Practice 1 (Part 1, 2, or 3 - see previous 3 pages).

- In this diagram example, the centre forward **(9)** makes a third man run into the "Receiving Zone" to receive the right back's **(66)** pass, turns, and dribbles past the mannequin (defender) to shoot and score.

Session for **JÜRGEN KLOPP** Tactics - 3 Player Combinations with a Third Man Run Against Deep Defences

PROGRESSION
3. Three Player Combinations with a Third Man Run Against a Deep Defence in a Dynamic Tactical Game

Use any combinations from Practice 1 = 2 Goals

Description

- In the final practice of the session, we play a normal 11 v 10 game in half a pitch (+ 10 yards), except the white back 4 have to stay within the box during their defensive phase.

- The practice starts with the red team's GK and the aim is to use different combinations with a third man run to score against a deep and compact defence.

- If the reds score using any of the 3 different combinations described in the first practice of this session, the goal counts double.

- The aim for the white defending team is to win the ball and then try to score within 12 seconds. In this situation, the reds must make a very quick transition from attack to defence.

- If the reds score, the whites score, or the ball goes out of play, restart from the red GK and the white back 4 must return to their starting positions inside the box.

JÜRGEN KLOPP TACTICAL ANALYSIS

SOLUTION 8

Attacking on the Flanks Against Deep and Compact Defences

Content from analysis of Liverpool F.C. during the 2018-2019 Champions League winning season and the 2019-2020 Premier League winning season

- Analysis based on recurring patterns of play observed within the Liverpool team.
- Tactical solutions displayed as examples of the team's tactics being used effectively.
- Real match examples of Liverpool scoring a goal using this specific attacking tactical solution.
- Each action, pass, individual movement with or without the ball, and the positioning of each player on the pitch including their body shape, are presented.
- The analysis is then used to create a full progressive session to coach this tactical situation.

Attacking on the Flanks Against Deep and Compact Defences

What?

Liverpool create chances and score by using the full width of the pitch to attack their opponent's defence.

Why?

Against teams who play with a compact defensive organisation in the width of the box or teams with individual and/or subgroup weaknesses in defending wide areas.

How?

Liverpool transfer the ball to the flanks and use different tactics defending on the situation. They use fast combination play or dominate 1v1s to exploit the quality, speed, and ability of their wide players against defenders who are unable to stop them.

Target Areas (on the Flanks)

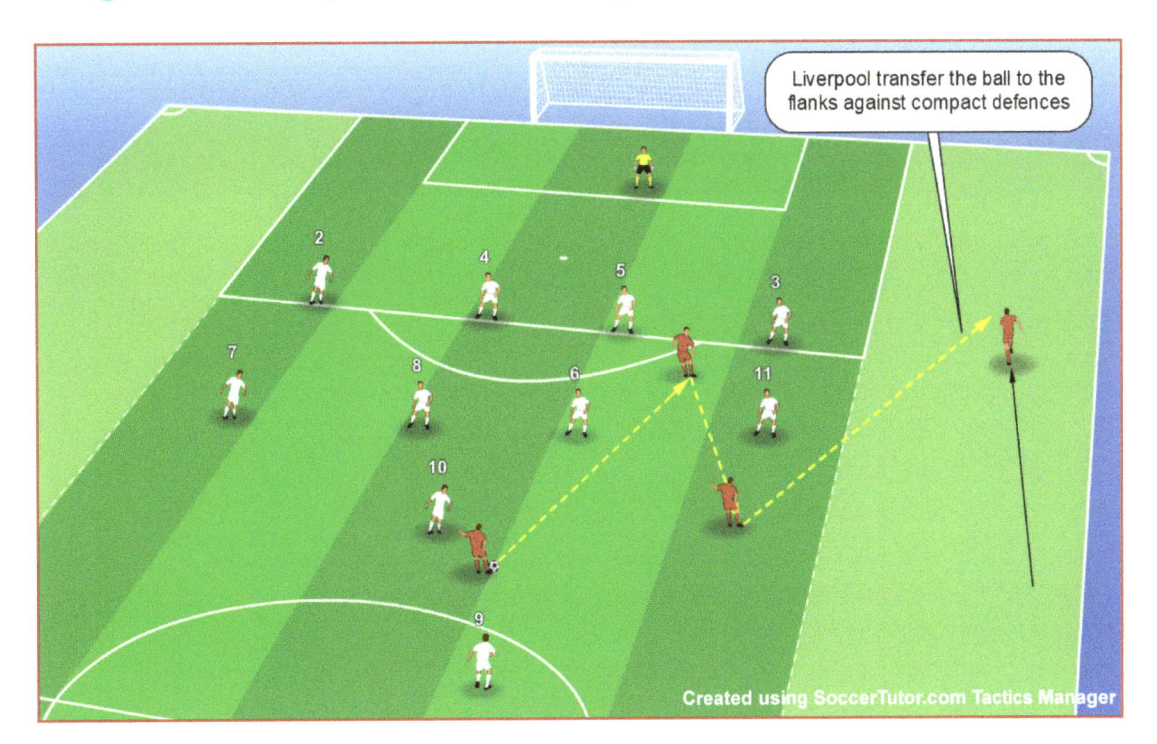

Liverpool transfer the ball to the flanks against compact defences

Tactical Solution 8 - Attacking on the Flanks Against Deep and Compact Defences

Tactical Solution A: Move the Ball Wide for the Full Back to Cross when Opponents are Deep Inside the Box

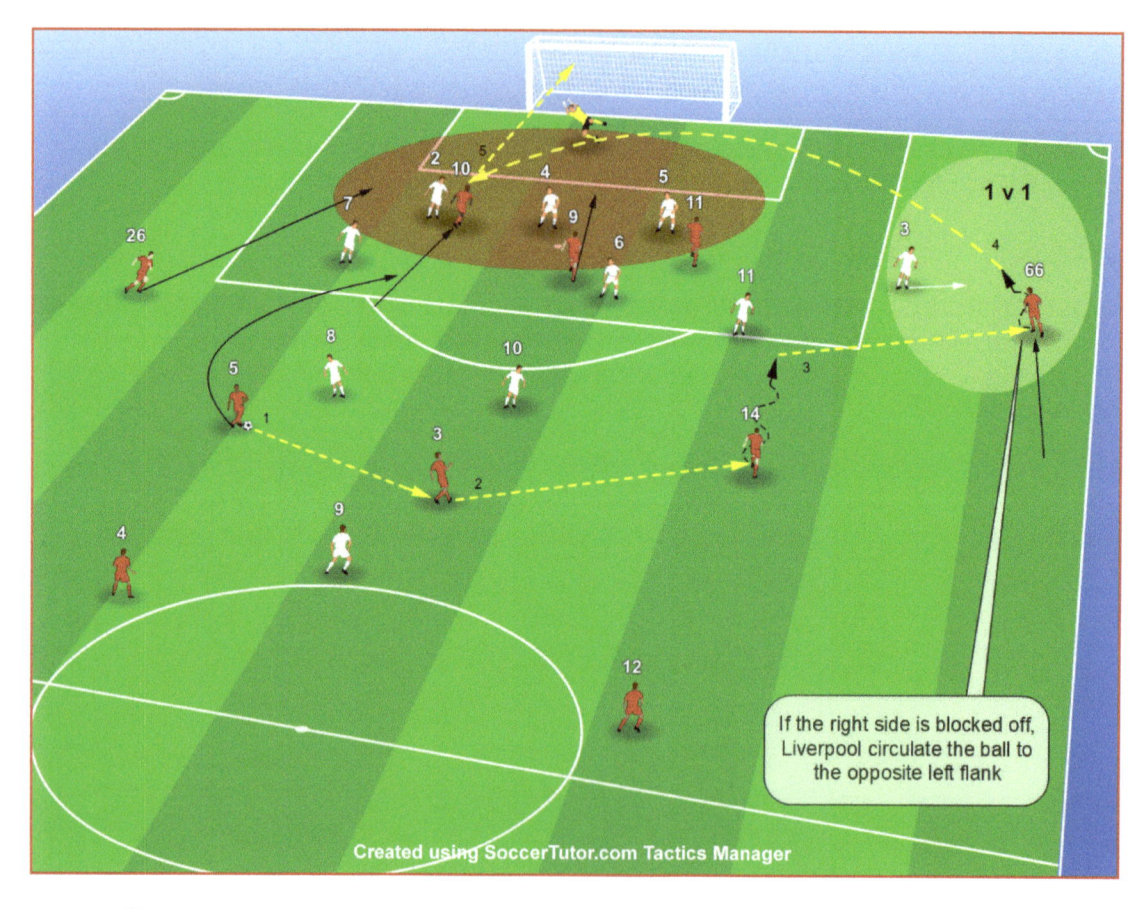

If the right side is blocked off, Liverpool circulate the ball to the opposite left flank

Liverpool keep possession in the opposition's half and force their opponents back.

The easiest solution Klopp's Liverpool use in this situation is to move the ball into a wide area (flank) to an unmarked full back, who crosses for the forwards and any other players who make runs into the box.

This can be done in different ways:

1. Quickly circulate the ball from one side of the pitch to the other (see diagram example).

2. Circulate the ball from one side of the pitch to the other, and then back again to the opposite side (switch) very quickly.

3. The ball carrier can dribble up to an opponent to draw him forward, and then pass the ball out wide to the full back.

After all 3 of these options, the full back delivers a cross into the box.

If the cross is cleared, the Liverpool players around the edge of the box move to receive the second ball and then pass to the full back out wide on the opposite side for another cross.

Tactical Solution 8 - Attacking on the Flanks Against Deep and Compact Defences

Tactical Solution B: Fast Combination Play for the Full Back to Receive in Behind when Opponents Defend Edge of Box

Deliver fast and high quality crosses for the Liverpool forwards always ready to sprint into the box

In this second example, the opposition are defending on the edge of the box, so aren't as deep.

Klopp's Liverpool use fast combination play in the central part of the pitch between 2-3 players.

The aim is to attract opponents towards them and then exploit the aggressive movement from the Liverpool full backs **Robertson (26)** and **A-Arnold (66)** in behind the opposition's defensive line.

Robertson (26) and **A-Arnold (66)** have speed, aggression, and quality that distinguishes them from other full backs.

They deliver fast and high quality dynamic crosses into the space between the defensive line (edge of penalty box) and the 6-yard box.

The Liverpool forwards are always ready to sprint into the box and finish these kinds of crosses.

In this example, the right back **(66)** delivers a cross along the ground to the penalty spot for the centre forward **(9)** to score.

Tactical Solution 8 - Attacking on the Flanks Against Deep and Compact Defences

Tactical Solution C (1): Through Ball to Wide Forward in Behind when Opponents Defend with 2 Players Out Wide

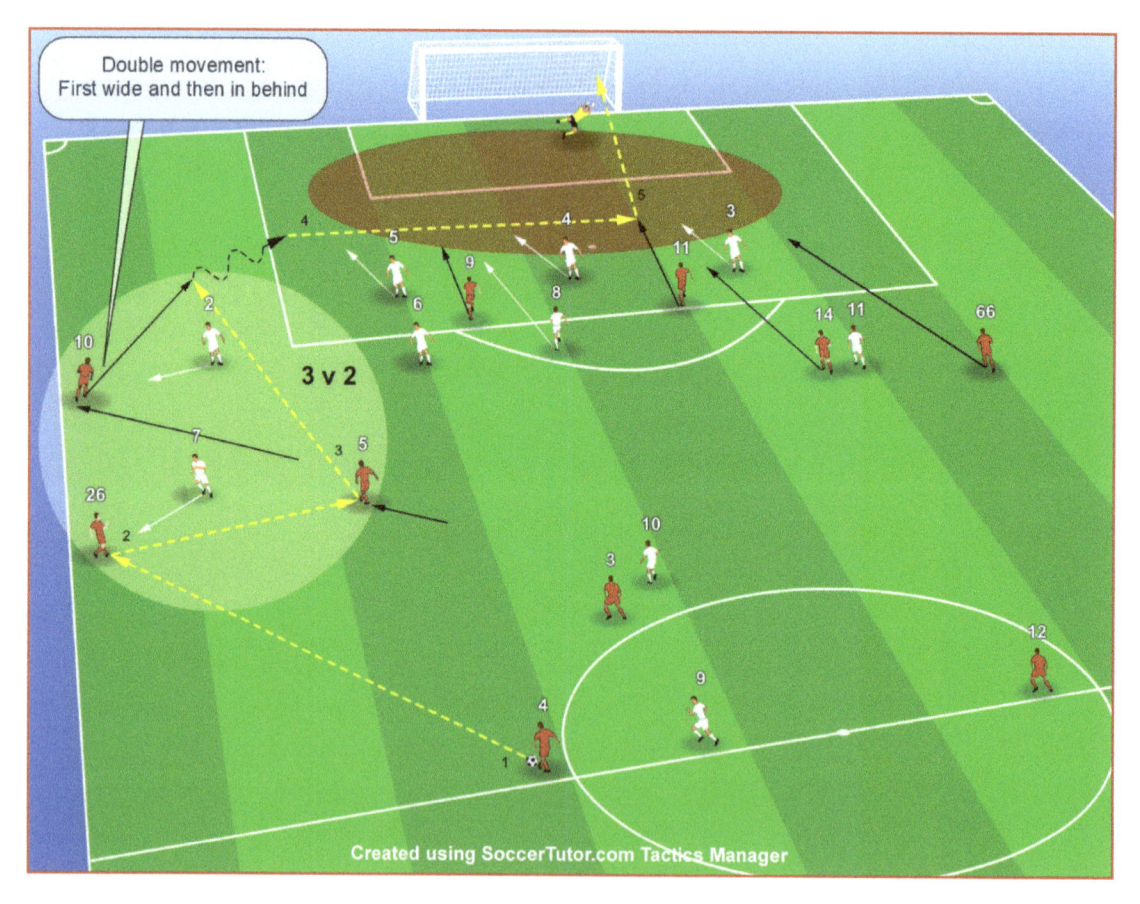

When the opposition are organised and defend well on the flank (with at least 2 players as shown), Klopp's Liverpool often use attacking combinations between 3 players to provide the best tactical solutions for this problem.

Normally the opposing full back is supported by the wide midfielder or wide forward on that side to stop Liverpool playing in behind and/or delivering a cross/cut back into the box.

Liverpool want to create a numerical advantage (3v2) with the full back, central midfielder and wide forward, or at least 2v2. They use cutting diagonal movements without the ball and inside/outside movements with the ball.

The aim is to use combination play to pass the ball in behind the opposing defender. Once that is achieved, the aim is to deliver a fast short cross for incoming teammates to finish the attack.

In this example, the left back **(26)** receives and plays inside to the central midfielder **(5)**. At the same time, the left forward **(10)** has made a diagonal movement towards the side-line. He then makes a run in behind, timed well for the central midfielder's **(5)** pass.

No.10 receives, enters the box, and delivers a low cross for the opposite wide forward **(11)** to score in the centre.

Tactical Solution 8 - Attacking on the Flanks Against Deep and Compact Defences

Tactical Solution C (2): Quick One-Two to Receive in Behind when Opponents Defend with 2 Players Out Wide

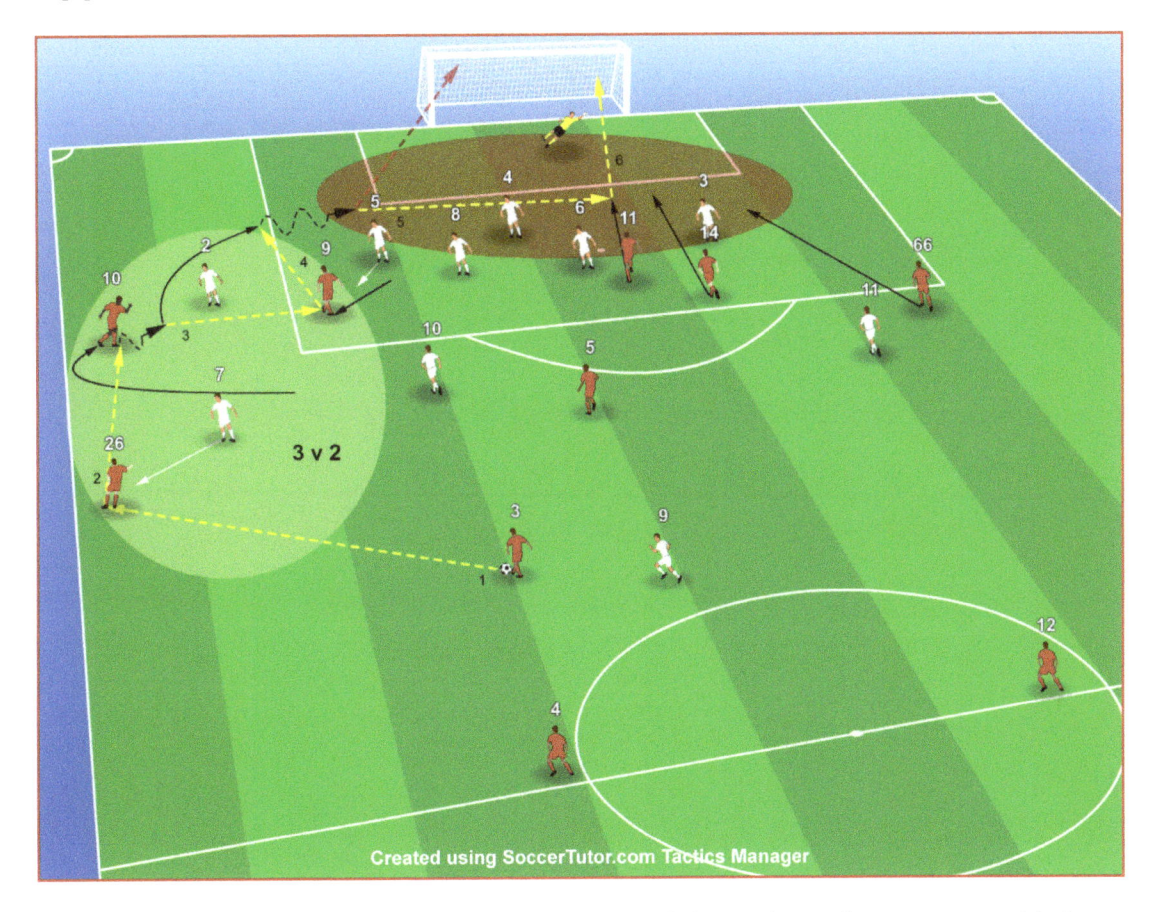

In this variation of the previous example (C1), Liverpool again use a 3 player combination to get in behind their opponents when they defend with 2 players on the flank.

The defensive midfielder **(3)** passes out wide to the left back **(26)**, who is pressed by the opposing winger (7). The left forward **(10)** makes a diagonal movement towards the side-line to provide support and receive the forward pass. He is then pressed by the opposing full back (2).

The centre forward **(9)** sees the situation and moves across to create a 3 v 2 advantage and is followed by the white centre back (5).

The left forward **(10)** plays a one-two with the centre forward **(9)**, receives the return pass inside the box, and moves towards the goal.

No.10 can either pass the ball across the box for a teammate or try to score himself (red arrow).

Tactical Solution 8 - Attacking on the Flanks Against Deep and Compact Defences

Tactical Solution C (3): Creating and Winning a 1 v 1 Duel when Opponents Defend with 2 Players Out Wide

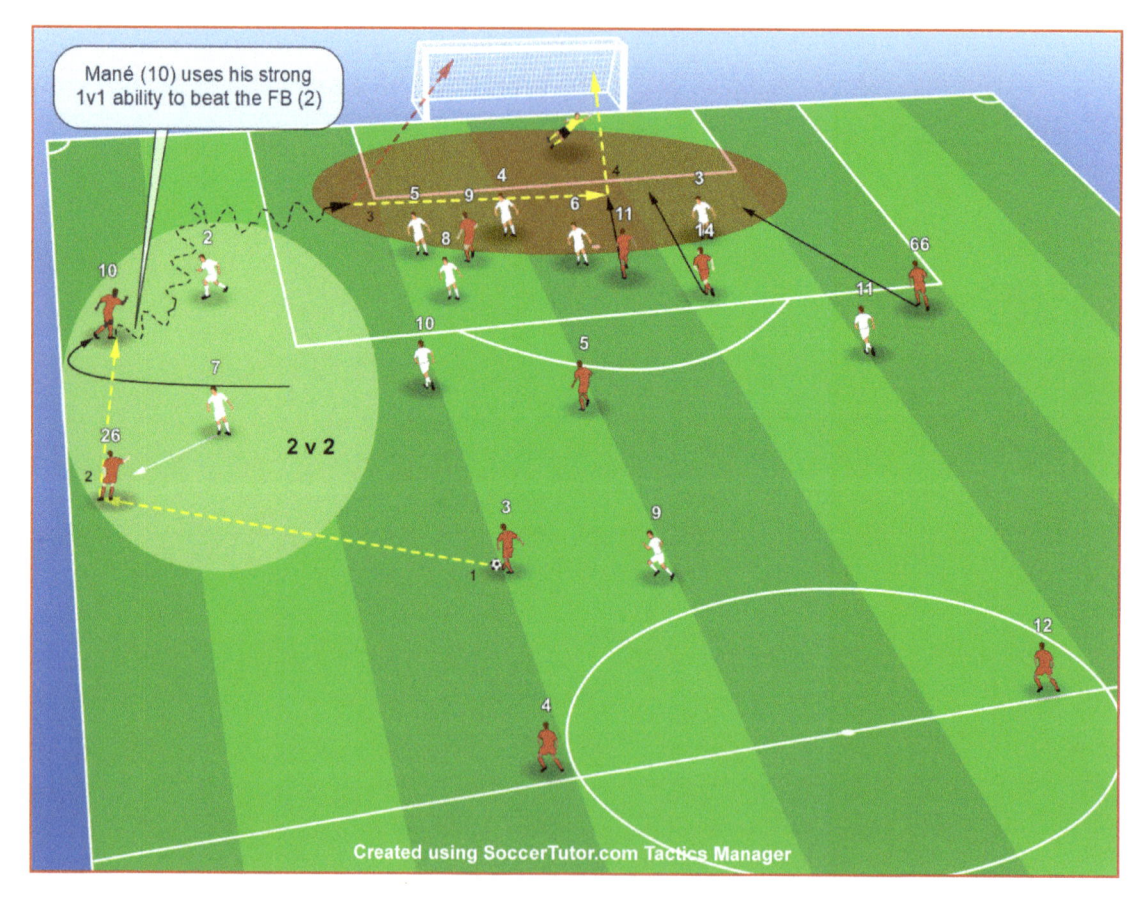

This third and final example for Tactical Solution C is a variation of the previous one (C2).

The Liverpool centre forward **(9)** doesn't move wide to provide support and instead positions himself in the middle of the box.

Therefore, there is a 2 v 2 situation on the flank, so the left forward **(10)** uses his strong 1 v 1 ability to beat the opposing full back.

As in the previous example, the left forward **(10)** dribbles into the box with the same options to either pass the ball across the box for a teammate or try to score himself (red arrow).

The left forward **(10)** has to be aware of the white centre back No.5, who may choose to move across and close him down.

NOTE: On the left flank, the left forward **Mané (10)** always uses this option to win the 1 v 1 and dribble into the box. However, when this situation occurs on the right side of the pitch, Liverpool have an extra option of winning a 1 v 1 and delivering a cross from outside the box. This is because **Salah (11)** and **Firmino (9)** have a high technical quality to deliver crosses.

Tactical Solution 8 - Attacking on the Flanks Against Deep and Compact Defences

Statistical Analysis of Liverpool Attacking on the Flanks Against Deep and Compact Defences

Liverpool scored **41 goals** in this tactical situation
(Premier League and Champions League 2018-2019 and 2019-2020 seasons)

VS. DEEP AND COMPACT DEFENCES
TACTICAL SOLUTION = ATTACK ON THE FLANKS

DATE	HOME	AWAY	SCORE	GOAL (MIN)	SCORER	ASSIST
1st Sep 2018	Leicester City	Liverpool	1-2	0-1 (10')	**Mané**	Robertson
15th Sep 2018	Tottenham	Liverpool	1-2	0-2 (54')	**Firmino**	Mané
18th Sep 2018	Liverpool	PSG	3-2	1-0 (30')	**Sturridge**	Robertson
3rd Nov 2018	Arsenal	Liverpool	1-1	0-1 (61')	**Milner**	Mané
24th Nov 2018	Watford	Liverpool	0-3	0-1 (67')	**Salah** *	Mané
8th Dec 2018	Bournemouth	Liverpool	0-4	0-3 (68')	**Own Goal**	Robertson
16th Dec 2018	Liverpool	Man Utd	3-1	2-1 (73')	**Shaqiri** *	Mané
21st Dec 2018	Wolves	Liverpool	0-2	0-1 (18')	**Salah**	Fabinho
26th Dec 2018	Liverpool	Newcastle	4-0	3-0 (79')	**Shaqiri**	A-Arnold
04th Feb 2019	West Ham	Liverpool	1-1	0-1 (22')	**Mané**	Milner
09th Feb 2019	Liverpool	Bournemouth	3-0	1-0 (24')	**Mané**	Milner
27th Feb 2019	Liverpool	Watford	5-0	1-0 (9')	**Mané**	Arnold
27th Feb 2019	Liverpool	Watford	5-0	3-0 (66')	**Origi**	Robertson
10th Mar 2019	Liverpool	Burnley	4-2	1-1 (19')	**Firmino** *	Salah
17th Mar 2019	Fulham	Liverpool	1-2	0-1 (25')	**Mané**	Firmino

* The full analysis of these goals is shown on the following pages and the table continues on the next page (goals 16-41)...

Tactical Solution 8 - Attacking on the Flanks Against Deep and Compact Defences

Date	Home	Away	Score	Goal (Time)	Scorer	Assist
5th Apr 2019	Southampton	Liverpool	1-3	1-1 (36')	**Keïta**	A-Arnold
9th Apr 2019	Liverpool	Porto	2-0	2-0 (26')	**Firmino**	A-Arnold
14th Apr 2019	Liverpool	Chelsea	2-0	1-0 (51')	**Mané**	Henderson
17th Apr 2019	Porto	Liverpool	1-4	0-1 (26')	**Mané**	Salah
4th May 2019	Newcastle	Liverpool	2-3	1-2 (28')	**Salah**	A-Arnold
7th May 2019	Liverpool	FC Barcelona	4-0	3-0 (56')	**Wijnaldum**	Shaqiri
12th May 2019	Liverpool	Wolves	2-0	1-0 (17')	**Mané**	A-Arnold
9th Aug 2019	Liverpool	Norwich	4-1	1-0 (7')	**Own Goal**	Origi
9th Aug 2019	Liverpool	Norwich	4-1	2-0 (19')	**Salah**	Firmino
17th Aug 2019	Southampton	Liverpool	1-2	0-1 (45+1')	**Mané**	
14th Sep 2019	Liverpool	Newcastle	3-1	1-1 (28')	**Mané**	Robertson
28th Sep 2019	Sheffield Utd	Liverpool	0-1	0-1 (70')	**Wijnaldum**	Origi
2nd Oct 2019	Liverpool	RB Salzburg	4-3	1-0 (9')	**Mané**	Firmino
2nd Oct 2019	Liverpool	RB Salzburg	4-3	2-0 (25')	**Robertson** *	A-Arnold
2nd Oct 2019	Liverpool	RB Salzburg	4-3	3-0 (36')	**Salah**	Firmino
20th Oct 2019	Man Utd	Liverpool	1-1	1-1 (85')	**Lallana** *	Robertson
5th Nov 2019	Liverpool	Genk	2-1	1-0 (13')	**Wijnaldum**	Milner
10th Nov 2019	Liverpool	Man City	3-1	3-0 (51')	**Mané**	Henderson
4th Dec 2019	Liverpool	Everton	5-2	5-2 (90')	**Wijnaldum**	Firmino
10th Dec 2019	RB Salzburg	Liverpool	0-2	0-1 (57')	**Keïta**	Mané
26th Dec 2019	Leicester City	Liverpool	0-4	0-3 (74')	**Firmino**	A-Arnold
1st Feb 2020	Liverpool	Southampton	4-0	1-0 (47')	**Chamberlain**	Firmino
24th Feb 2020	Liverpool	West Ham	3-2	1-0 (9')	**Wijnaldum**	Arnold
24th Feb 2020	Liverpool	West Ham	3-2	2-2 (68')	**Salah**	Robertson
11th Mar 2020	Liverpool	Atlético Madrid	2-3	1-0 (43')	**Wijnaldum**	Chamberlain
26th Jul 2020	Newcastle	Liverpool	1-3	1-1 (38')	**van Dijk**	Chamberlain

Tactical Solution 8 - Attacking on the Flanks Against Deep and Compact Defences

Analysis from Man Utd 1-1 Liverpool (Lallana 85') - 20th Oct 2019, Premier League

Tactical Solution A: Move the Ball Wide for the Full Back to Cross when Opponents are Deep Inside the Box

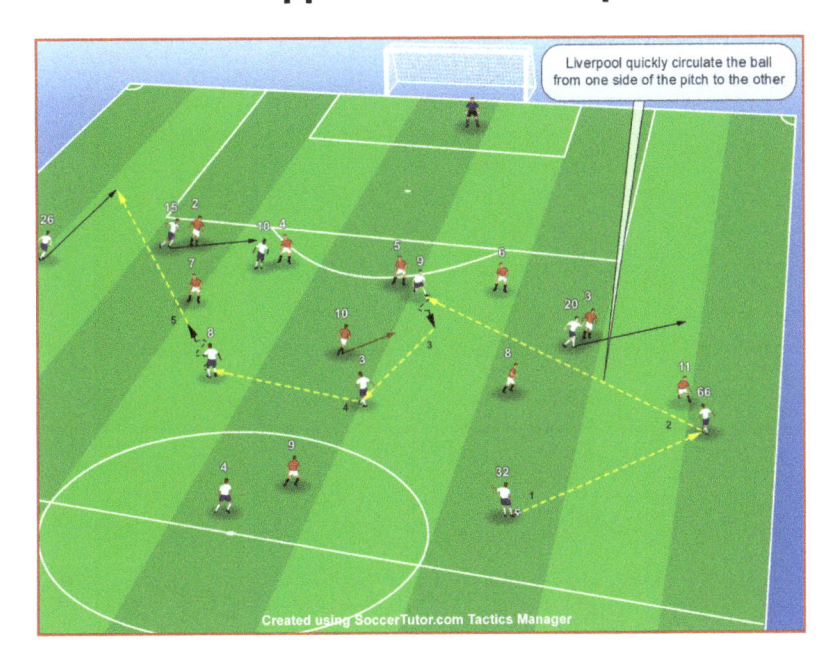

Centre back **Matip (32)** passes to right back **A-Arnold (66)** who is pressed. He passes to the centre forward **Firmino (9)**, who is marked, so he passes back to the defensive midfielder **Fabinho (3)**.

Fabinho (3) passes across to **Keïta (8)**, who dribbles forward up to his opponent, and then passes out wide to the unmarked left back **Robertson (26)** in an advanced wide position.

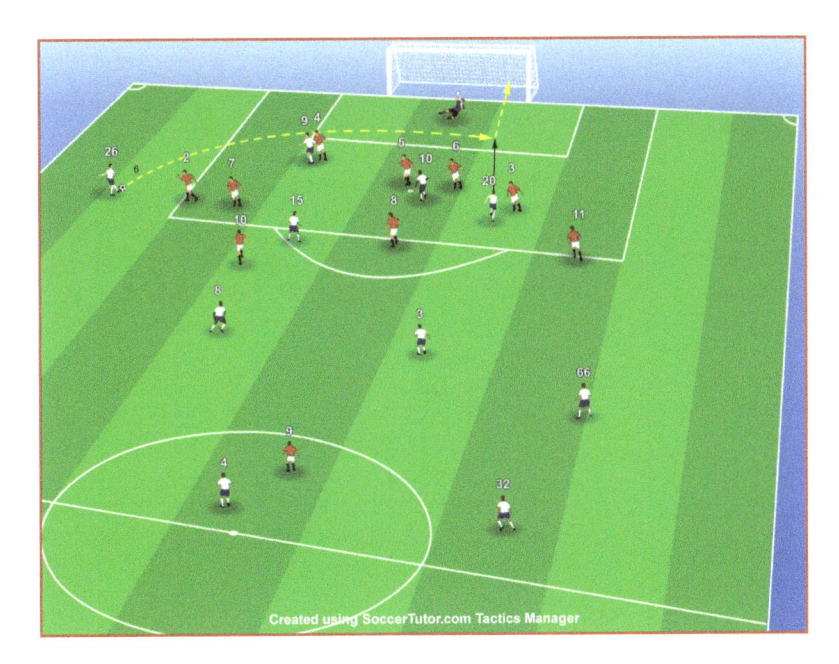

The Man Utd players have all dropped back and their defenders all are all deep inside their box.

Robertson (26) delivers a cross and **Lallana (20)** scores from close range.

If the cross had been cleared, the Liverpool players around the edge of the box would have moved to receive the second ball and then passed to the full back out wide on the opposite side (**A-Arnold - 66**) for another cross.

JÜRGEN KLOPP LIVERPOOL ATTACKING TACTICS

Tactical Solution 8 - Attacking on the Flanks Against Deep and Compact Defences

Analysis from Liverpool 4-3 RB Salzburg (Robertson 25') - 2nd Oct 2019, Champions League

Tactical Solution B: Fast Combination Play for the Full Back to Receive in Behind when Opponents Defend Edge of Box

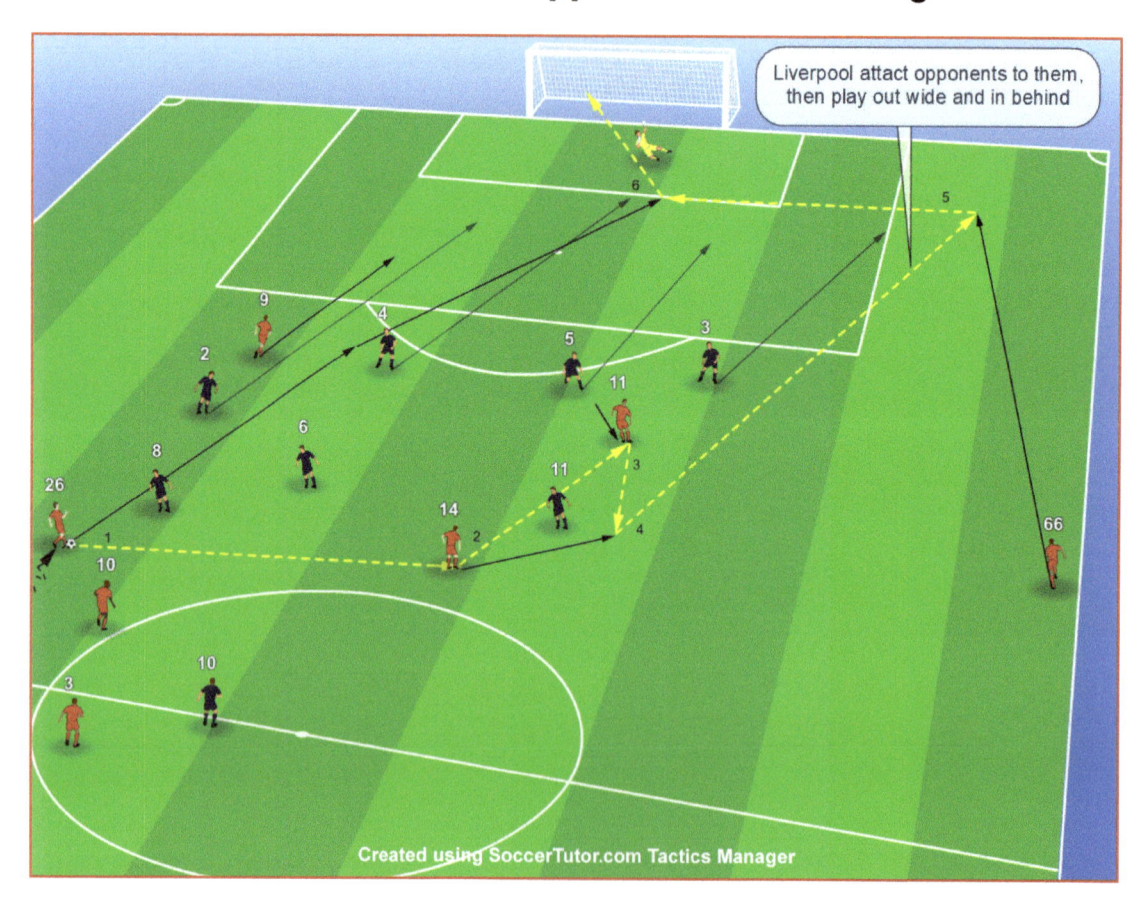

Liverpool attact opponents to them, then play out wide and in behind

In this example, the RB Salzburg defensive line is near the edge of the box. Klopp's Liverpool use fast combination play in the central part of the pitch between 2-3 players.

The aim is to attract opponents towards them and then exploit an advanced run from an attacking full back in behind the defensive line.

The left back **Robertson (26)** dribbles forward into the opponent's half and is put under pressure by the opposing central midfielders. He therefore passes inside to central midfielder **Henderson (14)**, who is unmarked.

Henderson (14) plays a quick one-two combination with the right forward **Salah (11)** who drops off to provide an option and is followed by the centre back.

Henderson (14) plays a hard pass along the ground for the advanced run of the right back **A-Arnold (66)**, who receives high up the flank and in behind the defensive line. He delivers a fast and high quality cross into the space behind the RB Salzburg defenders.

Robertson (26) has continued his run forward and scores from close range.

Tactical Solution 8 - Attacking on the Flanks Against Deep and Compact Defences

Analysis from Watford 0-3 Liverpool (Salah 67') - 24th Nov 2018, Premier League

Tactical Solution C (1): Through Ball to Wide Forward in Behind when Opponents Defend with 2 Players Out Wide

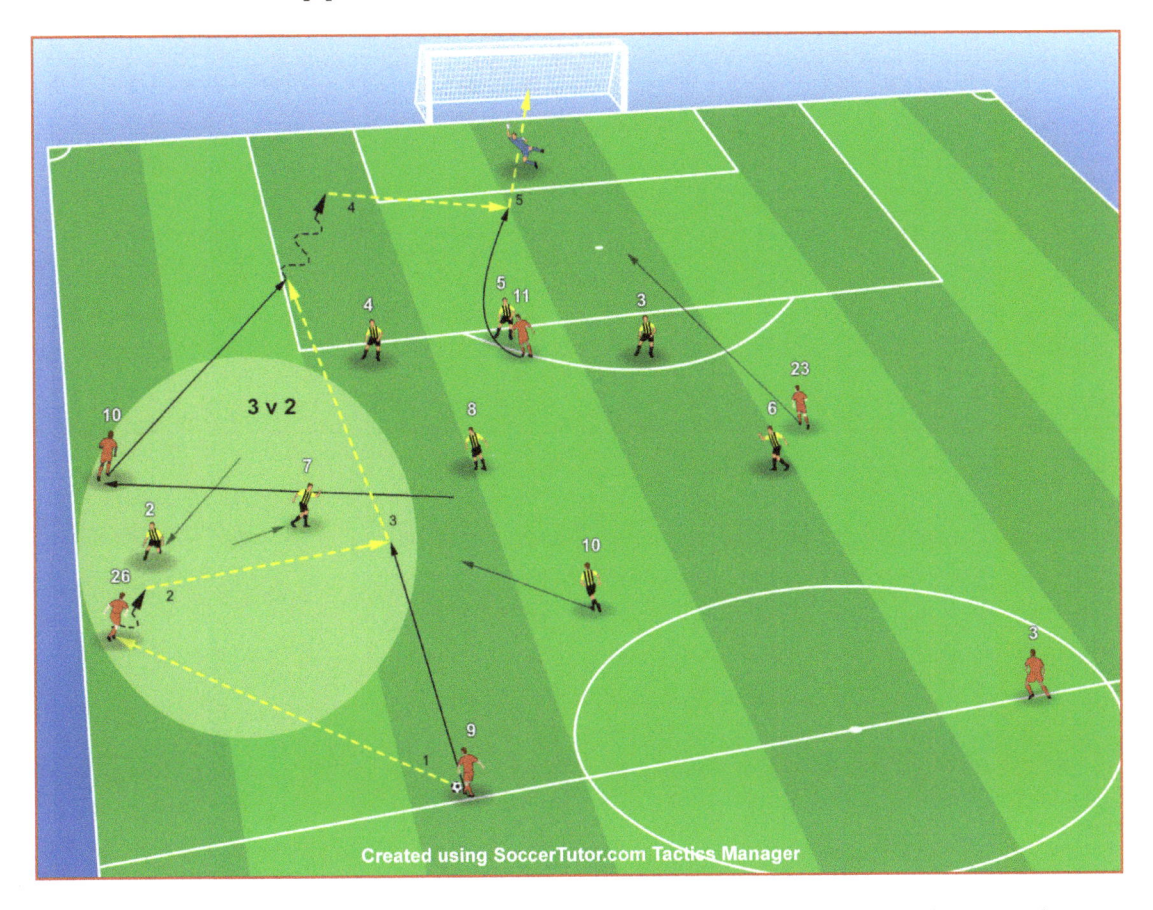

Watford are well organised and are defending with 2 players on the flank, as shown.

In this kind of situation, Liverpool look to use quick combination play between 3 players. Liverpool want to try and create a numerical advantage (3 v 2) on the flank and then play a pass in behind the defenders on that side.

In this example, the left back **Robertson (26)** receives near the side-line from **Firmino's (9)** pass. At the same time, the left forward **Mané (10)** has made a diagonal movement towards the side-line.

Firmino (9) moves forward and receives the return pass from **Robertson (26)**, as shown.

Mané (10) is unmarked and makes a run (second movement) in behind, timed well for **Firmino's (9)** pass into the box.

Mané (10) receives, dribbles forward, and cuts the ball back for the opposite wide forward **Salah (11)** to score from close range.

Tactical Solution 8 - Attacking on the Flanks Against Deep and Compact Defences

Analysis from Liverpool 4-2 Burnley (Firmino 19') - 10th Mar 2019, Premier League

Tactical Solution C (2): Quick One-Two to Receive in Behind when Opponents Defend with 2 Players Out Wide

In this example, Liverpool switch the play from the left to the right side.

Centre back **van Dijk (4)** passes to central midfielder **Lallana (20)** near the side-line.

Lallana (20) dribbles inside and then switches play with a long pass to the unmarked right forward **Salah (11)**.

The Burnley players quickly shift across and make sure to defend with 2 players on the flank.

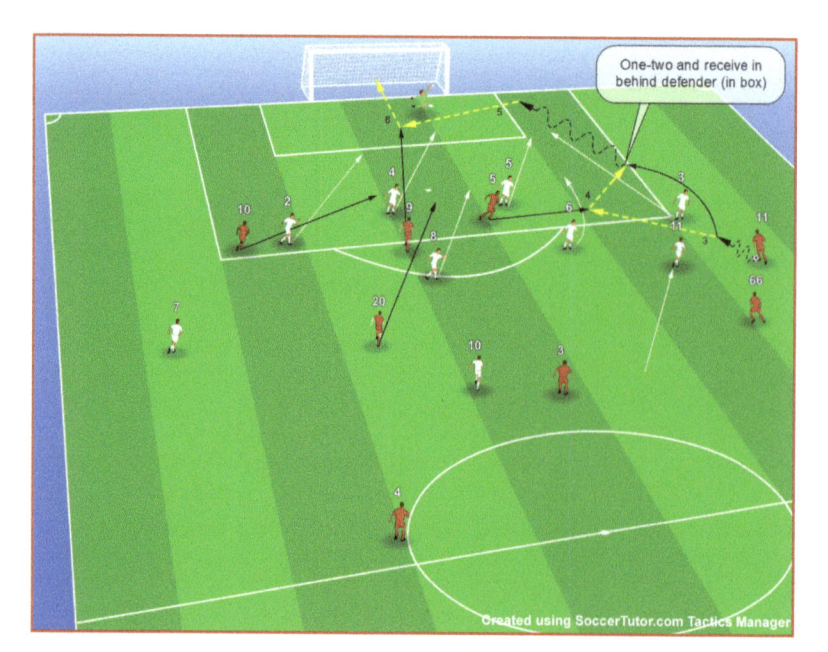

The left forward **Salah (11)** plays a one-two with central midfielder **Wijnaldum (5)**, receives the return pass inside the box, and dribbles towards the by-line.

Salah (11) passes the ball across the 6-yard box and the centre forward **Firmino (9)** taps the ball into an empty net.

Tactical Solution 8 - Attacking on the Flanks Against Deep and Compact Defences

Analysis from Liverpool 3-1 Man Utd (Shaqiri 73') - 16th Dec 2018, Premier League

Tactical Solution C (3): Creating and Winning a 1v1 Duel when Opponents Defend with 2 Players Out Wide

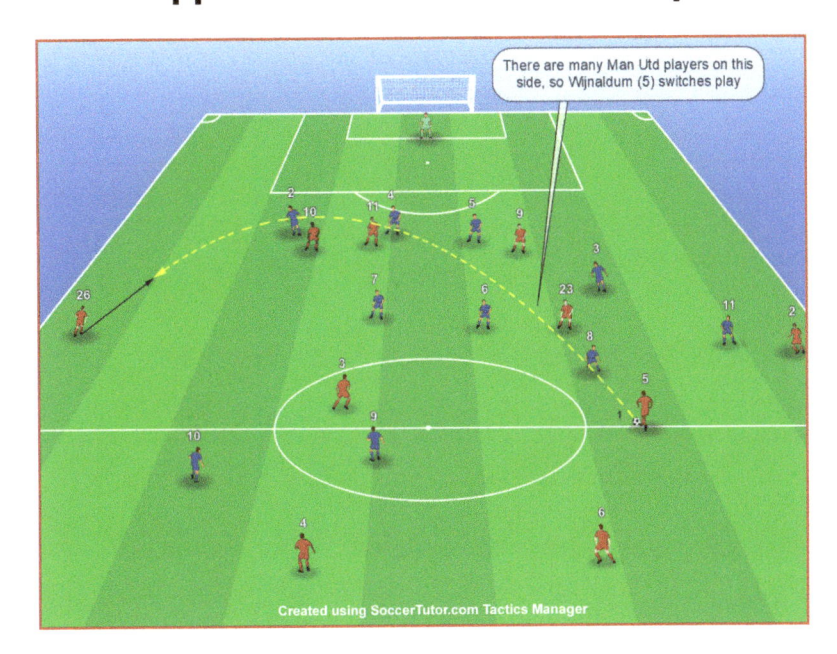

There are many Man Utd players on this side, so Wijnaldum (5) switches play

Liverpool are in possession on the right side of the pitch, where Man Utd have many players.

Therefore, the central midfielder **Wijnaldum (5)** decides to switch play to the weak side where the left back **Robertson (26)** can receive unmarked.

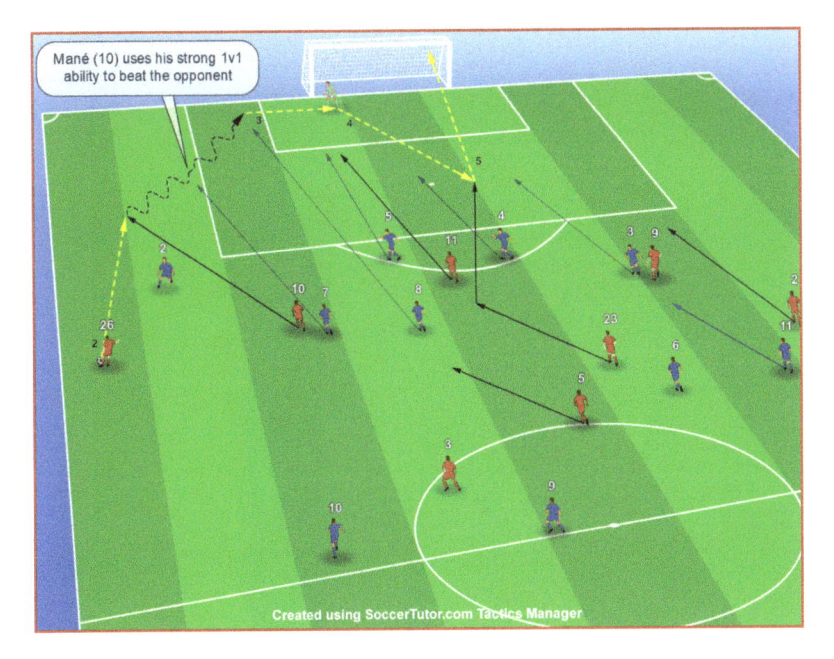

Mané (10) uses his strong 1v1 ability to beat the opponent

Once **Robertson (26)** has received, there is a 2v2 situation on the left side. The Man Utd right back (2) moves to close him down, and the right midfielder (7) is tracking **Mané (10)**.

Robertson (26) passes in behind the right back for **Mané's (10)** run, who receives in a 1v1 situation and beats his opponent to get into the box.

He cuts the ball back and it is deflected off the GK's legs to the oncoming **Shaqiri (23)**, who scores.

JÜRGEN KLOPP LIVERPOOL ATTACKING TACTICS

SESSION 8A BASED ON THE TACTICS OF JÜRGEN KLOPP

Move the Ball Wide for the Full Back to Cross when Opponents are Deep Inside the Box

Session for **JÜRGEN KLOPP** Tactics - Attacking on the Flanks Against Deep and Compact Defences

SESSION FOR THIS TACTICAL SITUATION (2 PRACTICES)
1. Move the Ball Wide for the Full Back to Cross in a Continuous High Intensity Game (+ Defend Mini Goals)

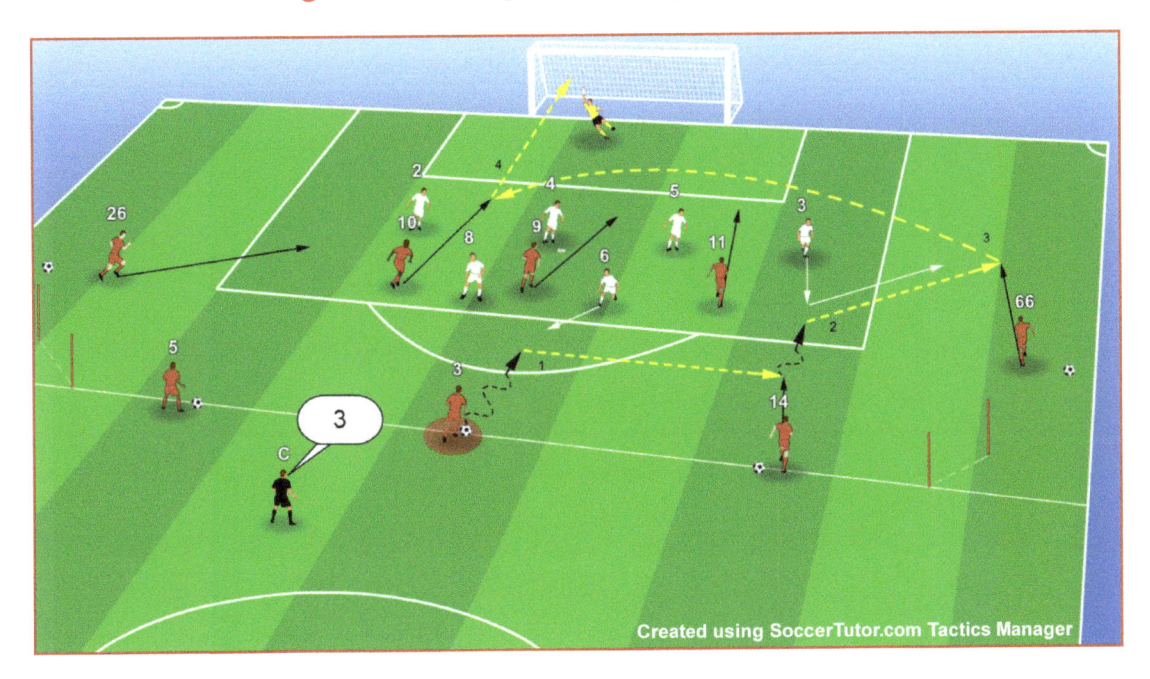

Description

- Mark out a line 10 yards from the box and position 2 mini goals at an angle as shown. The red attacking team use a 2-3-3 formation (from Liverpool's 4-3-3).

- The white defending team are in a 4-2 formation + GK (all inside the box).

- The reds have 2 full backs wide, 3 central midfielders on the line, and 3 forwards inside the box. The games starts when the Coach calls out a number (26, 5, 3, 14, or 66), and that player carries the ball forward to start.

- The reds can score in any way (1 point), but if they score from a full back's cross, they get 2 points. The reds have unlimited touches.

- If the whites win the ball, they try to score in a mini goal (2 points). They are limited to 2-3 touches.

- The game is continuous, and the players must return back to their positions immediately after a phase finishes, ready for the Coach's next signal. Play for e.g. 4-5 minutes and count how many goals the attacking team scores before switching the team roles.

Coaching Points

1. The white players must force play wide.
2. If a full back starts the attack, he must dribble forward and cross before he is closed down.
3. If a full back is closed down, quickly circulate the ball to the opposite full back.
4. Focus on accurate and well-weighted crosses + fast and quality finishing inside the box.
5. Execute with high rhythm, synchronisation of all movements, and good communication (verbal and visual).

Session for **JÜRGEN KLOPP** Tactics - Attacking on the Flanks Against Deep and Compact Defences

PROGRESSION
2. Move the Ball Wide for the Full Back to Cross in a Continuous High Intensity Game (+ Defend Large Goals)

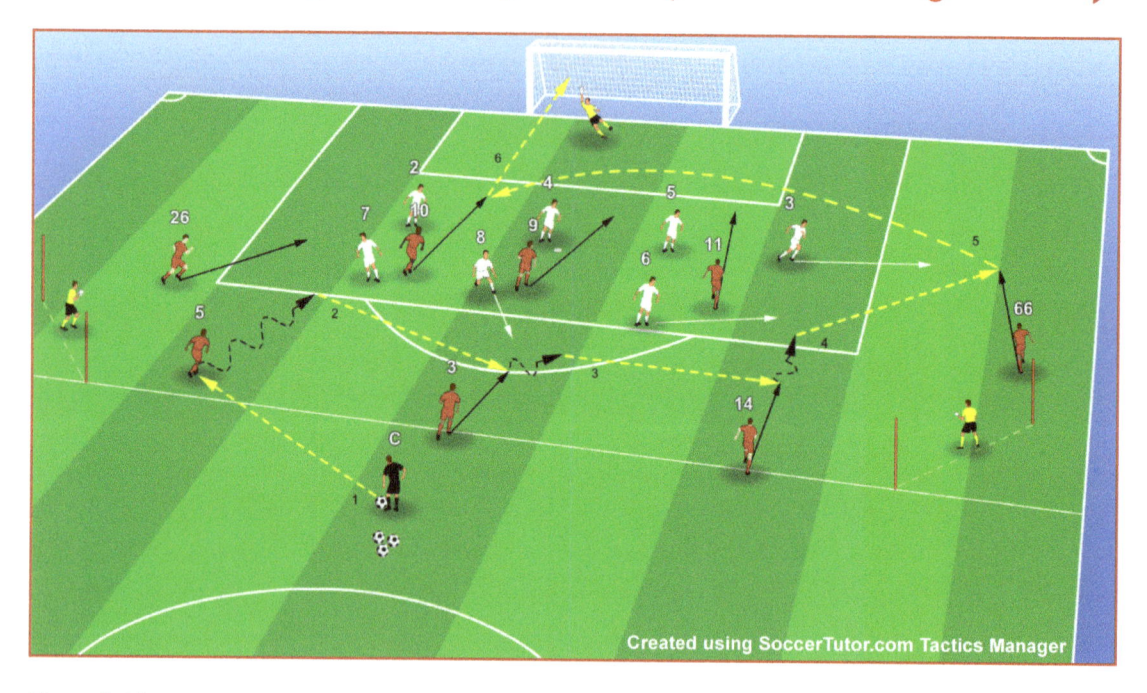

Description
- In this progression of the previous practice, we add 1 more midfielder for the white defending team. The Coach starts with a pass.
- We also use large goals at an angle in the corners with GKs. The diagram example shows pole gate goals, but you can use full sized normal goals if you have them available.
- The game is continuous, and the players must return back to their positions immediately after a phase finishes, ready for the Coach's next ball.
- Play for e.g. 5-6 minutes and count how many goals the attacking team scores before switching the team roles.
- The reds can score in any way (1 point), but if they score from a full back's cross = 2 points.
- If the whites win the ball, they try to score in either goal within 6-7 seconds (1 point).

Coaching Points
The coaching points from the previous page apply for this progression as well.

SESSION 8B BASED ON THE TACTICS OF JÜRGEN KLOPP

Fast Combination Play for the Advanced Full Back to Receive in Behind the Defensive Line

Session for **JÜRGEN KLOPP** Tactics - Attacking on the Flanks Against Deep and Compact Defences

SESSION FOR THIS TACTICAL SITUATION (2 PRACTICES)

1. Combination Play for the Full Back to Receive in Behind Against a Compact Defence (Unopposed)

1a: Three Player Combination on the Flank with Early Cross

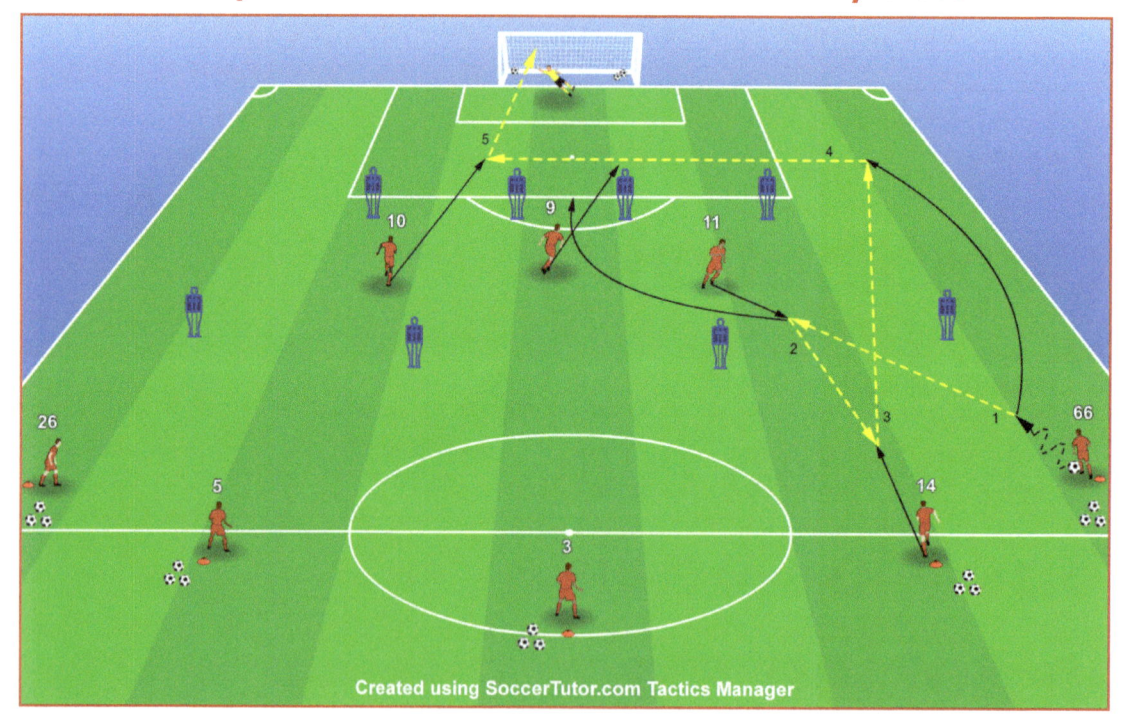

Practice Set-up

In half a pitch, there are 2 full backs, 3 central midfielders and 3 forwards from Liverpool's 4-3-3 + 8 mannequins in a 4-4 defensive formation.

The practice is continuous with the players working on 3 different combinations (a, b, and c) to exploit the full width of the pitch using the advanced full back to cross into the box.

Description (1a)

1. The right back **(66)** starts by dribbling forward and passing inside to the right forward **(11)**, who drops off to receive.

2. The right forward **(11)** lays the ball back for the forward run of the central midfielder **(14)**.

3. The central midfielder **(14)** passes the ball in between the 2 mannequins for the forward run of the right back **(66)** in behind.

4. The right back **(66)** delivers a low cross across the box (in the space between edge of penalty box and 6-yard box). The centre forward **(9)** runs towards the near post and the opposite wide forward (left) **No.10** runs to the far post. The right forward **(11)** also moves into the box after his lay-off pass.

5. In this example, the ball goes to the back post and the left forward **(10)** scores past the GK.

6. After the attack finishes, all players run back to their positions. Repeat the same sequence on the left starting with the left back **(26)**.

JÜRGEN KLOPP LIVERPOOL ATTACKING TACTICS

Session for **JÜRGEN KLOPP** Tactics - Attacking on the Flanks Against Deep and Compact Defences

1b: DM Dribbles Forward, Lay-off and Full Back's Cut Back

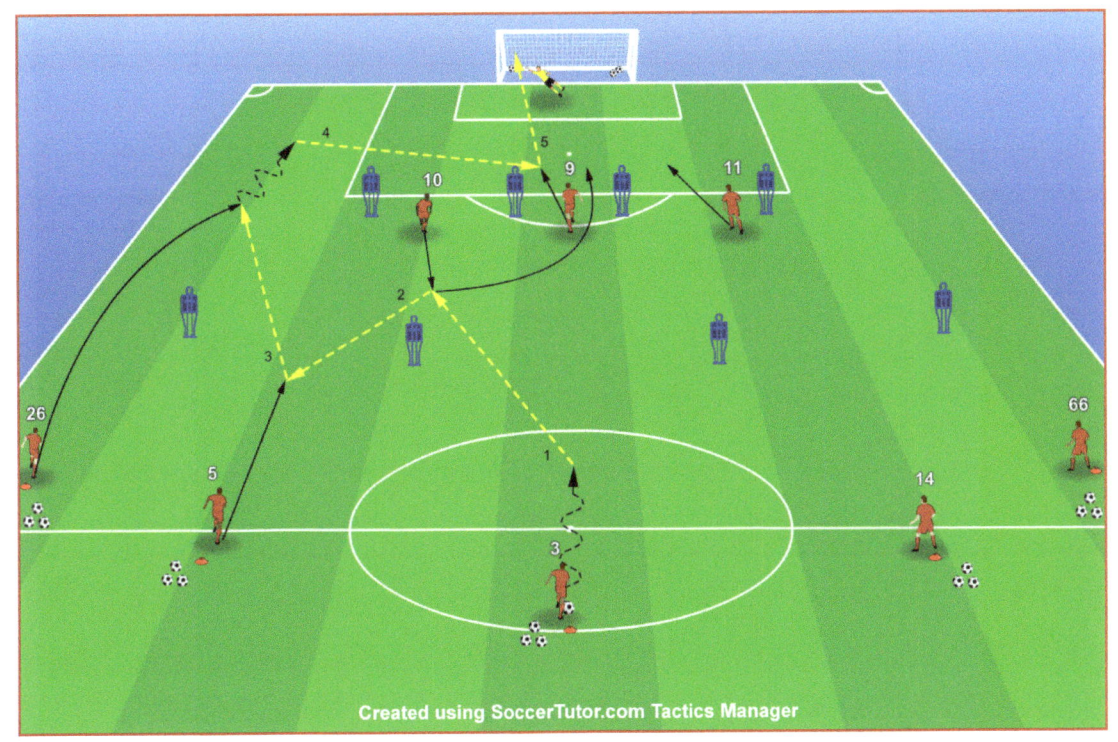

Practice Set-up

This is a variation of the previous practice (1a) and the practice set-up is exactly the same.

Description (1b)

1. The defensive midfielder **(3)** starts by dribbling forward and passing to the left forward **(10)**, who drops off to receive.

2. The left forward **(10)** lays the ball back for the forward run of the central midfielder **(5)**.

3. The central midfielder **(5)** passes the ball in between the 2 mannequins for the forward run of the left back **(26)**. The centre forward **(9)** runs towards the near post and the right forward **(11)** runs to the far post. The left forward **(10)** also moves into the box after his lay-off pass.

4. The left back **(26)** receives, dribbles the ball forward and cuts the ball back.

5. In this example, the ball is cut back for the centre forward **(9)**, who scores with a first time finish.

6. After the attack finishes, all of the players run back to their positions. The same sequence is repeated on the opposite side (right). It starts with the defensive midfielder **(3)** dribbling forward and passing to the right forward **(11)**, who drops back to receive.

Session for **JÜRGEN KLOPP** Tactics - Attacking on the Flanks Against Deep and Compact Defences

1c: Transfer Ball from One Side to the Other + Full Back's Cut Back

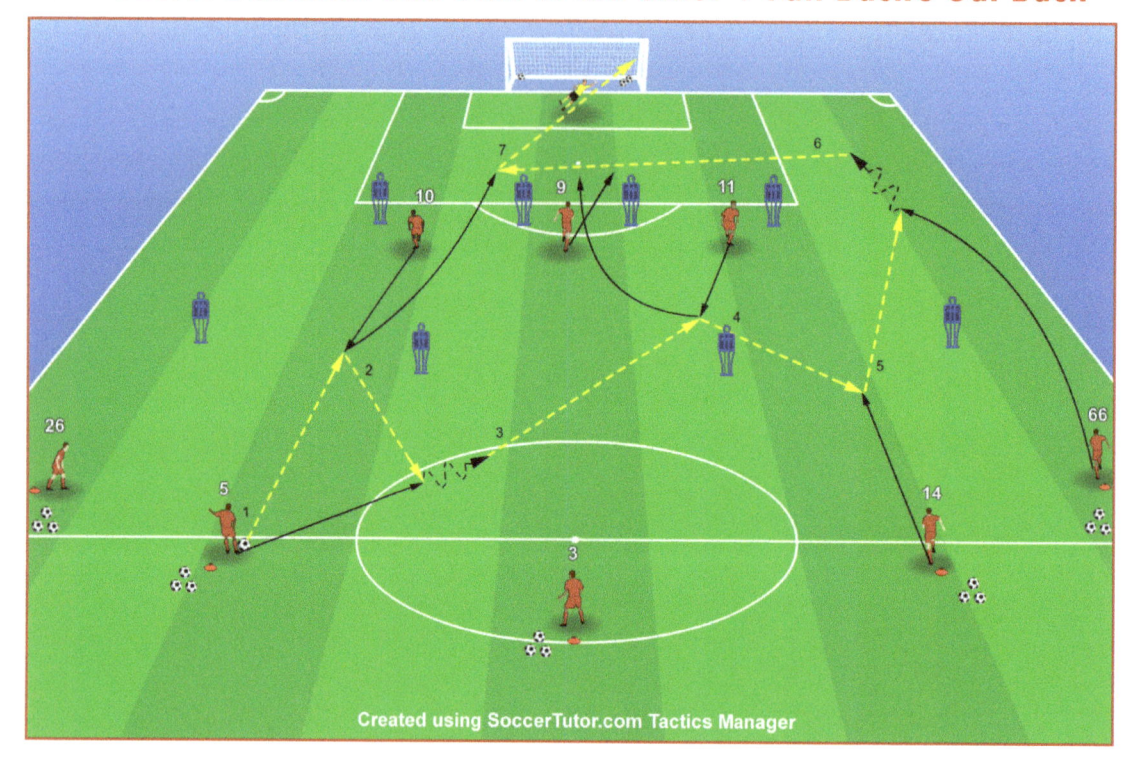

Practice Set-up

This is a variation of the previous 2 practices (1a & 1b), but the practice set-up is exactly the same.

Description (1c)

1. The central midfielder **(5)** starts by passing to the left forward **(10)**, who drops back to receive.

2. The left forward **(10)** lays the ball back for the central midfielder **(5)** to run onto (completing a one-two combination).

3. The central midfielder **(5)** passes across to the right forward **(11)**, who drops off to receive.

4. The right forward **(11)** lays the ball back for the run of the other central midfielder **(14)**.

5. The central midfielder **(14)** passes the ball in between the 2 mannequins for the forward run of the right back **(66)**.

6. The right back **(66)** receives, dribbles the ball forward and cuts the ball back. The centre forward **(9)** runs to the near post and the left forward **(10)** to the far post. The right forward **(11)** moves into the box after his lay-off pass.

7. In this example, the left forward **(10)** scores with a first time finish at the far post.

8. After the attack finishes, all the players run back to their positions. The same sequence is repeated from the opposite side (right).

Coaching Points

1. Accurate and well-weighted passes/crosses.
2. Quality first touch finishing in the box.
3. High intensity, concentration, and rhythm needed for all movements (synchronisation).
4. Communicate (verbal and visual) with heads up at all times.

Session for **JÜRGEN KLOPP** Tactics - Attacking on the Flanks Against Deep and Compact Defences

PROGRESSION
2. Combination Play for the Full Back to Receive in Behind Against a Compact Defence in a Time Limit Game

Reds have e.g. 5 mins to score as many goals as possible (Coaches feed balls)

Objective: Exploiting the full width of the pitch against a deep and compact defence.

Description
- In half a pitch (reduced length), mark out 2 wide zones for the full backs, as shown.
- The red attacking team have 2 full backs, 3 midfielders and 3 forwards from Liverpool's 4-3-3 formation, and the white defending team are in a 4-2 formation (+GK).
- This is a continuous game, and the Coaches have many balls. One of them starts by passing to a red player and the aim is to score as many goals as possible within the time limit e.g. 5 minutes.
- The reds must exploit the full width (wide zones) to play to either full back in behind, so they can deliver a cross into the box.
- Only the full backs (**No66** or **No.26**) can move into the wide zones.
- The white defending team's aim is to concede as few goals as possible within the time limit. If they win the ball, they pass to a Coach or kick the ball out of play. When this happens, a Coach passes a new ball in immediately and a new attack for the red team starts.

Coaching Points
1. The accuracy and weight of the passes and crosses need to be correct (in time and space).
2. Quality one touch finishing inside the box.
3. The players must communicate with their heads up and must be very focused.
4. The game must be executed with a high rhythm and a dynamic tempo.

SESSION 8C BASED ON THE TACTICS OF JÜRGEN KLOPP

Attacking on the Flank when Opponents Defend with 2 Players Out Wide

Session for **JÜRGEN KLOPP** Tactics - Attacking on the Flanks Against Deep and Compact Defences

SESSION FOR THIS TACTICAL SITUATION (3 PRACTICES)
1. Attacking on the Left Flank Against a Compact Defence in a Position Specific Conditioned Game

Description

- In half a pitch, we mark out 2 wide channels on the left, as shown. The same area on the right is a non-playing area.
- The red attacking team are in a 3-3-3 from Liverpool's 4-3-3 formation (with no right back involved). The white defending team are in a 3-3-1-1 formation (with no left back or left midfielder involved).
- Start with the GK and the reds exploit the full width on the left flank and use attacking combinations between the left back (26), left central midfielder (5) and left forward (10).
- These 3 players look to play through their opponent's defence (get in behind) and create goal scoring opportunities.
- In the diagram example, the left central midfielder (5) plays to the left forward (10) in behind, who cuts the ball back for the right central midfielder (14) to score.
- **RULES**: Maximum of 2 red players in each wide channel at a time (3 total across both) + only the white right back (2) and right midfielder (7) can defend in either channel.
- The white defending team aim to win the ball and then score within 10 seconds (counter).

Session for **JÜRGEN KLOPP** Tactics - Attacking on the Flanks Against Deep and Compact Defences

VARIATION
2. Attacking on the Right Flank Against a Compact Defence in a Position Specific Conditioned Game

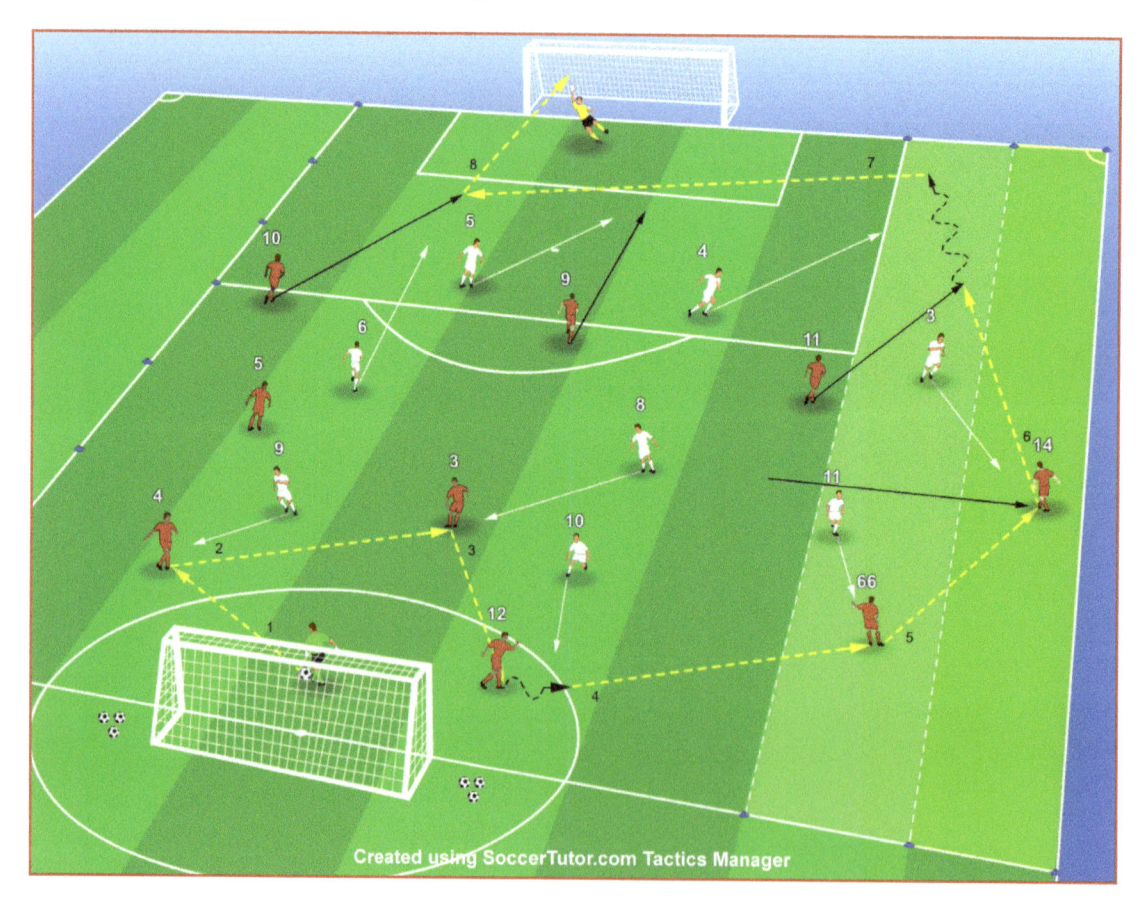

Description

- This is a variation of the practice on the previous page, and we now work on attacking on the right flank instead of the left.

- We replace the red left back with a right back **(66)** and the reds are still in a 3-3-3 from Liverpool's 4-3-3 formation

- We also replace the white right back and right midfielder with a left back (3) and left midfielder (11).

- The exact same aims and rules apply but the reds now work on 3 player combinations on the right flank.

- In the diagram example, the reds move the ball from left to right, and then the right central midfielder **(14)** plays to the right forward **(11)** in behind, who dribbles forward and delivers a low cross for the left forward **(10)** to score at the back post.

Session for JÜRGEN KLOPP Tactics - Attacking on the Flanks Against Deep and Compact Defences

PROGRESSION
3. Attacking on Both Flanks Against a Compact Defence in a Zonal 11v11 Tactical Game

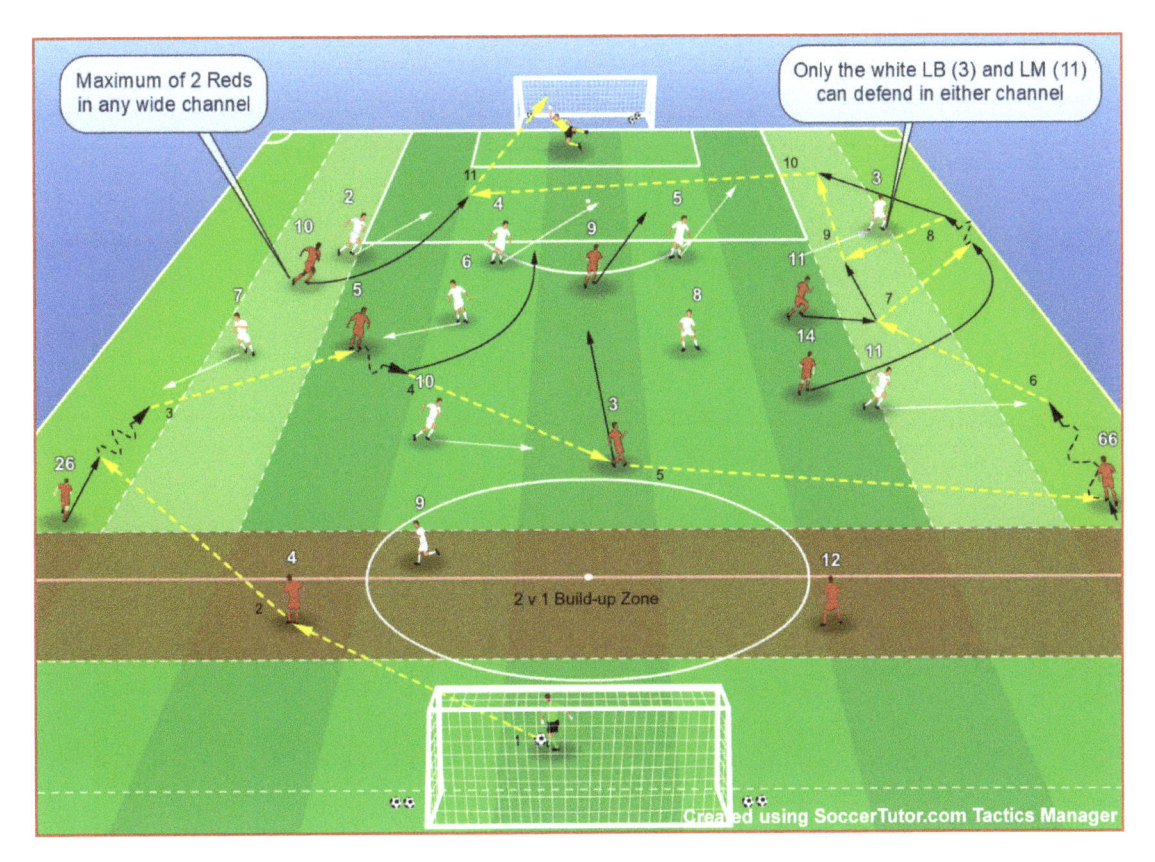

Maximum of 2 Reds in any wide channel

Only the white LB (3) and LM (11) can defend in either channel

2 v 1 Build-up Zone

Description

- In the final practice of this session, we now play an 11v11 game in half a pitch + 20 yards. Mark out a horizontal 10 yard zone and 4 wide channels (2 on each side), as shown.

- The game always starts with the red team's GK, who passes to a centre back (**No.4** or **No.5**) in the horizontal zone. Either the left back **(26)**, the right back **(66)** or defensive midfielder **(3)** move to help the red centre backs build up play if necessary.

- The reds exploit the full width on either flank and use attacking combinations between the full back, central midfielder and wide forward.

- These 3 players look to play through their opponent's defence (get in behind) and create goal scoring opportunities. The white defending team aim to win the ball and then score within 10 seconds (counter).

- In the diagram example, the right central midfielder **(14)** moves wide to receive and plays a one-two with the right forward **(11)** to get in behind. He then delivers a low cross for the left forward **(10)** to score at the back post.

- **RULES**: Maximum of 2 red players in each wide channel at a time (3 total across both) + only the white right back (2) and right midfielder (7) can defend in either channel.

TRANSITION FROM DEFENCE TO ATTACK

JÜRGEN KLOPP TACTICAL ANALYSIS

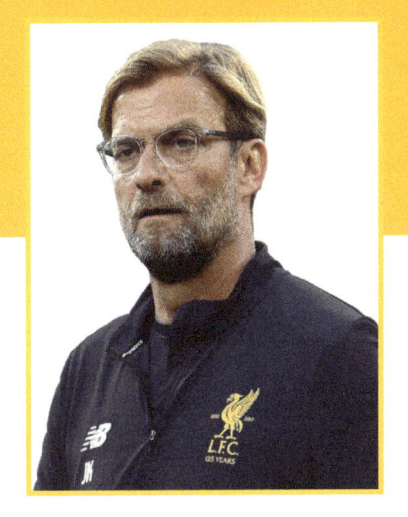

SOLUTION 9

Exploit Free Spaces in the Opposition's Half During a Counter Attack from the Low Zone

Content from analysis of Liverpool F.C. during the 2018-2019 Champions League winning season and the 2019-2020 Premier League winning season

- Analysis based on recurring patterns of play observed within the Liverpool team.
- Tactical solutions displayed as examples of the team's tactics being used effectively.
- Real match examples of Liverpool scoring a goal using this specific attacking tactical solution.
- Each action, pass, individual movement with or without the ball, and the positioning of each player on the pitch including their body shape, are presented.
- The analysis is then used to create a full progressive session to coach this tactical situation.

Tactical Solution 9 - Exploit Free Spaces During a Counter Attack from the Low Zone

Exploit Free Spaces in the Opposition's Half During a Counter Attack from the Low Zone

What?
Look to exploit free spaces in the opposition's half immediately after winning the ball.

Why?
The opposition have a lot of players in Liverpool's half with only 2 players (centre backs) at the back. When they lose the ball, they become a disorganised defence.

How?
A player receives out wide or in the centre part of the pitch, and then dribbles forward at speed. Teammates make fast supporting runs into the opponent's half to finish the counter attack as quickly as possible, often with 2-3 players combining.

Target Areas (Wide Areas)

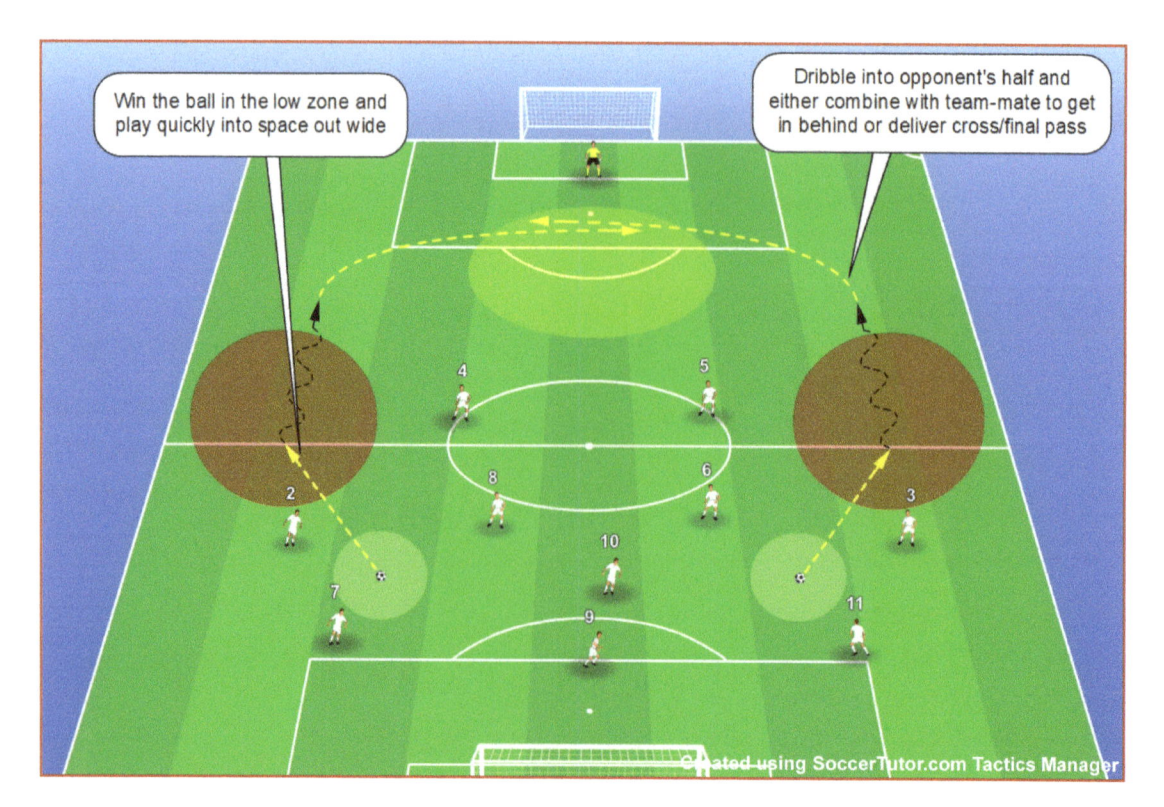

Win the ball in the low zone and play quickly into space out wide

Dribble into opponent's half and either combine with team-mate to get in behind or deliver cross/final pass

JÜRGEN KLOPP LIVERPOOL ATTACKING TACTICS

Tactical Solution 9 - Exploit Free Spaces During a Counter Attack from the Low Zone

Target Area (Through the Centre)

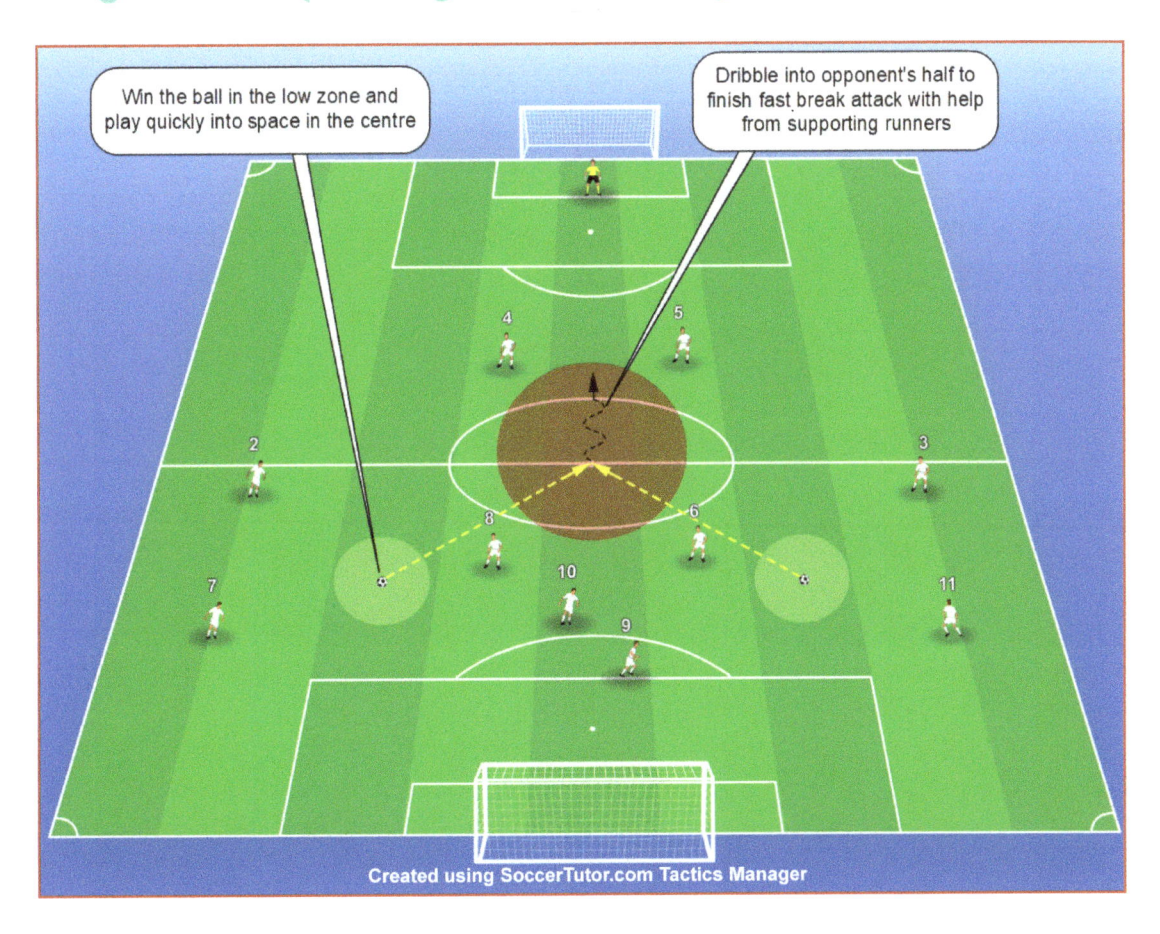

Win the ball in the low zone and play quickly into space in the centre

Dribble into opponent's half to finish fast break attack with help from supporting runners

JÜRGEN KLOPP LIVERPOOL ATTACKING TACTICS

Tactical Solution 9 - Exploit Free Spaces During a Counter Attack from the Low Zone

Tactical Solution A: Win the Ball, Pass Out Wide, Dribble the Ball Forward, and Cross into the Box

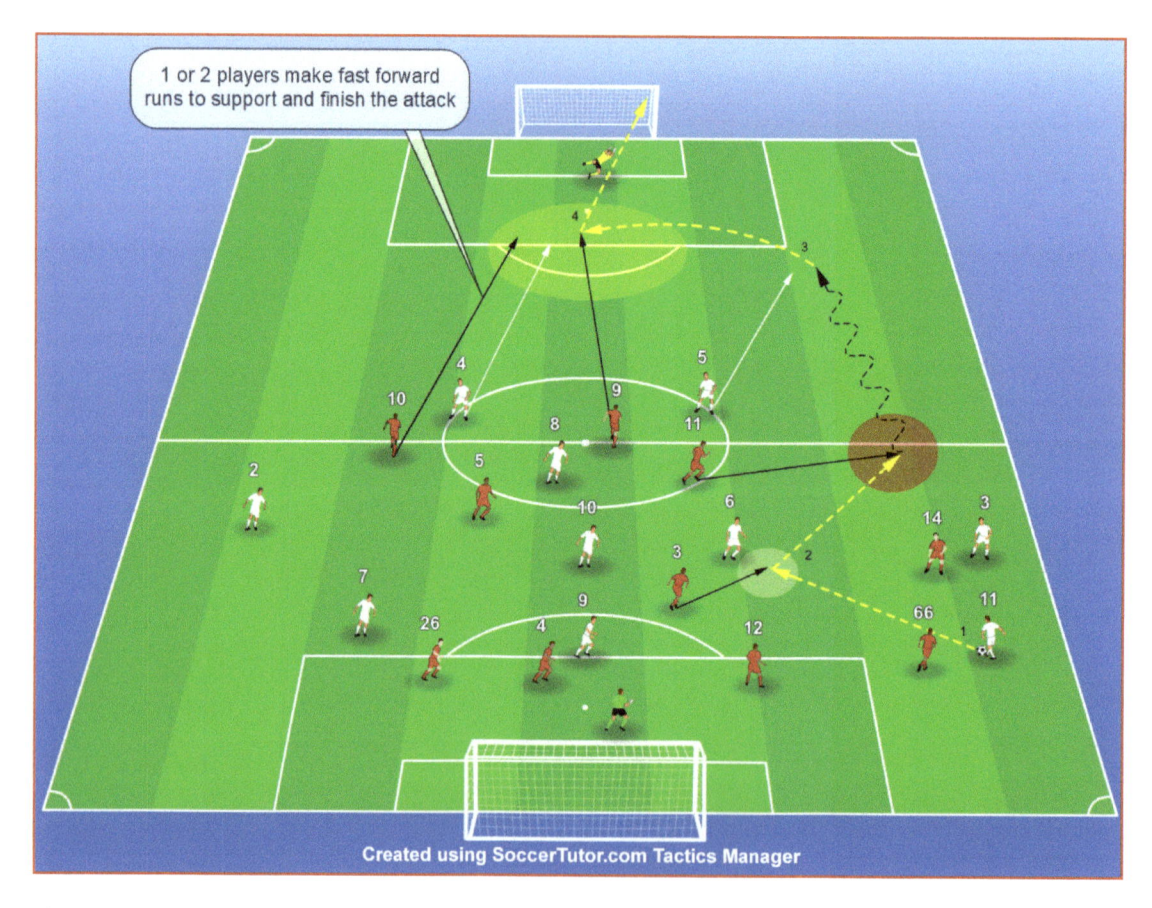

1 or 2 players make fast forward runs to support and finish the attack

The opposition are attacking with many players in Liverpool's half. Only the 2 white centre backs are in their own half and there is a lot of free space behind them.

In this example, the opposing winger's pass inside is intercepted by Liverpool's defensive midfielder **(3)** in the centre of the pitch.

When Liverpool win the ball in this kind of situation, the aim is most often to play a quick pass to a player out wide.

That player (right forward **No.11** e.g. **Salah**) has space to dribble forward with the ball at speed into the opposition's half.

At the same time, 1-2 players sprint forward to provide support and attacking solutions (taking up positions inside the box) to help finish the counter attack.

In this example, the centre forward **(9)** makes a good run into the centre of the box. The right forward **(11)** is tracked by the white centre back No.5, so delivers the ball into the box at the right time for the centre forward **(9)** to score.

Tactical Solution 9 - Exploit Free Spaces During a Counter Attack from the Low Zone

Tactical Solution B: Win the Ball, Pass Out Wide, Dribble the Ball Forward, One-Two to Get in Behind and Score

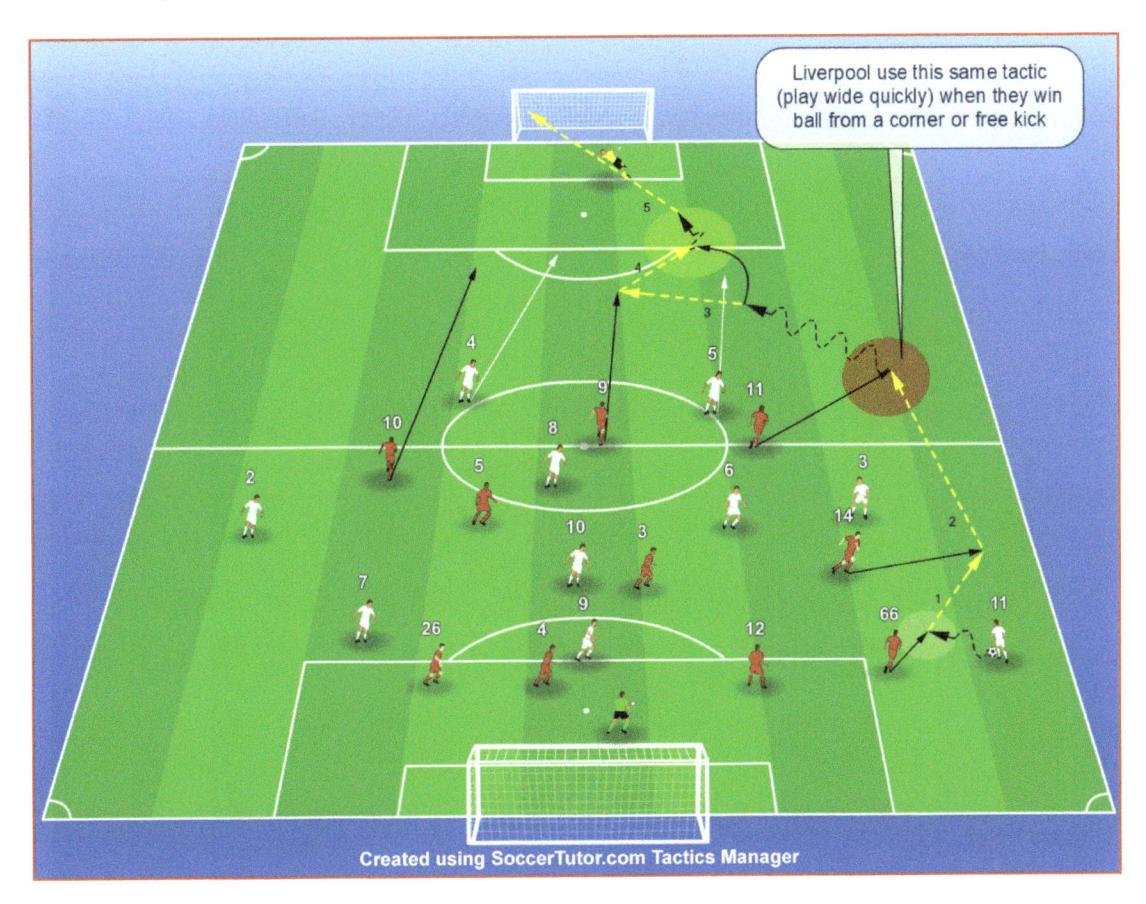

Tactical Solution B shows Liverpool in a very similar situation, winning the ball in the low zone again. This time however, the player dribbling forward decides to combine with a supporting teammate to receive in behind and score (instead of crossing the ball into the box). He can also choose to use an individual attack.

In this example, the opposing winger is tackled by Liverpool's right back **(66)**. He quickly passes to the central midfielder **(14)**, who moves close to the by-line to receive.

As mentioned in Tactical Solution A (previous page), Liverpool aim to exploit space out wide.

The central midfielder **(14)** passes forward to the right forward **(11)**, who moves to receive in the space out wide in the opponent's half. **No.11** has space to dribble forward with the ball at speed and the centre forward **(9)** sprints forward to provide support.

The right forward **(11)** is closed down, so he plays a one-two combination with the centre forward **(9)** to receive in behind, move forward with the ball, and then score past the GK.

Similar situations would occur when Liverpool won the ball back from their opponent's set-pieces. This would replicate the situation shown here of many opposing players pushed forward in their half, with only 2 players back to defend.

Tactical Solution 9 - Exploit Free Spaces During a Counter Attack from the Low Zone

Tactical Solution C (1): Win the Ball, Pass into the Centre, Dribble the Ball Forward, and Pass in Behind for Supporting Runners

The opposing centre backs are quite deep, so there is space for No.9 to receive in the centre

Tactical Solution C (1) again shows Liverpool winning the ball in the low zone.

Compared to the previous 2 examples (Tactical Solutions A and B), the 2 opposing white centre backs are in deeper positions when Liverpool's defensive midfielder (**3**) wins the ball.

In this situation, Liverpool's aim is to pass quickly to the centre forward (**9**) in the available space in the centre (red highlighted area).

In the diagram example, the defensive midfielder (**3**) intercepts the white right back's (**2**) pass. As he is closed down by the central midfielder (**8**), he passes quickly to the left forward (**10**).

From there, **No.10** executes the main aim in this situation, which is to play to the centre forward **No.9** in the available space.

Once **No.9** receives, he dribbles forward as the opposing centre backs back off towards their own goal.

3 Liverpool players make supporting runs, and the centre forward (**9**) has 2 options:

1. Pass in between the 2 centre backs and in behind for the run of the left forward (**10**).

2. Pass to the right of the centre backs and in behind for the run of the right forward (**11**).

Tactical Solution 9 - Exploit Free Spaces During a Counter Attack from the Low Zone

Tactical Solution C (2): Win the Ball and Pass in Behind to the Forward who Makes a Curved Run to Receive

The centre forward (9) makes a curved run to exploit this space and receive in behind

In this variation of the previous example (Tactical Solution C1), the centre forward **(9)** decides to move off into a wider position and into the available space away from the centre backs.

In the diagram example, the centre back **(12)** moves forward to intercept a long pass. He then passes quickly to the right forward **(11)**.

No.11 looks up, sees the curved run of the centre forward **(9)** into the space on the right side, and then plays a well-weighted pass into his path.

No.9 is able to receive in space and use his speed to dribble into the box ahead of the centre backs and score past the GK.

The 2 wide forwards **(10 & 11)** have again made supporting runs to help finish the counter attack if they are needed.

JÜRGEN KLOPP LIVERPOOL ATTACKING TACTICS

Statistical Analysis of Liverpool Exploiting Free Spaces During Counter Attacks from the Low Zone

Liverpool scored **20 goals** in this tactical situation
(Premier League and Champions League 2018-2019 and 2019-2020 seasons)

WIN BALL IN LOW ZONE VS. DISORGANISED OPPONENTS

EXPLOIT FREE SPACES IN OPPONENT'S HALF (COUNTER ATTACK)

DATE	HOME	AWAY	SCORE	GOAL (MIN)	SCORER	ASSIST
20th Aug 2018	Crystal Palace	Liverpool	0-2	0-2 (90 +3')	**Mané**	Salah
27th Oct 2018	Liverpool	Cardiff	4-1	4-1 (87')	**Mané** *	Salah
11th Nov 2018	Liverpool	Fulham	2-0	1-0 (41')	**Salah**	A-Arnold
24th Nov 2018	Watford	Liverpool	0-3	0-3 (88')	**Firmino**	Mané
5th Dec 2018	Burnley	Liverpool	1-3	1-3 (90 +1')	**Shaqiri**	Salah
8th Dec 2018	Bournemouth	Liverpool	0-4	0-2 (48')	**Salah**	Firmino
5th Apr 2019	Southampton	Liverpool	1-3	1-2 (80')	**Salah**	Henderson
17th Apr 2019	Porto	Liverpool	1-4	0-2 (65')	**Salah**	A-Arnold
31st Aug 2019	Burnley	Liverpool	0-3	0-3 (80')	**Firmino**	Salah
10th Nov 2019	Liverpool	Man City	3-1	1-0 (06')	**Fabinho**	
4th Dec 2019	Liverpool	Everton	5-2	1-0 (06')	**Origi**	Mané
4th Dec 2019	Liverpool	Everton	5-2	2-0 (17')	**Shaqiri**	Mané
4th Dec 2019	Liverpool	Everton	5-2	4-1 (45')	**Mané**	A-Arnold
24th Dec 2019	Liverpool	Watford	2-0	1-0 (38')	**Salah**	Mané
2nd Jan 2020	Liverpool	Sheffield Utd	2-0	2-0 (64')	**Mané** *	Salah
19th Jan 2020	Liverpool	Man Utd	2-0	2-0 (90 +3')	**Salah**	Alisson
29th Jan 2020	West Ham	Liverpool	0-2	0-2 (52')	**Chamberlain**	Salah
1st Feb 2020	Liverpool	Southampton	4-0	4-0 (90')	**Salah**	Firmino
24th Jun 2020	Liverpool	Crystal Palace	4-0	4-0 (69')	**Mané**	Salah
22nd Jul 2020	Liverpool	Chelsea	5-3	5-3 (84')	**Chamberlain** *	Robertson

* The full analysis of these goals is shown on the following pages...

Tactical Solution 9 - Exploit Free Spaces During a Counter Attack from the Low Zone

Analysis from Liverpool 5-3 Chelsea (Chamberlain 84') - 22nd July 2020, Premier League

Tactical Solution A: Win the Ball, Pass Out Wide, Dribble the Ball Forward, and Cross into the Box

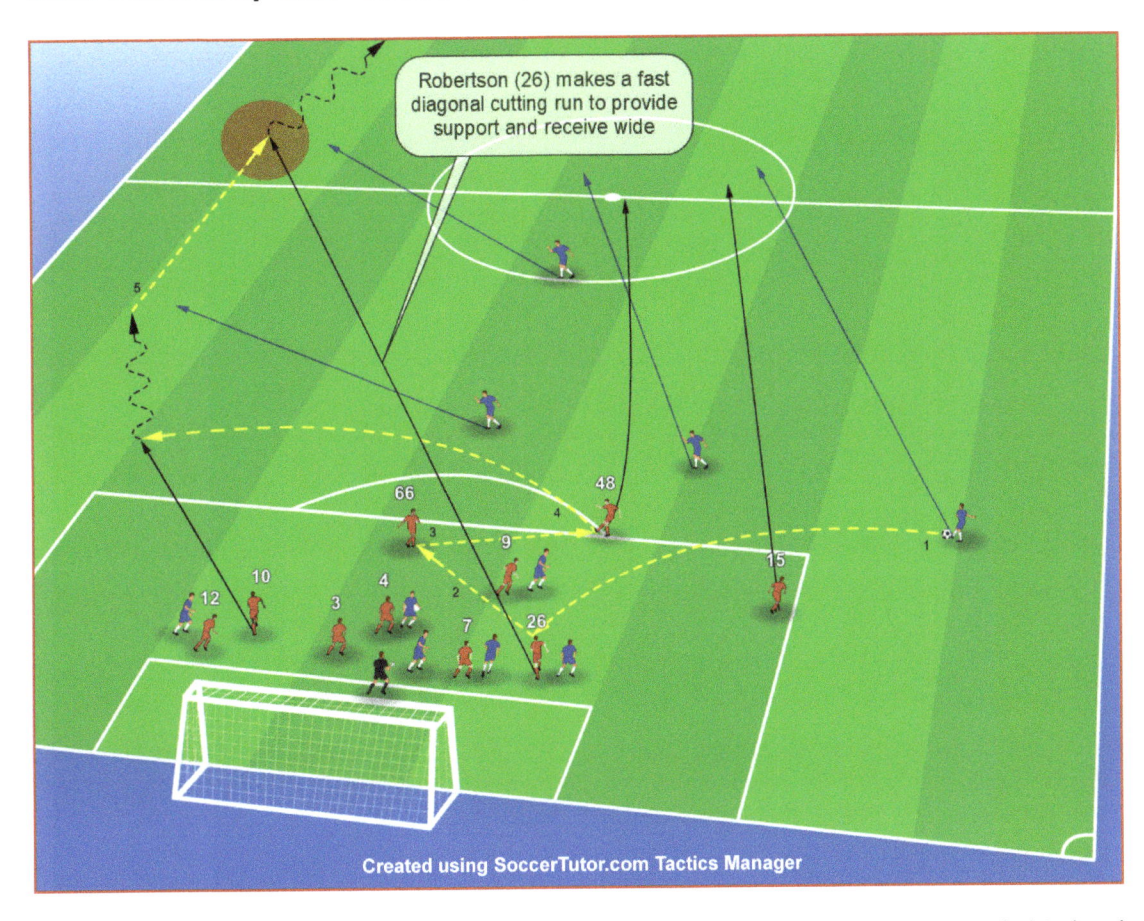

Liverpool left back **Robertson (26)** heads the ball clear from Chelsea's free kick to right back **A-Arnold (66)**. He moves the ball to **Jones (48)** on the edge of the box, who passes out wide and into the path of left forward **Mané (10)**.

Robertson (26) makes a fast diagonal cutting run behind the opponent to provide support and an attacking solution. **Mané (10)** passes into the channel for him to run onto.

Robertson (26) shows great acceleration to dribble past the approaching Chelsea centre back.

He wins his 1 v 1 battle easily to get in behind and has all the Chelsea players running back towards their own goal.

Both central midfielders **Jones (48)** and **Chamberlain (15)** sprint forward to provide support and hopefully help finish the attack.

JÜRGEN KLOPP LIVERPOOL ATTACKING TACTICS

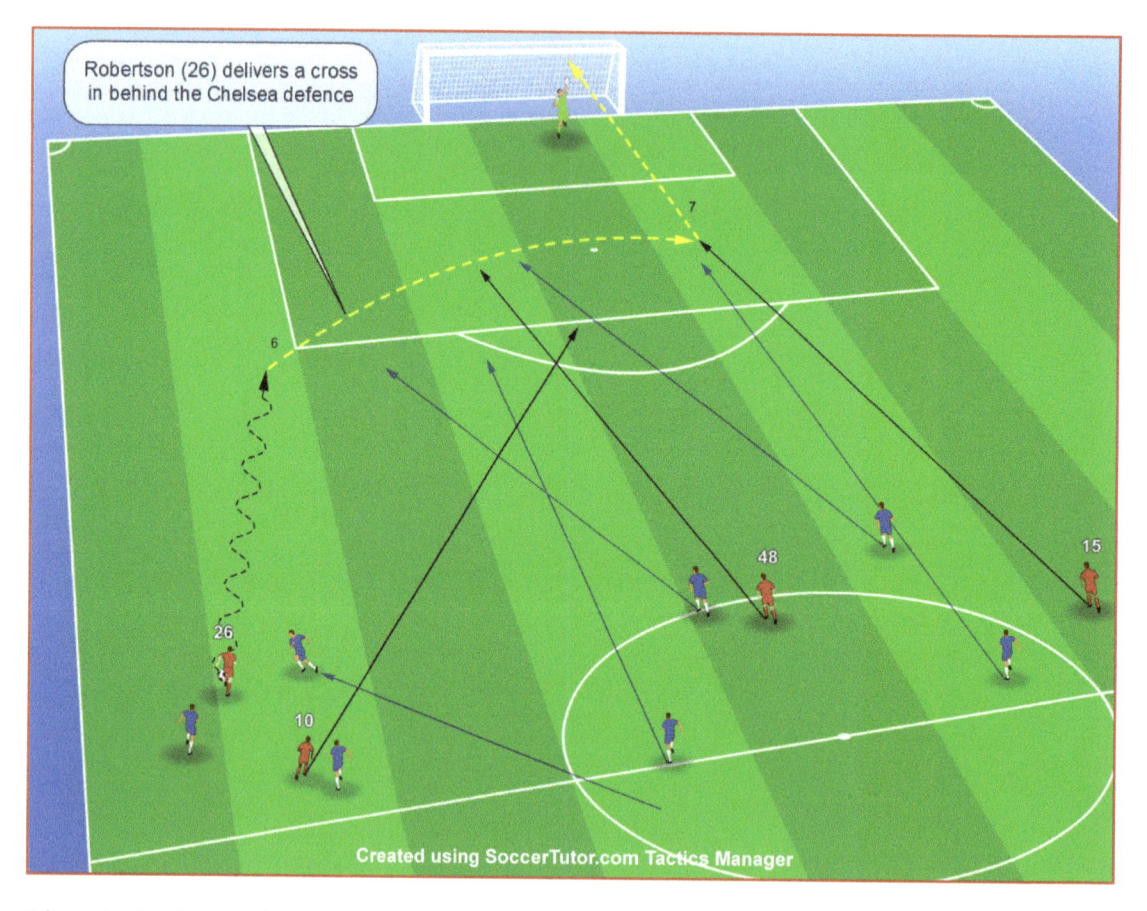

Tactical Solution 9 - Exploit Free Spaces During a Counter Attack from the Low Zone

After winning his 1 v 1 battle, **Robertson (26)** dribbles up to the box and delivers a cross in the channel between the Chelsea defensive line and the GK.

Jones (48) and **Chamberlain (15)** make runs into the box to try and score. **Mané (10)** also sprints forward to provide support.

The ball reaches **Chamberlain (15)** towards the back post, who finishes very well with a first time shot.

Tactical Solution 9 - Exploit Free Spaces During a Counter Attack from the Low Zone

Analysis from Liverpool 2-0 Sheffield Utd (Mané 64') - 2nd Jan 2020, Premier League

Tactical Solution B: Win the Ball, Pass Out Wide, Dribble the Ball Forward, One-Two to Get in Behind and Score

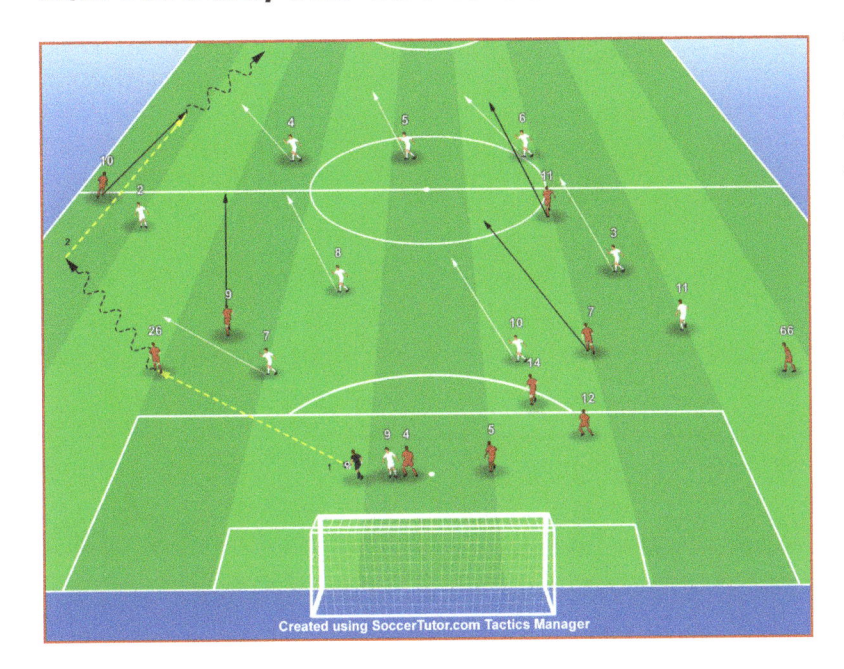

The GK **Alisson** has the ball after a Sheffield Utd attack. Liverpool look to act quickly and score with a fast counter attack before the Sheffield United players can get back into good defensive positions.

Alisson rolls the ball out to left back **Robertson (26)**, who dribbles forward towards the side-line. The left forward **Mané (10)** sprints forward to receive the ball in a wide position in Sheffield Utd's half.

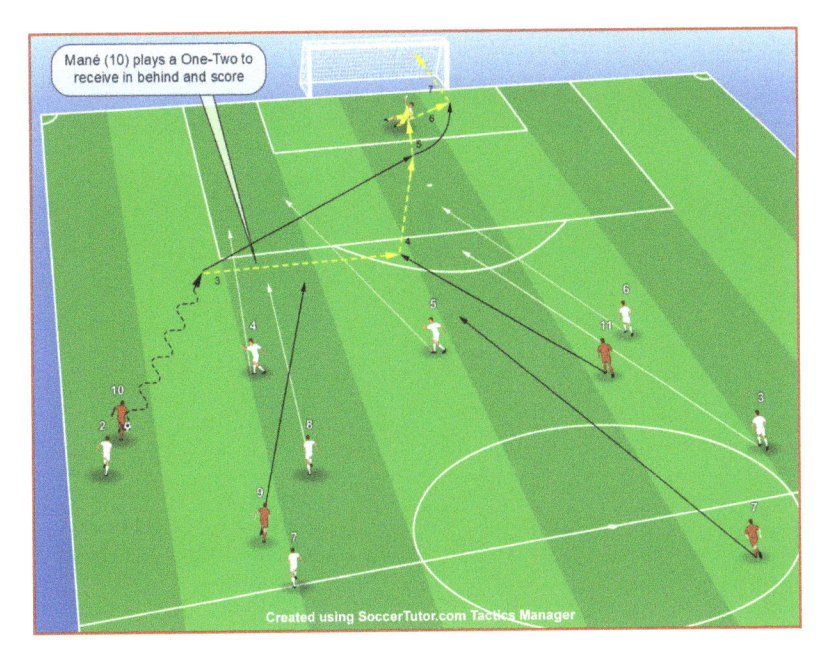

Mané (10) dribbles up to the box and then passes inside to **Salah (11)** at the edge of the box. **Firmino (9)** and **Milner (7)** have also sprinted forward to provide support/options.

Mané (10) runs in behind to receive the return pass and complete the one-two combination.

Mané (10) slides in to finish and the GK saves the ball. It bounces to the right and **Mané (10)** is able to get up and score easily in the empty net.

JÜRGEN KLOPP LIVERPOOL ATTACKING TACTICS

Tactical Solution 9 - Exploit Free Spaces During a Counter Attack from the Low Zone

Analysis from Liverpool 4-1 Cardiff (Mané 87') - 27th Oct 2018, Premier League

Tactical Solution C: Win the Ball, Pass into the Centre, Dribble Forward, and Pass in Behind for Supporting Runner

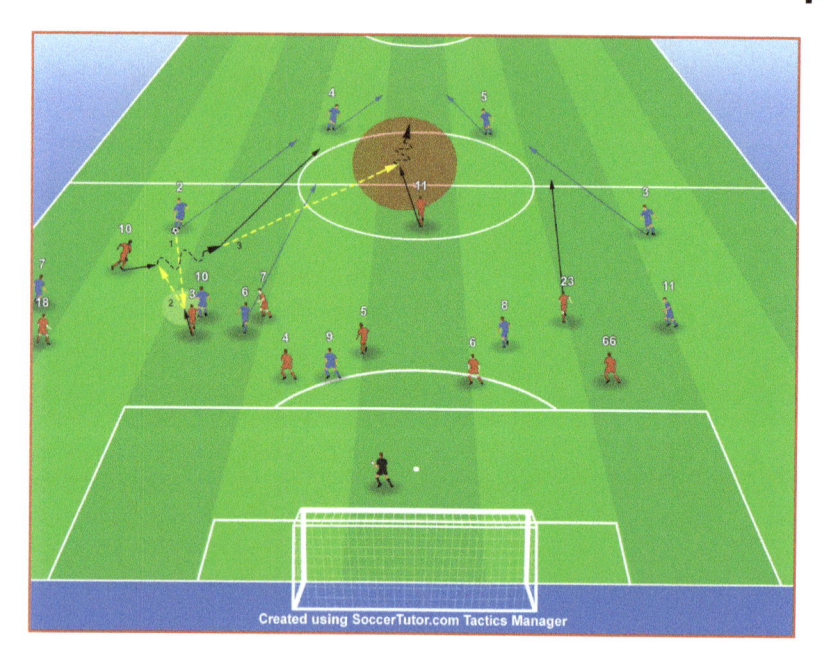

In this example, the defensive midfielder **Fabinho (3)** sprints forward and wins the ball before Cardiff's No.10 receives the pass and the ball goes to left forward **Mané (10)**.

From there, **Mané (10)** dribbles inside and passes to the centre forward **Salah (11)** in the available space.

Salah (11) dribbles forward as the opposing centre backs back off towards their own goal.

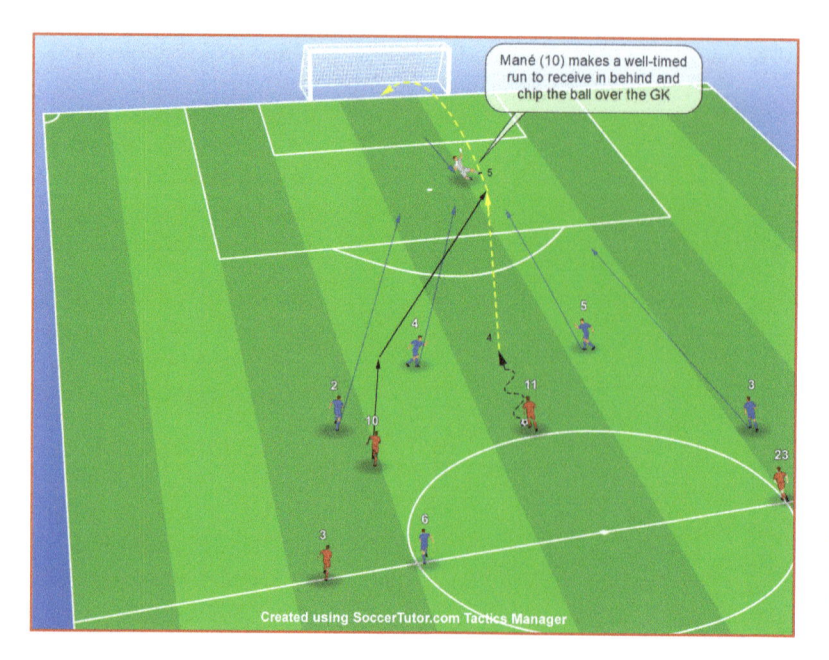

3 Liverpool players make supporting runs into the opponent's half to help finish the attack.

Salah (11) dribbles forward with the opposing centre backs still moving towards their own goal.

Mané (10) makes two intelligent movements to stay onside and receive the final pass in behind (and in the box). As the GK closes him down, he cleverly chips it over him to score.

SESSION 9 BASED ON THE TACTICS OF JÜRGEN KLOPP

Exploit Free Spaces in the Opposition's Half During a Counter Attack from the Low Zone

Session for **JÜRGEN KLOPP** Tactics - Exploit Free Spaces During a Counter Attack from Low Zone

SESSION FOR THIS TACTICAL SITUATION (4 PRACTICES)
1. Fast Break Attack from a Wide Position in an Unopposed Finishing Practice

1a: Cross into the Box

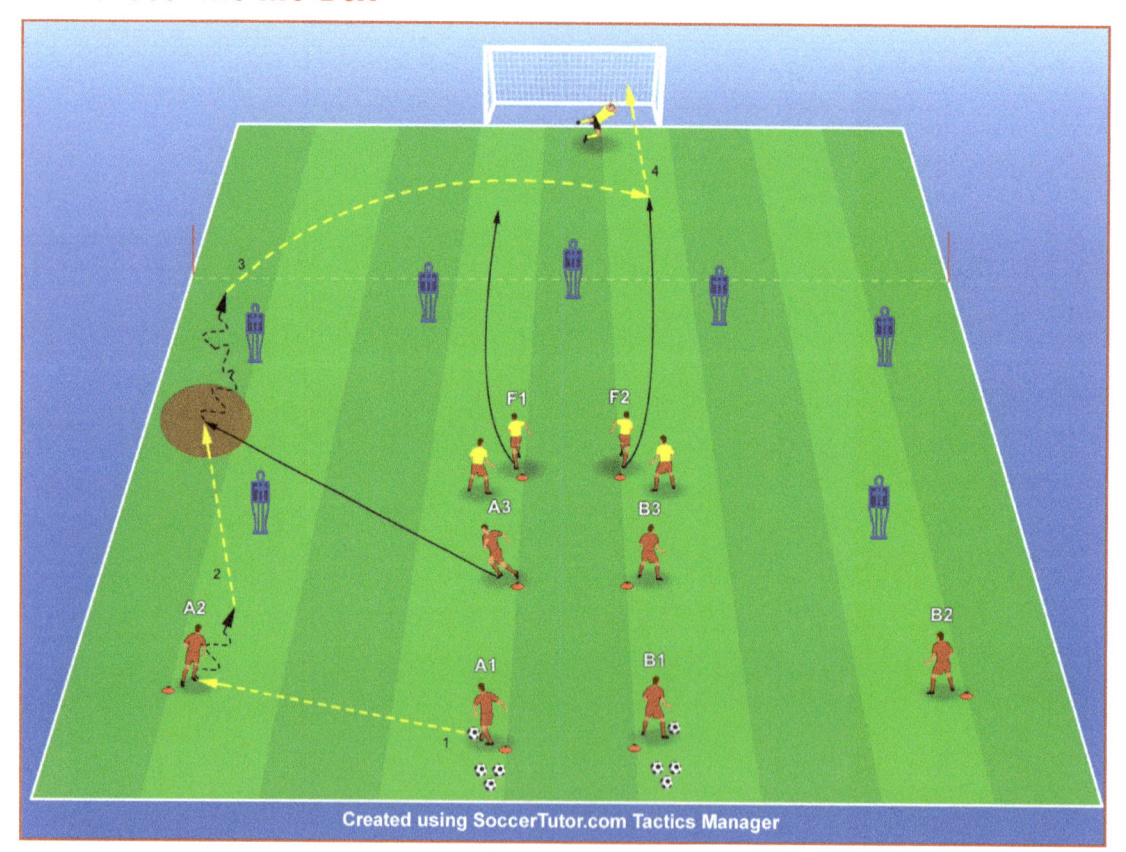

Description (1a)

In a 45 x 55 yard area, we have 7 mannequins and a large goal + GK. The 10 players start in the positions next to the cones, as shown.

The practice starts from either side (left side in diagram example).

1. Player 1 passes to Player 2.
2. Player 2 dribbles forward and Player 3 makes a fast diagonal cutting run in behind the mannequin to support him.
3. Player 2 passes the ball to Player 3.
4. Player 3 receives and dribbles at the next mannequin. At the right time, he dribbles past the mannequin (1 v 1). F1 and F2 sprint forward to support the attack.
5. Player 3 delivers a cross into the end zone for either F1 or F2 player to score.
6. When the attack is finished, the practice continues with the exact same sequence from the right side.

JÜRGEN KLOPP LIVERPOOL ATTACKING TACTICS

Session for **JÜRGEN KLOPP** Tactics - Exploit Free Spaces During a Counter Attack from Low Zone

1b: One-Two to Get in Behind and Score

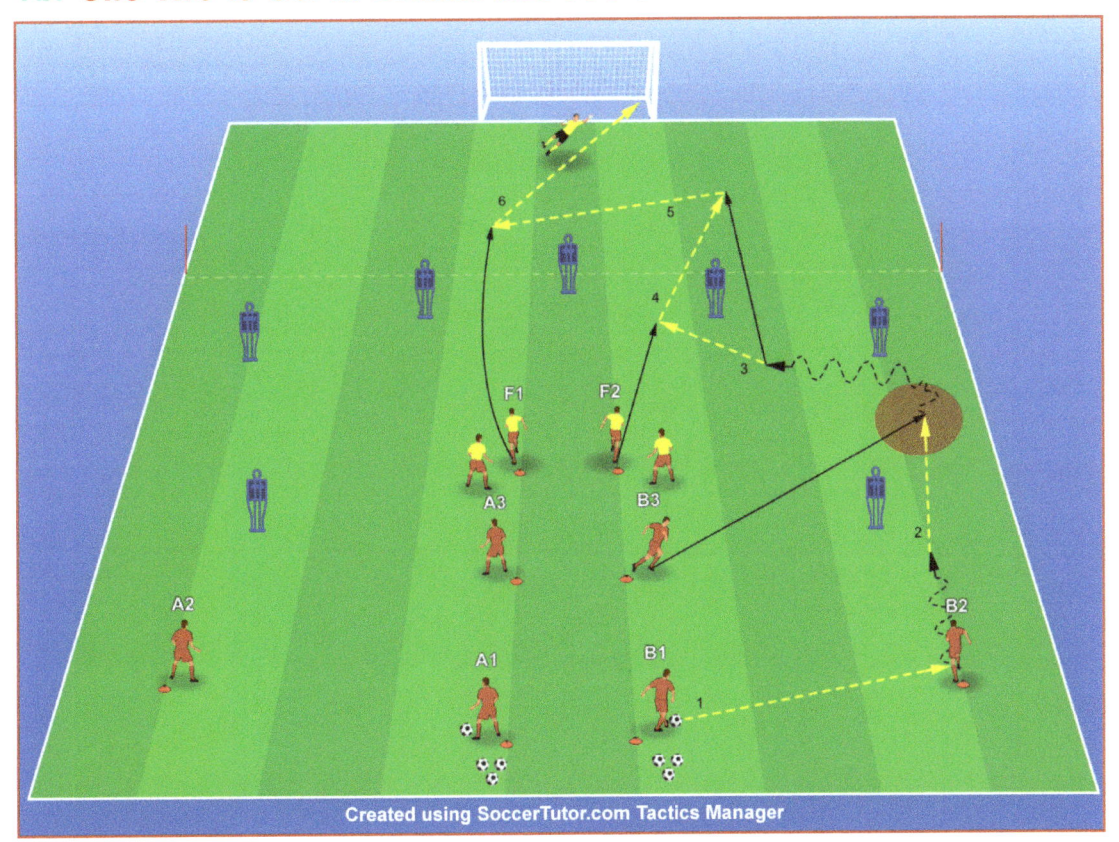

Description (1b)

In this variation, everything works exactly the same way up until Player 3 makes a cutting run and receives Player 2's pass.

1-3. Same as previous variation (1a).

4. Player 3 receives and dribbles inside past the mannequin.

5. Approaching the next mannequin, Player 3 then plays a one-two with F2, who has sprinted forward.

6. Player 3 receives the return pass in behind the defensive line and inside the end zone.

7. Player 3 either shoots or passes across F1 to score.

8. When the attack is finished, the practice continues with the exact same sequence from the left side.

Coaching Points

1. Passes need to be well-weighted and aimed just in front of their teammates, so they can step forward and receive.
2. The practice should be done at a high tempo throughout.
3. The key is the rhythm and timing of the movements, together with the passes.
4. Synchronisation in the movements and actions of all players.

Session for **JÜRGEN KLOPP** Tactics - Exploit Free Spaces During a Counter Attack from Low Zone

PROGRESSION
2. Fast Break Attack from a Wide Position in a High Intensity Functional Transition Game

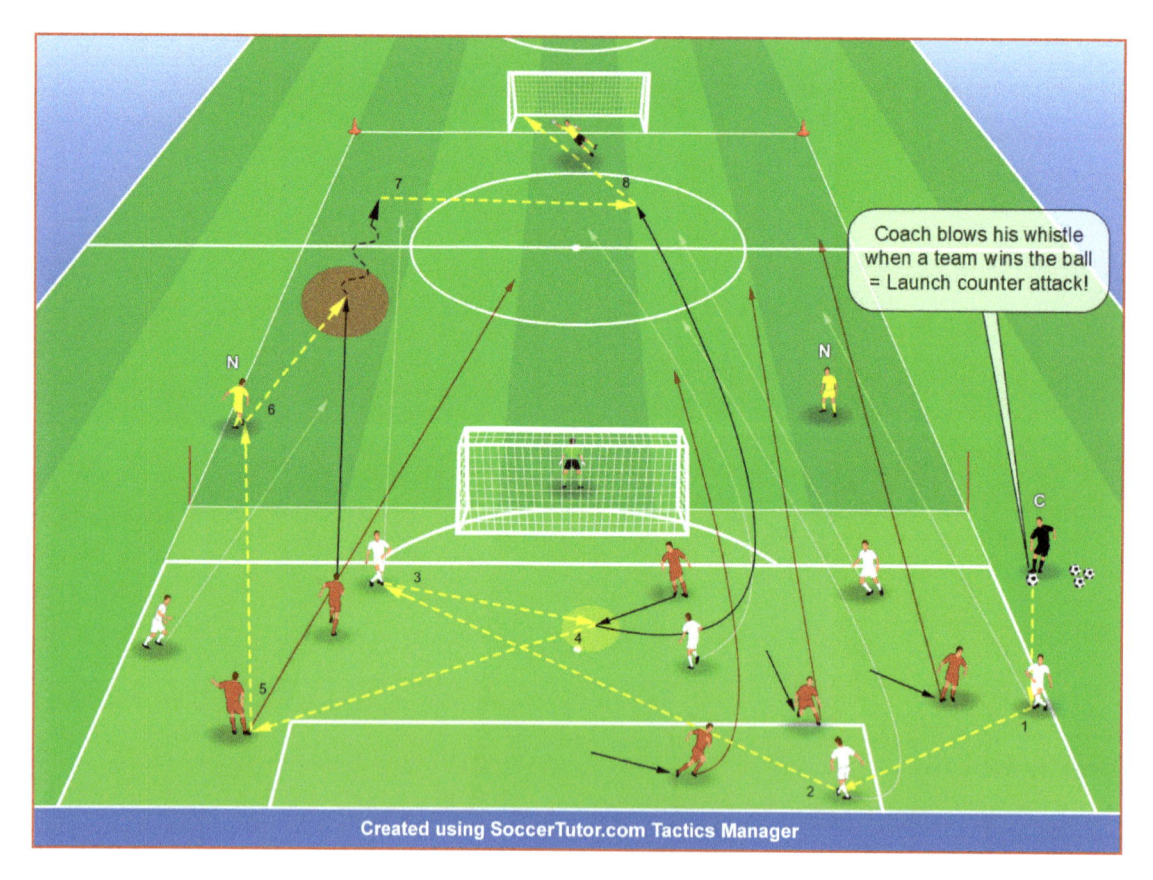

Coach blows his whistle when a team wins the ball = Launch counter attack!

Description

- In the large zone, there are 2 large goals with GKs + 2 yellow neutral players. In the small zone, we start with a 6v6 situation.

- The practice starts in the small zone with the Coach's pass and one team in possession (whites). The 6 white players aim to complete 8 passes (1 point).

- When the Coach blow his whistle, the team in possession try to pass to a neutral player as quickly as possible. The Coach tries to blow his whistle at the moment a team wins the ball, as we are focusing on counter attacks.

- All players move into the large zone. The reds win the ball in this example and their players sprint forward to score on the counter attack.

- The neutral player (limited to 2 touches) passes into the path of a red player's run. That player dribbles forward from a wide position and either delivers a cross or combines with teammates to create a chance and score (see examples on previous 2 pages).

- The white team must track back and defend their goal. If they win the ball back, they try to score themselves in the other goal.

Session for **JÜRGEN KLOPP** Tactics - Exploit Free Spaces During a Counter Attack from Low Zone

PROGRESSION
3. Exploiting Free Space Out Wide During a Counter Attack from the Low Zone in an 11v11 Dynamic Game

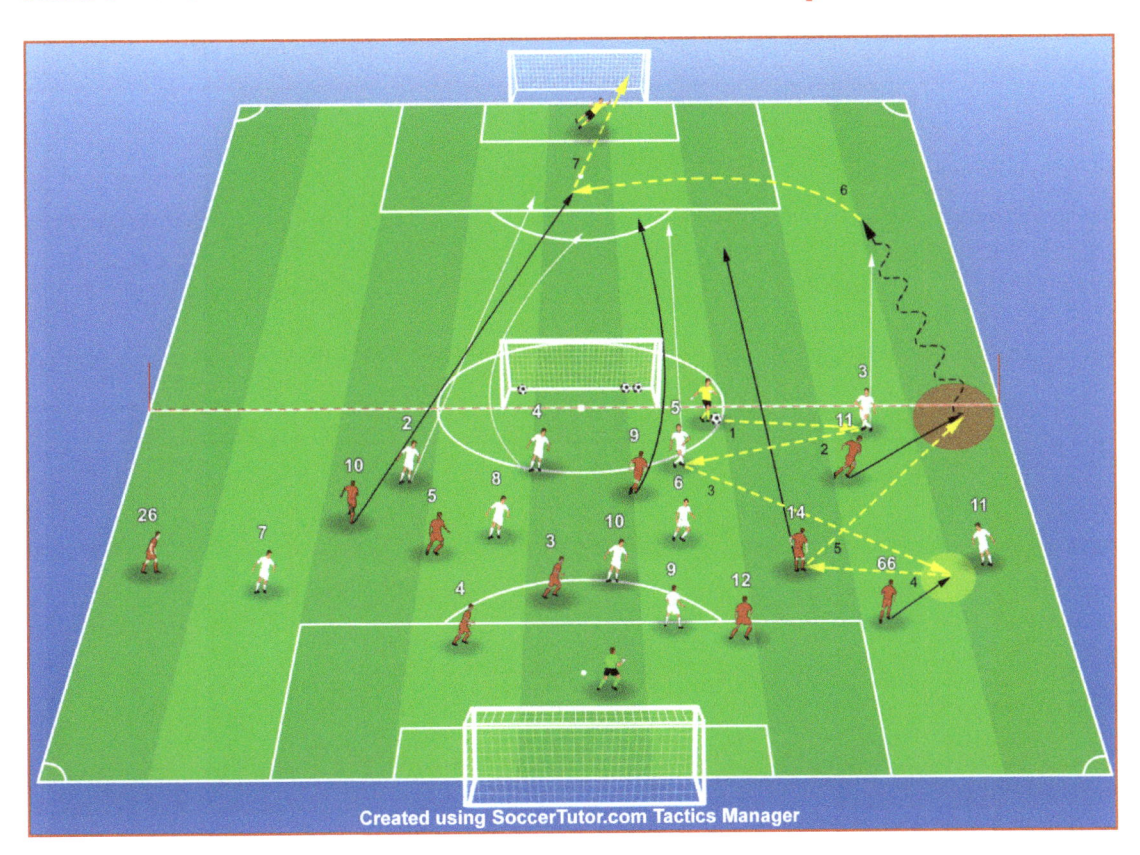

Description
- In this progression, there are 3 large goals with GKs and 2 teams of 10 outfield players (10v10) on a full pitch. The reds use Liverpool's 4-3-3 and the whites use the 4-4-2.
- The practice starts with the white GK and we play a normal 11v11 game in half a pitch.
- When the red team win the ball and the Coach decides to blow his whistle, the reds exploit the space in the other half of the pitch with a fast break attack (counter attack).
- They initially play the ball wide. The player that receives (**No.11** in diagram) dribbles forward and either delivers a cross, combines with teammates to create an opportunity, or uses an individual attack (see analysis examples and previous practices).
- When the attack finishes or the ball goes out of play, the team restarts in the same way. Change the team roles after a set time.

Rules
1. All players have 2-3 touches in the first phase but unlimited touches for the counter attack.
2. Make sure there is a time limit to finish the counter attack e.g. 12-15 seconds.

Session for **JÜRGEN KLOPP** Tactics - Exploit Free Spaces During a Counter Attack from Low Zone

4. Exploiting Free Space in the Centre During a Counter Attack from the Low Zone in an 11 v 11 Two Zone Game

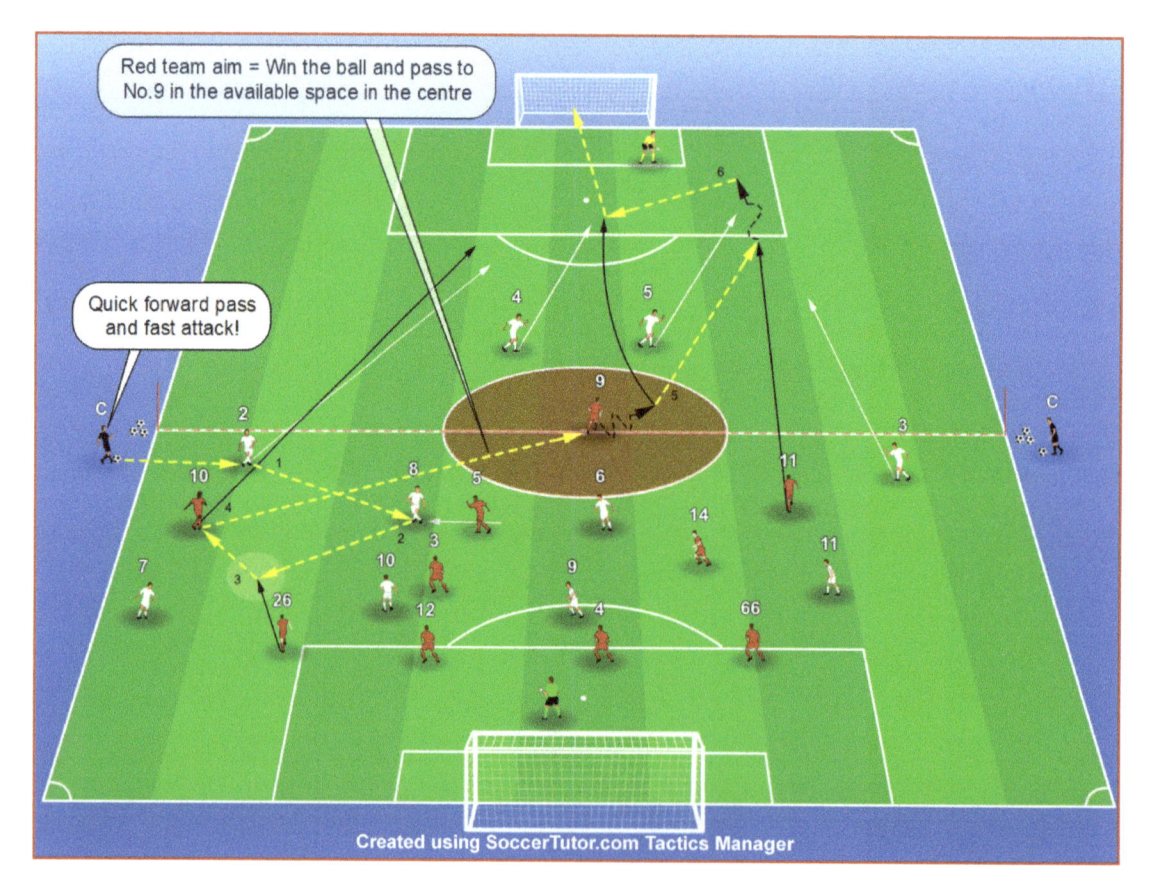

Description

- In this final practice of the session, we work on exploiting free space in the centre during a counter attack when the opposing centre backs are in deeper positions within their own half.
- Divide the pitch into 2 halves, as shown.
- The red team are in Liverpool's 4-3-3 formation and the whites are in whichever formation you want to practice playing against e.g. 4-2-3-1 in diagram example.
- The Coach starts by passing to a white full back. The white team attack with 8 outfield players and try to score.
- The red team's aims is to win the ball and then pass to the centre forward (**9**) in the available space in the centre.
- Once **No.9** receives, he dribbles forward as the opposing centre backs back off towards their own goal. At least 2 red players (**No.10** & **No.11** in diagram) sprint forward to provide support and help finish the fast break attack.

Coaching Points

1. See analysis for counter attack examples.
2. Defend: Keep compact with small distances and close the passing channels in front of box.
3. Attack: Quick forward pass, and fast attack!

JÜRGEN KLOPP
TACTICAL ANALYSIS

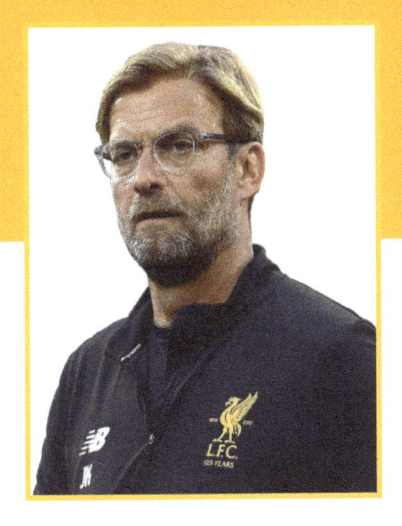

SOLUTION 10

Exploit Unbalanced Opponents in the Transition to Attack from the Middle Zone

Content from analysis of Liverpool F.C. during the 2018-2019 Champions League winning season and the 2019-2020 Premier League winning season

- Analysis based on recurring patterns of play observed within the Liverpool team.
- Tactical solutions displayed as examples of the team's tactics being used effectively.
- Real match examples of Liverpool scoring a goal using this specific attacking tactical solution.
- Each action, pass, individual movement with or without the ball, and the positioning of each player on the pitch including their body shape, are presented.
- The analysis is then used to create a full progressive session to coach this tactical situation.

Tactical Solution 10 - Transition to Attack from Middle Zone (Unbalanced Opponents)

Exploit Unbalanced Opponents in the Transition to Attack from the Middle Zone

What?

Liverpool look to take immediate advantage of their opponent's defensive imbalance.

Why?

The opposition have lost the ball and are positioned in such a way that leaves space to exploit in between their defenders and in behind.

How?

Fast attack immediately after winning the ball and exploit the free spaces in between the centre backs and full backs, or between the 2 centre backs (see both diagram examples).

Target Areas (Between Full Back and Centre Back)

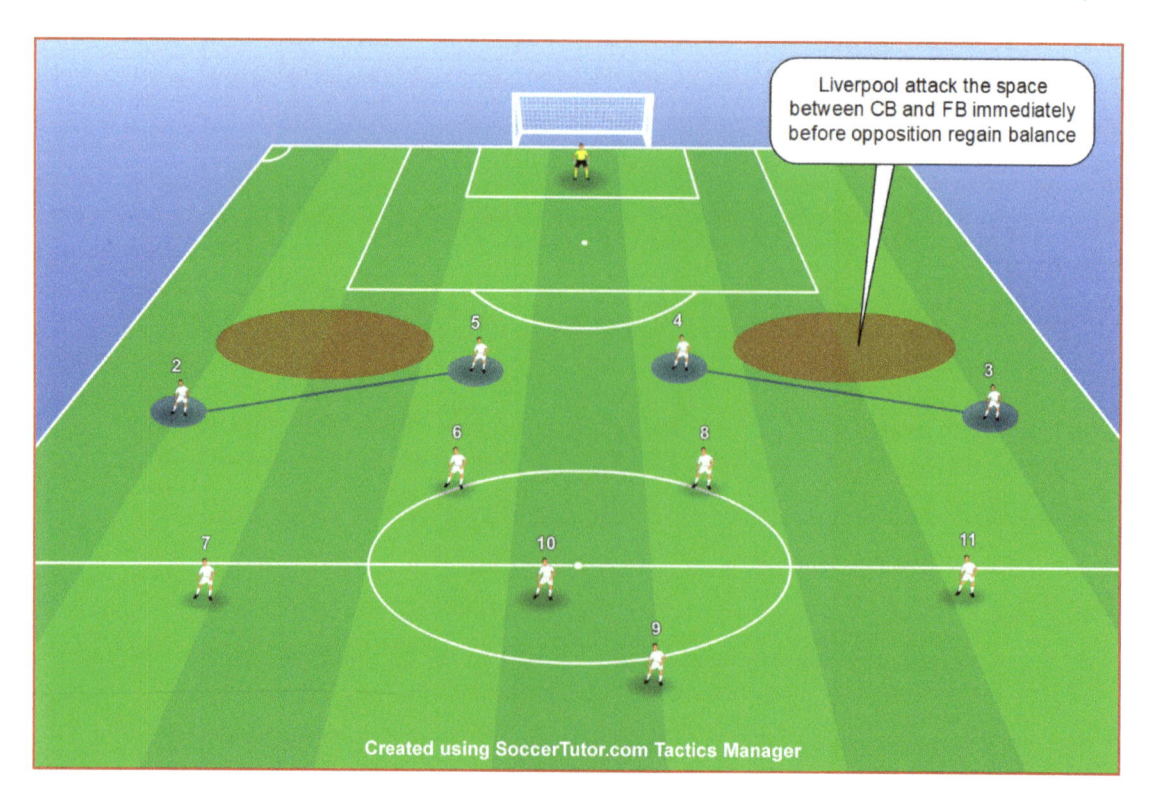

Liverpool attack the space between CB and FB immediately before opposition regain balance

Tactical Solution 10 - Transition to Attack from Middle Zone (Unbalanced Opponents)

Target Areas (in Between the 2 Centre Backs)

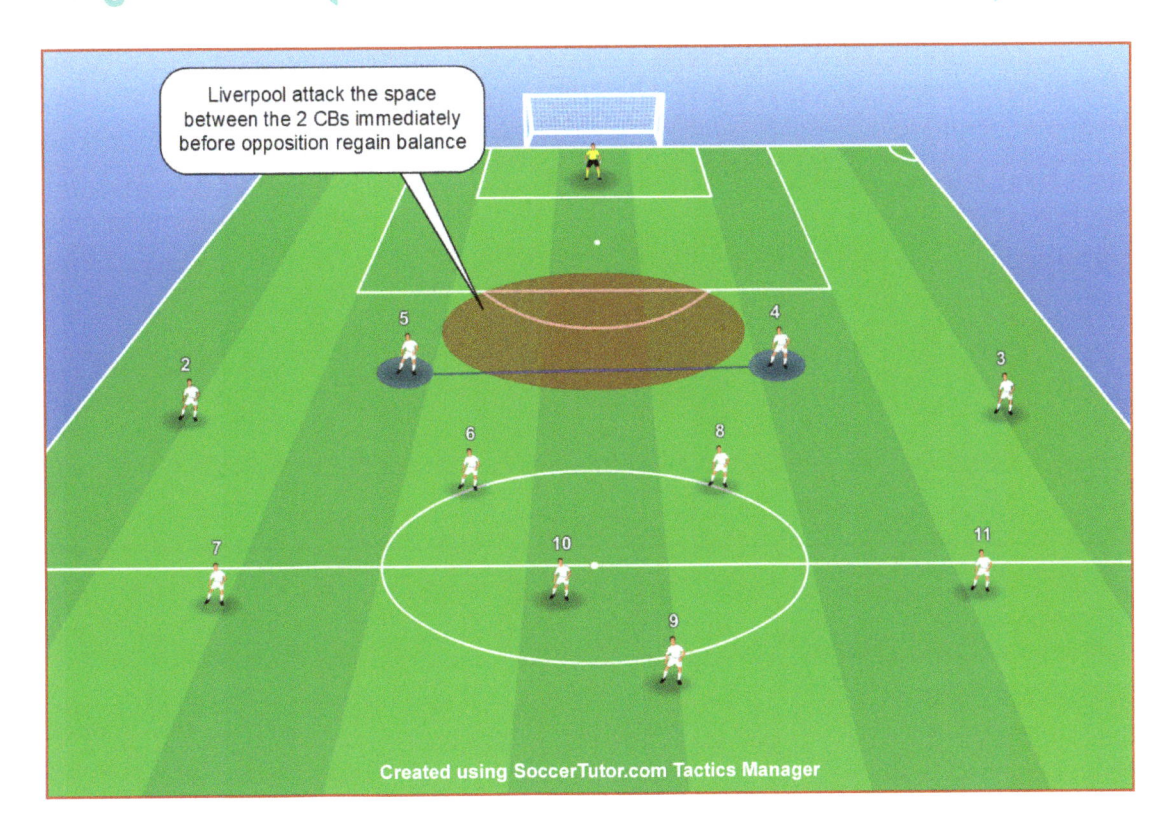

Liverpool attack the space between the 2 CBs immediately before opposition regain balance

Tactical Solution 10 - Transition to Attack from Middle Zone (Unbalanced Opponents)

Tactical Solution A: Win Ball in Middle Zone + Fast Break Attack to Exploit the Space in Between the Centre Back and Full Back

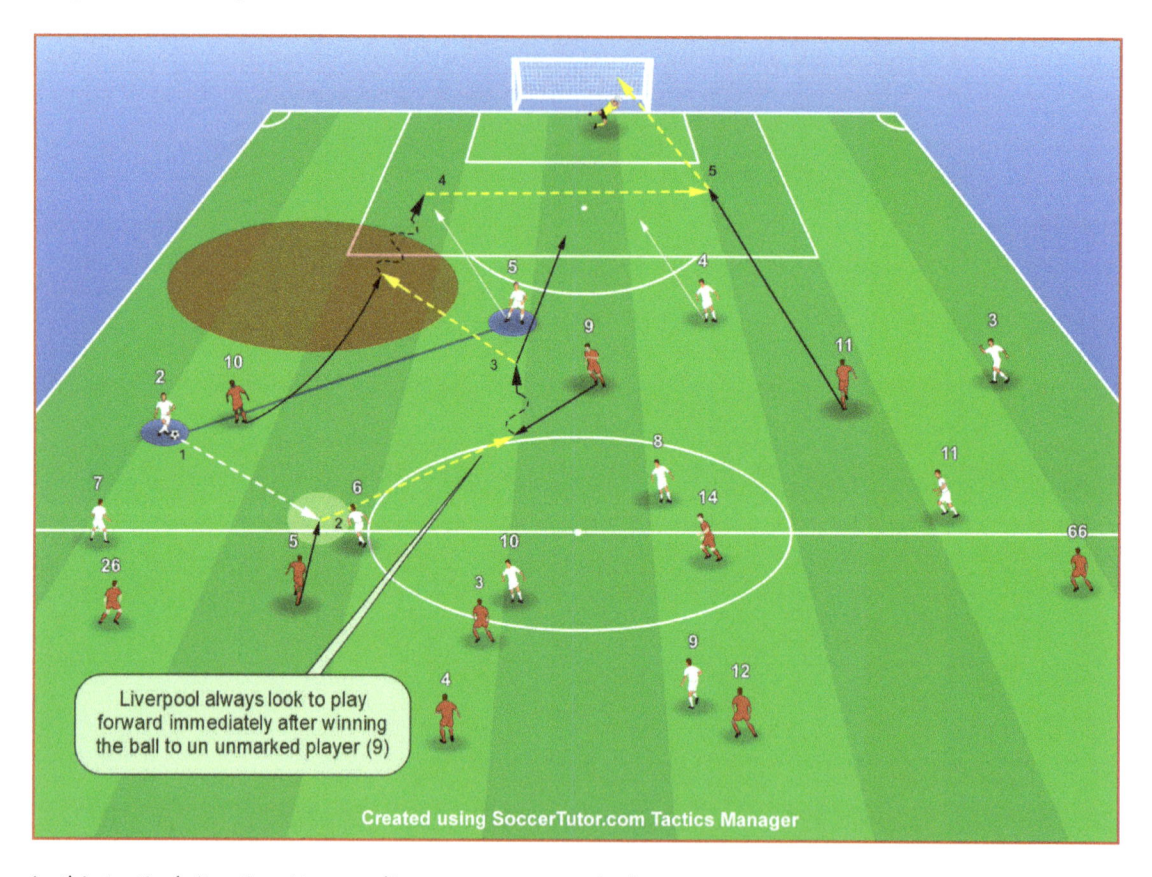

Liverpool always look to play forward immediately after winning the ball to un unmarked player (9)

In this tactical situation, Liverpool's opponents lose the ball in the middle zone and they are left in an unbalanced situation because there are large spaces (gaps) between their centre backs and full backs.

After winning the ball, Liverpool aim to move the ball very quickly to a player in a better position higher up the pitch, who is unmarked. In the diagram example, the central midfielder (**5**) wins the ball in the centre and immediately passes forward to the centre forward (**9**), who drops back to receive.

If the player that receives (**No.9** in diagram) has time and space, he dribbles forward towards the goal and at the opposing centre backs.

At the same time, 2-3 teammates make fast support runs to provide attacking solutions and create an overload to finish the attack as quickly as possible.

In this example, the centre forward (**9**) dribbles at the white centre back No.5 and draws his attention, and then plays a pass to the left forward (**10**) at the right time into the space available.

The left forward (**10**) dribbles forward and passes the ball across for the opposite wide forward (**11**) to score at the back post.

Tactical Solution 10 - Transition to Attack from Middle Zone (Unbalanced Opponents)

Tactical Solution B: Win Ball in Middle Zone + Direct Pass in Behind to Exploit Space Between the Centre Backs

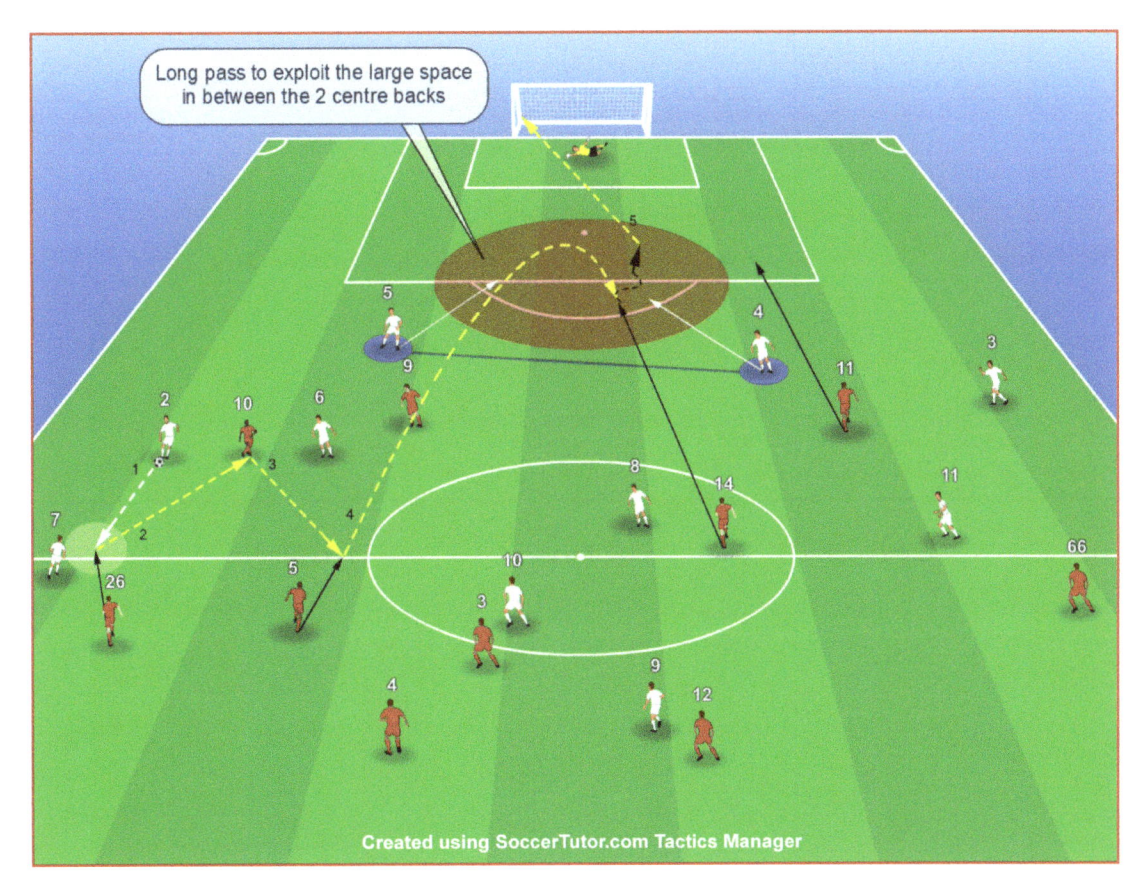

In this second tactical situation, Liverpool win the ball in a wide position and use fast combination play to move the ball to the central midfielder **(5)**, who receives unmarked with time and space.

The left forward **(10)** plays the ball back to central midfielder **No.5** as he is in a better position and is facing the opposition's goal, with a full view of the attacking options.

Instead of there being large gaps between the centre backs and full backs to exploit like in the example on the previous page, Liverpool's opponents have a large gap in between their 2 centre backs.

The right forward **(11)** makes a run in behind and the other central midfielder **(14)** makes an advanced run into the free space, as shown.

The central midfielder **(5)** plays a long pass into the free space in between the 2 white centre backs and in behind the defensive line for the run of **No.14**.

The central midfielder **(14)** receives and can either try to score or pass to a teammate if they are in a better position than him. In this example, **No.14** dribbles forward into the box and scores past the GK.

JÜRGEN KLOPP LIVERPOOL ATTACKING TACTICS

Tactical Solution 10 - Transition to Attack from Middle Zone (Unbalanced Opponents)

Statistical Analysis of Liverpool Exploiting Unbalanced Opponents in Transition to Attack from Middle Zone

Liverpool scored **11 goals** in this tactical situation
(Premier League and Champions League 2018-2019 and 2019-2020 seasons)

WIN BALL IN MIDDLE ZONE vs. UNBALANCED OPPONENTS
FAST ATTACK TO EXPLOIT GAPS/SPACES BETWEEN DEFENDERS

DATE	HOME	AWAY	SCORE	GOAL (MIN)	SCORER	ASSIST
29th Dec 2018	Liverpool	Arsenal	5-1	2-1 (16')	**Firmino**	
9th Feb 2019	Liverpool	Bournemouth	3-0	2-0 (34')	**Wijnaldum** *	Robertson
10th Mar 2019	Liverpool	Burnley	4-2	3-1 (67')	**Firmino**	Salah
31st Aug 2019	Burnley	Liverpool	0-3	0-2 (37')	**Mané**	Firmino
23rd Oct 2019	Genk	Liverpool	1-4	0-3 (77')	**Mané**	Salah
23rd Nov 2019	Crystal Palace	Liverpool	1-2	0-1 (49')	**Mané**	Robertson
7th Dec 2019	Bournemouth	Liverpool	0-3	0-3 (54')	**Salah**	Keïta
1st Feb 2020	Liverpool	Southampton	4-0	2-0 (60')	**Henderson**	Firmino
7th Mar 2020	Liverpool	Bournemouth	2-1	2-1 (33')	**Mané**	Van Dijk
8th Jul 2020	Brighton	Liverpool	1-3	0-2 (08')	**Henderson** *	Salah
15th Jul 2020	Arsenal	Liverpool	2-1	0-1 (20')	**Mané**	Robertson

* The full analysis of these goals is shown on the following pages...

Tactical Solution 10 - Transition to Attack from Middle Zone (Unbalanced Opponents)

Analysis from Brighton 1-3 Liverpool (Henderson 8') - 8th July 2020, Premier League

Tactical Solution A: Win Ball + Fast Break Attack to Exploit the Space in Between the Centre Back and Full Back

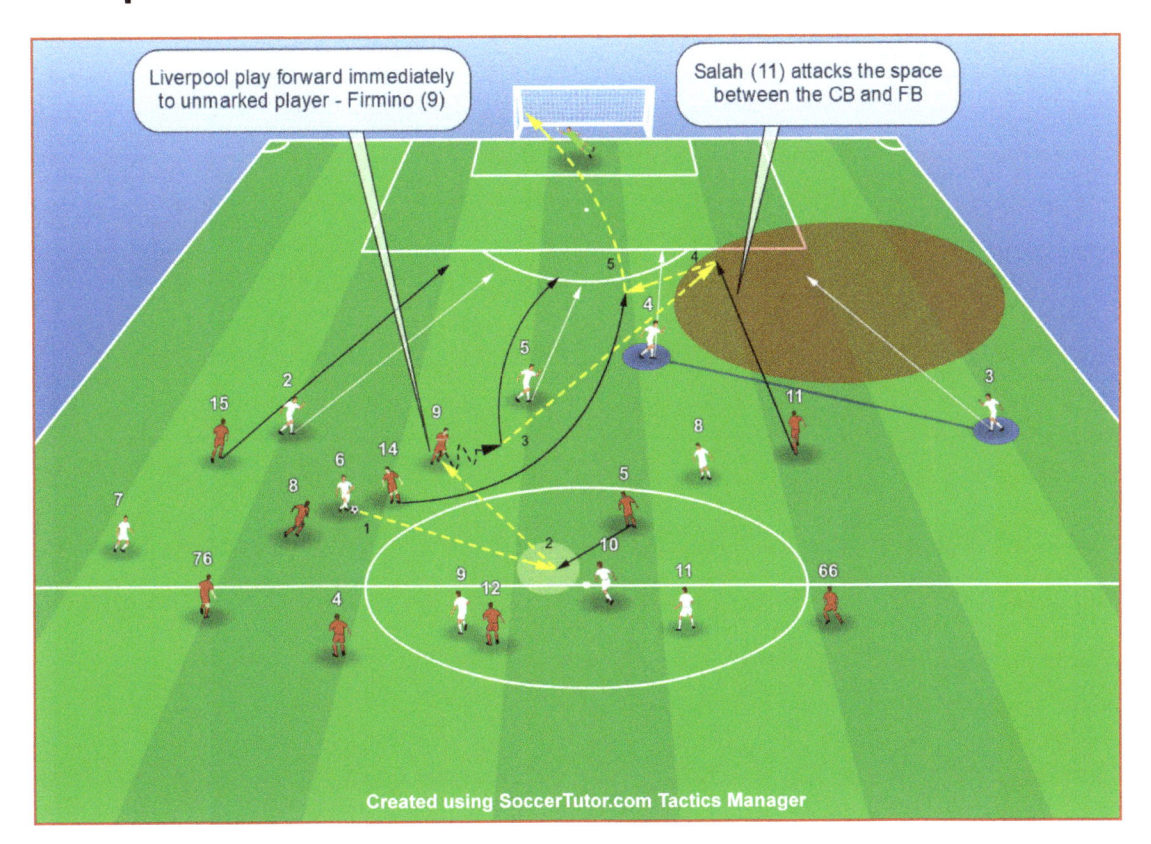

Liverpool press in the middle zone in a compact shape with small distances between the lines and their players. A Brighton midfielder makes a poor pass under pressure and Liverpool's central midfielder **Wijnaldum (5)** wins the ball.

With his first touch, **Wijnaldum (5)** passes to centre forward **Firmino (9)**, who is in a better position higher up the pitch.

Firmino (9) turns quickly and sees right forward **Salah's (11)** position in the large space between Brighton's centre back and left back.

Firmino (9) passes immediately in behind to **Salah (11)**, who receives on the run.

Normally in this type of situation, **Salah (11)** would be able to dribble into the box and either shoot or pass across for a teammate to finish. However, in this example the Brighton defenders do well to prevent this - the left back tracks back quickly and the left centre back blocks the path towards goal.

Henderson (14) and **Chamberlain (15)** have sprinted forward quickly to provide support. **Salah (11)** passes back into **Henderson's (14)** path so he can shoot with his first touch.

Henderson (14) scores with an excellent shot into the far corner of the net.

Tactical Solution 10 - Transition to Attack from Middle Zone (Unbalanced Opponents)

Analysis from Liverpool 3-0 Bournemouth (Wijnaldum 34') - 9th Feb 2019, Premier League

Tactical Solution B: Win Ball + Direct Pass in Behind to Exploit Space Between the Centre Backs

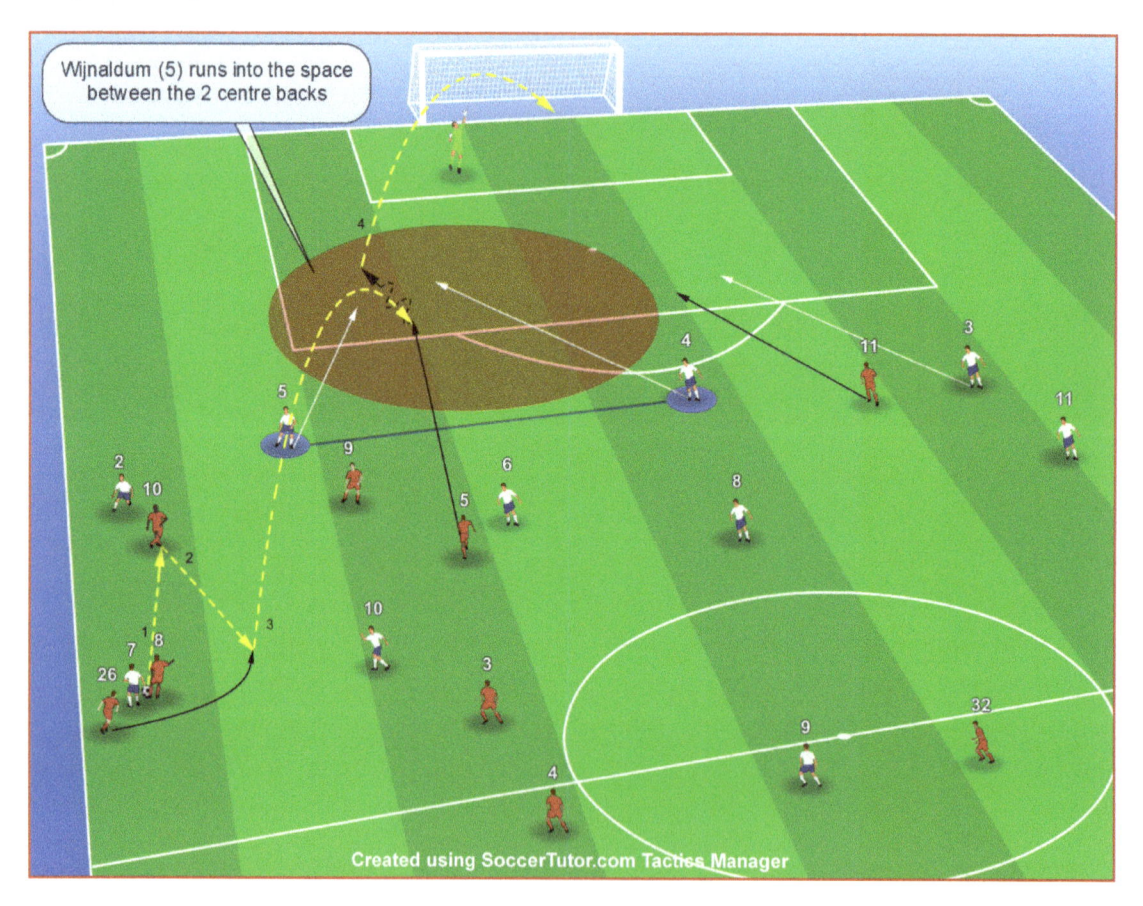

Liverpool are pressing in the middle zone on the left side of the pitch. The left back **Robertson (26)** and central midfielder **Keïta (8)** press the Bournemouth winger (7), who is facing his own goal without any passing options.

Keïta (8) is able to tackle the winger and the ball moves forward to Liverpool's left forward **Mané (10)**. **Mané (10)** has his back to the goal and **Robertson (26)** provides him with a better solution, so he passes first time back to him.

Central midfielder **Wijnaldum (5)** recognises the tactical situation and moves in behind the midfield line and starts his run into the large space between the 2 Bournemouth centre backs.

The left back **Robertson (26)** also recognises the situation very quickly and wants to exploit the gap between the 2 centre backs before they are able to reorganise.

Robertson (26) takes a quick first touch and then plays an aerial pass in between the 2 centre backs and in behind the defensive line for the run of central midfielder **Wijnaldum (5)**, who receives the ball inside the box and produces an excellent lob finish (half-volley) over the GK.

SESSION 10 BASED ON THE TACTICS OF JÜRGEN KLOPP

Exploit Unbalanced Opponents in the Transition to Attack from the Middle Zone

Session for JÜRGEN KLOPP Tactics - Transition to Attack from the Middle Zone (Unbalanced Opponents)

SESSION FOR THIS TACTICAL SITUATION (5 PRACTICES)

1. One-Touch Combination Play in a Continuous Short Passing Circuit

1a: Finish with Dribbling to Opposite Group

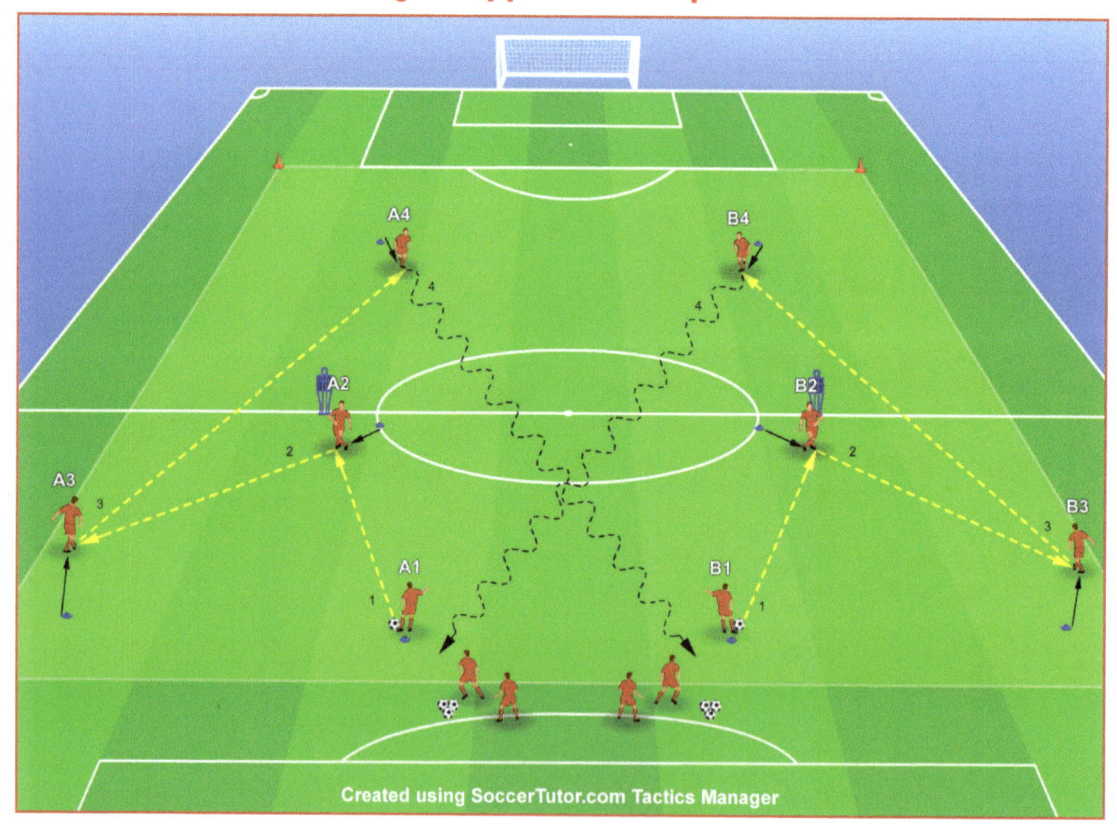

Description (1a)

We work with 12 players and start with 2 groups of 6 (A and B).

The sequence starts simultaneously with 2 balls from Player 1 in each group.

1. Player 1 passes forward to Player 2.
2. Player 2 passes back and wide to Player 3.
3. Player 3 passes forward to Player 4 with a diagonal pass.
4. Player 4 takes a first touch out in front and dribbles diagonally at speed to the start position of the other group.

Rotation

All players move to the next position:
1 -> 2 -> 3 -> 4 -> Opposite group

©SOCCERTUTOR.COM

JÜRGEN KLOPP LIVERPOOL ATTACKING TACTICS

Session for **JÜRGEN KLOPP** Tactics - Transition to Attack from the Middle Zone (Unbalanced Opponents)

1b: Finish with One-Two + Pass to Opposite Group

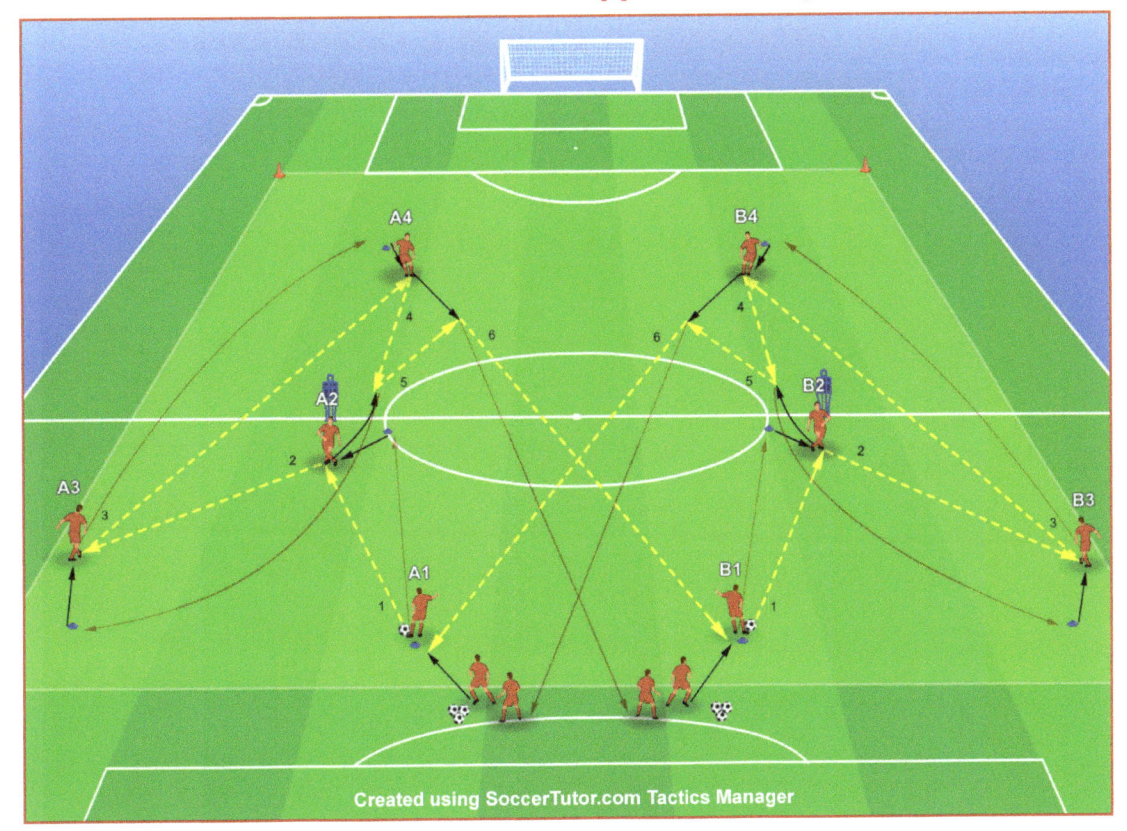

Description (1b)

- This is a variation of the passing circuit on the previous page (1a). We add a one-two and a final pass to replace the dribbling. The sequence is the same up until Player 3's pass forward to Player 4.

- Player 4 now plays a one-two combination with Player 2, who turns and moves past the mannequin.

- Player 4 moves to meet Player 2's return pass and passes to the start position of the other group.

Rotation

All players move to the next position:
1 -> 2 -> 3 -> 4 -> Opposite group

Coaching Points

1. Players need to make sure their first touch is made on the move to maintain the fluency of the practice.

2. Passes need to be well-weighted and aimed just in front of their teammates to step forward on to.

3. The practice should be done at a high tempo with a high rhythm and good synchronisation of the movements together with the passes.

4. Make sure the players communicate with their teammates and heads are up.

JÜRGEN KLOPP LIVERPOOL ATTACKING TACTICS

Session for **JÜRGEN KLOPP** Tactics - Transition to Attack from the Middle Zone (Unbalanced Opponents)

PROGRESSION
2. One-Touch Combination Play in a Continuous Finishing Circuit

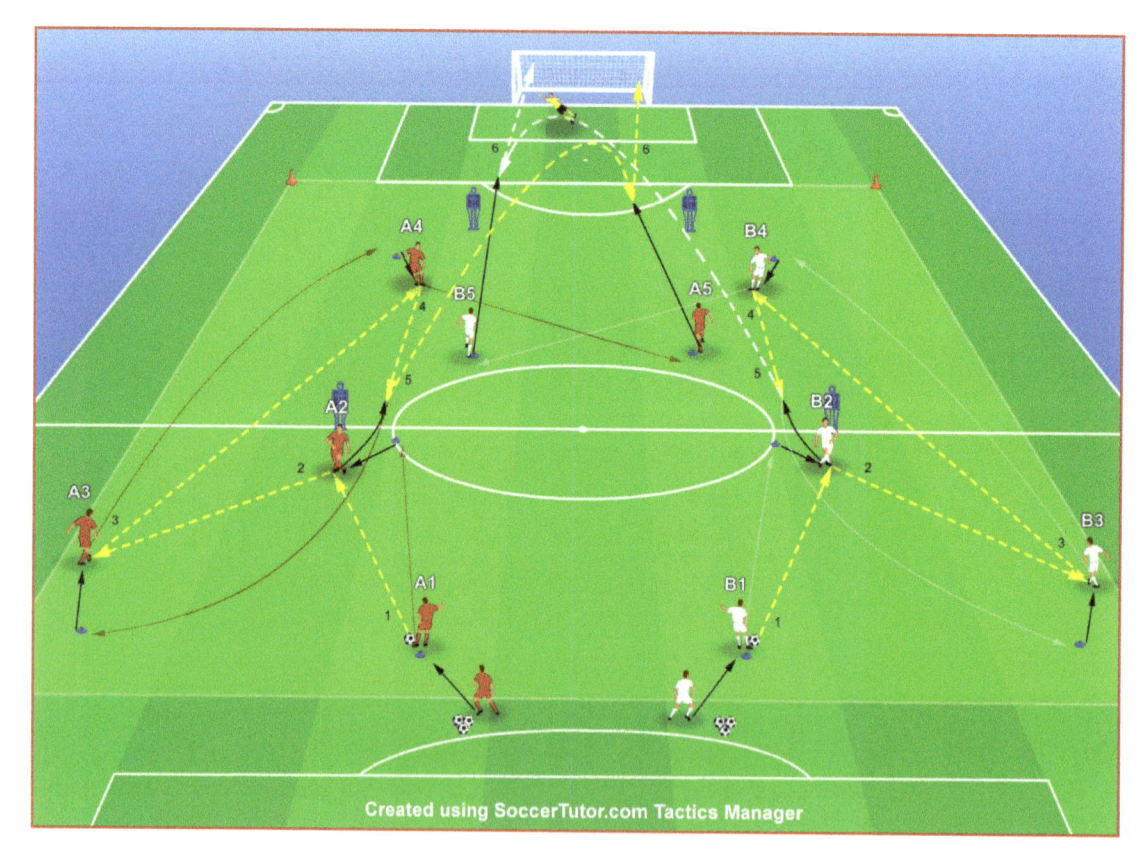

Objective: Combination play within a fast attack in a continuous finishing practice.

Description

In the marked out area shown, we work with 12 to 14 players split into 2 groups (A and B). The sequence starts simultaneously with 2 balls from Player 1 in each group.

1. Player 1 passes forward to Player 2.
2. Player 2 passes back and wide to Player 3.
3. Player 3 passes forward to Player 4.
4. Player 4 passes back to Player 2 (lay-off), who turns past the mannequin to receive.
5. Player 2 plays an aerial pass into the space between the 2 centre backs (mannequins) and in behind the defensive line.
6. Player 5 from the opposite side times his fast run into the box to meet the pass and score past the GK.

Rotation

All players move to the next position:
1 -> 2 -> 3 -> 4 -> 5 -> 1

Session for JÜRGEN KLOPP Tactics - Transition to Attack from the Middle Zone (Unbalanced Opponents)

PROGRESSION
3. Continuous 3v2 Attacking Overloads in a Fast Break Attack Dual Game

Description

- In a 25 x 35 yard area, we have 2 large goals and GKs + 16 outfield players: 8 end players (1-4), 4 attackers (A-D) and 4 defenders.

- The practice starts with **Player 1**, who dribbles the ball forward and passes to the most advanced attacker **(A)**. **Player A** passes back to the deeper attacker **Player B**.

- **Player B** dribbles forward at the 2 white defenders. At the same time, **Player 1** sprints forward to provide an attacking solution on the left side and **A** makes a movement in behind. We now have a **3v2 situation** for the reds to finish their attack.

- When the attack finishes (goal, ball goes out of play, GK saves, or whites win it), **C** and **D** take the place of **A** and **B**. **Player 2** restarts with an attack towards the opposite goal.

- **Player 3** starts the next attack, and then **Player 4**, so we play continuous 3v2 fast break attacks.

Coaching Points

1. The timing of the pass to best exploit the numerical advantage is key.

2. The best attacking solution depends on the decisions made by the defenders:
    - If the defender closes the ball carrier down, he should play out wide to a teammate.
    - If the defenders move to cover the wide areas, drive towards goal to score yourself.

Session for **JÜRGEN KLOPP** Tactics - Transition to Attack from the Middle Zone (Unbalanced Opponents)

PROGRESSION
4. Win the Ball in the Middle Zone and Fast Break Attack in a 3 Zone Dynamic Transition Game (10 v 9 +GK)

Aim: Win ball + quickly exploit gaps between defenders to score

Description

- Mark out the middle third of a full pitch, as shown. At one end, there are 3 mini goals and at the other end there is an end zone with a large goal + GK.

- The red team have 10 players in Liverpool's 4-3-3 formation and the white team have 9 outfield players in a 4-2-3 (from 4-2-3-1).

- The game starts from the GK and the white team try to find the best attacking solutions to score in one of the 3 mini goals.

- The aim for the red team is to apply team pressing in the middle zone to win the ball and then launch a fast break attack to score within a maximum of 12-14 seconds.

- The focus is on exploiting large gaps between centre backs and full backs, or between the 2 centre backs like in the diagram example.

- The left back **(26)** wins the ball, passes to the left forward **(10)**, who lays the ball back for the central midfielder **(5)** to play into the space in the middle. The other central midfielder **(14)** makes a fast and well-timed run into the end zone to receive and score.

- **Rule:** The red players are limited to 3 touches and the whites have unlimited touches.

Session for **JÜRGEN KLOPP** Tactics - Transition to Attack from the Middle Zone (Unbalanced Opponents)

PROGRESSION
5. Win the Ball in the Middle Zone and Fast Break Attack in a 3 Zone Dynamic Transition Game (11 v 9 +GK)

Description

- In this progression of the previous practice, we replace the 3 mini goals with a large goal and GK for the red team. In this example, you can see the reds launch a fast break attack when there are large gaps between the white centre backs and full backs.

- The left back **(26)** wins the ball again but this time he plays a diagonal forward pass to the centre forward **(9)**, who lays the ball back for the oncoming central midfielder **(14)**.

- The central midfielder **(14)** has options to his left and right (to **No.10** or **No.11**), who are both positioned in large gaps between the white defenders.

- In this example, the central midfielder **(14)** plays a pass in between the white centre back (5) and left back (3) for the run of the red right forward **(11)** to receive in behind and dribble into the box.

- The right forward **(11)** can either shoot or pass for a teammate to score, like in the diagram example to **No.10**.

- **Rule:** The red players are limited to 3 touches and the whites have unlimited touches.

JÜRGEN KLOPP TACTICAL ANALYSIS

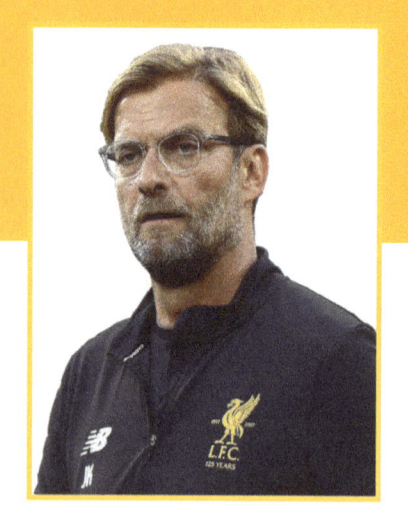

SOLUTION 11

Fast Break Attack After Winning the Ball in the High Zone

Content from analysis of Liverpool F.C. during the 2018-2019 Champions League winning season and the 2019-2020 Premier League winning season

- Analysis based on recurring patterns of play observed within the Liverpool team.
- Tactical solutions displayed as examples of the team's tactics being used effectively.
- Real match examples of Liverpool scoring a goal using this specific attacking tactical solution.
- Each action, pass, individual movement with or without the ball, and the positioning of each player on the pitch including their body shape, are presented.
- The analysis is then used to create a full progressive session to coach this tactical situation.

©SOCCERTUTOR.COM

JÜRGEN KLOPP LIVERPOOL ATTACKING TACTICS

Tactical Solution 11 - Fast Break Attack After Winning the Ball in the High Zone

Fast Break Attack After Winning the Ball in the High Zone (Opponent with Unbalanced Defence)

What?

Liverpool apply a high press and try to force their opponents into making an error, win the ball, and then launch a fast break attack against an unbalanced defence.

Why?

Against opponents that have difficulties building up play under pressure and have bad reactions in these kind of transition situations. Liverpool's attackers are very quick and have a lot of quality/ability to beat opposing defenders.

How?

Win the ball high up the pitch as quickly as possible and provide support with fast runs to exploit the free spaces and the opponent's unbalanced defence.

Target Areas (Spaces to Exploit High Up the Pitch)

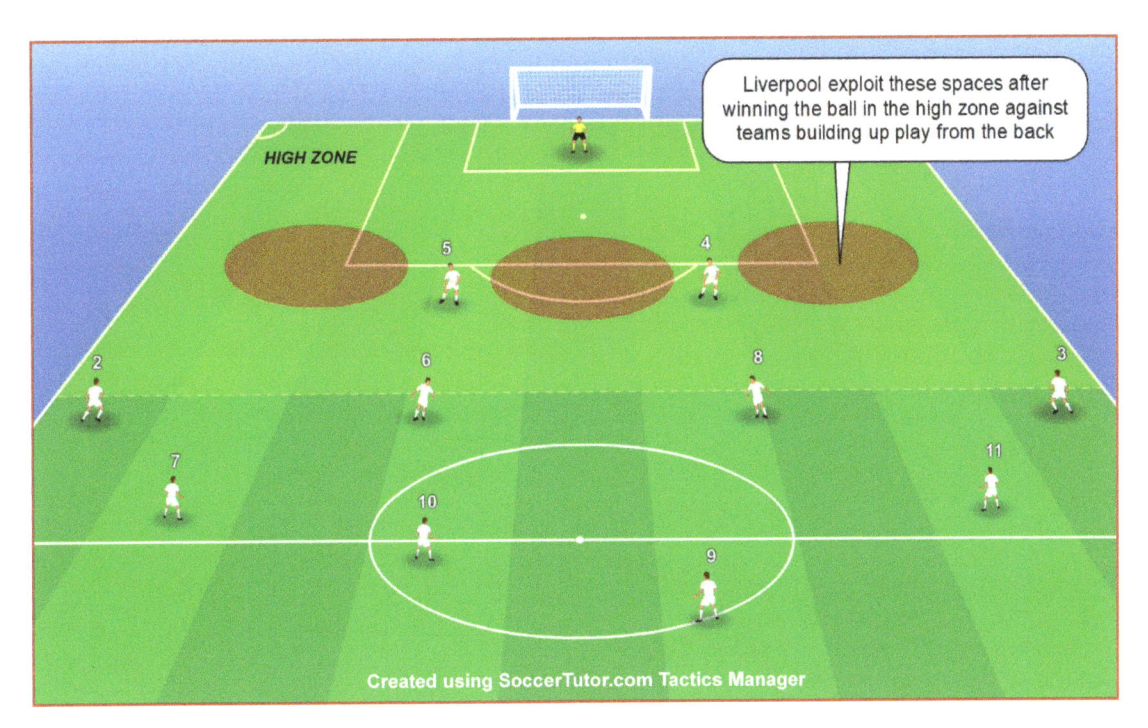

Liverpool exploit these spaces after winning the ball in the high zone against teams building up play from the back

Tactical Solution 11 - Fast Break Attack After Winning the Ball in the High Zone

Tactical Solution: Fast Break Attack After Winning the Ball in the High Zone to Finish Quickly Before Opponents Reorganise

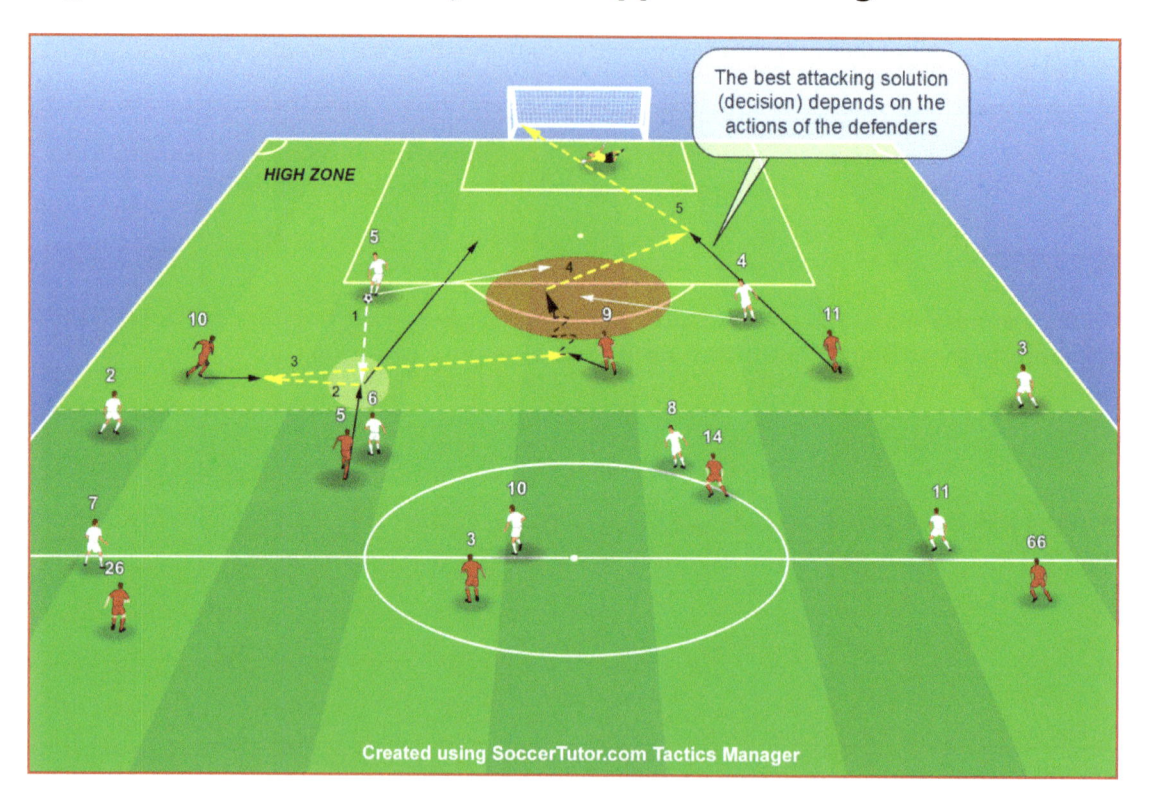

In this tactical situation, Liverpool's opponents open up the space of the pitch and try to build up play from the back.

Liverpool's 3 forwards, which are most often **Mané (10)**, **Firmino (9)** and **Salah (11)**, block some passing lanes and force their opponents to pass into an area where Liverpool's midfielders can press more effectively. Exactly how this works changes with each different tactical situation they experience during a match.

The player that wins the ball (central midfielder **No.5** in diagram example) immediately passes to the nearest free player.

The player that receives that first pass (left forward **No.10** in diagram) aims to play the ball to the forward with the best position to exploit the available spaces high up the pitch.

Once the forward in the best position (centre forward **No.9** in diagram) receives, he dribbles up to the defensive line with 2-3 teammates making fast runs to exploit the space in behind.

The best attacking solution (decision) depends on the actions of the opposing defenders.

If the opposing centre backs move to close down the ball carrier, he passes to a teammate with free space to finish the attack e.g. The centre forward's **(9)** pass in behind to the right forward **(11)** in the diagram example.

Tactical Solution 11 - Fast Break Attack After Winning the Ball in the High Zone

Statistical Analysis of Liverpool's Fast Break Attacks After Winning the Ball in the High Zone

Liverpool scored **13 goals** in this tactical situation
(Premier League and Champions League 2018-2019 and 2019-2020 seasons)

WIN BALL AFTER HIGH PRESS
FAST ATTACK TO EXPLOIT UNBALANCED OPPONENT (SCORE QUICKLY)

DATE	HOME	AWAY	SCORE	GOAL (MIN)	SCORER	ASSIST
25th Aug 2018	Liverpool	Brighton	1-0	1-0 (23')	**Salah** *	Firmino
18th Sep 2018	Liverpool	PSG	3-2	3-2 (90 +1')	**Firmino**	van Dijk
24th Oct 2018	Liverpool	Red Star Belgrade	4-0	1-0 (20')	**Firmino**	Robertson
24th Oct 2018	Liverpool	Red Star Belgrade	4-0	4-0 (80')	**Mané** *	Sturridge
10th Mar 2019	Liverpool	Burnley	4-2	2-1 (29')	**Mané**	
26th Apr 2019	Liverpool	Huddersfield	5-0	1-0 (01')	**Keïta**	Salah
17th Aug 2019	Southampton	Liverpool	1-2	0-2 (71')	**Firmino**	Mané
2nd Oct 2019	Liverpool	RB Salzburg	4-3	4-3 (69')	**Salah**	Firmino
7th May 2019	Liverpool	FC Barcelona	4-0	2-0 (54')	**Wijnaldum**	A-Arnold
14th Sep 2019	Liverpool	Newcastle	3-1	2-1 (40')	**Mané**	Firmino
7th Mar 2020	Liverpool	Bournemouth	2-1	1-1 (24')	**Salah**	Mané
8th Jul 2020	Brighton	Liverpool	1-3	0-1 (06')	**Salah**	Keïta
22 Jul 2020	Liverpool	Chelsea	5-3	1-0 (23')	**Keïta**	Wijnaldum

* The full analysis of these goals is shown on the following pages...

Tactical Solution 11 - Fast Break Attack After Winning the Ball in the High Zone

Analysis from Liverpool 4-0 Red Star Belgrade (Mané 80') - 24th Oct 2018, Champions League

Tactical Solution (1): Fast Break Attack After Winning the Ball in the High Zone (Left Forward Finishes)

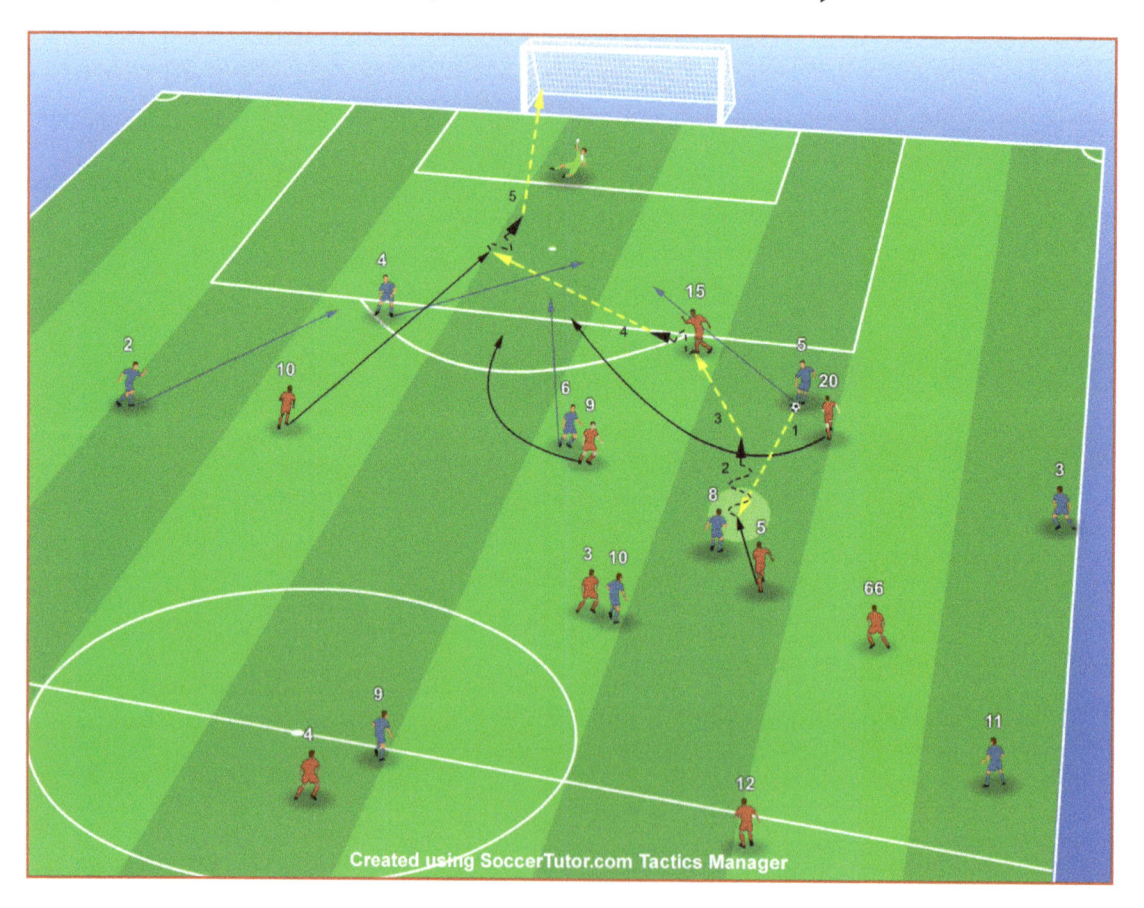

In this example, Liverpool apply a high press against opponents building up from the back. Central midfielder **Wijnaldum (5)** anticipates the centre back's poor pass towards the central midfielder, so steps in front of him to intercept.

As the Red Star Belgrade defence is spread out while building up play from the back, they are disorganised when **Wijnaldum (5)** wins the ball.

Wijnaldum (5) passes to the centre forward **Sturridge (15)**, who is the most advanced Liverpool player and is positioned between the 2 opposing centre backs.

Both centre backs move closer to **Sturridge (15)** and 3 Liverpool players make fast movements to provide him with support and attacking options.

Sturridge (15) is able to quickly turn and then pass at the correct time into the space to the left for **Mané (10)**, who is in a better position in relation to the goal. **Mané (10)** takes a quick first touch and then slots the ball past the oncoming GK with his second touch.

From the time **Wijnaldum (5)** wins the ball to **Mané (10)** scoring is just 5 seconds.

Tactical Solution 11 - Fast Break Attack After Winning the Ball in the High Zone

Analysis from Liverpool 1-0 Brighton (Salah 23') - 25th Aug 2018, Premier League

Tactical Solution (2): Fast Break Attack After Winning the Ball in the High Zone (Right Forward Finishes)

Liverpool are again applying a high press against their opponents (Brighton), who are trying to build up play from the back.

Central midfielder **Milner (7)** anticipates the centre back's poor pass towards the central midfielder, so moves forward to tackle him as soon as he receives.

Milner (7) wins the ball, and it goes to the left forward **Mané (10)** in the centre.

Mané (10) passes first time to **Firmino (9)**.

Mané (10) and **Salah (11)** make fast runs to provide support and attacking solutions.

Firmino (9) passes to his right to the right forward **Salah (11)**.

Salah (11) produces a great controlled first time finish into the bottom far corner of the net.

From the time **Milner (7)** wins the ball to **Salah (11)** scoring is just 4 seconds.

SESSION 11 BASED ON THE TACTICS OF JÜRGEN KLOPP

Fast Break Attack After Winning the Ball in the High Zone

Session for **JÜRGEN KLOPP** Tactics - Fast Break Attack After Winning the Ball in the High Zone

SESSION FOR THIS TACTICAL SITUATION (3 PRACTICES)
1. High Intensity Transition Play in a 3v3 (+3) Dynamic Possession Game

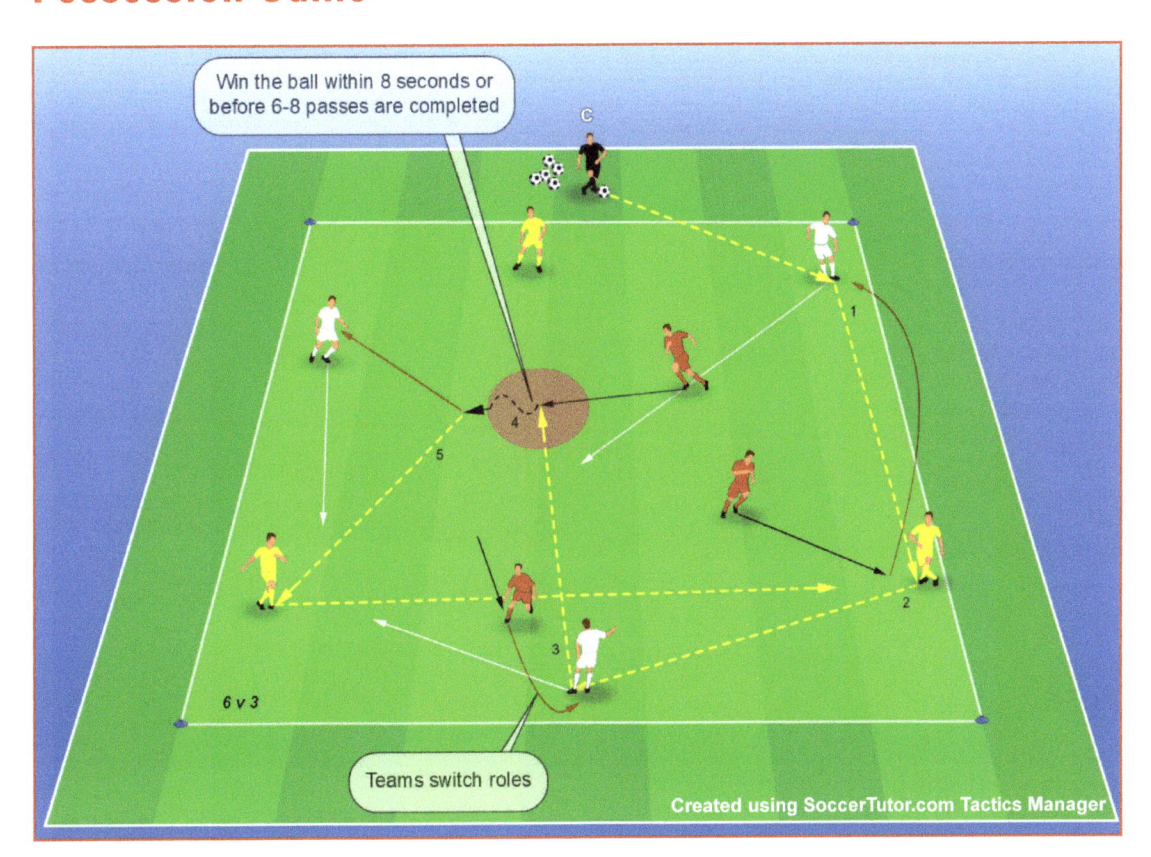

Win the ball within 8 seconds or before 6-8 passes are completed

6 v 3

Teams switch roles

Description

- In a 12 x 12 yard area, we work with 3 teams of 3 players each. The Coach starts and 2 teams are in possession (whites and yellows) in a 6v3 situation. If the red players win the ball, they switch roles with the team that lost it.

- The team that loses the ball makes a fast transition from attack to defence. If they are able to win the ball back within 8 seconds (or before 6-8 passes are completed), they switch roles with the team that lost it.

- If they recover the ball after 8 seconds (or 6-8 passes), they stay as the defensive team for a new ball and the practice continues.

Coaching Points

1. The nearest player applies intense aggressive pressing on the ball carrier and tries to block the passing lines to the other players.

2. The 2 other defending players must press in a triangle shape and try to avoid passes being played between them.

3. Correct pressing angles and good anticipation of where the next pass will go are needed.

4. If the ball is passed between 2 defending players, all 3 players must react quickly (and collectively) to the new situation.

Session for JÜRGEN KLOPP Tactics - Fast Break Attack After Winning the Ball in the High Zone

PROGRESSION
2. High Intensity 6 v 10 Dynamic Transition Game with Mini Goals

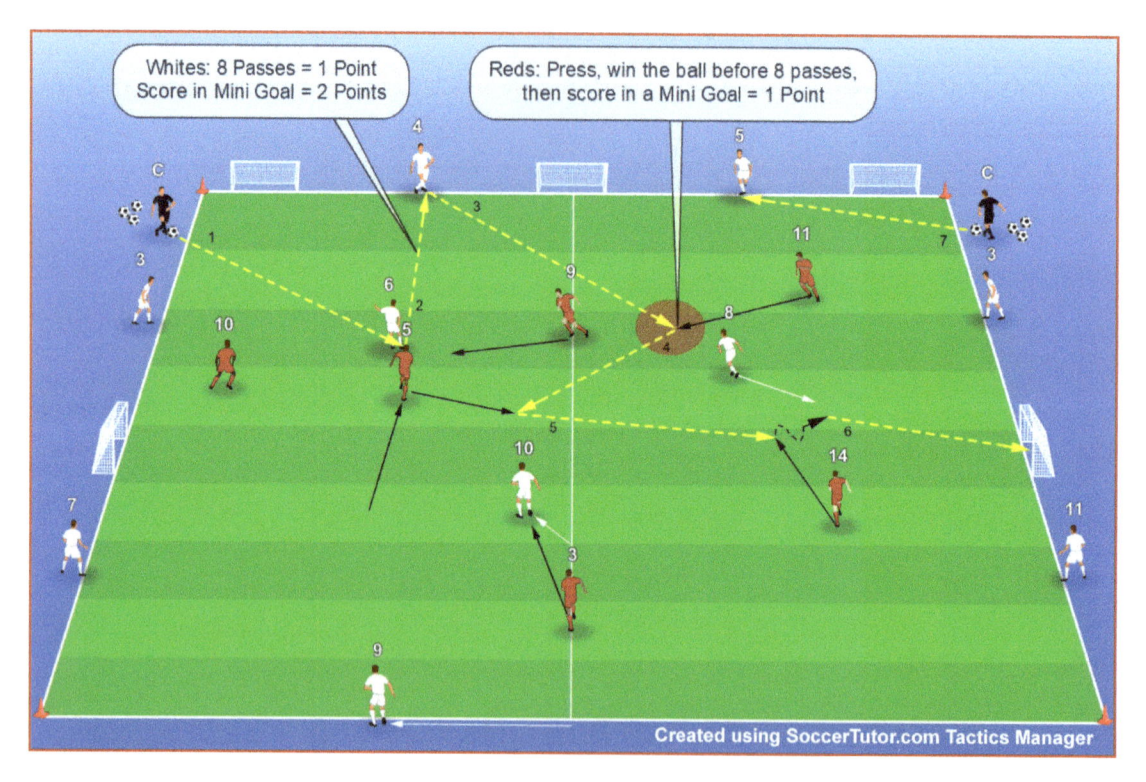

Whites: 8 Passes = 1 Point
Score in Mini Goal = 2 Points

Reds: Press, win the ball before 8 passes, then score in a Mini Goal = 1 Point

Description

- In a 25 x 30 yard area, we divide into 2 equal zones + 5 mini goals in the positions shown.

- The red team have 6 players in a 3-3 (from Liverpool's 4-3-3 without back 4) and the whites have all 10 outfield players from the 4-2-3-1 formation.

- The white back 4, the 2 wingers (7 & 11) and the centre forward (9) play outside the area. They have 1 central midfielder (6 & 8) in each zone. The attacking midfielder (10) can move freely across both zones.

- We have 2 Coaches with many balls and the practice starts with one of them passing to a white player.

- The white team aim to first complete 8 passes (1 point) and then try to score in any of the 5 mini goals (2 points).

- The red team aim to press the ball area and win the ball as quickly as possible. If this happens before the whites complete 8 passes, they try to score in any mini goal (1 point).

- If the reds win the ball after 8 passes have been completed, restart with the Coach passing a new ball to the white team.

- When the reds score in a mini goal, the Coach passes a new ball to the whites immediately, so the reds have to make a fast transition from attack to defence (high press to recover the ball as soon as possible).

Session for **JÜRGEN KLOPP** Tactics - Fast Break Attack After Winning the Ball in the High Zone

PROGRESSION
3. High Intensity Transition Play in a 9 v 10 Position Specific Conditioned Game

If reds don't recover ball within 8 seconds, a Coach passes a new ball to a white player

Description

In this final practice of the session, we play a game in the area shown, reducing the full width of the pitch. The red team have 9 outfield players in a 2-3-3 formation (from Liverpool's 4-3-3 without the centre backs). The white team have 9 outfield players in a 4-4-1 or 4-2-3 formation.

We work on 2 different tactical situations:

1. **EXAMPLE 1 (DIAGRAM EXAMPLE):** The red GK starts and the reds try to score. If they lose the ball, they must recover it within 8 seconds (fast into transition from defence to attack).

If not, a Coach passes a new ball into the white team and the reds must apply a high press with the same aim i.e. win the ball within 8 seconds and launch fast break attack.

2. **EXAMPLE 2 (NOT IN DIAGRAM):** The white GK starts, and the whites try to score. The reds press and must win the ball before the whites are able to complete 6 passes to be allowed to move into transition from defence to attack.

If not, a Coach passes a new ball into the white team and the reds must apply a high press, or the play restarts from the red GK.

FREE TRIAL

SOCCER TUTOR.COM

TACTICS MANAGER
Create your own Practices, Tactics & Plan Sessions!

www.SoccerTutor.com/TacticsManager
info@soccertutor.com

PC   Mac   iPad   Tablet   Web

SOCCERTUTOR.COM

Football Coaching Specialists Since 2001

COACHING TRANSITION PLAY Vol. 2
Full Sessions from the Tactics of Pochettino, Sarri, Jardim & Sampaoli

Michail Tsokaktsidis

SoccerTutor.com - The Web's #1 Soccer Coaching Specialists Since 2001

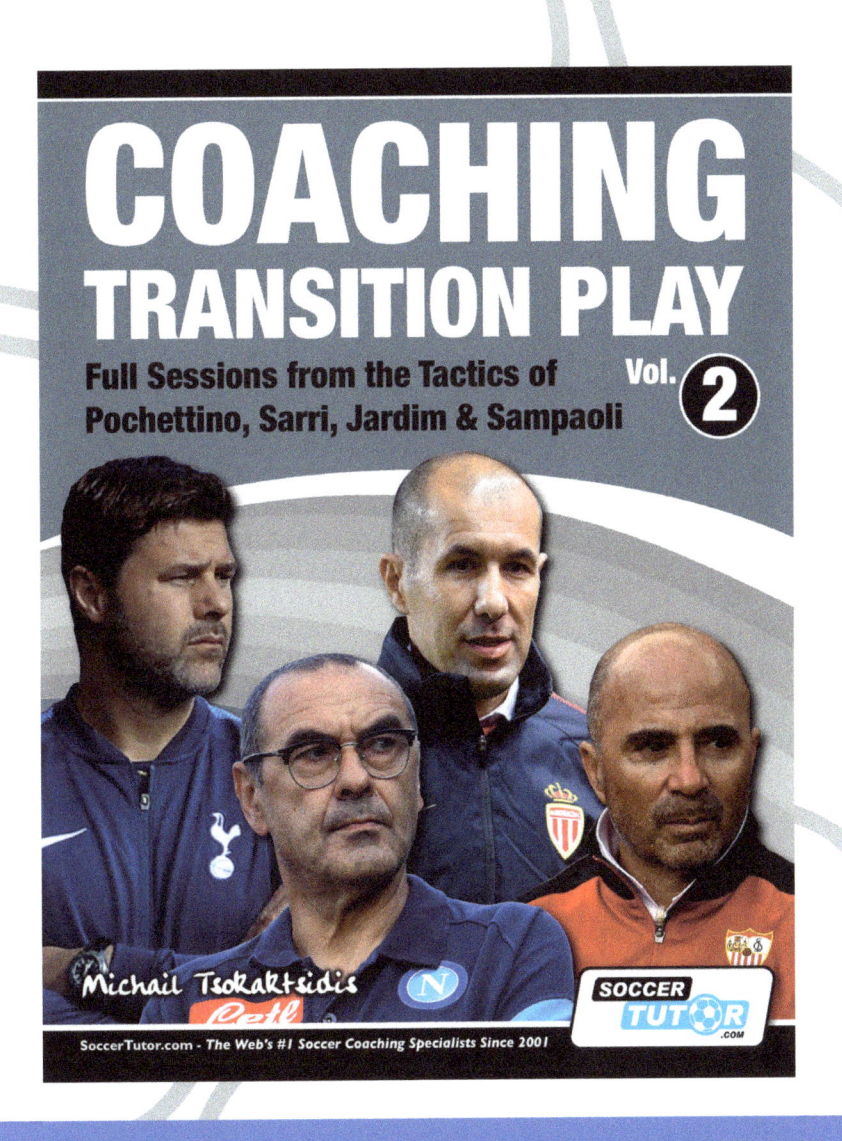

Available in Full Colour Print and eBook!
PC | Mac | iPhone | iPad | Android Phone/Tablet | Kobo | Kindle Fire

FREE COACH VIEWER APP

www.SoccerTutor.com
info@soccertutor.com

Lightning Source UK Ltd.
Milton Keynes UK
UKHW050220220222
399010UK00003B/47